Springer Series on Behavior Therapy and Behavioral Medicine

Series Editor: Cyril M. Franks, Ph.D.
Advisory Board: John Paul Brady, M.D., Robert P. Liberman, M.D., Neal E. Miller, Ph.D., and Stanley Rachman, Ph.D.

Vol. 1	**Multimodal Behavior Therapy** *A. A. Lazarus*	
Vol. 2	**Behavior Therapy Assessment** *E. J. Mash and L. G. Terdal, editors*	
Vol. 3	**Behavioral Approaches to Weight Control** *E. E. Abramson, editor*	
Vol. 4	**A Practical Guide to Behavioral Assessment (O.P.)**	
Vol. 5	**Asthma Therapy:** A Behavioral Health Care System for Respiratory Disorders *T. L. Creer*	
Vol. 6	**Behavioral Medicine:** Practical Applications in Health Care *B. G. Melamed and L. J. Siegel*	
Vol. 7	**Multimodal Handbook for a Mental Hospital:** Designing Specific Treatments for Specific Problems *L. F. Brunell and W. T. Young, editors*	
Vol. 8	**Eating and Weight Disorders:** Advances in Treatment and Research *R. K. Goldstein, editor*	
Vol. 9	**Perspectives on Behavior Therapy in the Eighties** *M. Rosenbaum, C. M. Franks, and Y. Jaffe, editors*	
Vol. 10	**Pediatric and Adolescent Behavioral Medicine:** Issues in Treatment *P. J. McGrath and P. Firestone, editors*	
Vol. 11	**Hypnosis and Behavior Therapy:** The Treatment of Anxiety and Phobias *J. C. Clarke and J. A. Jackson*	
Vol. 12	**Child Obesity:** A New Frontier of Behavior Therapy *M. D. LeBow*	
Vol. 13	**Punishment and Its Alternatives:** A New Perspective for Behavior Modification *J. L. Matson and T. M. DiLorenzo*	
Vol. 14	**The Binge–Purge Syndrome:** Diagnosis, Treatment, and Research *R. C. Hawkins II, W. J. Fremouw and P. F. Clement, editors*	
Vol. 15	**Behavioral Assessment in Behavioral Medicine** *W. W. Tryon, editor*	
Vol. 16	**Behavior Therapy Casebook** *M. Hersen and C. Last, editors*	
Vol. 17	**The Covert Conditioning Handbook** *J. R. Cautela and A. J. Kearney*	
Vol. 18	**Problem-Solving Therapy:** A Social Competence Approach to Clinical Intervention *T. J. D'Zurilla*	
Vol. 19	**The Psychological Management of Chronic Pain:** A Treatment Manual *H. C. Philips*	
Vol. 20	**Paradigms in Behavior Therapy:** Present and Promise *D. B. Fishman, F. Rotgers, and C. M. Franks, editors*	
Vol. 21	**Innovations in Child Behavior Therapy** *M. Hersen, Ph.D., editor*	
Vol. 22	**Adolescent Behavior Therapy** *E. L. Feindler and G. R. Kalfus, editors*	
Vol. 23	**Unifying Behavior Therapy:** Contributions of Paradigmatic Behaviorism *G. Eifert and I. Evans, editors*	
Vol. 24	**Learned Resourcefulness:** On Coping Skills, Self-Control and Adaptive Behavior *M. Rosenbaum, editor*	
Vol. 25	**Aversive and Nonaversive Interventions:** Controlling Life-Threatening Behavior by the Developmentally Disabled *S. L. Harris and J. S. Handleman, editors*	
Vol. 26	**Anxiety Across the Lifespan:** A Developmental Perspective *C. G. Last, editor*	
Vol. 27	**Promoting Health and Mental Health in Children, Youth, and Families** *D. S. Glenwick and L. A. Jason, editors*	

PROMOTING HEALTH AND MENTAL HEALTH IN CHILDREN, YOUTH, AND FAMILIES

David S. Glenwick, PhD
Leonard A. Jason, PhD
Editors

SPRINGER PUBLISHING COMPANY
New York

Copyright © 1993 by Springer Publishing Company, Inc.

All rights reserved

No part of this publication may be reproduced, stored in a retrieval system or transmitted in any form or by any means, electronic, mechanical, photocopying, recording, or otherwise, without the prior permission of Springer Publishing Company, Inc.

Springer Publishing Company, Inc.
536 Broadway
New York, NY 10012–3955

93 94 95 96 97 / 5 4 3 2 1

Library of Congress Cataloging-in-Publication Data

Promoting health and mental health in children, youth, and families /
  David S. Glenwick, Leonard A. Jason, editors.
    p.   cm.
  Includes bibliographical references and index.
  ISBN 0–8261–7310–1
  1. Clinical health psychology   2. Health promotion   3. Mental health promotion   4. Health Promotion.   I. Glenwick, David.
II. Jason, Leonard.
  [DNLM: 1. Behavior Therapy   2. Family Health   3. Mental Health Services.   W1 SP685NB v. 27 1993 / WM 425 P965 1993]
R726.7.P76   1993
362.2'042--dc20
DNLM/DLC
for Library of Congress   93–14539
                                                                 CIP

Printed in the United States of America

To Michael Jordan Glenwick,
who helps me perceive the world in fresh ways
every day
DSG

To Jay and Lynn Jason,
for passing on to me their good humor and
perspective on life
LAJ

Contents

Foreword by Alan E. Kazdin ix
Contributors xiii

Part I Introduction

1. Behavioral Approaches to Prevention in the Community:
   A Historical and Theoretical Overview 3
   David S. Glenwick and Leonard A. Jason

Part II Targeting Specific Health and Mental Health Problems

2. School-Based Interventions for Promoting Social
   Competence 17
   Jean Rhodes and Susan Englund
3. Prevention of Child Physical and Sexual Abuse 33
   Sandy K. Wurtele
4. Childhood Injury Prevention 51
   Lizette Peterson, Michelle Zink, and Jane Downing
5. Prevention of Substance Abuse 75
   Steven H. Kelder and Cheryl L. Perry
6. Preventing Teenage Pregnancy 99
   *W. LaVome Robinson, Peggy Watkins-Ferrell,
   Patricia Davis-Scott, and Holly Ruch-Ross*
7. Prevention of AIDS 125
   Jeffrey A. Kelly and Debra A. Murphy

8 Increasing Road Safety Behaviors   149
    E. Scott Geller

Part III Innovative Strategies for Promoting Health

9   Media-Based Behavior Change Approaches for Prevention   181
    Richard A. Winett
10 Applications of Social Support to Preventive Interventions 205
    G. Anne Bogat, Linda A. Sullivan, and
    Jacqueline Grober
11 Promoting Health Through Community Development   233
    Stephen B. Fawcett, Adrienne L. Paine,
    Vincent T. Francisco, and Marni Vliet

Index   257

Foreword

In the last decade, there has been increased attention paid to the scope of mental health and physical health problems that affects individuals at different points over the entire life span. Research on the precursors, prevalence, and continuity of dysfunction has provided important inroads in identifying individuals who are at risk and who could profit from some form of preventive efforts. Even with imperfect ability to predict onset, course, and outcomes for many physical and mental health problems, interventions at varied points from infancy through late adulthood have emerged. Of course, prevention is not merely focused on averting problems. In addition, prevention reflects interest in increasing positive health and adaptation, as reflected in improved quality of life, coping, and adjustment. It is likely that the difficult shoals of "normal" development can be better navigated with improved social, coping, and problem-solving skills.

Discussions of prevention often begin with the view that preventive interventions are needed because of the inherent limitations of treatment. Treatment, whether for physical or psychological dysfunction, is inefficient because of the focus on individuals, it is costly because of the intensity of application and professional effort, and it is less likely to be effective because the problem of dysfunction has crystallized. Prevention is argued to be the preferred mode of intervention because it is proactive, applied to many individuals, and does not wait for potentially intractable problems to form.

However, the significance of prevention as an area of work lies deeper. Preventive efforts represent a critical point at which science and application combine and interact, perhaps at their best. Theory and research are used as the basis to develop preventive interventions that are applied to persons who can profit directly from the effects. The structure of various settings, including the school and community, are often changed in the process to promote improved functioning. Yet prevention is not the mere application of theory and research findings. Prevention trials themselves provide tests of intervention models. Applications of interventions often examine theoretical issues and mechanisms of change. When findings depart from theoretical predictions, our conceptualization of the problem, population, and setting may be enhanced. The net effect is to raise further theoretical and research questions. Prevention trials play a crucial role not only in helping people directly, but also in testing models that will lead to improved understanding and intervention.

The concept of goals of prevention are laudatory, but can anything really be accomplished to improve the human condition? Drs. David Glenwick and Leonard Jason have presented us with a compendium of precisely such advances. In the chapters that follow, researchers who have contributed directly to the advances in the field present several significant areas of work. The topics, such as prevention of child physical and sexual abuse, teen pregnancy, injury and death from automobile accidents, and the spread of acquired immunodeficiency syndrome (AIDS), are obviously significant in their own right. These and other problem domains addressed in the book have sweeping implications for the health and functioning of others and, of course, for society at large, A successful intervention that, for example, prevents the spread of AIDS not only improves the well-being of individuals who are the target of the intervention, but also affects others as well (e.g., offspring, mates, significant others).

In this volume we learn about many problem areas and the range of their impact on individuals, families, and society at large. The impact of intervention programs is described to provide a current statement of advances and limitations within a given area. At the same time, the presentations provide an in-depth portrait of a specific prevention program so that the nature of the task, effort, and characteristics of the interventions themselves are more vivid. Documentation of the current status of research by different domains of functioning and with different types of interventions and concrete illustrations of individual programs make this book quite special.

The task of prevention extends well beyond developing effective interventions, daunting as that itself can be. Several types of problems emerge in relation to political, administrative, ethical, and financial issues. To an optimist, these issues are challenges; to the pessimist, perhaps they are insurmountable obstacles; to the present contributors, they are opportunities to learn. A special strength of the book is the distillation of information, principles, and guidelines in relation to implementation of preventive interventions. The chapters combine research acumen with voices of experience about how to implement and to incorporate preventive interventions into community life and society at large. Within the contributions are practical recommendations to ensure that preventive interventions can be operated through existing social institutions.

The very topic of prevention brings hope for advances for significant problems that affect individuals and society and for improving the quality of life generally. Specific advances documented in the chapters that follow show that this hope is not misplaced or based on a promissory note never to be paid. This book represents an even stronger basis for hope. The commitment of the editors and contributors, leaders in the field, to theory, research. and evaluation means that even though currently many major questions cannot be answered, we are on the path toward addressing them. The commitment to evaluation of processes and outcomes and to assessment of long-term follow-up are important investments. The book charts specific advances and models the approach we shall need to place prevention on firm empirical footing.

ALAN E. KAZDIN
Yale University

Contributors

G. Anne Bogat is an associate professor of clinical psychology at Michigan State University. She received her Ph.D. in clinical psychology from DePaul University. Her research interests include social support, the evaluation of sexual abuse prevention programs, issues in cross-cultural research, and intergenerational influences of parenting.

Patricia A. Davis Scott, a registered nurse, is the Director for Training and Technical Assistance at the National Committee to Prevent Child Abuse. From 1990–1992, she served as Associate Executive Director of Planned Parenthood in Chicago. She has extensive experience in the areas of community-based interventions, adolescent pregnancy, and school-based health service delivery.

Jane Downing is a doctoral student in sociology at the University of Missouri at Columbia. Her primary research interest is the sociology of child and family development.

Susan Englund is a doctoral student in psychology at the University of Illinois at Urbana-Champaign. Her research interests include family relationships during adolescence, the psychology of women, and feminist issues in community psychology.

Stephen B. Fawcett is a professor of human development and Director of the Work Group on Health Promotion and Community Development of the Schiefelbusch Institute for Life Span Studies at the University of Kansas. He received his Ph.D. in clinical psychology from the University of Kansas. He has published extensively in the areas of community development, empowerment, social policy, self-help, independent living, and health promotion.

Vincent T. Francisco is a doctoral student in human development at the University of Kansas. He is primarily interested in research in community development, particularly in the areas of coalition development and the evaluation of programs focusing on the reduction of risks for cardiovascular disease, substance abuse, and adolescent pregnancy.

E. Scott Geller is a professor of psychology at Virginia Polytechnic Institute and State University. He received his Ph.D. in experimental psychology from Southern Illinois University. Dr. Geller has published widely on the application of behavioral science to safety, health, and environmental problems in corporate and community settings. He is a past Editor of the *Journal of Applied Behavior Analysis*.

David S. Glenwick is a professor of psychology and Director of the Graduate Program in Clinical Psychology at Fordham University. He received his Ph.D. in clinical psychology from the University of Rochester. His principal research interests are (a) the development and evaluation of community-based prevention and intervention programs and (b) coping and stress in children and families. Dr. Glenwick is the Editor of *Criminal Justice and Behavior*.

Jacqueline Grober is a doctoral student in psychology at Michigan State University.

Leonard A. Jason is a professor of psychology at DePaul University. He received his Ph.D. in clinical psychology from the University of Rochester. Dr. Jason is a past President of the Division of Community Psychology of the American Psychological Association and a past Editor of *The Community Psychologist*. He has published numerous articles and chapters on preventive school-based interventions, substance abuse prevention, media interventions, and program evaluation.

Steven H. Kelder is an assistant professor in the School of Public Health at University of Texas Health Science Center in Houston. He received his Ph.D. in behavioral epidemiology from the University of Minnesota. His research has centered on youth substance-abuse prevention, cardiovascular disease prevention, and worksite health promotion.

Jeffrey A. Kelly is a professor of psychiatry and mental health sciences at the Medical College of Wisconsin, where he is the Director of the Community Health Behavior Program. Dr. Kelly received his Ph.D. in clinical psychology from the University of Kentucky. His research focuses on HIV/AIDS prevention.

Debra A. Murphy is an assistant professor of psychiatry and mental health sciences at the Medical College of Wisconsin, where she is also Associate Director of the Community Health Behavior Program. Dr. Murphy received her Ph.D. in clinical psychology from Florida State University. Her research interests include HIV/AIDS prevention and mental health aspects of AIDS.

Adrienne L. Paine is Associate Director of the Work Group on Health Promotion and Community Development of the Schiefelbusch Institute for Life Span Studies at the University of Kansas. She received her Ph.D. in developmental psychology from the University of Kansas. Dr. Paine's primary research activities are in the areas of community development, social support, and empowerment.

Cheryl L. Perry is a professor in the Division of Epidemiology in the School of Public Health at the University of Minnesota. She received her Ph.D. in education from Stanford University. Her interests include psychosocial aspects of health promotion and disease prevention, alcohol and drug-abuse prevention, and behavioral epidemiology.

Lizette Peterson is a professor of psychology at the University of Missouri at Columbia. She received her Ph.D. in clinical psychology from the University of Utah. Dr. Peterson is the Editor of *Behavior Therapy*. Her primary area of research is the prevention of disorders in children.

Jean Rhodes is an assistant professor of psychology at the University of Illinois at Urbana-Champaign. She received her Ph.D. in clinical-community psychology from DePaul University. Her research interests focus on adolescent risk, protective factors, resilience, and social support.

W. LaVonne Robinson is an associate professor of psychology at DePaul University. She received her Ph.D. in clinical psychology from the University of Georgia. Her research interests center on the prediction of risk and resiliency in African-American youth, the development and evaluation of school-based delivery models to promote adolescent well-being, and the prevention of pregnancy and HIV/STD.

Holly S. Ruch-Ross received her Sc.D. from the Harvard School of Public Health. She has been the Director of Research for the Ounce of Prevention Fund in Chicago. Her current research interests include risk and resiliency among adolescents in high-risk settings, as well as the evaluation of interventions designed to promote healthy adolescent development.

Linda A. Sullivan is a senior research analyst with R.L. Polk & Co. in Taylor, Michigan. She received her Ph.D. in social psychology from Michigan State University. Her research interests include (a) sex differences in the exchange of social support and (b) the relationship between alcoholism and social support.

Marni Vilet is senior vice president of the Kansas Health Foundation in Wichita. In that capacity, she is involved in grant administration, program development, community organizing, and leadership training. She received her master's in health education from Wichita State University.

Paggy Watkins-Ferrell is Clinical Director of CAUSES, a child abuse treatment and prevention program in Chicago. She received her Ph.D. in clinical-community psychology from DePaul University. Her research has involved the development and evaluation of pregnancy and HIV/AIDS prevention programs.

Richard A. Winett is a professor of psychology and the Director of the Center for Research in Health Behavior at Virginia Polytechnic Institute and State University. He received his Ph.D. in clinical psychology form SUNY at Stony Brook. Dr. Winett has published widely in the areas of disease prevention and health promotion.

Sandy K. Wurtele is an assistant professor of psychology at the University of Colorado at Colorado Springs. She received her Ph.D. in clinical psychology from the University of Alabama. Her research centers on the prevention of child sexual abuse.

Micehlle Zink is a doctoral student in psychology at the University of Missouri at Columbia. Her primary research interest is in children's affective development.

PART I

Introduction

CHAPTER 1

Behavioral Approaches to Prevention in the Community: A Historical and Theoretical Overview

David S. Glenwick and Leonard A. Jason

Approximately 15 years ago, behavioral psychologists began to turn their attention away from an exclusive focus on individuals and small groups (i.e., "patients" or "clients") and toward the development of higher order levels of intervention (Geller, Winett, & Everett, 1982; Glenwick & Jason, 1980). The underlying belief was that by modifying organizations, neighborhoods, communities, and society in general, one could ultimately indirectly impact more people than was possible by person-centered interventions (Glenwick & Jason, 1984; Nietzel, Winett, MacDonald, & Davidson, 1977). This broadened focus on environmental factors or person–environment transactions was at least partly due to the recognition that many systemic influences made it impossible to implement and maintain our intervention programs successfully (Jeger & Slotnick, 1982; Krasner, 1980). For example, many school administrators place limitations on teachers' creativity or independence. In such an atmosphere, even the best-designed prevention initiatives can flounder. However, when the school and classroom social climate provide teachers with the right combination of support and autonomy, and when teachers and administrators are enthusiastic about their work, there is a greater likelihood of successful health and mental health interventions (Jason, 1992).

In addition to this expansion in the *target* of interventions to include social and environmental systems, there was also an expansion in the *time point* of interventions (Jason & Glenwick, 1984; Winett, 1986). That is, instead of waiting for persons' problems to become strongly established to the point where such services as therapy and remediation are required, behavioral psychologists began to explore the possibilities of intervening before problems become evident to prevent their appearance in the first place, and, ideally, to enhance the growth of competencies in both individuals and social systems. This shift in emphasis was from repairing and rehabilitating those who have acquired labels and diagnoses indicative of disability to building in strengths to ward off the development of dysfunction (Caplan, 1964). Illustrative of such a primary preventive focus would be a curriculum intended to teach entire classes of grade-schoolers how to be effective problem solvers. Secondary prevention falls in between these end points on the time dimension and deals with keeping early-stage problems from becoming more serious ones (Zax & Cowen, 1977). An example would be an intervention aimed at helping elementary school youngsters with social skill deficits become more interpersonally adept so that they would not later require referral for traditional mental health services.

Since our initial survey of the field in 1980, application of behavioral principles to alter community systems and subsystems has continued to develop. Not only have well-controlled investigations increased in number, but the purview of behavioral psychologists has grown as well, addressing aspects of health and mental health that had been considered barely, if at all, in the 1970s (Greene, Winett, Van Houten, Geller, & Iwata, 1987). This book represents an attempt not only to provide an update of behavioral community research in those areas covered in our earlier reviews (Glenwick & Jason, 1980, 1984), but also to demonstrate how the field has branched out in innovative ways into new and exciting areas. Inspection of the table of contents reveals social problems to which behavioral psychologists had paid scant attention a decade ago but which are now the target of considerable applied research. These include, for instance, the prevention of child abuse, childhood accidents, adolescent pregnancy, and substance abuse. Indeed, in one case—acquired immunodeficiency syndrome (AIDS)—the problem itself had not yet begun to surface by 1980.

What is especially impressive about the research encompassed by this book is that it has been conducted during a period in which funding for human services in general, and novel preventive programs in particular, has been severely curtailed. For example, in mental health, funds for community mental health centers' consultation and education units—the base of much preventive work of the 1960s and 1970s—were often sharply reduced or even eliminated totally in the 1980s. Other areas, such as crime and delinquency and transportation, which had previously received substantial federal monies for preventive or community-wide programs, also suffered cutbacks. However, as the work summarized in the following chapters highlights, the field has continued to progress because of such factors as the initiative of committed researchers and the willingness of grassroots and community-based alternative sources of support (e.g., nonprofit organizations, foundations, and local government) to fill the gap created by federal and state reductions. There is a growing sentiment for change in the types of human services offered and in the mechanisms by which they are provided, stemming in part from the vast numbers of human casualties created by the social policies of the 1980s and the inadequacy of the response of traditional human service delivery programs (Price, Cowen, Lorion, & Ramos-McKay, 1988). This reawakened interest in prevention is illustrated by such documents as the U.S. Department of Health and Human Services' recent report (United States Department of Health and Human Services, 1991) asserting that (a) many of our social ills involve the failure to date of governmental and community systems to promote healthy life-styles, and (b) prevention of dysfunction by promoting behavioral competencies and discouraging health-endangering behaviors is the only way that our society can ever hope to gain control of our burgeoning social problems and contain spiraling health care costs.

THEORETICAL FOUNDATIONS OF PREVENTION

Within psychology, a philosophy of prevention first gained currency in the 1960s and 1970s. Such pioneers of community psychology as Albee (1967), critiquing the status quo in human services, observed that the number of human service professionals trained by our institutions of higher education would be increasingly insufficient to meet the ever-growing population of those experiencing some form of suffering or being judged by society as in need of services. Additionally, it was argued by Albee (1967) and others that by devoting most of our resources to serving persons with long-standing disorders, we were giving ourselves the daunting challenge of attempting to cure refractory, entrenched problems—problems with which our track record of success had been less than glowing. Furthermore, not only were traditional services inadequate in amount and limited in efficacy, but they were also distributed inequitably in our society, with unempowered subgroups receiving a disproportionately lesser share of services and resources (Heller et al., 1984; Rappaport, 1977).

As an alternative to the traditional delivery model—in which professionals provide rehabilitative health and mental health services to individuals or small groups who are already evidencing crystallized, and often chronic, disorders—a preventively oriented, community psychology model arose. This model, first formulated at a conference in Swampscott, Massachusetts, in 1965 (Levine & Perkins, 1987), stressed the need to complement conventional delivery approaches with a broader perspective. Such a perspective, as described earlier in this chapter, would emphasize prevention and would widen our scope of intervention to encompass higher target levels. Also, exclusive reliance on professional service providers would be decreased by the training of paraprofessionals (e.g., volunteers in schools) and natural change agents (i.e., those already on the front lines, such as teachers and policemen) in the promotion of health and mental health in the populations which they serve. The core belief was that by either (a) modifying social systems to make them more responsive and health inducing, or (b) teaching persons how to live behaviorally healthier life-styles, the flow of human casualties could be reduced (Cowen, 1973). Thus, it was hoped that through community-based prevention and promotion, services could be implemented that were cost-effective, with fewer resources ultimately having to be devoted to remediating hard-to-cure, entrenched problems.

The applied interventions contained in this book exemplify the application of behavioral principles and learning theory to this preventive- and community-oriented strategy. Preventive and community psychology suggest the directions to travel and the destinations one should seek, that is, the promotion of health and mental health competencies in large segments of our society. Behavioral psychology provides a vehicle for getting there, a technology of what one can do within the framework of a preventive- and community-oriented model. This research is especially exciting and promising on three counts: (a) its melding of theory and action, (b) its willingness to tackle social problems heretofore largely ignored by both behavioral and community psychologists, and (c) its incorporation of innovative approaches (such as the media, community development, and social support promotion) as intervention mechanisms.

CURRENT TRENDS IN BEHAVIORAL APPROACHES TO PREVENTION

In the chapters that follow, several recurrent themes emerge that appear characteristic of the field as it enters its adolescence. The first is the importance of involving the target populations themselves (i.e., the consumers and recipients of programs) in all phases of the intervention process (Kelly, 1990). There is a growing willingness by behavioral psychologists involved in health and mental health promotion to turn to the target populations for input concerning such aspects as problem identification, information on the problem, intervention design, and intervention acceptability. The result is a more collaborative process in which (a) consensus between the applied interventionist (i.e., the behavioral psychologist) and the target population is sought at each step, and (b) the intervention process is more sensitive to the local culture and environment.

The values that underlie such collaborative efforts emphasize a willingness to understand people from their viewpoint. By actively working with people as engaged participants rather than as subjects, researchers and interventionists can empower those whom they are trying to help. Such involvement of participants in the design and implementation of interventions increases the possibility that they will have the skills to continue solving their problems even after the outside interventionists have left the scene (Jason & Crawford, 1991).

Another feature is the increasing collaboration occurring between behavioral psychologists and other professions/disciplines concerned with prevention and promotion. Among these are educators, medical personnel, communications experts, and epidemiologists (Martin, 1991). Behavioral psychologists are evidencing greater awareness that by themselves they possess only a limited perspective on a particular social problem and that collaboration with other professions and disciplines can have synergistic effects, producing a more potent intervention than would otherwise be possible (Jason, Hess, Felner, & Moritsugu, 1987).

The increased fostering of target groups' sense of personal control is another hallmark of much recent research. Preventive interventions by behaviorists historically have been criticized for their reliance on external control (a derivative of behaviorism's traditional operant emphasis on response consequences). Current projects, however, are beginning to place conspicuous emphasis on encouraging internal control—that is, control by the participants—as part of the behavior change process. Thus, target populations are given the skills to act on and mold their environments rather than to be passively shaped by the environment (Albino, 1983). The process becomes a bidirectional, transactional one between individuals and the ecological context of which they are a part.

Accompanying this facilitation of internal control and personal choice, there has been a greater inclusion of subjective variables in the evaluation process. That is, rather than depend solely on observable behavior change as an indicator of a project's success, behavioral psychologists in the health/mental health promotion field have become more accepting of the importance of cognitive variables and constructs, such as social validity (Wolf, 1978) and self-efficacy (Bandura, 1974), which are only indirectly measurable. These, behaviorists are realizing, can be valuable both in evaluating previously overlooked aspects of change and in understanding the *process* by which change occurs or fails to occur. For example, if a project's goals, intervention mechanisms, or outcomes (the primary components of social validity) are unacceptable to the target population, then the project may be doomed from the start. As a second illustration, the presence of "psychological reactance" and the absence of "intrinsic motivation" (cognitive constructs drawn from social psychological theory) can help account for the failure to achieve long-term positive effects in some behavioral community interventions.

A fifth distinguishing characteristic of the present generation of applied behavioral interventions is a greater emphasis on antecedent behavior change procedures as opposed to consequence procedures (i.e., ones that employ rewards or penalties) (Greene et al., 1987). Behavioral psychologists have developed an awareness of how changing setting factors (i.e., aspects of the contexts and environments in which behavior occurs) can increase the likelihood of desirable behavior change. Thus, many of the projects outlined in the following chapters incorporate into the environment such components as modeling, role-playing exercises, problem-solving training, and prompting as ways of fostering the development of health and mental health competencies.

In summary, the field today seems to be marked by greater heterogeneity and tolerance with regard to such questions as (a) how interventions are developed, (b) with whom one develops them, (c) what behavior change techniques are employed, (d) how much interventions need to depend on external versus internal controls, and (e) what process and outcome variables are appropriate to measure when evaluating projects. As can be seen from the preceding discussion, the various characteristics of behavioral interventions are in actuality quite interconnected both conceptually and methodologically with one another.

FUTURE DIRECTIONS IN THE BEHAVIORAL PROMOTION OF HEALTH AND MENTAL HEALTH

Despite the laudable increase in flexibility that is apparent in the trends highlighted in the previous section, noteworthy challenges remain for behaviorists interested in facilitating health and mental health in communities. The first is the need to develop more multilevel interventions, that is, interventions that are not limited to only one level but encompass two or more levels. Thus, for example, a substance abuse prevention program could involve both the media (a community-level component) and participating schools (an organizational-level component) (Rhodes & Jason, 1988). Multilevel interventions potentially have the twin virtues of targeting many persons while influencing them with maximally effective behavior change techniques.

A second challenge stems from the unfortunate, but not surprising, finding that many creative projects mounted by behavioral psychologists during the past 15 years have all too seldom been adopted by the host settings on an ongoing basis (Levine & Perkins, 1987). The challenge is to devise cost-effective, user-friendly interventions and to work with the target populations involved to enhance their desire and ability to retain the program without, or with minimal, outside assistance. Such empowerment efforts increase stakeholders' sense of ownership of the program and the probability that the program will become incorporated into the setting's routine mode of functioning (Fawcett, 1990).

As important as program maintenance is the challenge of program dissemination, both within and outside of psychology, to relevant applied researchers, human service organizations, governmental bodies, and so forth. Transmitting information about effective preventive programs and techniques to those who might profit by such knowledge is a vital initial step in the adoption process, and will require behavioral psychologists to venture beyond conventional psychology outlets such as journals and conventions. Particularly in these times of large budget deficits and retrenchment in funding for social programs, it is crucial to attend to the public policy implications of our interventions and to consider how to maximize their impact. Attempting to influence legislative or regulatory policies, for example, can be one way of initiating higher-level changes and expanding the reach of our programs (Jason, 1991).

As commented on earlier, behavioral psychologists engaged in prevention have developed an increasing openness toward collaboration with professions and disciplines outside of psychology. However, there remains room for further incorporation of concepts and theories from other subdisciplines *within* psychology. The challenge is to draw creatively from those areas that would appear to have especial heuristic value. These include social psychology (e.g., the concepts of psychological reactance and intrinsic motivation), environmental/ecological psychology (e.g., the idea of the interdependence of systems), and developmental psychology (e.g., the notion of transactional influence processes between persons and their environmental contexts) (Jason, 1992).

A final challenge concerns the importance of appreciating the complexity of settings and the impact of such complexity on both researchers and participants. The term *contextualism* has received much currency in recent writings on the philosophy of psychology as a science. It refers to the idea that knowledge is relative to a given frame of reference (Kingry-Westergaard & Kelly, 1990). According to this view, rather than discovering knowledge of the objective world, investigators are gathering knowledge of their interactions with the world. This somewhat humbling perspective suggests that several of the traditional goals of behavioral research—such as the external control of phenomena, the identification of universal principles, and the replicability of specific findings—may be elusive when mounting applied interventions (Jason, 1992). For example, the complexity of social environments may limit the robustness of general principles identified in laboratory settings and may alter or moderate their expression. Thus, the characteristics of the social settings in which we work, and the multiple contingencies that may simultaneously be in effect in any setting, need to be carefully analyzed to uncover the operative factors influencing behavior in that setting (Patterson, 1982). Illustratively, research on multiple contingencies indicates that contingent reinforcement in a particular environment can produce either high or low response rates depending on the other concurrently available sources of reinforcement (McDowell, 1982). An awareness of the complexity of settings can aid preventively oriented behavioral researchers in better comprehending and considering those contextual issues (e.g., entry issues, the process of target problem selection, larger systemic forces influencing the selected problem) that frequently determine a project's outcome (Bogat & Jason, in press).

The potential impact of behavioral principles and strategies on health and mental health promotion would appear to be considerable. Indeed, much current activity in health and education is already grounded in the application of learning theory by intervention agents and service deliverers who would hardly view themselves as behaviorists. The challenge is to develop more interventions in which behavioral approaches are applied more systematically and thoughtfully. Such interventions are exemplified by the projects highlighted in the following chapters. Increasing behavioral psychology's influence in the promotion of health and mental health represents an exciting opportunity for contributing to social change in the coming decade.

PURPOSE AND ORGANIZATION OF THIS BOOK

Our goal in putting together the current work is to reach two crucial audiences. The first consists of scholars and students wishing a summary of the existing research on health and mental health promotion from a behavioral perspective. Many of those comprising this audience may themselves be among those conducting community-based preventive interventions of the sort described herein. Our second audience is made up of those on the front lines—program developers and evaluators, human service administrators, and community organizers and advocates—seeking innovative, practical approaches to health and mental health promotion.

The chapters that follow are grouped into two parts. The first part contains seven chapters that address specific health and mental health issues—social competence in the schools, physical and sexual abuse, childhood accidents, substance abuse, adolescent pregnancy, AIDS, and vehicular safety. These topics are ones in which substantial investigation has been carried out. However, although they typify current research in the field, they are meant to be illustrative rather than exhaustive of the totality of preventively oriented applied behavioral research. For example, biologically and physiologically oriented interventions are not the explicit topic of any of the chapters. There are, however, many significant discoveries occurring in investigations of the nervous, endocrine, and immune systems (Cohen & Williamson, 1991; Kiecolt-Glaser & Glaser, 1989). Investigators in the field of psychoneuroimmunology (Kiecolt-Glaser, Garner, Speicher, Penn, & Glaser, 1984), for instance, have reported that under certain conditions (such as stress, bereavement, or loneliness) there are reductions in disease-fighting immune cells, whereas social support and relaxation training can enhance the immune system. Thus, it may be possible one day to use preventive strategies to boost the functioning of individuals vulnerable to disease.

The second part (chapters 9–11) considers three innovative strategies for health/mental health promotion—the media, social support, and community development. These strategies have applicability as intervention mechanisms for addressing the specific social problems in chapters 2 to 8, as well as a broad range of problems not considered in depth in this book.

All of the remaining chapters are structured in the same manner to provide consistency of organization. Each is divided into four sections reflecting the book's dual audience. The initial section defines the problem (e.g., AIDS) or strategy (e.g., the media) that is that chapter's subject, presenting its salient features and emphasizing why it merits attention. The second section is a critical review of the empirical literature on the topic, highlighting accomplishments and central findings, on the one hand, but also the shortcomings of research to date, on the other.

Each chapter then describes in detail an applied intervention project in its area, considering the ethical, logistical, political, and financial issues involved in actually designing and implementing such a project in the "real world." The objective of this third section is to convey a sense of both (a) the potential pitfalls that can endanger a project's success and (b) concrete recommendations for preventing and surmounting such stumbling blocks.

Finally, the chapters conclude with a fourth section discussing unresolved issues and future research directions, pointing the way to the next steps that empirical investigations and applied interventions might profitably take. Our hope is that the readers of this book will be among those involved in taking these steps into the field's future development.

REFERENCES

Albee, G. W. (1967). The relation of conceptual models to manpower needs. In E. L. Cowen, E. A. Gardner, & M. Zax (Eds.), *Emergent approaches to mental health problems* (pp. 63–73). New York: Appleton-Century-Crofts.

Albino, J. E. (1983). Health psychology and primary prevention: Natural allies. In R. D. Felner, L. A. Jason, J. N. Moritsugu, & S. S. Farber (Eds.), *Preventive psychology: Theory, research and practice* (pp. 221–233). New York: Pergamon.

Bandura, A. (1974). Behavior theory and models of man. *American Psychologist, 29,* 859–869.

Bogat, G. A., & Jason, L. A. (in press). Dogs bark at those they do not recognize: Towards an integration of behaviorism and community psychology. In J. Rappaport & E. Seidman (Eds.), *Handbook of community psychology.* New York: Plenum.

Caplan, C. (1964). *Principles of preventive psychiatry.* New York: Basic Books.

Cohen, S., & Williamson, G. M. (1991). Stress and disease in humans. *Psychological Bulletin, 109,* 5–24.

Cowen, E. L. (1974). Social and community interventions. In P. Mussen & M. Rosenzweig (Eds.), *Annual Review of Psychology* (Vol. 24, pp. 423–472). Palo Alto, CA: Annual Reviews.

Fawcett, S. B. (1990). Some emerging standards for community research and action: Aid from a behavioral perspective. In P. Tolan, C. Keys, F. Chertok, & L. Jason (Eds.), *Researching community psychology: Issues of theory and methods* (pp. 64–75). Washington, DC: American Psychological Association.

Geller, E. S., Winett, R. A., & Everett, P. B. (1982). *Preserving the environment: New strategies for behavior change.* New York: Pergamon.

Glenwick, D. S., & Jason, L. A. (Eds.). (1980). *Behavioral community psychology: Progress and prospects*. New York: Praeger.
Glenwick, D. S., & Jason, L. A. (1984). Behavioral community psychology: An introduction to the special issue. *Journal of Community Psychology, 12*, 103–112.
Greene, B. F., Winett, R. A., VanHouten, R., Geller, E. S., & Iwata, B. (Eds.). (1987). *Behavior analysis in the community: 1968–1986 from the Journal of Applied Behavior Analysis*. Lawrence, KS: Society for the Experimental Analysis of Behavior.
Heller, K., Price, R. H., Reinharz, S., Riger, S., Wandersman, A., & D'Aunno, T. (1984). *Psychology and community change: Challenges of the future* (2nd ed.). Homewood, IL: Dorsey.
Jason, L. A. (1991). Participating in social change: A fundamental value for our discipline. *American Journal of Community Psychology, 19*, 1–16.
Jason, L. A. (1992). Eco-transactional behavioral research. *Journal of Primary Prevention, 13*, 37–72.
Jason, L. A., & Crawford, I. (1991). Toward a kinder, gentler, and more effective behavioral approach in community settings. *Journal of Applied Behavior Analysis, 24*, 649–651.
Jason, L. A., & Glenwick, D. S. (1984). Behavioral community psychology: A review of recent research and applications. In M. Hersen, R. M. Eisler, & P. M. Miller (Eds.), *Progress in behavior modification* (Vol. 18, pp. 85–121). New York: Academic Press.
Jason, L. A., Hess, R. E., Felner, R. D., & Moritsugu, J. N. (Eds.). (1987). *Prevention: Toward a multidisciplinary approach*. New York: Hawthorn.
Jeger, A. M., & Slotnick, R. S. (Eds.). (1982). *Community mental health and behavioral-ecology: A handbook of theory, research, and practice*. New York: Plenum.
Kelly, J. (1990). Changing contexts and the field of community psychology. *American Journal of Community Psychology, 18*, 769–792.
Kiecolt-Glaser, J., Garner, W., Speicher, C. E., Penn, G., & Glaser, R. (1984). Psychosocial modifiers of immunocompetence in medical students. *Psychosomatic Medicine, 46*, 7–14.
Kiecolt-Glaser, J. K., & Glaser, R. (1989). Psychoneuroimmunology: Past, present, and future. *Health Psychology, 8*, 677–682.
Kingry-Westergaard, C., & Kelly, J. G. (1990). A contextualist epistemology for ecological research. In P. Tolan, C. Keys, F. Chertok, & L. Jason (Eds.), *Researching community psychology: Issues of theory and methods* (pp. 23–31). Washington, DC: American Psychological Association.
Krasner, L. (Ed.). (1980). *Environmental design and human behavior: A psychology of the individual in society*. New York: Pergamon.
Levine, M., & Perkins, D. V. (1987). *Principles of community psychology: Perspectives and applications*. New York: Oxford University Press.
Martin, P. R. (Ed.). (1991). *Handbook of behavior therapy and psychological science: An integrative approach*. New York: Pergamon.
McDowell, J. J. (1982). The importance of Herrnstein's mathematical statement of the law of effect for behavior therapy. *American Psychologist, 37*, 771–779.
Nietzel, M. T., Winett, R. A., MacDonald, M. L., & Davidson, W. S. (1977). *Behavioral approaches to community psychology*. New York: Pergamon.
Patterson, G. R. (1982). *Coercive family process*. Eugene, OR: Castalina.
Price, R. H., Cowen, E. L., Lorion, R. P., & Ramos-McKay, J. (Eds.). (1988). *Fourteen ounces of prevention*. Washington, DC: American Psychological Association.
Rappaport, J. (1977). *Community psychology: Values, research, and action*. New York: Holt, Rinehart and Winston.

Rhodes, J. E., & Jason, L. A. (1988). *Preventing substance abuse among children and adolescents.* New York: Pergamon.
United States Department of Health and Human Services (1991). *Healthy people 2000: National health promotion and disease prevention objectives* (DHHS Publication No. PHS 91-50213). Washington, DC: U.S. Government Printing Office.
Winett, R. A. (1986). *Information and behavior: Systems of influence.* Hillsdale, NJ: Lawrence Erlbaum.
Wolf, M. M. (1978). Social validity: The case for subjective measurement or how applied behavior analysis is finding its heart. *Journal of Applied Behavior Analysis, 11,* 203–214.

PART II

Targeting Specific Health and Mental Health Problems

CHAPTER 2

School-Based Interventions for Promoting Social Competence

Jean Rhodes and Susan Englund

DESCRIPTION OF THE PROBLEM

Schools are ideal settings for implementing behavioral, social competence interventions (Lorion, 1989; Rutter, Maughan, Mortimore, & Ouston, 1979; Weissberg, Caplan, & Harwood, 1991). The unifying administrative structure of schools provides opportunities to reach many youth during their formative years of social development (Cowen, Hightower, Pedro-Carroll, & Work, 1989). Many programs are easily implemented in classroom contexts, and school curricula provide an efficient vehicle for widespread dissemination (Cowen et al., 1989). In addition, teachers and other adults in the setting can serve as powerful identification figures or mentors for students, and can teach, model, and shape socially competent behavior. Finally, schools offer a vehicle for identifying potential social competence problems, which often begin or intensify during a child's school years (Maughan, 1988; Rutter, 1982; Weissberg et al., 1991). Such problems are associated with increased risk for negative behavioral and mental health outcomes (Weissberg, Caplan, & Sivo, 1989). Because teachers work closely with large groups of similarly aged children, they have standards of adaptive and maladaptive social behavior.

Despite this natural fit, school administrators and teachers have not completely embraced the idea of implementing social competence programs within school settings. This is due, in part, to the competing goals and pressures faced by schools. On the one hand, public pressure to improve scholastic achievement has led many schools to follow conventional curricula. Conversely, changes in the structure of families and communities have placed schools in the position of assuming a growing responsibility for their students' well-being. Schools have been forced to extend well beyond basic educational mandates to address larger social problems, such as AIDS, substance abuse, teenage pregnancy, and antisocial behavior (DeFreise, Crossland, Pearson, & Sullivan, 1990; Zins & Forman, 1988). Both the public and teachers recognize that improving youth's social competence may ultimately improve their capacity to achieve in school (Weissberg et al., 1991).

Innovative, school-based strategies that are sensitive to diverse student needs, as well as to the constraints and limited resources of schools, can help to address these competing demands. If such programs can improve students' social functioning, health behavior, and academic performance, particularly in the face of growing budgetary constraints, then the investment of resources would appear well spent.

REVIEW AND CRITIQUE OF THE LITERATURE

Cowen et al. (1989) have described several strategies for promoting social competence in school settings. One strategy is to teach and model directly the skills or social competencies that promote adjustment, and prevent or delay the initiation of problem behaviors. A second is to modify the classroom or overall school environment in ways that improve outcomes. A third is to develop interventions for students who are at risk because of their exposure to acute or chronic stressors, and to strengthen their coping skills. In the following sections we review behaviorally based social competence programs representing each of these strategies. We then provide a detailed case example to illustrate the third strategy. Readers interested in additional descriptions of social competence interventions are referred to two edited books by Price, Cowen, Lorion, and Ramos-McKay (1988) and Lorion (1989).

Skills Training

Classroom-based skills training is the most commonly used approach to promoting social competence (Weissberg et al., 1991). Skills training programs are designed to teach and model such skills as effective communication, peer pressure resistance, and assertiveness. They often include role playing, rehearsal, modeling, and peer instruction, and can be applied to a range of social situations. Although most of the early skills-based programs (e.g., Evans, Hansen, & Mittlemark, 1977; Jason, 1979) were designed to prevent cigarette smoking, programs are currently being implemented to promote general social competence and to prevent a range of problem behaviors among preschoolers and kindergartners through middle school and high school students.

Shure and Spivack (1988), for example, have developed an interpersonal cognitive problem-solving program for preschoolers and kindergartners. The program uses scripts, games, and exercises to foster the development of problem-solving skills. The training is designed to teach children to consider alternative solutions and consequences to problems and solution–consequence pairing. As youngsters understand and produce problem concepts, they can evaluate appropriate responses to interpersonal problems. The program can be informally integrated into the ongoing classroom instruction and continued as long as the children are in school. Studies with inner-city preschoolers have found relationships among certain cognitive problem-solving skills, teacher-rated adjustment, and improvements in children's adjustment (Shure & Spivack, 1988).

At the middle and high school levels, Botvin and colleagues have developed a curriculum-based program called Life Skills Training. This program seeks to facilitate the development of generic life skills, as well as skills and knowledge more specifically related to substance use. The general cognitive–behavioral skills incorporated into this program include techniques for (a) enhancing self-esteem (e.g., goal setting, behavioral change techniques, increasing positive self-statements; (b) resisting persuasive appeals (e.g., identifying persuasive appeals, formulating counterarguments); (c) coping with anxiety (e.g., relaxation training, mental rehearsal); (d) verbal and nonverbal communication skills; and (e) a variety of other social skills (e.g., initiating social interactions, communication skills, complimenting, assertiveness skills). These skills are taught using a combination of instruction, modeling, and rehearsal. Participation in the program has been found to be associated with significant reductions in tobacco, alcohol, and marijuana use among participants. Such changes appear to be more enduring when multiple years of training are provided (Botvin & Tortu, 1988).

Although these two examples represent sustained, multimethod approaches, many skills-based social competence programs have been brief and have relied on single-method intervention strategies. There is growing recognition, however, that more long-term comprehensive interventions may be required to bring about enduring behavioral changes among school-aged populations (Weissberg et al., 1991).

It should also be noted that some researchers have voiced concerns that skills-based techniques concentrate too narrowly on the individual and do not attend adequately to the powerful influences of schools, families, neighborhoods, and communities (Fantuzzo & Rohrbeck, 1992; Martens & Witt, 1988; Rhodes & Jason, 1988). Focusing on the child or adolescent, as opposed to the contributing social conditions, places the problem at the level of the individual, with the implicit suggestion that this is where the solution should begin (Rhodes & Jason, 1990). In addition to targeting individuals, skills training programs are beginning to attempt to influence supports within school settings and the broader environmental context (Weissberg et al., 1991).

Changing School Environments

In contrast to strategies that concentrate on students' skills, environmental approaches seek to develop or modify the classroom practices and school climate in ways that enhance social and educational competence. A basic assumption underlying such strategies is that regularities and contingencies within the school setting can directly influence its students' behavior. Efforts often center on identifying competence-promoting structural features and then arranging the school in ways that maximize school achievement (Comer, 1988). Rutter et al., (1979) for example, found that, irrespective of its size or physical characteristics, successful schools had several distinctive features. These included an emphasis on scholastic achievement, well-defined roles for teachers, rule and procedural flexibility, incentives and rewards for positive achievement, and conditions that fostered student responsibility.

Programs attempting to improve school climate are sometimes implemented during school transitions, when students are at heightened risk for academic and social maladjustment. During a transition, students can easily become confused about the size and complexity of their new school format or insecure about their role expectations. In addition, students often have concerns about their capacity to make and sustain new friendships or may fear academic failure (Hamburg, 1986). Given these stressors, several researchers (e.g., Felner & Adan, 1988; Felner, Ginter, & Primavera, 1982; Jason, 1992; Reyes, 1992) have implemented environmentally based programs designed to improve the adjustment of youth to new school settings.

In an effort to facilitate the adaptation of students during school transitions, Felner and his colleagues have developed and tested the School Transitional Environment Program (STEP). STEP has two primary components: (a) organizing the school environment so as to minimize the level of change and confusion, and (b) redefining the roles of homeroom teachers and guidance counselors to facilitate the provision of more support to students during school transitions (Felner & Adan, 1988). Evaluations of the program at the end of the first year of a high school transition indicated that, in contrast to matched comparison students, STEP students exhibited no declines in their academic performance, self-concept, or school attendance (Felner et al., 1982).

Reyes (1992) is currently implementing a similar program in an inner-city, predominantly minority school system. The program begins in the eighth grade and consists of three primary components: (a) increasing parents' awareness of high school regularities, (b) familiarizing the students with the new high school setting, and (c) providing teachers with specific techniques for dealing with students' heightened vulnerability. At the secondary school level, efforts are made to influence the environment so as to reduce its potential complexity. To this end, three additional components are emphasized: (a) redefining the role of the homeroom teacher such that he or she provides additional support, (b) reorganizing the school environment so as to reduce system flux (e.g., by minimizing daily classroom changes), and (c) providing parents with ongoing feedback on student progress. Such programs are expected to reduce the stress of school transition and, ultimately, to lower the incidence of school dropout. Preliminary evidence offers support for the efficacy of this approach with urban, Hispanic students.

In addition to efforts that concentrate on modifying the school environment, researchers are beginning to target the community contexts in which schools are embedded. Jason (1991), for example, provided compelling evidence for the effectiveness of a smoking intervention that sought to discourage merchants from selling cigarettes to minors. Incentives were provided to merchants in the surrounding community to work with the school system to deter minors from purchasing cigarettes. Merchant sales to minors in the target community dropped by 70% and rates of student usage by 50%.

Targeting At-Risk Youth

The general skills-based and environmental approaches described earlier are designed to target all youth with the hope of preventing the onset of problems. Although many high-risk youth benefit from participation in such programs, there are some who require additional intervention to strengthen their adaptive skills and forestall negative outcomes. The third strategy entails developing interventions for students who are at risk by virtue of their exposure to stressful life circumstances (Cowen et al., 1989).

Stressful life circumstances can have adverse psychological effects on children, predisposing them for later serious psychological and physical disorders (Cowen & Work, 1988; Garmezy & Rutter, 1983; Rutter, 1983). For example, the negative psychological effects of parental divorce, family discord, parental death, and childhood injury and hospitalization have all been linked with later negative adjustment (Cowen & Work, 1988; Kornberg & Caplan, 1980; Peterson & Mori, 1985; Wallerstein, 1983). Whereas the primary prevention programs reviewed previously are appropriate for most young people, it may be necessary to provide more intensive and differentiated interventions for those who are sustaining ongoing or acute life stressors.

One such program is the Children's Support Group (CSG) program, which is part of the Divorce Adjustment Project (Stolberg & Mahler, 1989). Stolberg and colleagues have pointed out that many of the stressors and tasks confronting divorcing adults disrupt their parenting skills and divert their attention away from child-rearing responsibilities. Thus, although the emotional impact of divorce on children often requires increased parental availability, it is frequently impossible for parents to provide this added buffering (Stolberg & Mahler, 1989). The Divorce Adjustment Project (Lorion, 1989; Stolberg & Garrison, 1985) incorporates a two-part, preventive intervention. First, children's support groups, designed to provide emotional support and to teach cognitive-behavioral skills aimed at increasing children's insight into parent and family interactions, are conducted in the school during the day. Concurrent with this program is the Single Parents' Support Group program, designed to promote adult adjustment and to train effective parenting strategies. The CSG program has been shown to be effective in reaching its prevention goals, with children's social competence improving significantly compared with a no-treatment control group (Stolberg & Mahler, 1989).

School-based prevention programs aimed at improving prenatal practices and promoting the social competence of pregnant students also exemplify this third approach. The following section provides a detailed case example that highlights the procedural, ethical, and political issues that arise when implementing an intervention for high-risk youth in a school setting.

CASE EXAMPLE

Program Rationale

Adolescent child bearing is associated with heightened risk for health and social adjustment problems. Adolescent mothers are exposed to a wider range of stressors and are at greater risk for distress than either older mothers or childless adolescents (Brown, Adams, & Killam, 1981; Elster, McAnary, & Lamb, 1983; Hayes, 1987). These young women must cope not only with the demands of motherhood but with the various social, educational, and developmental tasks of adolescence (Panzarine, 1986). Pregnant and parenting adolescents are at risk for school dropout, welfare dependency, and repeated early pregnancies (Hayes, 1987). Moreover, babies born to adolescents are more likely than other babies to be premature and to have low birthweights (Coll, 1990). These negative outcomes are even more likely to occur among African-American adolescents and their offspring, who often face additional adversities resulting from economic hardship and discrimination (McLoyd, 1990; Olds, 1988; Tucker, 1978).

Efforts to promote socially competent behavior among pregnant adolescents are needed. Research has indicated that adolescents are unusually receptive to training and support when they are going through the profound biological, psychological, and social changes produced by pregnancy (Hayes, 1987). Programs aimed at building supportive relationships may help to encourage the use of health services, reduce substance use, and promote long-term improvements in the parents' educational and social functioning (Baldwin & Cain, 1980; Colletta, 1981; Furstenberg & Crawford, 1978). For example, case management support services have been found to be associated with decreased alcohol and drug consumption, improved psychological functioning, and increased use of prenatal health care during pregnancy. Similarly, nurse home-visitation programs that provide support and behavioral parent education have led to dramatic improvements in the lives of pregnant teens and their infants (Olds, 1988; Provence & Naylor, 1983; Rush, Stein, & Insoln, 1980).

In addition to these more professionalized programs, there has been a rapid expansion of programs that pair pregnant teens with volunteer mentors from within the community. The mentors provide ongoing support to their protégées and serve as positive role models who encourage the adoption of prosocial, healthy behavior. Mentors appear to be effective in forestalling or preventing some of the problems associated with adolescent pregnancy and parenthood (Rhodes, Ebert, & Fischer, 1992).

Program Description

Currently, Rhodes et al. (1992) are investigating the Parent Mentor Program, which is being implemented in an alternative public high school for pregnant students. The students, nearly all of whom (98.6%) are African-American, attend the alternative school for the duration of their pregnancy, after which they transfer back to their regular high schools. Volunteer mentors are recruited to the Parent Mentor Program through an intensive community outreach and are paired with students on a one-to-one basis. The mentors offer ongoing support and systematic congitive-behavioral training, based largely on Kanfer's self-management model (Kanfer & Goldstein, 1986; Kanfer & Hagerman, 1987; Kanfer & Schefft, 1988). The self-management model seeks to help protégées in their current circumstances and to develop the skills they need to work toward the goals they ultimately want to achieve.

Motivation

An essential precursor to using self-management techniques is to ensure that the protégées are sufficiently motivated to work toward achieving their goals. Mentors help their protégées increase motivation in several ways. They assist the young women in clarifying their values and long- and short-term goals. The young women are encouraged to think about the kind of lives they would like to have in the future, and then are helped to determine systematically how those dreams might become reality. Mentors help to build hope by assisting the protégées in developing a plan for moving from their current life situation to the better life for which they are hoping. The plan is grounded in the protégées' values and priorities, and consists of a series of small, attainable steps. It is not a rigid blueprint, but a flexible outline that is easily altered if the priorities, circumstances, or desires of the young woman change. This process of building a plan based on reasonable steps is designed to help the protégée grow as she moves toward her goals. As hope grows, so does motivation and the probability of success in achieving her life goals.

Self-Management Strategy

The self-management strategy consists of three parts: self-monitoring, self-evaluation, and self-reinforcement. Self-monitoring includes paying close attention to some unwanted behaviors and noting the conditions under which they are most likely to occur. The protégée might record the time that a certain behavior occurred, what happened immediately before and following it, and how she felt before, during, and after it happened. By recording the circumstances surrounding the behavior, the young woman can become more aware of the factors sustaining it. For example, if she wants to quit smoking for the sake of her own health and that of her unborn baby, but has trouble stopping, she may discover through self-monitoring that she tends to smoke when she feels nervous. After discovering such a pattern, she and her mentor could discuss some alternative anxiety-reducing activities. She may be able to decrease her smoking gradually by substituting another behavior for smoking at these times.

When some pattern of unwanted behavior is detected and the protégée has begun to alter it, she can begin to engage in self-evaluation and self-reinforcement. Self-evaluation refers to attending specifically to one's attempts to modify a behavior and making special note of the progress one is making. The mentor can be an important figure in this technique, helping her partner to notice and appreciate the positive gains she is making. Self-reinforcement refers to rewarding oneself for a job (or a step) well done. The reward may be a few words of self-praise or may be a small material reward that the protégée chooses for herself as a treat.

In addition to these self-management strategies, the young women are introduced to specific problem-solving rules. These rules are designed to help the mentors and their protégées decide how to approach problems or difficult situations. The rules are presented as a way of thinking about one's life that promotes hope, as well as movement toward positive growth and change. The young women are encouraged to look for the aspects about their situations that they can change and to act on changing them. They are encouraged to make changes one small step at a time and to keep an open mind regarding the future. The mentors also teach their protégées a variety of skills including stress management, problem solving, and strategies for dealing with intense emotions.

Finally, the mentors are supplied with a guidebook that cites information and resources that their protégées may need during their pregnancies. With the assistance of the guidebook, the mentors are able to give their protégées information and direct them to places where they can receive further information and services. The program is set up in such a way as to encourage mentors to integrate the information from the guidebook with their understanding of the self-management techniques and the other skills they teach their protégées. For example, if a mentor looked under "Alcohol" in her guidebook, in addition to information about alcohol and pregnancy and listings for further information and local self-help groups, she would find a suggestion to refer back to the self-management model to help her protégée deal with the problem.

Overall, the self-management strategy is a useful tool because it teaches the protégées some of the skills they will need to help themselves in a variety of situations. The advantages of this type of approach are many. The high degree of participation by the protégée in setting her own goals increases her motivation to work toward these goals. As she works hard and begins to see progress, she becomes more enthusiastic about her plan. With the support of her mentor she can notice the progress that she is making, thereby increasing her self-esteem and sense of independence. Any mistrust the protégée may have of her adult mentor may be softened by the mentor's encouragement of the protégée's full participation in the decisions and goals that are made. Finally, the considerable allowance for individual variation and choice within the structured self-management model offers the young women opportunities to make their own choices within the context of a friendly, caring, and supportive relationship.

Evaluation

We are currently in the process of evaluating the effectiveness of this intervention model. Over the next several years, we will randomly assign every student in the school to an experimental (mentor) or comparison (no mentor) condition. The health and psychosocial functioning of the women with assigned mentors will be contrasted with that of women who have no mentor. Ultimately, we expect that women with assigned mentors will demonstrate improved psychosocial functioning relative to the comparison group.

Ethical Issues

Several ethical issues are raised regarding this program's implementation within the alternative school setting. First, there is the question of whether the structured program may undermine the natural wisdom of the indigenous, volunteer mentors. One of the program's strengths is that so many of the volunteer mentors were themselves adolescent mothers. As such, they possess the experiential understanding and credibility that make them strong role models and information sources for their young protégées. As Borkman (1984) pointed out, people with experiences in common are often easily able to form close bonds with one another. Thus, the benefits of the mentoring relationship may come from the emotional connection and support rather than from anything in particular the mentor might say or do. Introducing a structured agenda into the mentoring relationships could undermine the mentor's status and sense of personal efficacy and weaken their experiental authority. They may come to feel they have little to offer without the self-management technique—or may focus on that technique to the exclusion of their own experience. Conversely, whether or not the mentors use a structured program in their interactions with their partners, the influence of their shared backgrounds is likely to remain. It is hoped that the self-management strategy will be used as a supplement to the mentors' natural wisdom.

A second issue concerns the fact that we are advocating an individual solution to what is clearly a much broader social problem. In doing so, we may be sending a message to both the young women and others that adolescent pregnancy and the circumstances surrounding it are problems of individuals rather than society. Nonetheless, at this time, societal solutions are not forthcoming, and the young women are in immediate need of assistance. We have identified some skills that can potentially help young, pregnant women as well as some natural helpers who can teach them the skills. Problems as complex as adolescent pregnancy need to be addressed from a variety of perspectives—including working with individuals to effect change.

Finally, although most of the participants in the Parent Mentor Program are urban African-American women, the self-management procedure was formulated as a therapeutic technique with white clinical populations (Kanfer & Schefft, 1988). To minimize cultural biases inherent in the program, we are working in collaboration with a cohort of African-American mentors and protégées to transform and develop the self-management training into a program that is culturally sensitive and relevant to the students' lives.

Implementation Issues

It should be pointed out that an effective behavioral intervention strategy alone cannot ensure a program's success. The success of any school-based strategy depends also on its implementation. The potential for positive effects can be diminished when program implementers are poorly trained, have inadequate organizational support for program delivery, or fail to develop productive, collaborative relationships with school personnel (Fantuzzo & Rohrbeck, 1992; Rhodes & Jason, 1988). In many cases, programs are designed and implemented by university- or agency-based researchers who conduct evaluation research in the school. The researcher typically enters the setting with a model and hopes that the school officials, teachers, and students will adopt it (Dryfoos, 1990). This approach can be successful or disastrous, depending on the level of trust and cooperation established among the various persons involved. In the following sections, we will discuss some of these factors and how they may influence the success or failure of behavioral interventions in the school setting.

Collaboration

A key to gaining the trust of school personnel is to enter the setting in a spirit of collaboration. This includes making efforts to allow school officials to identify their own problems. The implementers can then assist school officials by providing appropriate behavioral strategies to address these problems. Collaboration also entails demonstrating a genuine respect for the school personnel's important role in the implementation process. Teachers and staff are the experts regarding their school ecology and social validity issues. They can assist the implementers in developing an adequate appreciation of the classroom or school ecology, and the ways in which implementation might be affected by internal and external factors.

Identifying Sources of Resistance

Even with a collaborative stance, subtle and not-so-subtle variables can impede a program's success within a setting. For example, although a principal or board of education may agree to participate in a university-conceived program, there may be reluctance to provide the necessary time and support. Examples of this might include repeated scheduling difficulties during the initial and follow-up evaluations or lack of support from key teachers or staff. Under such circumstances, even the most carefully designed behavioral program may not stand a chance. School systems (like many administrative structures) tend to seek a state of equilibrium, and a program may be seen as a drain on resources and a threat to the system's stability. Careful observance of existing policies and regularities can help reduce or minimize the threat of instability (Parsons & Meyers, 1985; Rhodes & Jason, 1988).

Implementers must also be aware of the power conflicts that may exist among school officials, and be able to gain the administration's trust and support. Understanding the internal and external power structures is a crucial step in this process. Internally, the program implementer should identify the key personnel within a setting as well as potential sources of opposition. For example, an important element of success within a school setting is the establishment of positive, collaborative relationships with individuals serving as the "gatekeepers." Gatekeepers, such as the principal, guidance counselor, or certain teachers, may oversee and sanction the implementers' entry into the school. Some have been assigned this role formally, whereas others adopt it more informally (Glidewell, 1959). It is critical to find out where the real power and decision making resides. If a teacher who has been in the system for a long time, and has considerable support among other teachers, opposes the intervention, it may fail even if the principal is supportive.

In addition to understanding the internal power structures, the implementer should be familiar with external factors that may have a significant impact on program functioning (Caplan, 1974). In Chicago, for example, each public school is governed by a 12-member local school council, consisting of parents, community members, teachers, and the principal. The council oversees personnel, budgetary, and programming decisions. Before any program is implemented within a given school, it must gain the majority approval of the school council. Neighborhood and community groups can also have a significant impact on interventions, as can churches, local and state policies, and government agencies. These forces can influence a school's goals and philosophy, as well as its structural and internal dynamics. If, for example, the school board imposes a shift in education to a "back to basics" approach, a proposed school-based, behavioral intervention for promoting social competence may be cut to provide additional time for basic curricula. Finally, the implementer should be familiar with past attempts to introduce interventions into a particular school setting. If, in the past, many other programs have been tried and failed, the school personnel might be reluctant to attempt another intervention (Rhodes & Jason, 1988).

Throughout this chapter, we have presented several examples of promising school-based, behavioral interventions designed to promote students' social competence. Implementing such interventions within a school system is a complex process, and there are countless factors that may affect success. As we have discussed, the development of collaborative relationships within school settings can ensure the integrity of program implementation.

FUTURE DIRECTIONS

We have provided several promising examples of behavioral programs designed to promote students' social competence. These approaches typically target all youth with the hope of preventing the onset of a wide range of problems. We also highlighted programs that target youth who appear to be most at risk for later social adjustment difficulties by virtue of their exposure to stressful life circumstances. It was suggested that these youth may require additional intervention to strengthen their coping skills and delay or prevent negative outcomes. In both cases, long-term comprehensive interventions appear to be required to bring about behavioral changes in school-aged children and adolescents.

Efforts to develop enduring, comprehensive social competence programs will continue to challenge researchers and practitioners. Such work will, no doubt, be shaped by the nation's rapidly worsening socioeconomic conditions. Unemployment, poverty, and crime are tragically affecting the lives of thousands of youth and undermining the vitality of their families, neighborhoods, schools, and social systems. In light of these changes, it will be important for researchers and practitioners to increase and intensify our prevention efforts. In the course of these efforts, we face critical questions concerning the most realistic, cost-effective ways to address social competence problems.

To date, our research, intervention, and funding priorities have concentrated on the individual, largely ignoring the crucial contributing role of contextual variables. The poverty-related nature of many social and health problems, however, makes it necessary to widen and even alter our traditional approaches. There is a need to examine and address individual social competencies in context or even shift the major interest to a predominantly structural or ecological orientation.

This will require interventions that are both sensitive to the complex interplay of various levels of behavioral influences and responsive to the regularities of the school system.

REFERENCES

Baldwin, W., & Cain, V. S. (1980). The children of teenage parents. *Family Planning Perspectives, 12,* 34–43.
Borkman, R. (1984). Mutual self-help groups: Strengthening the selectively unsupportive personal and community networks of their members. In A. Gortner & F. Riessman (Eds.), *The self-help revolution* (pp. 205–215). New York: Human Sciences Press.
Botvin, G. J., & Tortu, S. (1988). Preventing adolescent substance abuse through life skills training. In R. H. Price, E. L. Cowen, R. P. Lorion, & J. Ramos-McKay (Eds.), *Fourteen ounces of prevention: A casebook for practitioners* (pp. 98–110). Washington, DC: American Psychological Association.
Brown, H., Adams, R., & Kellam, S. (1981). A longitudinal study of teenage motherhood and symptoms of distress: The Woodlawn community epidemiology project. In R. G. Simmons (Ed.), *Research in community mental health.* New York: JAI Press.
Caplan, G. (1974). *Support systems and community mental health.* New York: Behavioral Sciences Press.
Coll, C. G. (1990). Developmental outcome of minority infants: A process-oriented look into our beginnings. *Child Development, 61,* 270–289.
Colletta, N. D. (1981). Social support and the risk of maternal rejection by adolescent mothers. *Journal of Psychology, 109,* 191–197.
Comer, J. P. (1988). Educating poor minority children. *Scientific American, 259,* 42–48.
Cowen, E. L., Hightower, A. D., Pedro-Carrol, J., & Work, W. C. (1989). School-based models for primary prevention programming with children. In R. P. Lorion (Ed.), *Protecting the children: Strategies for optimizing emotional and behavioral development* (pp. 133–160). New York: Haworth Press.
DeFries, G. H., Crossland, C. L., Pearson, C. E., & Sullivan, C. J. (1990). Comprehensive school health programs: Current status and future prospects. *Journal of School Health, 60,* 16–34.
Dryfoos, J. G. (1990). *Adolescents at risk: Prevalence and prevention.* New York: Oxford University Press.
Elias, M. J., & Weissberg, R. P. (1989). School-based social-competence promotion as a primary prevention strategy: A tale of two projects. *Prevention in Human Services, 7,* 177–200.
Elster, A. B., McAnanary, E. R., & Lamb, M. E. (1983). Parental behavior of adolescent mothers. *Pediatrics, 71,* 494–503.
Evans, R., Hansen, W. B., & Mittlemark, M. B. (1977). Increasing the validity of self-reports of smoking behavior in children. *Journal of Applied Psychology, 62,* 521–523.
Fantuzzo, J. W., & Rohrback, C. A. (1992). *Self-managed groups: Fitting self-management approaches into classroom systems.* Manuscript submitted for publication.
Felner, R., & Adan, A. (1988). The school transitional environment project: An ecological intervention and evaluation. In R. H. Price, E. L. Cowen, R. P. Lorion, & J. Ramos-

McKay (Eds.), *Fourteen ounces of prevention: A casebook for practitioners* (pp. 111–122). Washington, DC: American Psychological Association.

Felner, R. D., Ginter, M., & Primavera, J. (1982). Primary prevention during school transitions: Social support and environmental structure. *American Journal of Community Psychology, 10*, 277–290.

Felner, R. D., Primavera, J., & Cauce, A. M. (1981). The impact of school transitions: A focus for preventive efforts. *American Journal of Community Psychology, 9*, 449–459.

Furstenberg, F. F., & Crawford, A. G. (1978). Family support: Helping teenage mothers to cope. *Family Planning Perspectives, 10*, 322–333.

Glidewell, J. C. (1959). The entry problem in consultation. *Journal of Social Issues, 15*, 51–59.

Hamburg, B. A. (1986). Subsets of adolescent mothers: Developmental, biomedical, and psychosocial issues. In J. B. Lancaster & B. A. Hamburg (Eds.), *School-age pregnancy and parenthood: Biosocial dimensions* (pp. 115–145). New York: Aldine De Gruyter.

Hayes, C. D. (1987). *Risking the future: Adolescent sexuality, pregnancy, and childbearing*. Washington, DC: National Academy Press.

Jason, L. A. (1979). Preventive community interventions: Reducing school children's smoking and decreasing smoke exposure. *Professional Psychology, 10*, 744–752.

Jason, L. A. (1992). *School transitions: A strategic time to help children*. San Francisco: Jossey-Bass.

Kanfer, F. H., & Goldstein, A. P. (Eds.). (1986). *Helping people change: A textbook of methods* (3rd ed.). New York: Pergamon.

Kanfer, F. H., & Hagerman, S. M. (1978). A model of self-regulation. In F. Halisch & J. Kuhl (Eds.), *Motivation, intentions, and volition* (pp. 87–125). New York: Springer Verlag.

Kanfer, F. H., & Scheftt, B. K. (1988). *Guiding the process of therapeutic change*. Champaign, IL: Research Press.

Kornberg, M. S., & Caplan, G. (1980). Risk factors and preventive interventions in child therapy: A review. *Journal of Prevention, 1*, 73–133.

Lorion, R. P. (1989). Basing preventive interventions on theory: Stimulating a field's momentum. In R. P. Lorion (Ed.), *Protecting the children: Strategies for optimizing emotional and behavioral development* (pp. 7–32). New York: Haworth Press.

Martens, B. K., & Witt, J. C. (1988). Expanding the scope of behavioral consultation: A systems approach to classroom behavior change. *Professional School Psychology, 3*, 271–281.

Maughan, B. (1988). School experiences as risk/protective factors. In M. Rutter (Ed.), *Studies of psychosocial risk: The power of longitudinal data* (pp. 200–220). New York: Cambridge University Press.

McLoyd, V. C. (1990). The impact of economic hardship on black families and children: Psychological distress, parenting, and socioemotional development. *Child Development, 61*, 311–346.

Olds, D. L. (1988). The prenatal/early infancy project. In R. H. Price, E. L. Cowen, R. P. Lorion, & J. Ramos-McKay (Eds.), *Fourteen ounces of prevention* (pp. 9–23). Washington, DC: American Psychological Association.

Panzarine, S. (1986). Stressors, coping, and social supports of adolescent mothers. *Journal of Adolescent Health, 7*, 153–161.

Parsons, R. D., & Meyers, J. (1985). *Developing consultation skills*. San Francisco: Jossey-Bass.

Peterson, L., & Mori, L. (1985). Prevention of child injury: An overview of targets, meth-

ods, and tactics for psychologists. *Journal of Consulting and Clinical Psychology, 53,* 586–595.
Price, R. H., Cowen, E. L., Lorion, R. P., & Ramos-McKay, J. (Eds.). (1988). *Fourteen ounces of prevention: A Casebook for Practitioners.* Washington, DC: American Psychological Association.
Provence, S., & Naylor, A. (1983). *Working with disadvantaged parents and children: Scientific issues and practice.* New Haven, CT: Yale University Press.
Reyes, O. (1992). *An ecological drop-out prevention program.* Unpublished manuscript.
Rhodes, J. E., Ebert, L., & Fischer, K. (1992). Natural mentors: An overlooked resource in the social networks of young African-American mothers. *American Journal of Community Psychology, 20,* 445–461.
Rhodes, J. E., & Jason, L. A. (1988). *Preventing substance abuse among children and adolescents.* Elmsford, NY: Pergamon.
Rhodes, J. E., & Jason, L. A. (1990). A social stress model of substance abuse. *Journal of Consulting and Clinical Psychology, 58,* 395–401.
Rush, D., Stein, Z., & Insoln, M. (1980). A randomized controlled trial of prenatal supplementation in New York City. *Pediatrics, 65,* 683–697.
Rutter, M. (1982). Psychosocial resilience and protective mechanisms. *American Journal of Orthopsychiatry, 57,* 316–331.
Rutter, M., Maughan, B., Mortimore, P., & Ouston, J. (1979). *Fifteen thousand hours: Secondary schools and their effects on children.* Cambridge, MA: Harvard University Press.
Shure, M. B., & Spivack, G. (1988). Interpersonal cognitive problem solving. In R. H. Price, E. L. Cowen, R. P. Lorion, J. Ramos-McKay (Eds.), *Fourteen ounces of prevention: A casebook for practitioners* (pp. 69–82). Washington, DC: American Psychological Association.
Stolberg, A. L., & Mahler, J. L. (1989). Protecting children from the consequences of divorce: An empirically derived approach. In R. P. Lorion (Ed.), *Protecting the children: Strategies for optimizing emotional and behavioral development* (pp. 161–176). New York: Haworth Press.
Tucker, C. (1978). Parental perceptions of child rearing problems. *Child Psychiatry and Human Development, 8,* 145–161.
Wallerstein, J. S. (1983). Children of divorce: Stress and development tasks. In N. Garmezy & M. Rutter (Eds.), *Stress, coping and development in children* (pp. 265–302). New York: McGraw-Hill.
Weissberg, R. P., Caplan, M., & Harwood, R. L. (1991). Promoting competent young people in competence-enhancing environments: A systems-based perspective on primary prevention. *Journal of Consulting and Clinical Psychology, 59,* 830–841.
Weissberg, R. P., Caplan, M. Z., & Sivo, P. J. (1989). A new conceptual framework for establishing school-based social-competence programs. In L. A. Bond & B. E. Compas (Eds.), *Primary prevention and promotion in the schools* (pp. 255–260). New York: Sage.
Zins, J., & Forman, S. G. (Eds.) (1988). Mini-series on primary prevention: From theory to practice. *School Psychology Review, 17,* 539–634.

CHAPTER 3

Prevention of Child Physical and Sexual Abuse

Sandy K. Wurtele

DESCRIPTION OF THE PROBLEM

This chapter reviews behavioral approaches to preventing two types of child maltreatment—physical abuse and sexual abuse. Physical abuse has included two major categories: (a) major physical injuries, which include severe bruises/cuts/lacerations, burns/scalds, bone fractures, internal injuries, poisonings, brain damage/skull fracture, subdural hemorrhage or hematoma, and dislocation/sprains; and (b) minor physical injuries, which include minor cuts/bruises/welts, twisting/shaking, or similar injuries that do not constitute a substantial risk to the life of the child (American Humane Association, 1988). Sexual abuse has been defined by the National Center on Child Abuse and Neglect (1978) as contacts or interactions between a child and a perpetrator when the child is being used for the sexual stimulation of the perpetrator or another person.

Incidence

Both physical and sexual abuse are considered to be serious social problems affecting children, families, and society. Although statistics on the frequency of occurrence vary considerably, reports of physical abuse consistently outnumber those of sexual abuse. For example, the second National Incidence Study (Department of Health & Human Services, 1988; Sedlak, 1990) estimated that 269,700 children experienced physical abuse in 1986, whereas the estimated incidence for sexual abuse during that same time period was 119,300 children. The American Association for the Protection of Children reported that approximately 28% of all child abuse and neglect reports in 1986 involved charges of physical abuse, and 16% involved charges of sexual abuse (American Humane Association, 1988).

Sex and Age of Victim

The two forms of abuse differ in their sex distribution, as relatively equal numbers of males and females experience physical abuse, but more females experience sexual abuse (or at least more females are reported). Regarding age distribution, the incidence of physical abuse resulting in major physical injuries decreases with increasing age. For example, children with major injuries tend to be younger ($M =$ 5.54 years) than children experiencing minor injuries ($M = 8.29$; American Humane Association, 1988). Fatalities as a result of abuse also decrease with increasing age (American Humane Association, 1988; Crittenden & Craig, 1990). Sexual abuse victims tend to be older ($M = 9.19$; American Humane Association, 1988) than physical abuse victims.

Perpetrator Characteristics

Perpetrators of the two types of maltreatment differ. According to the American Humane Association (1988), perpetrators of sexual abuse are more likely to be male (82.4%) than female (17.6%). For physical abuse, the male–female ratio is about 1:1 (50.5% male vs. 49.5% female), although perpetrators of major physical injuries are more likely to be female (56.8% female vs. 43.2% male), perhaps related to females' greater contact with younger children. Perpetrator relationship to the child victim also varies according to the type of maltreatment. For physical abuse, perpetrators are primarily parents (81.9%) compared with other relatives (5.5%) and unrelated perpetrators (12.6%), whereas for sexual abuse, the distribution is more even across parents (42%), relatives (22.8%), and acquaintances (35.2%; American Humane Association, 1988).

Although child abuse occurs at all socioeconomic (SES) levels, a disproportionate percentage of maltreated children come from lower SES families. For example, children from families earning less than $15,000 a year were more than 5 times as likely to be maltreated and more than 7 times as likely to be seriously injured or impaired (Department of Health & Human Services, 1988).

Consequences

Both physical and sexual abuse have been associated with a variety of detrimental consequences. Consequences of physical abuse can include insecure infant–mother attachment formation; neurological and ocular damage; cognitive deficits and developmental delays (especially in fine motor and language skills);

socioemotional problems, such as lack of trust and empathy, low self-esteem, depression, and poor relationships with adults and peers; school-related problems including misconduct and academic underachievement; antisocial behaviors including juvenile delinquency and aggressiveness; and self-mutilative or other self-destructive behaviors (Ammerman, Cassisi, Hersen, & Van Hasselt, 1986; Cicchetti, 1987; Crittenden, 1988; Erickson, Egeland, & Pianta, 1989; Youngblade & Belsky, 1990). The final and severest consequence of physical abuse is death, with an average of three fatalities reported daily (Daro & Mitchel, 1990).

Initial consequences of child sexual abuse can include affective disturbances (e.g., anxiety, depression, shame and guilt, hostility, anger), physical problems (e.g., genital injury, urinary tract infections), cognitive disturbances (e.g., low school achievement, poor concentration, dissociation), and sociobehavioral disturbances (e.g., withdrawal, aggression, disturbed peer relations, strong dependency needs, oversexualized behavior) (Alter-Reid, Gibbs, Lachenmeyer, Sigal, & Massoth, 1986; Miller-Perrin & Wurtele, 1990; Wyatt & Powell, 1988). The emotional damage resulting from both types of maltreatment may last a lifetime.

Response to the Problem

Clearly, the physical and sexual abuse of children are seriously disturbing problems that warrant response and intervention. An initial response was an expanded service system for victims, their families, and perpetrators. Unfortunately, treatment programs are not always successful in protecting children from continued abuse. Cohn and Daro's (1987) review of federally funded demonstration treatment programs indicated that a high percentage (30–47%) of parents maltreated their children while undergoing treatment, and the likelihood for future maltreatment continued to exist for more than one half of the families served. Recidivism rates of child molesters range from 1% (Giarretto, 1982) to 40% (Marshall & Christie, 1981). It has become clear that treatment efforts in general will not eradicate these problems. More recently, the concern has expanded into prevention efforts, and a wide array of programs aimed at primary or secondary prevention (Caplan, 1964) have been developed.

REVIEW AND CRITIQUE OF THE LITERATURE

Physical Abuse

In the area of physical abuse, efforts to reduce the number of new cases (i.e., primary prevention) have included (a) interventions that enhance parental competencies, resources, and coping skills, such as parent education programs in hospitals and communities; and (b) programs that prevent the onset of abusive behavior, such as community-wide media campaigns, crisis services, and community enhancement of social networks (Rosenberg & Reppucci, 1985). Some of these primary prevention interventions have targeted parents deemed to be at high risk for abusing their children. Risk factors associated with physical abuse include but are not limited to low SES, single and teenaged parenthood, isolation from support networks, and complicated pregnancies (Belsky, 1980). A variety of interventions have been used with populations thought (epidemiologically) to be at risk for abusing their children including facilitating bonding by encouraging increased postpartum contact (O'Connor, Vietze, Sherrod, Sandler, & Altemeier, 1980) and bolstering parents' support networks by providing regular home visitations by either nurse practitioners (Olds, Henderson, Tatelbaum, & Chamberlin, 1986) or trained parent volunteers (Boger, Richter, & Weatherston, 1983; Taylor & Beauchamp, 1988).

Only recently have behavioral methods been explored as an early intervention and prevention strategy. The conceptual model for treating and preventing child abuse underlying early strategies was the social-situational model (Parke & Collmer, 1975). This model proposes that unique characteristics of both the parent and the child interact to bring about maltreatment in particular situations (e.g., high levels of stress). Derived from social learning theory, the social-situational model suggests that parents physically abuse their children in a futile effort to achieve control over the child's behavior. Factors that contribute to this process include limited and ineffective parental disciplinary tactics and aggressive, hyperactive, or noncompliant behaviors of children. It is well established that compared with nonabusing parents, abusive parents exhibit deficits in child management skills (Bousha & Twentyman, 1984; Burgess & Conger, 1978; Trickett & Kuczynski, 1986). In addition, abused children emit more threats and physically negative behaviors (Reid, Taplin, & Lorber, 1981), are more aggressive and noncompliant (Herrenkohl & Herrenkohl, 1981; Oldershaw, Waters, & Hall, 1986; Trickett & Kuczynski, 1986), and display fewer positive behaviors (Oldershaw et al., 1986) compared with nonabused children. (Although it is difficult to distinguish cause from consequences, such child behaviors can serve to maintain dysfunctional parental care.)

According to this transactional model of mutual influence (Sameroff & Chandler, 1974), a pattern of interactions can result in which the child's aversive behaviors (e.g., noncompliance) increase parental frustrations and elicit more punitive tactics, which, in turn, increases the child's "provocative" (Mannarino & Cohen, 1990) behaviors (e.g., angry outbursts), thus increasing the probability of physical abuse and trapping the parent and child in a "coercive cycle" (Patterson, 1982) that maintains the abuse. Such a pattern is reflected in survey data (Gil, 1969, 1970) showing that abusive episodes often occur during disciplinary encounters. For example, comparing the reasons for physically abusive and nonabusive disciplinary incidents, Herrenkohl, Herrenkohl, and Egolf (1983) found that physical abuse was more frequently associated with the child's refusing to do something, fighting or arguing with a sibling, playing with dangerous objects, creating some inconvenience (e.g., bed-wetting), lying or stealing, or being aggressive. Child fatalities during early childhood have also resulted from beatings associated with noxious child behavior (Crittenden & Craig, 1990). From this perspective, children in abusive families are difficult to manage, and their parents have not learned (or do not perform) effective child management skills to control them. Therefore, early behavioral research focused on training abusive or potentially abusive parents in effective and nonviolent child management skills to reduce coercive interactions.

Early investigations into the utility of a behavioral approach used case studies and targeted already abusing parents (e.g., Wolfe & Sandler, 1981). These studies provided preliminary support for the social learning model's prediction that improvement in parents' child management skills may result in less coercive child-rearing methods and fewer child behavior problems in the home. By providing intensive child management training to abusive parents, aversive behavior toward their children was reduced, positive behaviors (of both parents and children) increased, and further abuse was prevented.

As empirical research began revealing the multidimensional nature of child maltreatment (see Ammerman, 1990, for a review of etiological models of child maltreatment), prevention approaches began targeting such maltreatment correlates as social isolation, parent-child conflict, ineffective coping with anger arousal, and inadequate social and self-control skills, and also began working with a larger sample of child-abusing parents (e.g., Barth, Blythe, Schinke, & Schilling, 1983; Wolfe, Sandler, & Kaufman, 1981).

As an example of a more preventively oriented intervention, Wolfe, Edwards, Manion, and Koverola (1988) implemented a parent training program with a group of young parents and children who had been identified as being "at risk" for child maltreatment. "At-risk" status was determined by scores on the Child Abuse Potential Inventory (CAPI; Milner, 1986), evidence of major problems in the parenting role (e.g., anger, lack of parenting knowledge), and home observations confirming problematic child behavior. Thirty women, mostly single and of low income, with young children aged 9 to 60 months were randomly assigned to either the behavioral parent training program or the information-only comparison program offered by the child protection agency. The parent training condition included individual training in child management skills (to increase social rewards and decrease aversive behaviors) and enhancement of the child's adaptive functioning (e.g., language and social interaction skills). These mothers also were taught in vivo desensitization (e.g., relaxation, diversion) with their children present. Additionally, they received the standard agency services (i.e., information group meetings and periodic home visits from their caseworkers). Self-report measures indicated that significant improvements in parenting risk (CAPI scores) and child behavior problems at posttest and at 3-month follow-up were evident only for mothers who participated in parent training in addition to information groups. Home observation data on frequencies of praise, criticism, and physical negative behavior revealed that both treatment and comparison groups provided a more stimulating environment for their children after treatment. Caseworkers rated the parent-training mothers as managing significantly better and being at lower risk of maltreatment than the comparison mothers. The agency had closed the cases for six of the treatment versus only two of the comparison subjects by the 1-year follow-up.

Working with mothers identified by community professionals as at risk of engaging in child abuse, Barth and colleagues (Barth, 1989; Barth, Hacking, & Ash, 1988) focused on helping clients reduce environmental stressors and build formal and informal service and resource networks. They also provided modeling or instruction on parenting skills, goal setting, and problem solving. Paraprofessional "parenting consultants" visited clients in their homes and helped them identify goals for improved self- and child care (e.g., becoming involved with school or work, using community services, learning and using knowledge of child development, and preparing for the baby's birth). Clients specified tasks that would move them closer to the achievement of their goals, and social-learning approaches were used to promote task achievement. For example, when working with depressed mothers, the parenting consultants helped them focus on positive activities, pleasant events, and physical exercise (Barth, 1985). The achievement of tasks was related to a reduction in CAPI scores in Barth (1989), although reports of child abuse were similar for treatment and control groups in Barth et al. (1988).

Research reviewed thus far has concentrated on two sets of factors thought to contribute to child physical abuse, namely, parental characteristics (e.g., ineffective child management or problem-solving techniques, poor self-control), and child characteristics (e.g., noncompliance). Recently, a third set of factors—disturbances in the family ecosystem—has been recognized as contributing to child abuse. The family ecosystem can be disturbed because of such problems as unemployment, marital distress, hazardous homes, medical problems, and parental social isolation or "insularity" (Wahler, 1980). These and other pressures can intensify the effects of child misconduct and serve as functional contributors to abuse.

The necessity of considering these three factors (the parent, the child, and the family ecosystem) was the basic tenet of Project 12-Ways, an ecobehavioral approach to the treatment and prevention of child abuse and neglect (J. R. Lutzker, 1984). "Ecobehavioral" means that behavior must be examined within the contexts of the environments in which it exists. Project 12-Ways can be considered "ecobehavioral" as it provided in vivo services (e.g., in homes, schools) in many different areas including child management training, stress-reduction skills training, assertiveness training, self-control instruction, job-finding skills training, money management, health maintenance and nutrition instruction, home safety improvement, training for children lagging in developmental skills (e.g., toilet training), marital and leisure time counseling, alcohol treatment referral, social support groups, and prenatal/postnatal care for single parents (e.g., Barone, Greene, & J. R. Lutzker, 1986; J. R. Lutzker, Megson, Webb, & Dachman, 1985; S. Z. Lutzker, J. R. Lutzker, Braunling-McMorrow, & Eddleman, 1987). The intervention package offered to a particular family was based on an assessment of that family's needs and circumstances, the goal being to provide a package that appeared to have the greatest likelihood of success (J. R. Lutzker, McGimsey, McRae, & Campbell, 1983). The intent was to help families build an environment that would reduce the likelihood of abuse and neglect.

Though demonstrating the impact of various services on individual families involved in, or at risk for abuse, the preceding reports did not answer the question of whether Project 12-Ways had any large-scale impact on child abuse and its reoccurrence. For example, did families that terminated treatment for abuse refrain from subsequent abuse? Lutzker and Rice (1987) examined recidivism data over 5 years for 352 Project 12-Ways families and 358 comparison families. Overall, the percentage of recidivistic families was 21.3% for Project 12-Ways families and 28.5% for the comparison families, a difference that was statistically significant. Although the differences may not have been clinically large, they must be viewed in light of the nonrandom assignment of families (i.e., the severer cases may be referred to Project 12-Ways). Although this approach has not been shown to prevent child abuse in all families, the provision of multiple kinds of services in multiple settings appears to be a logical approach, and its applicability to at-risk groups seems promising. Indeed, Project Ecosystems, a replication of Project 12-Ways, is directed at families with developmentally disabled children who are at risk for abuse and neglect (Newman & J. R. Lutzker, 1990).

Sexual Abuse

The prevention of child sexual abuse has taken a different tack, in both the type and target of prevention efforts. Most of the work has been at the primary prevention time point and has targeted children, by teaching them means of identifying sexual advances and strategies for preventing their own abuse. Programs are most often presented in classrooms to groups of children, with accompanying presentations sometimes made to teachers and parents (e.g., Hill & Jason, 1987). Program format has varied along a continuum from those employing a didactic approach and emphasizing children's understanding of prevention concepts to those stressing acquisition of certain behavioral skills.

Early attempts provided children with basic information about sexual abuse in a didactic fashion. In several studies (e.g., Conte, Rosen, Saperstein, & Shermack, 1985; Kolko, Moser, & Hughes, 1989; Wolfe, MacPherson, Blount, & Wolfe, 1986), children observed a live (e.g., given by deputy sheriffs or medical students) or filmed presentation about sexual abuse and then participated in discussions. The results indicated that children increased their knowledge about sexual abuse, although these knowledge gains were of low magnitude.

Other researchers have explored whether children learn better from programs that incorporate a more active mode of training. For example, Wurtele, Marrs, and Miller-Perrin (1987) compared a program that included participant modeling (PM) with a similar program using symbolic modeling (SM). Twenty-six kindergarten children were randomly assigned to one of the two programs. The PM program taught self-protective skills through modeling and active rehearsal; the SM program taught the same skills, but the children observed as skills were modeled by an experimenter. The findings provided evidence for the greater efficacy of PM relative to SM for the teaching of personal safety skills. Such results support the inclusion of active rehearsal in prevention programs for young children.

Other researchers have compared didactic and behavioral approaches to teaching personal safety skills. For example, Wurtele, Saslawsky, Miller, Marrs, and Britcher (1986) randomly assigned 71 children from grades kindergarten, first, fifth, and sixth to (a) participate in the Behavioral Skills Training program (BST; Wurtele, 1986), which involved discrimination training of appropriate/inappropriate genital touches, in addition to training (i.e., modeling, behavioral rehearsal, and feedback) in self-protective responses; (b) observe a film about sexual abuse; (c) participate in a combination of (a) and (b); or (d) participate in an attention-control program. The children were assessed on acquisition of knowledge about sexual abuse and of personal safety skills. The BST program, alone or in combination with the film, significantly enhanced knowledge gain over that resulting from a control presentation. Findings on the safety skills measure approached significance, with BST children scoring higher than controls. The BST children's scores also increased on both measures over a 3-month follow-up period.

More recently, Blumberg, Chadwick, Fogarty, Speth, and Chadwick (1991) randomly assigned 264 kindergarten through third-grade children to one of three programs: (a) a role-play program that used role play, modeling, rehearsal, and discussion to teach sexual abuse prevention concepts; (b) a multimedia program that used stuffed animals, puppets, films, and discussion to teach children about sexual, physical, and emotional abuse; or (c) a control program about fire prevention. Only children in the role-play program improved significantly in their ability to discriminate between appropriate and inappropriate touches. Unfortunately, in both Wurtele et al. (1986) and Blumberg et al. (1991) the various conditions differed considerably in their content and format, making it difficult to determine what accounted for the superiority of the programs incorporating more active modes of training.

By holding the teaching format constant, Wurtele, Kast, Miller-Perrin, and Kondrick (1989) explored whether content differences would affect preschoolers' abilities to learn from a personal safety program. One hundred preschoolers were randomly assigned to either the BST program, a feelings-based program, or to an attention-control program. Both treatment programs used instruction, modeling, rehearsal, and feedback, but their content varied. In the feelings-based program, children were instructed to use their feelings to distinguish between "OK" touches (i.e., those that feel good) and "not-OK" touches (i.e., those that feel bad or confusing). In contrast, the BST program provided children with a concrete rule to protect their genitals and helped children use this rule to discriminate between OK and not-OK touching (or viewing) of the genitals. Compared with a control presentation, both training programs were effective in enhancing children's sexual abuse knowledge and in teaching them *how* to respond effectively to those inappropriate-touch situations common to the two programs. However, the two training programs differed in their relative abilities to teach children *when* to use their personal safety skills. Children taught to "trust their feelings" when making safety decisions were confused when asked to identify the appropriateness of two incongruous situations (i.e., when an appropriate touch feels bad and when an inappropriate touch feels good). It appears that the feelings-based approach, which is used in most prevention programs (Tharinger et al., 1988), may impede, rather than enhance, preschoolers' abilities to discriminate between appropriate and inappropriate touching of the genitals.

Other evaluations of prevention programs incorporating behavioral training procedures have appeared in the literature. For example, Wurtele (1990) randomly assigned twenty-four 4-year-old children to either the BST or an attention-control program. Compared with controls, 4-year-olds who participated in the training program demonstrated a better ability to identify inappropriate touches in novel situations, greater knowledge about sexual abuse, and higher levels of personal safety skills. Supplemental analyses indicated that BST subjects were more likely to say they would escape from a potential perpetrator and inform a resource person about the incident. In contrast, few control children indicated they would tell someone about the inappropriate situations. Gains in BST children's knowledge and skills were maintained at a 1-month follow-up.

Kraizer, Witte, and Fryer (1989) evaluated the five-part *Safe Child Program* (Kraizer, 1988) with 670 children, ages 3 to 10. The program included teacher-directed role playing, discussion, and activities to enhance mastery of prevention skills. Experimental and control children were pretested and posttested using an in vivo simulation technique to measure behavioral change. In this technique, a confederate put his or her arm around the child and tried various techniques to persuade the child to allow such touching. Scoring was based on the child's verbal response (e.g., saying "no") and body language (e.g., standing up, moving the examiner's hand). Experimental children improved in their verbal and nonverbal skills, whereas control children's scores remained stable and low. Information about random assignment, whether raters were kept blind as to subjects' group status, and interrater reliability was not provided, thus limiting this study's potential contributions. It is notable, however, for its inclusion of an in vivo simulation technique for assessing gains in behavioral skills.

In summary, programs incorporating more active modes of training have resulted in greater knowledge and skill gains than those employing a more didactive approach. It must be noted, however, that on measures of their personal safety skills, young children are not achieving 100% accuracy in recognizing and responding in potentially abusive situations, even though their performance has been significantly better than that of control children. Although only moderate knowledge and skill gains are not surprising given the programs' limited duration (usually 1.5 hours), it does require that we turn our attention to improving gains even further.

CASE EXAMPLE

Results from our survey of 375 parents of preschoolers (Wurtele, Kvaternick, & Franklin, 1992) suggest that parents want to be involved in sexual abuse prevention efforts with their children. Almost all (94%) believed preschoolers should learn about sexual abuse prevention both at home and school. Very few parents (less than 10%) believed that only experts, not parents, should teach children about sexual abuse. Their suggestion that children should be taught about sexual abuse when young (on average, 3.4 years) also implied that parents want to play an active role in prevention efforts. Their reasons for not discussing sexual abuse related to a lack of knowledge, vocabulary, or materials. This finding suggests the need for educating parents about sexual abuse and providing them with assistance and materials to teach their children personal safety skills.

We have recently been exploring the possibility of recruiting parents from the community to serve as personal safety instructors. There are several advantages to home-based safety instruction. By focusing on target behaviors (i.e., teaching their children how to recognize and resist abusive advances), behavioral interventions may have systemic effects (e.g., reducing the secrecy surrounding the topic of child sexual abuse; stimulating parent-child discussions about sexuality in general). Parents can integrate discussions of sexual abuse with what their children already know and can be sensitive to their children's abilities regarding comprehension and skill acquisition. Given parents' ongoing contact with their children, the parent-as-trainer approach may also enhance generalization and maintenance.

We have made available a parent version of our BST program to parents whose preschoolers were enrolled in a private, middle-class preschool (Wurtele, Currier, Gillispie, & Franklin, 1991) and in a Head Start preschool serving low-income parents (Wurtele, Gillispie, Currier, & Franklin, 1992; Wurtele, Kast, & Melzer, 1992). Our first concern was whether parents would be willing to teach their children personal safety skills, given the controversial nature of the topic. In all three studies, we found a high rate of participation (more than 90%), which may have been related to several characteristics of the setting and the program. Preschools serve as a naturally occurring community system for introducing such a program, and the support of the preschool teachers and administrators for the program most likely increased participation. When we initially contacted parents about teaching the program, a few were hesitant to do so, saying that they lacked the knowledge or vocabulary to discuss the topic. When they were told that a script was included, they were willing to teach the program. According to parental report, having a script to read helped them feel more comfortable discussing sexual abuse with their children. The price of the program, at least in monetary terms, was unbeatable, as it was provided free to parents. Parents may not be willing to teach an expensive program or one that is too demanding of their time. The site of the program was also ideal, as parents taught the program in the comfort of their own homes. Teaching it at home also made it possible for them to teach their other (younger and older) children.

Maintaining telephone contact during the program may have provided additional support or enhanced motivation and compliance. Whether program effects would occur with parents not provided with such personal contact has not been determined (see Peterson, Mori, Selby, & Rosen, 1988). If such contact is necessary, it may be a major impediment to the ecological validity and the widespread implementation of this kind of prevention program. To enhance children's attention during the program and to help parents track their children's progress, we included in the program the child's "token time" packet, which contained 29 program objectives. As a skill or concept is mastered, the child pastes a sticker (token) in a box beside the objective. This device was rated very positively by parents and also provided us with a check on parental compliance in teaching the program.

Although parental refusal to teach the program was not a problem in these studies, it may be a problem in implementing a home-based teaching approach on a widespread basis, particularly with abusing and severely dysfunctional families. A home-based program may not be appropriate for use with such families, for whom school-based interventions may be required. Given the complexity of the child sexual abuse problem, multiple and diverse prevention approaches will be necessary.

FUTURE DIRECTIONS

There is emerging support for using a behavioral approach to prevent the physical and sexual abuse of children. In the area of physical abuse, extant research demonstrates the efficacy of competency-based prevention programs for reducing the likelihood of reabuse among abusive parents and the risk for first-time abuse by high-risk parents. Several questions need to be addressed in future investigations. For example, although perpetrators of physical abuse are mothers and fathers of all socioeconomic groups, research efforts have almost exclusively focused on mothers from low SES backgrounds. Thus, researchers need to evaluate these approaches with a broader client base. Yet to be addressed are effective methods for engaging and retaining these different types of clients in voluntary prevention programs. Similarly, most published reports describe prevention efforts targeted at parents of preschool and early elementary–aged children, with little attention directed toward parents of infants, adolescents, or handicapped children. For example, training new parents in caregiving, communication skills, and sensorimotor/language stimulation would appear to hold promise in enhancing children's adaptive functioning, improving the parent-child relationship, and reducing child abuse potential (Field, Widmayer, Greenberg, & Stoller, 1982; Helfer, 1987; S. Z. Lutzker et al., 1987). The efficacy of primary prevention efforts aimed at teaching parenting skills to adolescents who are not yet parents has yet to be explored. Researchers also need to address whether the target of physical abuse prevention programs should expand to children, as has been the case with sexual abuse.

Additionally, there is a need to define adequately "abusing" and "high-risk" subjects (Fink & McCloskey, 1990), and to provide consistently data on intended changes within the family system (proximal effects) along with distal data on reports of subsequent abuse. For proximal effects, it is important to document whether parent training increases positive behaviors of both parents and children. For distal effects, there is a need to conduct long-term follow-ups with participating families. Critical to the field's expansion is the development of reliable and easily administered assessment protocols and standardized measures of parenting skills and children's behaviors.

More research is needed to identify which strategies are most successful with what types of families (e.g., Brunk, Henggeler, & Whelan, 1987) and at what point(s) in the family's development. For example, with seriously disadvantaged families, whose difficulties go beyond their inability to manage their children's behavior, the provision of only child management training is unlikely to be effective. With multiproblem families, it may be more effective to first target those problems (e.g., inadequate social skills, emotional or physical problems, substance abuse) that are interfering with parents' ability to focus on child management training (e.g., Booth, Mitchell, Barnard, & Spieker, 1989). Given the multidetermined nature of child maltreatment, continued evaluation of the ecobehavioral's approach of providing multiple kinds of services in multiple settings is certainly warranted. An expansion across other domains in which the parent and child function may also enhance preventive effects (e.g., teaching children to engage in reciprocal behaviors supportive of parents' attempts at management; involving the child's preschool or school to foster greater between-environment consequences that a child receives for both prosocial and antisocial behavior; and providing assistance with families' economic, child care, employment, substance abuse, or marital problems; see Miller & Prinz, 1990).

Evidence is also beginning to accumulate in the sexual abuse prevention field suggesting that a behavioral approach can help children gain in knowledge about sexual abuse and in personal safety skills (i.e., recognizing, resisting, and reporting abuse). More attention to measuring proximal and particularly distal effects is needed. How to measure children's abilities to recognize, refuse, and report is an area needing greater attention. The feasibility, safety, and utility of in vivo simulation techniques to measure proximal effects have yet to be determined. Whether children can use their increased knowledge and skills to prevent sexual abuse is an unresolved issue. Long-term, large-scale follow-up studies are needed to determine if children are better able to protect themselves as result of program participation.

Also, we must widen our conceptualizations of child sexual abuse prevention and expand beyond the current focus on children as targets of prevention information. More responsibility for preventing child sexual abuse should be placed on adults, and behaviorally oriented preventive strategies could make a major contribution to those efforts. More systems-oriented interventions need to be designed, implemented, and evaluated including but not limited to (a) educating parents about aspects of the family that may increase (poor supervision, lack of privacy) or decrease (open communication) the probability of sexual abuse; (b) encouraging schools to integrate comprehensive sexuality and family life education into the standard curriculum; (c) enhancing public awareness of the problem and ways to prevent it (e.g., via the use of media); and (d) changing societal attitudes that condone the sexual exploitation of children. The prevention of both physical and sexual abuse will require attending to the confluence of factors that lead to child maltreatment: factors at the levels of the individual, family, community, and society. Ultimately, primary prevention of child physical and sexual abuse reflects a broader concern for child and family advocacy.

REFERENCES

Alter-Reid, K., Gibbs, M. S., Lachenmeyer, J. R., Sigal, J., & Massoth, N. A. (1986). Sexual abuse of children: A review of the empirical findings. *Clinical Psychology Review, 6,* 249–266.
American Humane Association. (1988). *Highlights of official child neglect and abuse reporting: 1986.* Denver, CO: Author.
Ammerman, R. T. (1990). Etiological models of child maltreatment: A behavioral perspective. *Behavior Modification, 14,* 230–254.
Ammerman, R. T., Cassisi, J. E., Hersen, M., & Van Hasselt, V. B. (1986). Consequences of physical abuse and neglect in children. *Clinical Psychology Review, 6,* 291–310.

Barone, V. J., Greene, B. F., & Lutzker, J. R. (1986). Home safety with families being treated for child abuse and neglect. *Behavior Modification, 10*, 93–114.

Barth, R. P. (1985). Beating the blues: Cognitive-behavioral treatment for depression in child-maltreating young mothers. *Clinical Social Work Journal, 13*, 317–328.

Barth, R. P. (1989). Evaluation of a task-centered child abuse prevention program. *Children and Youth Services Review, 11*, 117–131.

Barth, R. P., Blythe, B. J., Schinke, S. P., & Schilling, R. F. III. (1983). Self-control training with maltreating families. *Child Welfare, 62*, 313–324.

Barth, R. P., Hacking, S., & Ash, J. R. (1988). Preventing child abuse: An experimental evaluation of the Child Parent Enrichment Project. *Journal of Primary Prevention, 8*, 201–217.

Belsky, J. (1980). Child maltreatment: An ecological integration. *American Psychologist, 35*, 320–335.

Blumberg, E. J., Chadwick, M. W., Fogarty, L. A., Speth, T. W., & Chadwick, D. L. (1991). The touch discrimination component of sexual abuse prevention training: Unanticipated positive consequences. *Journal of Interpersonal Violence, 6*, 12–28.

Boger, R., Richter, R., & Weatherston, D. (1983). Perinatal positive parenting: A program of primary prevention through support of first-time parents. *Infant Mental Health Journal, 4*, 297–308.

Booth, C. L., Mitchell, S. K., Barnard, K. E., & Spieker, S. J. (1989). Development of maternal social skills in multiproblem families: Effects on the mother-child relationship. *Developmental Psychology, 25*, 403–412.

Bousha, D. M., & Twentyman, C. T. (1984). Mother-child interactional style in abuse, neglect, and control groups: Naturalistic observations in the home. *Journal of Abnormal Psychology, 93*, 106–114.

Brunk, M., Henggeler, S. W., & Whelan, J. P. (1987). Comparison of multisystemic therapy and parent training in the brief treatment of child abuse and neglect. *Journal of Consulting & Clinical Psychology, 55*, 171–178.

Burgess, R. L., & Conger, R. (1978). Family interactions in abusive, neglectful, and normal families. *Child Development, 49*, 1163–1173.

Caplan, G. (1964). *Principles of preventive psychiatry.* New York: Basic Books.

Cicchetti, D. (1987). Developmental psychopathology in infancy: Illustration from the study of maltreated youngsters. *Journal of Consulting and Clinical Psychology, 55*, 837–845.

Cohn, A. H., & Daro, D. (1987). Is treatment too late: What ten years of evaluative research tell us. *Child Abuse & Neglect, 11*, 433–442.

Conte, J. R., Rosen, C., Saperstein, L., & Shermack, R. (1985). An evaluation of a program to prevent the sexual victimization of young children. *Child Abuse & Neglect, 9*, 319–328.

Crittenden, P. M. (1988). Relationships at risk. In J. Belsky & T. Nezworski (Eds.), *Clinical implications of attachment theory* (pp. 136–174). Hillsdale, NJ: Lawrence Erlbaum.

Crittenden, P. M., & Craig, S. E. (1990). Developmental trends in the nature of child homicide. *Journal of Interpersonal Violence, 5*, 202–216.

Daro, D., & Mitchel, L. (1990). *Child abuse fatalities remain high: The results of the annual fifty state survey.* Chicago, IL: National Committee for Prevention of Child Abuse.

Department of Health and Human Services. (1988). *Study findings: Study of national incidence and prevalence of child abuse and neglect.* (DHHS Publication No. ADM 20-01099). Washington, DC: U.S. Government Printing Office.

Erickson, M. F., Egeland, B., & Pianta, R. (1989). The effects of maltreatment on the development of young children. In D. Cicchetti & V. Carlson (Eds.), *Child maltreatment: Theory and research on the causes and consequences of child abuse and neglect* (pp. 647–684). New York: Cambridge University Press.

Field, T., Widmayer, S., Greenberg, R., & Stoller, S. (1982). Effects of parent training on teenage mothers and their infants. *Pediatrics, 69*, 703–707.

Fink, A., & McCloskey, L. (1990). Moving child abuse and neglect prevention programs forward: Improving program evaluations. *Child Abuse & Neglect, 14*, 187–206.

Giarretto, H. (1982). A comprehensive child sexual abuse treatment program. *Child Abuse & Neglect, 6*, 263–278.

Gil, D. G. (1969). Physical abuse of children: Findings and implications of a nationwide survey. *Pediatrics, 44*, 857–864.

Gil, D. G. (1970). *Violence against children: Physical child abuse in the United States.* Cambridge, MA: Harvard University Press.

Helfer, R. E. (1987). The perinatal period, a window of opportunity for enhancing parent-infant communication: An approach to prevention. *Child Abuse & Neglect, 11*, 565–579.

Herrenkohl, E. C., Herrenkohl, R. C., & Egolf, B. P. (1983). Circumstances surrounding the occurrence of child maltreatment. *Journal of Consulting & Clinical Psychology, 51*, 424–431.

Hill, J. L., & Jason, L. A. (1987). An evaluation of a school-based child sexual abuse primary prevention program. *Psychotherapy Bulletin, 22*, 36–38.

Kolko, D. J., Moser, J. T., & Hughes, J. (1989). Classroom training in sexual victimization awareness and prevention skills: An extension of the Red Flag/Green Flag people program. *Journal of Family Violence, 4*, 25–45.

Kraizer, S. (1988). *The safe child program.* Palisades, NY: Health Education Systems.

Kraizer, S., Witte, S. S., & Fryer, G. E. Jr. (1989). Child sexual abuse prevention programs: What makes them effective in protecting children? *Children Today, 18*, 23–27.

Lutzker, J. R. (1984). Project 12-Ways: Treating child abuse and neglect from an ecobehavioral perspective. In R. F. Dangel & R. A. Polster (Eds.), *Parent training: Foundations of research and practice* (pp. 260–297). New York: Guilford Press.

Lutzker, J. R., McGimsey, J. F., McRae, S., & Campbell, R. V. (1983). Behavioral parent training: There's so much more to do. *The Behavior Therapist, 6*, 110–112.

Lutzker, J. R., Megson, D. A., Webb, M. E., & Dachman, R. S. (1985). Validating and training adult-child interaction skills to professionals and to parents indicated for child abuse and neglect. *Journal of Child and Adolescent Psychotherapy, 2*, 91–104.

Lutzker, J. R., & Rice, J. M. (1987). Using recidivism data to evaluate Project 12-Ways: An ecobehavioral approach to the treatment and prevention of child abuse and neglect. *Journal of Family Violence, 2*, 283–290.

Lutzker, S. Z., Lutzker, J. R., Braunling-McMorrow, D., & Eddleman, J. (1987). Prompting to increase mother-baby stimulation with single mothers. *Journal of Child and Adolescent Psychotherapy, 4*, 3–12.

Mannarino, A. P., & Cohen, J. A. (1990). Treating the abused child. In R. T. Ammerman & M. Hersen (Eds.), *Children at risk* (pp. 249–268). New York: Plenum.

Marshall, W., & Christie, M. (1981). Pedophilia and aggression. *Criminal Justice and Behavior, 8*, 145–158.

Miller, G. E., & Prinz, R. J. (1990). Enhancement of social learning family interventions for childhood conduct disorder. *Psychological Bulletin, 108*, 291–307.

Miller-Perrin, C. L., & Wurtele, S. K. (1990). Reactions to childhood sexual abuse: Implications for post-traumatic stress disorder. In C. Meek (Ed.), *Post-traumatic stress*

disorder: Assessment, differential diagnosis, and forensic evaluation (pp. 91–135). Sarasota, FL: Professional Resource Exchange.
Milner, J. S. (1986). *The Child Abuse Potential Inventory: Manual.* Webster, NC: Psytec.
National Center on Child Abuse and Neglect. (1978). *Child sexual abuse: Incest, assault, and sexual exploitation: A special report.* Washington, DC: U.S. Department of Health, Education and Welfare.
Newman, M. R., & Lutzker, J. R. (1990). Prevention programs. In R. T. Ammerman & M. Hersen (Eds.), *Children at risk* (pp. 225–248). New York: Plenum.
O'Connor, S., Vietze, P., Sherrod, K., Sandler, H., & Altemeier, W. (1980). Reduced incidence of parenting inadequacy following rooming-in. *Pediatrics, 66,* 176–182.
Oldershaw, L., Waters, G. C., & Hall, D. K. (1986). Control strategies and noncompliance in abusive mother-child dyads: An observational study. *Child Development, 57,* 722–732.
Olds, D. L., Henderson, C. R. Jr., Tatelbaum, R., & Chamberlin, R. (1986). Preventing child abuse and neglect: A randomized trial of nurse home visitation. *Pediatrics, 78,* 65–78.
Parke, R. D., & Collmer, C. W. (1975). Child abuse: An interdisciplinary analysis. In E. M. Hetherington (Ed.), *Review of child development research* (Vol. 5, pp. 509–590). Chicago: University of Chicago Press.
Patterson, G. R. (1982). *Coercive family process.* Eugene, OR: Castalia.
Peterson, L., Mori, L., Selby, V., & Rosen, B. N. (1988). Community interventions in children's injury prevention: Differing costs and differing benefits. *Journal of Community Psychology, 16,* 188–204.
Reid, J. B., Taplin, P. S., & Lorber, R. (1981). A social interactional approach to the treatment of abusive families. In R. B. Stuart (Ed.), *Violent behavior: Social learning approaches to prediction, management, and treatment* (pp. 83–101). New York: Brunner/Mazel.
Rosenberg, M. S., & Reppucci, N. D. (1985). Primary prevention of child abuse. *Journal of Consulting & Clinical Psychology, 53,* 576–585.
Sameroff, A. J., & Chandler, M. J. (1974). Reproductive risk and the continuum of caretaking casualty. In F. D. Horowitz, M. Hetherington, S. Scarr-Salapatek, L., & G. Siegel (Eds.), *Review of child development research* (Vol. 4, pp. 187–244). Chicago: University of Chicago Press.
Sedlak, A. J. (1990). *Technical amendment to the study findings—National incidence and prevalence of child abuse and neglect: 1988.* Rockville, MD: Westat.
Taylor, D. K., & Beauchamp, C. (1988). Hospital-based primary prevention strategy in child abuse: A multi-level needs addressment. *Child Abuse & Neglect, 12,* 343–354.
Tharinger, D. J., Krivacska, J. J., Laye-McDonough, M., Jamison, L., Vincent, G. G., & Hedlund, A. D. (1988). Prevention of child sexual abuse: An analysis of issues, educational programs, and research findings. *School Psychology Review, 17,* 614–634.
Trickett, P. K., & Kuczynski, L. (1986). Children's misbehaviors and parental discipline strategies in abusive and nonabusive families. *Developmental Psychology, 22,* 115–123.
Wahler, R. G. (1980). The insular mother: Her problems in parent-child treatment. *Journal of Applied Behavior Analysis, 13,* 207–219.
Wolfe, D. A., Edwards, B., Manion, I., & Koverola, C. (1988). Early intervention for parents at risk of child abuse and neglect: A preliminary investigation. *Journal of Consulting & Clinical Psychology, 56,* 40–47.
Wolfe, D. A., MacPherson, T., Blount, R., & Wolfe, V. V. (1986). Evaluation of a brief intervention for educating school children in awareness of physical and sexual abuse. *Child Abuse & Neglect, 10,* 85–92.

Wolfe, D. A., & Sandler, J. (1981). Training abusive parents in effective child management. *Behavior Modification, 5*, 320–335.

Wolfe, D. A., Sandler, J., & Kaufman, K. (1981). A competency-based parent training program for child abusers. *Journal of Consulting & Clinical Psychology, 49*, 633–640.

Wurtele, S. K. (1986). *Teaching young children personal body safety: The Behavioral Skills Training program.* Colorado Springs, CO: Author.

Wurtele, S. K. (1990). Teaching personal safety skills to four-year-old children: A behavioral approach. *Behavior Therapy, 21*, 25–32.

Wurtele, S. K., Currier, L. L., Gillispie, E. I., & Franklin, C. F. (1991). The efficacy of a parent-implemented program for teaching preschoolers personal safety skills. *Behavior Therapy, 22*, 69–83.

Wurtele, S. K., Gillispie, E. I., Currier, L. L., & Franklin, C. F. (1992). A comparison of teachers vs. parents as instructors of a personal safety program for preschoolers. *Child Abuse & Neglect, 16*, 127–137.

Wurtele, S. K., Kast, L. C., & Melzer, A. M. (1992). Sexual abuse prevention education for young children: A comparison of teachers and parents as instructors. *Child Abuse & Neglect, 16*, 865–876.

Wurtele, S. K., Kast, L. C., Miller-Perrin, C. L., & Kondrick, P. A. (1989). A comparison of programs for teaching personal safety skills to preschoolers. *Journal of Consulting & Clinical Psychology, 57*, 505–511.

Wurtele, S. K., Kvaternick, M., & Franklin, C. F. (1992). Sexual abuse prevention for preschoolers: A survey of parents' behaviors, attitudes, and beliefs. *Journal of Child Sexual Abuse, 1*, 113–128.

Wurtele, S. K., Marrs, S. R., & Miller-Perrin, C. L. (1987). Practice makes perfect? The role of participant modeling in sexual abuse prevention programs. *Journal of Consulting & Clinical Psychology, 55*, 599–602.

Wurtele, S. K., Saslawsky, D. A., Miller, C. L., Marrs, S. R., & Britcher, J. C. (1986). Teaching personal safety skills for potential prevention of sexual abuse: A comparison of treatments. *Journal of Consulting & Clinical Psychology, 54*, 688–692.

Wyatt, G. E., & Powell, G. J. (Eds.). (1988). *Lasting effects of child sexual abuse.* Newbury Park, CA: Sage.

Youngblade, L. M., & Belsky, J. (1990). Social and emotional consequences of child maltreatment. In R. T. Ammerman & M. Hersen (Eds.), *Children at risk* (pp. 109–146). New York: Plenum.

CHAPTER 4

Childhood Injury Prevention

Lizette Peterson, Michelle Zink, and Jane Downing

DESCRIPTION OF THE PROBLEM

Preventable injuries kill more children in the United States than all other causes of death combined. Injuries result in permanent disability for more than 30,000 children and require emergency medical treatment for 16 million children annually (Rodriguez, 1990). Any normal life-span cut short by death, or loss of mobility and health is tragic. It is doubly so with a child who has an entire lifetime ahead, who is not capable of protecting himself or herself against hazards that cause injury, and whose injury could have been avoided if certain environmental or behavioral modifications had been made. Yet, this is the picture of most child injuries.

The United States has a higher child mortality rate than other industrialized nations, owing to a large extent to preventable injury and violence (Centers for Disease Control, 1990). Such statistics suggest that protecting children from injury is not a clear priority in our society (Margolis & Runyan, 1983), despite substantial rhetoric to the contrary. This chapter considers some of the past and present interventions for preventing childhood injury including a detailed example of an intervention to increase safe behavior in children. The chapter then describes some of the barriers to intervention and some future possibilities for improved injury prevention programs in the United States.

Injury Prevention Categories

A little girl crosses a street for the first time by herself on the way to kindergarten. A young mother bathes her 3-month-old baby. A 16-year-old boy dives into a lake from a dock. All are candidates for various kinds of preventive interventions to avoid pedestrian injury, infant drowning, and spinal cord trauma. There is such a variety of interventions to increase safe responding that some system for categorizing prevention programs is desirable. One useful categorical system (Peterson & Mori, 1985) has organized programs by the *tactics, methods*, and *targets* they employ. This chapter adds to this system the *contingency*, or relationship, between desired change and an immediate, discriminable consequence delivered by the intervention. This classification system will first be described, and examples of programs filling differing cells within the method × contingency × target matrix will then be explored.

"Tactic" refers to the way in which the program consumer is contacted. A population-wide tactic reaches many persons, typically through multimedia campaigns that may involve messages on television, radio, or newspaper; or written material that is mailed or publicly distributed. High-risk group tactics involve the identification and treatment of a group of consumers or an environment in which there is an elevated probability of injury. Finally, milestone tactics orient toward a particular age or developmental juncture in which children may be particularly at risk or recipients particularly amenable to prevention. Milestone tactics often focus on children in school or public health settings.

"Method" refers to the type of prevention required of the consumer. The two end points on a continuum of methods currently in use have been labeled passive and active. Passive methods do not involve much direct action from the consumer but instead rely on product or environmental modifications. Active methods, in contrast, rely on behavior change on the part of caregivers and their children. Most prevention programs use a method somewhere on one side or the other of the continuum, but purely passive or active methods are rare. Because a preventive method is more likely to be routinely used when it requires less energy, time, and attention, passive methods are preferred over active methods when possible.

"Contingency" refers to the extent to which the intervention uses a direct and discernible consequence for the targets' compliance with the intervention. Legislated or mandated changes are usually regarded as strong contingencies. When applied to manufacturers, stiff, frequently enforced penalties for failure to comply with safety regulations create effective interventions. However, when applied to caretakers, enforcement of mandated change is more difficult. Thus, a conceptually strong contingency, such as legislated change, may in practice be strong or weak. Offering a direct positive consequence for change (such as rewarding a child's acquisition of safety behavior with stickers or small toys) is another conceptually strong contingency that may be strong or weak in practice, depending on the choice of rewards and the schedule of presentation. Finally, the most conceptually weak contingencies involve no direct consequence for effecting safety changes. Attempts to educate or persuade that rely on self-consequated change have in the past been relatively ineffective in decreasing children's injuries.

"Target" refers to the recipient of the intervention. Some interventions target the injury-causing agent (referred to as the "vector" in the injury literature), and these are more likely than not to use passive methods. Others attempt to influence the caregiver or focus directly on the child, and these interventions are more likely to employ active methods.

The tactics, methods, contingencies, and targets combine to produce a matrix of possible preventive interventions. A sample, rather than a comprehensive review, of such interventions can illustrate this system's utility, as well as provide an appreciation of the various kinds of programs currently in use.

REVIEW AND CRITIQUE OF THE LITERATURE

For discussion purposes, our literature review divides contingency strength into a dichotomy of stronger and weaker, and intervention methods into a dichotomy of passive and active. However, it should be remembered that these parameters are clearly continuous variables.

Passive Methods of Prevention

Conceptually Stronger Contingency—Injury Agent

Some of the most successful prevention methods have involved product modification, a passive method that is legislated, employing a strong contingency for the manufacturer's product to meet certain safety standards. For example, the number of childhood poisonings dropped precipitously following passage of the Poison Prevention Packing Act mandating child-resistant caps and limiting the amount of medication per container (Walton, 1982). Establishing flammability standards for children's sleepwear has resulted in a decrease in nonhouse-fire burns in children (Smith & Falk, 1987); and the Refrigerator Safety Act, banning doors that could not be opened from the inside, has virtually eliminated children's asphyxiation in refrigerators (Robertson, 1983).

Although clearly the most effective strategy, government agencies show great reluctance to mandate regulation. Fireworks (Smith & Falk, 1987), toys with small eye-piercing projectiles (Berger, 1981), and minibikes for children that travel up to 50 miles per hour (mph) (Rivara, 1982) are the agents for increasing numbers of child injuries each year, and yet concerns about both increased financial cost and decreased personal freedom remain effective barriers to legislated prevention efforts for such hazards.

Conceptually Weaker Contingency—Injury Agent

Some companies have been responsive to education efforts demonstrating the value of safety features for their products. Black and Decker Manufacturing Company, for example, publicly "advocates application of all state-of-the-art safety devices as standard equipment" (Vicker, 1982, p. 1). Similarly, Sorenson (1976) described a Danish manufacturing firm's voluntary product design change when learning that their vacuum cleaner electric plug was associated with infant mouth burns.

However, most safety experts regard such attitudes as the exception rather than the rule (Robertson, 1983). Without the strong contingency afforded by government sanctions, change is consequated only by a manufacturing firm's conscience or oblique beliefs that safety will sell products or avoid lawsuits. Some companies have continued to manufacture unsafe children's equipment even in the face of multiple lawsuits from injured children's parents. These manufacturers often cease production only when insurance companies cancel their coverage, a potent contingency (Smith & Falk, 1987). Other companies meet the letter of the law by enclosing small disclaimers on inner flaps of toys' packing with messages such as "Do not point or fire missiles into mouth or toward face" (Berger, 1981, p. 32), rather than attempting to remove the threat. Thus, as was noted in the previous section, passive change of the injury vector itself is preferred to other prevention methods, but in the absence of a clear positive consequence for the manufacturing firm, such change is sometimes difficult to obtain.

Conceptually Stronger Contingency—Caregiver

There are very few aspects of caregiving that are legislated, short of penalties for blatant child abuse and neglect. One of the few areas of legislated caregiver action is the use of child safety restraints.[1] Every state in the United States has now adopted mandatory child-restraint legislation. However, these laws are rarely enforced, and when they are, the fines are minimal. This renders a potentially strong contingency (legal penalties) weaker. As a result, the majority of parents still fail to use child restraints correctly and routinely (Roberts & Turner, 1986), although the use of safety restraints appears to be increasing (Morbidity and Mortality Weekly Report, 1988). Because automobile deaths are the leading killer of children in the United States, prevention in this area is vitally important. Legislation alone does not appear sufficient to protect most children from traveling in cars without safety restraints.

Conceptually Weaker Contingency—Caregiver

There have been a variety of educational programs that have targeted caregiver's use of one-time-only, passive interventions. These programs offer no direct consequence to the caregiver for adopting new, passive methods; the expectation is that the caregiver's own conscience or desire to parent effectively and safely will be its own reward. These passive methods typically are ineffective (Pless & Arsenault, 1987). For example, programs using educational interventions to try to persuade parents to install smoke detectors or to turn down water heater thermostats to avoid scalding burns have had mixed success, with many parents completing the low-cost task of lowering water temperature but few installing smoke detectors (Thomas, Hassanein, & Christophersen, 1984). It is possible to strengthen the contingency of home-based interventions, however. For example, programs having individual contact and offering clear positive consequences for adopting new passive methods, by giving away safety equipment such as smoke detectors (Gorman, Charney, Holtzman, & Roberts, 1985) and window guards (Spiegel & Lindaman, 1977), have successfully increased these safety features in at-risk homes. When targeting the caregiver, decreasing the cost of change imposed on the caregiver and increasing the positive consequences for change appear to be crucial.

Child

Passive methods that directly target the child with strong contingency, legislated methods have yet to be created. Although there are no tests of weaker contingency methods, there are now public campaigns to educate and persuade children to use safety devices. It remains to future research to see if interventions such as television messages proclaiming "If you want to be cool, a helmet's the rule" have a perceptible impact on children's safety behaviors.

Active Methods of Prevention

By definition, active methods are directed toward persons rather than toward the injury agent and thus there are no categories of active interventions directed toward injury agents. The nature of active intervention is to target the behavior of the caregiver or the child, either to remove risky responding or to increase safe behavior.

Conceptually Stronger Contingency—Caregiver

As noted earlier, there have been few strong contingencies applied to caregivers. Currently, most states have laws specifying the youngest age at which children can be left unsupervised (e.g., Masters, 1978). Most states prosecute parents who clearly violate community norms by failing to supervise young children in the bath or near traffic. Yet, none of these contingencies is likely to operate preventively. It seems unlikely that concern about prosecution will influence a neglectful parent's active safety interventions.

However, once violations have occurred and court-mandated treatment is applied, contingencies with power to influence caregiver behavior can come into play. Tertinger, Greene, and Lutzker (1984) worked with parents whose history of neglect resulted in referral to their Project 12-Ways (see also chapter 3 by Wurtele). One aspect of treatment involved the application of the Home Accident Prevention Inventory, an instrument that identified hazards in the home that warranted remediation. Parents received instruction, modeling, role-playing, and corrective feedback in a variety of areas,[2] ranging from the safe storage of firearms and poisons to the need to remove small objects from an infant's reach. Follow-up more than 1 year later showed a substantial decrease in child-accessible injury agents in those homes.

It is unlikely that communities will soon accept the widespread mandating of such safety programs in the absence of prior neglect or abuse, however, so this kind of solution seems relevant only to certain high-risk groups. Employing positive rather than negative consequences seems a preferable route, yet few researchers have directly targeted adult caregivers using an explicit positive contingency. In one successful exception, Roberts and Turner (1986) rewarded parents with lottery tickets that could be exchanged for prizes whenever they arrived at their day care placement with their preschooler in a safety restraint. The number of parents using restraints increased from low levels to sizable majorities (up to 80% at one center and 64% at the other). Although rates fell after the reward program was discontinued, they remained much higher than at baseline.

There seems to be some hesitancy to use explicit, strong contingencies to alter caregiver actions that safeguard the child. However, past research suggests that such contingencies are effective in increasing adults' own safety behavior (e.g., Streff & Geller, 1986). The least effective interventions have been those targeting caregiver behavior with educational and persuasive techniques in the absence of any tangible or direct consequence for action. Future work in this area may profitably consider ways of selecting and acquiring appropriate incentives for caregivers and techniques for maintaining safety behavior once acquired. Although challenging, these goals seem the most likely to produce change in caregivers' active preventive behaviors. Because many of the most important active caregiving behaviors occur in private (e.g., bathing the child; exposing the child to flames, scalds, or poisons in the kitchen), researchers must struggle, using strong contingencies during intervention, to produce repertoires of behavior that are likely to endure after the program's completion in the absence of explicit rewards. This may involve overrehearsal, in which safe behaviors become second nature, as easy to perform as unsafe behavior. It may also involve a gradual shift from external to internal control.

Conceptually Weaker Contingency—Caregiver

Most safety education programs belong in this category. A variety of differing approaches have been attempted including the use of slide-tape shows and pediatrician prescriptions for car safety restraints for children (Miller & Pless, 1977), a discussion with a safety expert and written instructions for home hazard removal (Dershewitz & Williamson, 1977), neighborhood discussion groups with trained team leaders and monthly newsletters (Schlesinger et al., 1966), and a national television campaign targeted at home safety (Colver, Hutchinson, & Judson, 1982). None of these methods used an explicit positive consequence for increasing safe behavior, and none demonstrated an increase in safety or a decrease in injuries.

Perhaps one of the best-conducted examples of a safety education program is Project Burn Prevention (McLaughlin, Vince, Lee, & Crawford, 1982). This project used a community-wide approach, selecting Lynn and Quincy, Massachusetts, as centers for intensive educational intervention. Three vehicles were used: (a) media within the entire Boston metropolitan area including both Quincy and Lynn (television announcements, radio talk shows, newspapers, posters in public buildings and on subways and buses); (b) community agencies in Quincy (film strips and cassettes presented at parent-teacher associations (PTAs), Rotary clubs, boy-girl scouts, apartment parties, and a community health fair); and (c) schools in Lynn (K–12 teacher guides with film strips, audiocassettes, games, and texts). The program was conducted during an 8-month period. Implementation data showed that the television spots were aired an average of 22 times each month by each of the four local stations. There were 26 newspaper articles published during this time, and 85,000 information books were distributed in Boston, 18,000 in Quincy (sufficient for 20% of the population), and 17,000 (sufficient for 19% of the population) in Lynn. The 19 volunteers conducted 63 programs contacting 1,100 people. However, all of the interventions sought to persuade and to educate in the absence of positive consequences for behavior change.

At the program's completion, a telephone survey revealed no educational improvement in adults' knowledge of burn prevention. No reductions in burn incidence or severity were found. Although there was evidence that the school programs increased student knowledge, the overall conclusion drawn by the authors was that the project had failed in its goal of burn prevention. Given the sophistication and scope of this intervention, this conclusion is very discouraging. It is unclear whether the population-wide tactic, the weak contingency method, or both may have contributed to this lack of success. The authors concluded their article with a strong statement about the effectiveness of passive methods in contrast to active methods, although acknowledging the importance of both. We would argue that focusing on the strength of the contingency associated with the active approach might improve its impact. Thus, future research targeting the caregiver should examine stronger contingency approaches before concluding that active approaches are ineffective.

Conceptually Stronger Contingency—Child

In contrast to the few studies using explicit contingencies with adults, most recent, successful interventions with children have relied on such approaches. Because this is the best-developed type of preventive intervention for children and the one most applicable to community psychologists, more examples are described here than in other sections to give the reader an appreciation for the range within this area. The case example in this chapter is also drawn from this area.

Although several compelling studies now exist showing the effectiveness of actual interventions using strong contingencies with children, progress in this area has been relatively recent. In 1978 Yeaton and Bailey published a description of a study entitled "Teaching Pedestrian Safety Skills to Young Children: An Analysis and One-Year Follow-up." A few children who were in early elementary school grades and who typically walked to and from school were selected from two schools. Children were taught safety rules that included the following steps: (a) wait at the curb, (b) look all ways, (c) watch vehicle distance (a distance of 7.6 meters was marked with tape), (d) walk, (e) continue to look, and (f) use crosswalk. The children first heard a didactic message that employed an ongoing explanation of appropriate looking and waiting behavior at the street corner. Then, an adult modeled the correct steps and asked the child to restate the steps verbally. Finally, the children demonstrated and rehearsed the appropriate behavior.

Before the intervention, children at School A correctly used 40% to 50% of the skills, and children at School B about 10% to 20%. Following the intervention, correct behavior increased to between 87% and 100% on the street where the children were taught and to between 65% to 75% of the untrained streets. At 1-year follow-up, the children from School A were still using around 80% of the rules correctly, whereas the younger children at School B were only using 50% of the rules correctly. However, after one session of remediation training, both schools demonstrated the same high level of skills shown after initial intervention.

This program required an average of 16 minutes for each of 11 training sessions. In all, less than 8 minutes per subject were expended. This in vivo approach to avoiding pedestrian injury, the leading cause of death in middle elementary school, was implemented by crossing guards who had received 1 hour of instruction. Such high subject contact in an intervention is typically regarded as very expensive, but by using existing personnel, costs could remain low, whereas opportunity for behavioral rehearsal and feedback would be high. The focus on very young children who are at the highest risk for pedestrian roadway injury, and the positive effects of the booster session, suggest a milestone approach that could continue to reduce risk for children served.

Similarly, Rosenbaum, Creedon, and Drabman (1981) targeted preschool children to improve their ability to identify injury emergencies. A variety of emergencies was selected including an unconscious adult on the kitchen floor, a person falling downstairs, and a fire on the kitchen stove. The children received the skills training in small groups and were rewarded with verbal praise for correct responding. Incorrect answers were followed by both feedback and a model of the correct answer. Children learned to discriminate emergencies from nonemergencies, pick up the telephone receiver, dial 911, and report their name, address, telephone number, nature of the emergency, number of people (if any) injured, and determine whether an ambulance was needed. Following the program, correct responding by the children had increased from about 60% of the safety responses to near 100%. High levels of proficiency were found in response to untaught situations, as well as to those situations focused on during the program. A 3-month follow-up showed excellent retention.

Recognition of, and ability to report, an emergency are only two of the many components necessary to exit a fire safely. Jones, Kazdin, and Haney (1981) described a multicomponent program for teaching third graders complex fire-exiting skills. Safe fire exiting involves a series of decisions that flexibly allow a child to select an unblocked path to safety. Jones et al. employed nine differing situations that varied such cues as whether or not (a) the child was coughing/eyes burning, (b) the child could leave through a window without assistance, (c) the exit door was hot, (d) the door was cool but hot air was rushing into the room, and (e) there was a fire in the exit path. The program taught the children through modeling, behavioral rehearsal, and simulation to respond correctly to each decision rule. Some of the situations necessitated nine correct responses, with others requiring as many as 20. Correct series of responses were consequated with verbal praise and stars to be traded later for a large prize. Subjects performed at very low levels ($\bar{X}$ = 4.5% correct) before training, but overall group performance had risen to 100% correct responding after training. Most compelling were the social validation measures from actual fire fighters, who rated children as much more likely to be severely burned and killed before training than after training.

These studies and several similar studies not reviewed here individually demonstrated that it was possible for young children to learn a variety of ways of avoiding hazards and remaining safe. Each sought to protect the children they served from one portion of the injuries for which the children were at risk. However, none of the studies took a holistic approach to injury prevention. This concern prompted some of our early work in multifaceted safety skills acquisition with children, outlined subsequently.

During the 1980s, concern about new risks to children grew. One source of risk was the increasing absence of parental supervision that occurred as expanding numbers of dual-career families emerged. Children were often left after school to supervise themselves. The numbers ranged from 2.1 to 15 million children estimated to be in self-care by the late 1980s (Nienhuis, 1987). Some authors (e.g., Long & Long, 1982) argued that this was a tragedy, but other reports more firmly grounded in data (e.g., Rodman, Pratto, & Nelson, 1985) suggested few traumatic and many well-adjusted outcomes. However, it was clear that children's risk of serious injury increased dramatically with the absence of parental supervision (Tokuhata, Colflesh, Digon, & Mann, 1972). Some experts described the absence of appropriate supervision as the most pressing national problem in the health care of children (Zigler, 1982).

Our initial work in this area was stimulated by the concern that many parents selecting self-care as an option for their children appeared to underestimate the potential safety risks involved and overestimate the degree to which their child was adequately prepared to meet the risks. We began by conducting a survey (Peterson, Mori, & Scissors, 1986; Peterson & Scissors, 1983) of 8- to 10-year-old children and their parents that focused on children's knowledge of home safety practices. Children of this age were targeted because 8 years of age marks the time at which state law allows the child to be in self-care legally. Children were individually interviewed, while parents completed a questionnaire matched to the child's interview. The questions began as general open-ended queries (e.g., "Do you [or Do your parents] have specific rules about how your child [you] are to answer the telephone? Can you tell me about them?") and progressed to very specific questions that focused on a given safety rule and asked if the child's parents would advocate the rule if the child was at home alone (e.g., "If I get a bad cut, I should contact my parents, yes or no?" "If I get a bad cut, I should wait for my parent to get home, yes or no?"). Though parents and children agreed that the children were aware of the rules, the children actually listed only between 18% and 39% of the general rules their parents specified. Also, for more than half (24 of 44) of the questions, at least 40% of the parents and children disagreed with one another, even though chance alone would predict that for 50% of the questions there should be agreement even if the child had no safety knowledge.

Armed with this assessment of needs, we began a series of studies to increase children's safety skills. Our first intervention (Peterson, 1984a) focused on 8- to 9-year-old children's skills in three basic domains: (a) dealing with emergencies (with specific modules on exiting a fire, seeking shelter from a tornado, and responding to a serious cut), (b) strangers (with specific modules on answering the telephone and the door), and (c) daily challenges (with specific modules on selecting safe play activities and preparing safe, nutritious snacks). Children met each night after school for 1 hour for a month. The early part of each module was spent introducing the concepts and modeling discriminations between correct and incorrect responses that were initially presented with both a picture and some words. Later, as the incorrect answers were faded, children learned to list the six correct rules, and ultimately the children rapidly executed the correct sequences of responses, both in training and immediately after training. Extensive verbal praise was used at each juncture, and children were rewarded with stickers and stars for each session in which they participated appropriately and could demonstrate mastery of the material. At 1-year follow-up, children remained very proficient at dealing with strangers and daily challenges (i.e., the activities with which they continued to have frequent experience), but they performed only slightly better than baseline at emergencies. However, a single booster session brought emergency responding up near criterion.

The second study (Peterson, 1984b) sought to streamline the behavioral, strong contingency method used and to contrast this method with a more traditional weak contingency method that was in active use in the community. In this study, half of the 7.5- to 10-year-old children received the Boy Scouts of America's "Prepared for Today" program, which used didactic teaching and discussion to increase safety behavior, and the other half received the streamlined behavioral intervention. Assessment concentrated on the topics presented in both programs including daily challenges (activities and food preparation), strangers (answering the door and telephone), emergencies (exiting a fire and responding to a cut), and looking after younger children. Individual undergraduate experimenters worked individually with the children twice a week for about 40 minutes, using extensive verbal praise, and at the end of each session a small food or activity reward. At the end of 8 weeks, both groups had improved over baseline; however, children receiving the behavioral intervention showed superior performance in every trained module, and a real-world probe in which a stranger attempted to gain entry to the house validated the gains. Good maintenance was seen at 5-month follow-up. Furthermore, data obtained on the children's fears relevant to safety issues revealed no increases in anxiety following training in this (or any subsequent) study.

Subsequent work extended the intervention to preschoolers (Mori & Peterson, 1986), attempted with only mild success to engineer generalization of training (Peterson & Mori, 1985), and demonstrated that the behavioral methods were successful in the classroom (Peterson & Thiele, 1988). We found that highly motivated parents could be very successful at increasing their children's safety skills in the home, that unmotivated parents were not very successful, and that even expertly done, strong contingency 1-day workshops performed by trained volunteers were inadequate to the challenge of increasing children's skills to safe lower limits (Peterson, Mori, Selby, & Rosen, 1988). Our most positive conclusion is that any motivated adult quickly can become a successful intervention agent. Our most frustrating conclusion is that real skill acquisition cannot be hurried; it requires much time and effort. Children need extensive rehearsal *beyond* the time when they first can perform the correct behaviors for skills to be maintained, and they do not readily translate one generic skill from one type of hazard to another. One of the greatest obstacles to widespread successful safety acquisition programs is the current reluctance on the part of program consumers to expend the time and effort that are required. The next section illustrates this difficulty.

Conceptually Weaker Contingency—Child

Most elementary schools have a loosely organized safety curriculum, often made up of volunteer visits to the classroom by a variety of safety experts. Thus, a fire department official may discuss exiting a house fire, a police officer may talk about pedestrian and bicycle safety, and the school nurse may lecture on some first-aid basics. Most of these individuals lack a background in child education, and it is extremely rare that the impact of such visits is assessed. (Indeed, we could find no published evaluation of these programs, despite their use nationwide.) It seems particularly ironic that the school system, presumably the body most sensitive to the need for sound pedagogical practices, would use the lecture-discussion format to teach safety skills. Such methods are not only ineffective but may also be dangerous because they increase parents' and children's beliefs about how well-prepared the children are to behave safely without delivering the skills that are then presumed (Peterson & Roberts, 1992). Evaluation of such programs seems an essential first step toward ensuring genuine increases in safe behavior.

In the last several years, there has been a movement toward community-based safety education as well. Hospitals and shopping malls have been among the sites for workshops designed to teach children to avoid injury and to treat minor injuries. Few evaluations of such programs have been conducted. Results from those programs that have been assessed often suggest that although children do make small skill gains, especially when behavioral rehearsal is employed, the increments are probably insufficient to protect the child and clearly do not match the gains the parent and child believe have occurred (Peterson et al., 1988).

Self-help safety materials targeting "latchkey" or unsupervised children have flooded the market in recent years with titles like *I Can Do It, Prepared for Today, In Charge: A Complete Handbook for Kids with Working Parents,* and *I'm in Charge*. Most are unevaluated and rely on discussing various courses of action with the child. Evaluations that exist suggest small, uneven increases in skill from such interventions (Peterson, 1984b).

The bottom line for weaker contingency interventions for both parents and children seems to be that they are relatively ineffective. Although there have been notable exceptions (e.g., classroom films, posters, and television spots focusing specifically on pedestrian midblock "dart-out" apparently reduced the number of this kind of injury in one community; Preusser & Blomberg, 1984), most injury specialists conclude that brief educational endeavors in the absence of other contingency changes are unsuccessful in preventing injury (Pless & Arsenault, 1987). Yet, in terms of sheer volume, these programs probably outnumber all other formal interventions. This poses a serious problem for injury prevention, as will be discussed subsequently.

Barriers to Injury Prevention Program Implementation

There are a variety of impediments to implementing successful injury prevention. Some of these difficulties include public attitudes toward injury, as well as the mistaken beliefs that present interventions are effective and sufficient, and that these sort of low-cost endeavors are the most cost-effective solution to the injury problem. Other difficulties include the nature of the problem itself and inadequacies in our awareness of injury process. Understanding these barriers seems a first step toward surmounting them.

Public Attitudes

Parents do not perceive their children as being at high risk for serious injury (Eichelberger, Gotschall, Feely, Harstad, & Bowman, 1990), nor do they report that they worry very much about such common causes of child injury as pedestrian trauma, drowning, burns, or falls (Peterson, Farmer, & Kashani, 1990). When asked in a yes/no format whether injuries are preventable, most parents suggest that they are (Eichelberger et al., 1990). However, when Peterson et al. used a scale ranging from 0 (all accidents are controlled by chance or fate and cannot be prevented) to 5 (some accidents can be prevented, about half cannot), to 10 (all accidents can be prevented by safer behavior and situations), parents suggested that some but not all accidents are preventable (the means for several different kinds of injuries fell between 6 and 7 on the scale). Further, parents are even less inclined to feel that they themselves are responsible for instituting preventive behavior (Peterson et al., 1990). Parents regard themselves as relatively well informed, yet they actually lack the information necessary to prevent many forms of child injury. Eichelberger et al. (1990) summarized their national survey results as indicating "parents' combined ignorance and indifference" (p. 719) toward injury prevention.

Beliefs About Present Interventions

Parents tend not only to overestimate their own knowledge but also to overestimate grossly their children's existing safety skills (Peterson et al., 1986). When asked where children obtained these presumed skills, the most common response is that they received skill training in the classroom, in the form of a presentation by a fire or police department official. A summary of 10 published studies from our laboratory documented that virtually every child had minimal skills in the 13 different skill areas addressed by the various studies summarized in that report

(Peterson, 1989). There is no reason to expect that other populations of children are substantially better equipped with safety skills. Our most alarming data came from a hospital-based workshop for children, in which skills whose acquisition in earlier studies had required a period of weeks were targeted in a single teaching session. Not surprisingly, the children in this workshop acquired minimal skills (Peterson et al., 1988). Following this intervention, however, the parents indicated that their children had successfully acquired the targeted skills, and there were statistically significant decreases in the children's ratings of fears of home-based hazards. Thus, far from supplying the requisite skills, this study may have placed children at more risk because of decreased parental supervision and child concern about hazards.

In addition to the typical overestimation of safety skills resulting from didactic, weak contingency, active intervention programs oriented toward adults and children, there is a widespread overestimation of the degree to which legislated safety standards protect children (Berger, 1981). There has been some very successful legislation previously described that protects children from a range of hazards, ranging from strangling in poorly made cribs (Consumer Product Safety Commission, 1979) to ingesting toxic amounts of medication (Walton, 1982). However, these actions are the exception rather than the rule. There is active opposition to injury prevention through product regulation; increased financial costs and concerns with personal freedom are among the reasons cited for such opposition (Berger, 1981; Garbarino, 1988). Gun legislation is among the most sensitive areas. Gun-related child (ages 10–14) homicides and suicides are on the increase. In addition, about 300 children a year are killed by unintentional firearm mishaps (Waller, Baker, & Szocka, 1989). Yet, the powerful National Rifle Association lobbies vigorously to support the production and sale of the handguns responsible for most of these injuries. There are less politically sensitive products as well that have resisted legislation. For example, some experts suggest that as many as 42% of injuries requiring emergency department attention in infants under 1 year of age may be due to "baby walkers," and such devices offer no developmental advantage to infants (O'Shea, 1986). However, they continue to be manufactured without regulation. Thin plastic bags have resulted in child suffocation for more than 25 years, with the only intervention being warning signs printed on some of the bags. Baker and Fisher (1980) reported that some parents continue to use such bags as mattress covers for young children. As Berger (1981) observed, the American public has a "serious misconception" about the degree to which safety legislation protects children. Such misconceptions increase the risks to children in the long run.

Cost-Benefit Analysis

There appears to have been some shortsightedness in many of the current injury reduction programs. As is often the case with prevention programs, there has been an emphasis on cost containment without appropriate evaluation of benefits derived. Programs that cost little and provide little benefit are no bargain and may actually cause harm, with parents believing they can provide less supervision and children believing they can tolerate more risks (Peterson & Roberts, 1992). Thus, the most essential change within injury prevention programs nationwide must be attention to evaluation, providing clear and quantifiable evidence of skills acquired and hazards that remain. Balancing immediate cost with clear long-term benefit to the child seems the first step toward promoting effective prevention. Yet, even this is not as easy or straightforward as it might appear.

Evaluation Challenges

Even though injuries are the leading killer of children in the United States, serious injuries are, thankfully, very low base-rate events. Thus, many thousands of children must be treated to demonstrate a reduction in the actual number of injuries. For some methods (e.g., strong contingency, legislated, targeted to the injury agent), this level of measurement is possible. For other methods (e.g., strong contingency, positive consequences for behavior, targeted to the child), funding rarely permits sufficient contact to afford a clear demonstration of injury prevention. It could be argued that increasing safe behavior is logically related to decreased injury, but this remains to be established empirically. Some experts, including those in our laboratory, believe that in some areas so little is known about the process of injury that prevention cannot be automatically assumed to be the outcome of increased safety. Many researchers are turning back from intervention to more descriptive studies, which, in turn, may provide a more complete basis for future intervention (Chassin, Presson, & Sherman, 1985). Such an orientation seems to offer the most hope for future interventions.

CASE EXAMPLE

Although different lessons can be learned from any intervention study, it is our experience that the greatest amount of learning occurs during one's first foray into an area. Thus, we will consider here our initial study on children's safety skill acquisition (Peterson, 1984a). We will punctuate the narrative with some semi-ironic "rules" that are perfectly clear to us now, after the fact, and that may organize the experience similarly for the reader.

Rule 1: *Even when the constituency (i.e., consumers supporting the program who will be served) is known, the intervention (if it is to endure) must operate through an existing social institution.* If the problem is conceived of as one in which children without parental supervision require skill acquisition to be safe, a logical social institution to have such a program would seem to be the public school system, which has the primary charge of children's skill acquisition and which already has a place in its curriculum for safety education. Thus, we approached our local school board enthusiastically with our intervention, which could extend and improve its mission.

Rule 2:   *Never underestimate the slowness or inflexibility of an unprepared bureaucracy.* We learned quickly that the authorities charged with education preferred to regard our request as research rather than an augmentation of their existing safety education programs. Multiple telephone calls were made to administrators who were unavailable and who failed to return the calls. Periodically, we met with school board officials, and described our program and its benefits. After nearly 3 months of such sporadic activity, the proposal was refused by the city schools, leading to Rule 3.

Rule 3:   *Social institutions should be expected to be wary about accepting additional charges, especially in sensitive or potential litigious areas.* The school board official entrusted with research authorization explained that the project had been denied because it focused on *home* safety, and certainly the safety of a child in the home was the responsibility of the parents and not the school. Students now have important additional educational requirements beyond the three *R*s, the official noted, and reminded us of the new program to teach elementary students computer keyboarding skills. Finally, he concluded that there had been concern expressed about the potential for legal difficulties if a child completing a course in safety were subsequently injured. However, the program proposed was a fine one, and he wished us luck.

Rule 4:   *Don't give up the ship.* If the prerogative for children's skill acquisition did not lay with the schools, but rather with the parents, a social institution made up of parents should be sought, as per Rule 1. We therefore met with several PTA groups to convince them of our program's importance. After several such presentations, the program was received enthusiastically by the city PTA president. The PTA as a group agreed to petition the board of education to allow our program to take place at school, after school hours. Thus, no valuable class time was required, and the school system would not be liable for any results. This petition was successful. We selected a school two blocks from the university campus to facilitate travel of the undergraduate instructors (now in training for 4 months) and students returning home following the intervention each day, and sent home more than 100 letters describing the project and requesting children's participation.

Rule 5:   *Do not let the enthusiasm of your program consumers mislead you concerning their investment in a costly intervention.* Although the groups of parents we had contacted had been most excited about our program, very few parents authorized their child's participation in the project. Of nearly 100 eligible children, only eight participated in the actual intervention. Explanations for nonparticipation included (a) my child is rarely left unsupervised, so he or she does not need such skills; (b) my child is frequently left unsupervised and has never been hurt, so he or she must already have such skills; and (c) my child is already involved in soccer, gymnastics, and girl or boy scouts. Our family cannot take on another activity right now. Our research group activated Rule 4 and continued.

Rule 6: *Stay flexible in design strategy.* We had initially conceived of a control group design, with two large groups of children learning safety skills or control skills. We quickly switched to a multiple-baseline design that presented differing modules at differing times to the eight children involved.

We met with the children to begin teaching and found that two of the children had very limited English, and one was frankly phobic about being left at home alone, although this child was left alone several times a week. Our planned strategy of didactic, modeling, and role-playing techniques suddenly seemed inadequate to the task.

Rule 7: *Stay flexible with the vehicle carrying the intervention.* We converted the materials to visual playing cards with both a picture and a brief narrative to accompany each safety rule. We did the same with common wrong answers. Thus, we began with a simple discrimination of correct and incorrect, in the context of playing with the cards (a nonthreatening and fun activity) that gradually shaped the children to correct responding.

Rule 8: *Be alert to obstacles to the program, once begun.* Following the first sessions, we found that two of the children had been told to walk home after the program, even though it was dark outside. One experimenter drove these children home. The other children were picked up by their parents. Although the school we had selected was close to the university campus, four of the children were bused in from homes near the city limits, more than 10 miles away. When they remained at school, there was no bus transportation home. After the third session, two parents noted that their children would have to drop out if transportation were not provided.

Soon, our experimenters were transporting six of the eight children around town, requiring insurance and mileage reimbursement from this unfunded project. Occasionally an experimenter would take a child home only to find the house dark and locked. The experimenter would then take the child to the experimenter's home, and return when he or she had made telephone contact indicating that the parent had arrived home.

Other obstacles included provision of makeup work for children when they were ill, dealing with a loud janitorial staff who was accustomed to an empty building after school, and attempting to keep the two groups of children uninformed about what the other group was learning (so that two different multiple baselines could be maintained at the same time). Various unusual naturally occurring events also took place. For example, on the evening the children were to begin the tornado module, a real tornado swept through the area, and the children spent a tense 90 minutes in the basement of the school with sirens going off continually and experimenters trying to reassure the children, first, that this was not just for practice, and, second, that they were not in immediate danger.

Rule 9: *Your program is only as good as your staff.* Throughout the site location, subject recruitment, design alteration, treatment expansion, and actual intervention, the undergraduate experimenters and assessors responded enthusiastically and innovatively to problems that arose, and were patient and creative in dealing with the children. The energy and time required to shape and reward even the best intervention staff cannot be overemphasized. A less enthusiastic group undoubtedly would have experienced even more difficulties. As best evidence of the staff's quality, a year after the project concluded, one of the experimenters returned and volunteered to conduct follow-up assessments and training with all eight subjects to ensure skill maintenance.

Rule 10: *Always program for generalization (both site to site and across time), and do not oversell your program.* One of our grave concerns had been whether skills taught at school in small groups by an attentive adult would be maintained when at home and alone. Therefore, we had asked children to imagine their own homes as they rehearsed and had gradually withdrawn experimenter support. Our follow-up data collected in the children's homes suggested that there was no problem with cross-site generalization. We spent considerable time with parents, noting that the skills the children had acquired would need frequent boosters and that the skills in no way substituted for parental supervision.

Rule 11: *Take what you have learned and restructure your intervention, keeping what is effective and improving on the weak points.* Our additional studies summarized earlier have attempted to expand on this initial study by varying by age of subject, type of skill, training of intervention agent, size of group, generalization of skill, and time required for the intervention.

Rule 12: *There is no such thing as a free lunch, and program dissemination must convince consumers of this.* Our application of this rule was to acknowledge finally that there were limits to the effectiveness of any intervention program in terms of the time and effort required to do the job. As we noted earlier, one common obstacle to implementing successful programs is that consumers continue to refuse to allocate sufficient time, resources, and skill to ensure successful prevention.

FUTURE DIRECTIONS

It is tempting to be unreasonably optimistic about the future. The number of fatal injuries to children has been decreasing slowly for years and in the 1980s decreased very slightly in every category except suicide and homicide (which increased) (Waller et al., 1989). Government funding and direct federally sponsored initiatives for injury prevention have grown in the last decade, although funding remains a small percentage of that expended to study diseases that affect far fewer children. There seems to be the beginnings of a new consumer awareness, at least for some forms of safety equipment, as can be seen by the passage of recent municipal legislation mandating helmet use for children riding bicycles or minibikes. Similarly, automobile manufacturers now advertise their air bags as standard safety equipment. This seems to fit well with the nation's increasing adoption of healthy life-style changes.

There are more grassroots initiatives dedicated to injury prevention than ever before. Industry-sponsored programs such as Johnson and Johnson's Safe Kids Coalition have been joined by other groups, many of which served as models for coalition development in the National Committee for Injury Prevention and Control's book *Injury Prevention: Meeting the Challenge* (1989). Emphasis on data-based prevention endeavors, with information on everything from how to increase interagency cooperation to how to structure a press release, is included in this text.

Thus, reasons for optimism exist, if only as trends that must be realized in the future. Some of the reasons for pessimism have already been presented, namely that the average American adult greatly underestimates the risk of injury to children, and overestimates both his or her own prevention knowledge and children's skill level. The correlates of childhood injury (e.g., poverty and parental absence) show no signs of decreasing. No single public institution is willing to accept the charge of injury prevention. Most of the existing prevention programs are not data based, are unevaluated, and are probably ineffective. Our knowledge of injury prevention remains inadequate to avoid many kinds of injury events, and only a small proportion of injury prevention studies currently can be funded.

There seems to be the beginnings of a change that we must nourish if the change is to continue. If interventions can be increasingly data based, those data may be used to increase public awareness of the need for sound prevention strategies. The greatest hope for the future lies in multiple-level intervention including increases in safety legislation, environmental planning with safety as a base, and early education of potential parents regarding safety issues, with subsequent strong contingency programs to increase both passive and active interventions. Perhaps most important to community psychologists, at-risk children must be contacted directly. The optimal vehicle would seem to be the public school systems, which, using existing strong contingency programs, could increase effectively safety skills acquisition in all children, with specific programming at different developmental milestones.

Children equipped with the habit of safe behavior, living within safer environments, and supervised by safety-conscious adults could enjoy decades of productive life that might otherwise be denied to some of them. This seems a most compelling goal for future research and intervention.

NOTES

1. Some researchers argue that child safety restraints would be better considered as an active rather than passive intervention, because they require refastening at each use. Because most researchers still consider barrier methods such as safety restraints to be passive interventions and because they are less active than attempting to alter the behavior of the child in their care, they are considered as a passive intervention here.
2. Many of the interventions suggested by the HAPI and by many of the educational programs examined later in this section might be considered passive interventions (e.g., storing poison in a locked container). The programs considered here, however, focused on multiple or repeated, discriminative changes in the parents' behavior, and thus they are considered under the heading of active interventions.

REFERENCES

Baker, S. P., & Fisher, R. S. (1980). Childhood asphyxiation by choking or suffocation. *Journal of the American Medical Association, 244*, 1343–1346.

Berger, L. (1981). Childhood injuries: Recognition and prevention. *Current Problems in Pediatrics, 12*, 1–59.

Centers for Disease Control. (1990). Special contribution: Childhood injuries in the United States. *American Journal of Diseases of Children, 144*, 627–648.

Chassin, L. A., Presson, C. C., & Sherman, S. J. (1985). Stepping backward in order to step forward: An acquisition-oriented approach to primary prevention. *Journal of Consulting and Clinical Psychology, 53*, 612–622.

Colver, A. F., Hutchinson, P. J., & Judson, E. C. (1982). Promoting children's home safety. *British Medical Journal, 285*, 1177–1180.

Consumer Product Safety Commission. (1979, February). *Impact of crib safety activities on injuries and deaths associated with cribs.* Washington, DC: Author.

Dershewitz, R. A., & Williamson, J. W. (1977). Prevention of childhood household injuries: A controlled clinical trial. *American Journal of Public Health, 67*, 1148–1153.

Eichelberger, M. R., Gotschall, C. S., Feely, H. B., Harstad, P., & Bowman, L. M. (1990). Parental attitudes and knowledge of child safety: A national survey. *American Journal of Diseases of Children, 144*, 714–720.

Garbarino, J. (1988). Preventing childhood injury: Developmental and mental health issues. *American Journal of Orthopsychiatry, 58,* 25–45.
Gorman, R. L., Charney, E., Holtzman, N. A., & Roberts, K. B. (1985). A successful city-wide smoke-detector give away program. *Pediatrics, 75,* 14–18.
Jones, R. T., Kazdin, A. E., & Haney, J. I. (1981). Social validation and training of emergency fire safety skills for potential injury prevention and life saving. *Journal of Applied Behavior Analysis, 14,* 249–260.
Long, L., & Long, T. (1982, September 20). The lonely life of latchkey children. *People Magazine,* pp. 63–65.
Margolis, L., & Runyan, C. (1983). Accidental policy: An analysis of the problem of unintentional injuries of childhood. *American Journal of Orthopsychiatry, 53,* 629–644.
Masters, M. (1978). *Revised statutes of the State of Missouri, 4,* 4707.
McLaughlin, E., Vince, C. J., Lee, A. M., & Crawford, J. D. (1982). Project Burn Prevention: Outcome and implications. *American Journal of Public Health, 72,* 241–247.
Miller, J. R., & Pless, I. B. (1977). Child automobile restraints: Evaluation of health education. *Pediatrics, 59,* 907–911.
Morbidity and Mortality Weekly Report. (1988). Progress toward achieving the national 1990 objectives for injury prevention and control. *Journal of the American Medical Association, 259,* 2069–2077.
Mori, L., & Peterson, L. (1986). Training preschoolers in home safety skills to prevent inadvertent injury. *Journal of Clinical Child Psychology, 15,* 106–114.
National Committee for Injury Prevention and Control. (1989). *Injury prevention: Meeting the challenge.* New York: Oxford University Press.
Nienhuis, M. (1987, February 18). 7.2% of children characterized as "latchkey" in 1984 census survey. *Education Week,* p. 6.
O'Shea, J. S. (1986). Childhood accident prevention strategies. *Forensic Science International, 30,* 99–111.
Peterson, L. (1984a). The "Safe at Home" game: Training comprehensive prevention skills in latchkey children. *Behavior Modification, 8,* 474–494.
Peterson, L. (1984b). Teaching home safety and survival skills to latch-key children: A comparison of two manuals and methods. *Journal of Applied Behavior Analysis, 17,* 279–294.
Peterson, L. (1989). Latchkey children's preparation for self-care: Overestimated, underrehearsed and unsafe. *Journal of Clinical Child Psychology, 18,* 36–43.
Peterson, L., Farmer, J., & Kashani, J. H. (1990). Parental injury prevention endeavors: A function of health beliefs? *Health Psychology, 9,* 177–191.
Peterson, L., & Mori, L. (1985). Prevention of child injury: An overview of targets, methods, and tactics for psychologists. *Journal of Consulting and Clinical Psychology, 53,* 586–595.
Peterson, L., Mori, L., & Scissors, C. (1986). Mom or dad says I shouldn't: Supervised and unsupervised children's knowledge of their parents' rules for home safety. *Journal of Pediatric Psychology, 11,* 177–188.
Peterson, L., Mori, L., Selby, V., & Rosen, B. (1988). Community intervention in children's injury prevention: Differing costs and differing benefits. *Journal of Community Psychology, 16,* 62–73.
Peterson, L., & Roberts, M. C. (1991). *Complacency, misdirection, and effective prevention of children's injuries. American Psychologist, 23,* 375–387.
Peterson, L., & Scissors, C. (1983, August). *Mom/Dad says no: Correspondence between parents' and children's at home rules.* Paper presented at the meeting of the American Psychological Association, Anaheim, CA.

Peterson, L., & Thiele, C. (1988). Home safety at school. *Child and Family Behavior Therapy, 10*, 1–8.

Pless, I. B., & Arsenault, L. (1987). The role of health education in the prevention of injuries to children. *Journal of Social Issues, 43*, 87–104.

Preusser, D. F., & Blomberg, R. D. (1984). Reducing child pedestrian accidents through public education. *Journal of Safety Research, 15*, 47–56.

Rivara, F. P. (1982). Minibikes: A case study in underregulation. In S. B. Bergman (Ed.), *Preventing childhood injuries* (pp. 61–63). Columbus, OH: Ross Laboratories.

Roberts, M. C., & Turner, D. S. (1986). Rewarding parents for their children's use of safety seats. *Journal of Pediatric Psychology, 11*, 25–36.

Robertson, L. S. (1983). *Injuries: Causes, control strategies, and public policy*. Lexington, MA: Lexington Books.

Rodman, H., Pratto, D. J., & Nelson, R. S. (1985). Child care arrangements and children's functioning: A comparison of self-care and adult-care children. *Developmental Psychology, 21*, 413–418.

Rodriguez, J. G. (1990). Childhood injuries in the United States: A priority issue. *American Journal of Diseases of Children, 144*, 625–626.

Rosenbaum, M. A., Creedon, D. L., & Drabman, R. S. (1981). Training preschool children to identify emergency situations and make emergency phone calls. *Behavior Therapy, 12*, 425–435.

Schlesinger, E. R., Dickson, D. G., Westaby, J., Lowen, L., Logrillo, V., & Maiwald, A. (1966). A controlled study of health education in accident prevention. *American Journal of Diseases of Children, 3*, 490–496.

Smith, G. S., & Falk, H. (1987). Unintentional injuries. In R. W. Ambler & N. B. Dold (Eds.), *Closing the gap: The burden of unnecessary illness* (pp. 143–163). New York: Oxford University Press.

Sorenson, B. (1976). Prevention of burns and scalds in a developed country. *Journal of Trauma, 16*, 249–258.

Spiegel, C. N., & Lindaman, F. C. (1977). Children can't fly: A program to prevent childhood morbidity and mortality from window falls. *American Journal of Public Health, 67*, 1143–1147.

Streff, F. M., & Geller, E. S. (1986). Strategies for motivating safety belt use: The application of applied behavior analysis. *Health Education Research: Theory and Practice, 1*, 47–59.

Tertinger, D. A., Greene, B. F., & Lutzker, J. R. (1984). Home safety: Development and validation of one component of an ecobehavioral treatment program for abused and neglected children. *Journal of Applied Behavior Analysis, 17*, 159–174.

Thomas, K. A., Hassanein, R. S., & Christophersen, E. R. (1984). Evaluation of group well-child care for improving burn prevention practices in the home. *Pediatrics, 74*, 879–882.

Tokuhata, G. K., Colflesh, V., Digon, E., & Mann, L. (1972, May). *Childhood injuries caused by consumer products*. Harrisburg, PA: Pennsylvania Department of Health, Division of Research and Biostatistics.

Vicker, R. (1982, August 23). Rise in chainsaw injuries spurs demands for safety standards but industry resists. *Wall Street Journal*, p. 1.

Waller, A. E., Baker, S. P., & Szocka, A. (1989). Childhood injury deaths: National analysis and geographic variations. *American Journal of Public Health, 79*, 310–315.

Walton, W. W. (1982). An evaluation of the Poison Prevention Packaging Act. *Pediatrics, 69*, 363–370.

Yeaton, W. H., & Bailey, J. S. (1978). Teaching pedestrian safety skills to young children: An analysis and one year follow-up. *Journal of Applied Behavior Analysis, 11,* 315–329.

Zigler, E. (1982, August). *Current social policy issues related to children and families.* Paper presented at the meeting of the American Psychological Association, Washington, DC.

CHAPTER 5

Prevention of Substance Abuse

Steven H. Kelder and Cheryl L. Perry

DESCRIPTION OF THE PROBLEM

Drug and alcohol use among adolescents has been, and will continue to be, a major social and health issue in contemporary American society. Every year since 1975, the Monitoring the Future Study has conducted a nationwide representative substance abuse survey of approximately 17,000 high school seniors (Johnston, O'Mally, & Bachman, 1990). In 1989, 54% of the respondents reported having tried an illicit drug, 33% having tried an illicit drug other than marijuana. Almost 44% had tried marijuana or hashish; 18% were monthly users. In fact, 84% of the seniors claimed marijuana would be "fairly easy" or "very easy" for them to obtain. With respect to cocaine, 10.3% had used some form of cocaine during their lifetime, and 2.8% were monthly users; 4.7% had tried crack cocaine, with 1.4% reporting monthly use. The survey also reported that use of legal drugs by adolescents has remained exceedingly high. More than 90% of the seniors had tried alcohol at least once in their life, with 33% reporting recent heavy use (five or more drinks in a row in the last 2 weeks); 65.7% had tried cigarettes, 29% were current smokers. These rates represent conservative estimates, as they do not include high school dropouts, among whom drug use is even more prevalent. Although the rates of legal and illegal substance use have been declining since 1975 (with the exception of alcohol), they are still unacceptably high and threaten the health, safety, and development of our nation's youth.

The results from the Monitoring the Future Study also suggest that the emphasis by both the federal government and mass media on teenage use of "headline drugs" such as crack and cocaine may be misplaced. Hard drugs have obvious health-compromising and developmental consequences and should be of concern, yet the three drugs that account for the largest portion of drug problems in the United States have not received the top priority they deserve. Clearly, as a group, the drugs of choice for adolescents are tobacco, alcohol, and marijuana. These substances are experimental with first, most frequently used, associated with the greatest morbidity and mortality, and are often strong "gateway" predictors of subsequent harder drug use (Kandel, 1977; Kandel & Logan, 1984). By virtue of their gateway status, widespread use, and substantial health consequences, prevention efforts should place a primary focus on tobacco, alcohol, and marijuana.

Adolescent substance use can lead to tragic consequences for the individual, his or her family, and society. Perry and Jessor (1985) have provided a useful framework for conceptualizing the broad health consequences of adolescent substance abuse. Four interrelated health domains—physical, social, psychological, and personal—allow for a more refined representation of these potential consequences. Physical health refers to processes of physical and physiological functioning and their adequacy and efficiency. In the area of physical health, suicides, homicides, and unintentional injuries account for approximately 80% of all adolescent deaths. Several studies reveal considerable involvement of alcohol and drugs in these deaths (Blum, 1987; Rosen, Xiangdong, & Blum, 1990). Moreover, motor vehicle accidents kill more teenagers than any other single cause of death, and most of these accidents involve alcohol. With respect to smoking, 85% of teenagers who completely smoke two cigarettes will become regular smokers and potentially suffer the major health consequences related to smoking (Silvis & Perry, 1987).

Social health refers to a person's social effectiveness, the adequacy with which the individual fulfills tasks, performs roles, and acquires the necessary skills for adaptive functioning within social settings. Jessor and Jessor (1977) found that substance use during adolescence is strongly associated with other problem behaviors, such as early sexual behavior, delinquency, deviant attitudes, and school dropout. Degree of involvement in criminal activities and alcohol use also appear to be related (Temple & Ladouceur, 1985). As Newcomb and Bentler (1989, p. 248) have reported with reference to their longitudinal studies on adolescent substance abuse: "High levels of teenage drug use reflected a tendency toward precocious development, characterized by early involvement in marriage, family and the work force, and forsaking of educational pursuits. Polydrug use as a teenager interfered with the development tasks of adolescence, which lead to poor or unsuccessful role acquisition as young adults (e.g., failed marriages and job instability)." Drug use also impedes psychosocial maturation and interferes with the critical development of identity formation, personal and interpersonal communication, and decision-making skills (Newcomb & Bentler, 1988b).

The third domain of health, psychological health, refers primarily to a subjective domain of self-appraisal of how one generally feels, that is, one's sense of well-being. Psychological health involves such areas as a sense of fitness and energy, feelings of well-being, a self-concept of personal competence, and a belief in an internal locus of control. The acute impact of substance use on psychological health includes mood changes, psychological dependency, impaired judgment and motor function, decreased attention span, memory loss, prolonged aimlessness, and a lack of clarity about goals (Kandel & Davies, 1987; Newcomb & Bentler, 1988a).

The final domain is that of personal or spiritual health. Personal health goes beyond adequate functioning in the other three domains. It refers to the individual as an integrated whole and emphasizes the possibility of inner capabilities, resources, and talents that are not tapped or elicited by the ordinary circumstances of everyday life. A concern with personal health implies that there is unrealized potential for fulfillment along various dimensions and that its stimulation would permit an individual's fuller development. Personal health often is associated with a belief in the potential for a greater meaning to one's life. Substance use influences personal or spiritual health by limiting prematurely the adolescent user's range of interests. Adolescents who increase their amount of time under the influence of alcohol or drugs have less time and willingness to pursue and participate in growth-enhancing experiences or needed introspection. With reference to this domain, it is also of interest that Jessor (1984) reported adolescents with a religious affiliation were less likely to use drugs.

Given the enormous costs and consequences of substance abuse across multiple domains of health, it seems critical to prevent the first use and experimentation of gateway substances. Today's supply-side "war on drugs" consists primarily of law enforcement, confiscation, and treatment of those dependent on illicit drugs. Yet, because these efforts focus mainly on illicit hard drugs, they are less likely to prevent the onset of the three gateway substances: tobacco, alcohol, and marijuana. A realistic prevention policy should place far greater emphasis on highly prevalent substances and those with the greatest potential for causing subsequent hard drug progression. The question, of course, is how.

REVIEW AND CRITIQUE OF THE LITERATURE

Early prevention programs assumed that adolescents simply lacked information about the negative effects of drug use. Underlying this approach was the belief that if students were sufficiently aware of the negative consequences they would make a rational decision not to drink or smoke. The information model was used to increase awareness of the adverse health, legal, and social consequences of substance use and typically made use of fear arousal or "scare tactics," as well as messages with moral overtones. The exaggerated claims about the negative and immoral effects of drugs (e.g., films such as *Reefer Madness*) frequently did more to undermine the credibility of adults and authority than to deter drug use. Later programs focused on individual deficiencies, such as a lack of self-esteem or undeveloped values. Research from over a dozen years evaluating these approaches has concluded they have had little effect on substance use behaviors and may even have encouraged experimentation (Kohn, Goodstadt, Cook, Sheppard, & Chan, 1982; Polich, Ellickson, Reuter, & Kahan, 1984; Rundell & Bruvold, 1988). Still, changing knowledge concerning the consequences of drug use continues to be the predominant form of drug education in schools (Murray et al., 1988).

Today's models of substance abuse prevention are driven by social-learning theory (Bandura, 1977; 1986) and go beyond the information and individual deficit models. These models consider the social context of initial use and subsequent abuse. The remainder of this chapter will describe these social influences models for adolescent substance abuse prevention; illustrate applications to tobacco, alcohol, and marijuana; and provide recommendations for future research and practice.

Social Influences Model of School Health Education

The literature on the antecedents of adolescent drug use suggests that social-environmental, personality, and behavioral factors are important determinants of future drug use (Perry & Jessor, 1985; Perry & Murray, 1985). These factors are determined reciprocally; that is, they are evidenced through dynamic and constant interaction between the individual and the larger social environment (Bandura, 1977; 1985). From this view, substance use is conceptualized as a socially learned, purposeful, and functional behavior. Because of this reciprocal nature, prevention programs should be designed to have an impact on environmental, personality, and behavioral risk factors. A summary of the most potent and predictive environmental, personality, and behavioral risk factors and their translation into prevention strategies is shown in Table 5.1. It is important to note that the identification of those factors that are predictive of onset is critical because they are also the factors that become the focus for intervention.

The adolescent's social environment provides the necessary conditions for drug use through observing the behavior of influential role models, through social support systems, and through access or barriers to drugs or nondrug alternatives. Experimentation with substances generally occurs within the context of a social situation, yet not all teens in high-risk environments choose to experiment or use tobacco, alcohol, or drugs regularly. It may be that personality and behavioral factors are critical in determining the adolescent's response to the environment. The relative value placed on more conventional goals (vs. drug taking), and the adolescent's ability to participate in nondrug alternatives, may be the pivotal determinants of substance use initiation. The findings from longitudinal research suggest using a broad-based three-factor prevention approach rather than concentrating on a single factor or subset of risk factors (Flay, 1985; Perry, 1986; Sussman, 1989). These research findings suggest that drug use has meaning to adolescents and serves specific functions for them. Specifically, the use of tobacco, alcohol, and marijuana offers an opportunity to challenge parental and societal authorities, demonstrate autonomy and independence, signal entry into a peer group, or simply relieve the stresses of growing up. Therefore, prevention efforts should attend to the functions served by drugs as well as to the more immediate social-environmental, personality, and behavioral risk factors of substance use.

Most school-based strategies for tobacco, alcohol, and marijuana prevention have seven major components, with the programs generally involving 6 to 12 classroom sessions. First, the students begin by identifying the short-term consequences of use, such as smelling badly, having an accident, or acting out of control. This generally is done through small group discussions so that the "consequences" are relevant to the age group. Second, the students discover that substance use is not a normative behavior for young adolescents. This is accomplished by comparing their expectations of how many of their peers are substance users with actual data and by discussing their overestimates of prevalence. Third, the reasons why adolescents use substances are explored. These reasons or functions include a desire to have fun, a way of making friends, a signal of maturity, or a method of coping with personal problems (Perry & Murray, 1985). Fourth, the

TABLE 5.1 Psychosocial Risk Factors Involved in Adolescent Substance Abuse Prevention

Environmental factors	
Parental influence:	Parental involvement and support
Cultural norms:	Promotion of a nonuse norm
Opportunities:	Appealing, substance-free activities
Role models:	Peer leaders; influential person's behavior
Social support:	From families and peers
Personality factors	
Knowledge:	Harmful consequences and alternatives
Values:	Relative importance of drugs vs. abstinence
Self-efficacy:	Confidence in being able to resist peer pressure
Locus of control:	Perception of being in charge of self
Meanings:	Functions that drugs serve
Behavioral factors	
Behavioral capability:	Refusal skills; alternative activity engagement
Intentions:	Statements about remaining substance free
Behavior repertoire:	Communication, decision making
Reinforcements:	Tangible rewards for nondrug alternatives

students learn how these meanings are established in our culture through advertising and through peer and adult role models. The methods used by advertisers to convince adolescents of tobacco or alcohol's functional values are presented through discussions of selected advertisements. Mock social situations are analyzed to identify the type of influences that exist. Fifth, the students learn and practice skills to resist these influences. They create antitobacco advertisements and skits (role playing) around possible social encounters. Sixth, near the end of most programs, the students make a public commitment (goal) to abstain. This commitment acts as a psychological anchor and explicitly creates an intention not to experiment with substances. Finally, all these activities are experiential—designed to require active participation—and often are led by trained same-age peer leaders.

The systematic use of peer leaders in smoking and drug abuse prevention programs is a notable component. Several researchers have found peer-led programs to be significantly more successful in reducing onset and use rates than the same program taught by classroom teachers or other adults (Klepp, Halper, & Perry, 1986; Perry & Grant, 1988; Murray, Davis-Hearn, Goldman, Pirie, & Luepker, 1988). Generally, in each of the intervention classrooms, several students are elected as students who are "liked and respected." Peer leaders chosen by classmates are familiar, positive role models who provide key social information and not merely facts. These students are trained to conduct more than half of the activities in the prevention program, particularly activities that involve sharing of social information. They lead small group discussions and brainstorming sessions, read and give directions for activities, report students' views to the class, and organize role plays and skits. Young adolescents can easily be trained to perform these functions, and the inclusion of peer leaders appears to enhance intervention effects.

Application of the Social Influences Model

In the United States, drug use tends to begin during preadolescence and early adolescence, with decreasing rates of initiation over time. By the end of the 9th grade, slightly more than half of all students have had their first experience with cigarettes and alcohol, and 25% with marijuana (Johnston, O'Mally, & Bachman, 1987). As past substance use is a strong predictor of subsequent use (Newcomb & Bentler, 1989), it is clear that the 6th through 10th grades are the optimum entry points for primary prevention. Programs before the 6th grade can provide an important base of information, but programs emphasizing skills development need to be more proximal to the age of initiation of substance use behaviors. One goal of substance use prevention programs is to delay onset of use until a later age when personal decision-making skills have become more discriminating. This section will review how several investigators have applied the social influences model to prevent tobacco, alcohol, and drug use.

Smoking Prevention

Most of the studies that have supplied the social influences model to smoking prevention have done so with sixth- through eighth-grade students and have demonstrated a significant impact on smoking-onset rates. Several recent comprehensive reviews of the smoking prevention literature, including two meta-analyses, have reported positive findings in the proportion of students who began to smoke when compared with an equivalent or randomly assigned control group (Botvin & Dusenbury, 1989; Flay, 1985; Pentz, MacKinnon, Flay, Hansen, Johnson, & Dwyer, 1989; Rundell & Bruvold, 1988; Tobler, 1988). In these studies, the impact on regular (i.e., weekly) smoking ranged from reductions of 43 to 60%, with maintenance of these effects generally 1 to 3 years postintervention. For example, Murray, Davis-Hearn, Goldman, Pirie, and Luepker (1988), assessing the Minnesota Smoking Prevention Program (MSPP), found that after 4 years a peer-led social influences program reduced daily and weekly smoking incidence by 35% to 50% compared with an adult-led, health consequences or existing curriculum comparison groups. The effects of the MSPP and other social influences programs appear to diminish over time, suggesting that additional booster education programs are needed during middle adolescence (Botvin, Renick, & Baker, 1983; Flay et al., 1989). Yet, even without booster sessions, the repeated success of these programs in at least delaying onset of tobacco smoking, across more than 20 research studies, is encouraging. (Further discussion of the MSPP is provided subsequently in the case example.)

In 1987 a National Cancer Institute advisory panel of expert smoking prevention researchers attempted to achieve consensus on the essential elements for school-based smoking prevention programs (Glynn, 1989). The panel concluded that sufficient data and experience existed to make eight recommendations considered necessary for successful school-based smoking prevention programs. The panel recommended: (a) giving smoking prevention at least five classroom sessions in each of 2 years and booster sessions in senior high school; (b) including information about the social influences of tobacco onset, short-term effects, and refusal skills; (c) fitting the program into existing curricula; (d) starting the program during the transition from elementary to middle school or junior high; (e) involving students in presenting the program; (f) encouraging parent participation; (g) training teachers thoroughly—ideally for a full day; and (h) using a prevention program that fits with established community norms and needs so that it will be adopted readily.

Alcohol and Drug Prevention

The reported impact of the social influences model on adolescent alcohol and drug use has been more limited (Moskowitz, 1989; Rundell & Bruvold, 1988; Tobler, 1988). Nevertheless, Project SMART, a peer-led social influences prevention program was effective in delaying the onset of tobacco, alcohol, and marijuana use (Hansen, Johnson, Flay, Graham, & Sobel, 1988). Pentz (1983) reported her social skills intervention program also had a positive effect on alcohol use and academic performance. In their four-country pilot alcohol education study, Perry and Grant (1988) obtained significantly lower alcohol use scores with an intervention group, when compared with a randomly assigned comparison group. Their study suggests that a peer-led social influences program can be efficacious across a variety of settings, economies, and cultures. In a larger study, Ellickson and Bell (1990) tested their social influences curriculum (called Project Alert) across widely diverse socioeconomic and demographic school environments. The program's results indicated that tobacco and marijuana use can be delayed effectively but that the onset of alcohol use is more difficult to arrest.

Life Skills Training

In light of the limited findings using the social influences model for alcohol use prevention, Botvin (1986) suggested that an expansion of the model to include other life skills might be necessary to delay onset. Although most social influences interventions focus on specific skills for resisting the social and environmental pressures to initiate substance use, Botvin's Life Skills Training (LST) program also includes a general set of skills for promoting individual competence. To function in today's society, adolescents are expected to have acquired a certain set of social skills. Interpersonal skills are necessary for the development of healthy social relationships, and failure to develop these skills may adversely affect an individual's performance in personal, work, or school situations. The ability to make logical decisions without being overly influenced by others, and to cope with anxiety and stress become more important as adolescents grow and increase their autonomy. As Botvin and Dusenbury (1989) noted:

> Susceptibility to negative environmental influences [to use substances] might also be reduced by increasing self-esteem, a sense of personal control, self-confidence, self-satisfaction, and assertiveness. It would also be important to teach adolescents specific skills (e.g., interpersonal skills, goal-setting, self-directed behavior change techniques) designed to increase the likelihood of achieving desired goals as well as an array of general coping skills (e.g., anxiety reduction techniques, self reinforcement techniques, positive thinking). (p. 155)

The LST program consists of 15 to 20 sessions for seventh-grade students, with additional booster sessions in the eighth and ninth grades. Table 5.2 provides a description of the seventh-grade program. The seventh grade is a time when students are experimenting with new behaviors and feel increasing pressure to engage in substance use. The LST program's specific objectives are to (a) provide students with skills to resist direct pressures to smoke, drink, or use marijuana; (b) decrease susceptibility to indirect social pressures by helping students develop greater autonomy, self-esteem, self-mastery, and self-confidence; (c) enable stu-

TABLE 5.2 Summary of the Life Skills Training Program Description

Number of sessions	Topic	Description
4	Substance Use: Myths and Realities	Common attitudes and beliefs about tobacco, alcohol, and marijuana use; current prevalence rates of adults and teenagers; the social acceptability of using these substances; the process of becoming a regular (habitual) user, and the difficulty of breaking these habits; the immediate physiological effects of smoking.
2	Decision-Making and Independent Thinking	Discussion of routine decision-making; description of a general decision-making strategy; social influences affecting decisions; recognizing persuasive tactics; and the importance of independent thinking.
2	Media Influence and Advertising Techniques	Discussion of media influences on behavior; advertising techniques and the manipulation of consumer behavior; formulating counterarguments and other cognitive strategies for resisting advertising pressure; cigarette and alcohol advertising as case studies in the use of these techniques.
2	Self-Image and Improvement	Discussion of self-image and how it is formed; the relationship between self-image and behavior; the importance of a positive self-image; alternative methods of improving one's self and self-image; beginning a self-improvement project.
2	Coping with Anxiety	Discussion of common anxiety-inducing situations; demonstration and practice of cognitive-behavioral techniques for coping with anxiety; instruction on the application of these techniques to everyday situations as active coping strategies.
2	Communication Skills	Discussion of the communication process; distinguishing between verbal and nonverbal communication; techniques for avoiding misunderstandings.
	Social Skills (A)	Discussion on overcoming shyness; initiating social contacts, giving and receiving compliments; basic conversational skills; initiating, sustaining, and ending conversations.
	Social Skills (B)	Discussion of boy-girl relationships and the nature of attraction; conversing with the opposite sex; social activities and asking someone out for a date.
	Assertiveness	Situations calling for assertiveness, reasons for not being assertive, verbal and nonverbal assertive skills; resisting peer pressures to smoke, drink, or use marijuana.

Note. From Substance Abuse Prevention and the Promotion of Competence (p. 163) by G. J. Botvin and L. Dusenbury. In G. W. Albee & J. M. Joffe (Eds.), *Primary Prevention of Psychopathology* (Vol. 12, pp. 146–178). NewBerry Park, CA: Sage. Copyright 1989 by Sage. Reprinted by permission.

dents to cope with anxiety induced by social situations; (d) increase students' knowledge by providing them with accurate information concerning the prevalence rates of tobacco, alcohol, and marijuana use; and (e) promote the development of attitudes and beliefs consistent with nonsubstance use (Botvin & Dusenbury, 1988). Because pressures to use substances continue into high school, a 10-session booster program for eighth graders and a five-session booster program for ninth graders were developed. The booster curricula review and reinforce the material covered in the seventh-grade program.

Botvin and Dusenbury (1989) reported on a series of six progressively larger and more complex quasi-experimental studies to delay substance use utilizing the LST program and peer leaders compared with similar reference schools. Results from these studies have provided encouraging evidence for the LST program's efficacy in preventing smoking onset (40–80% fewer smokers at posttest), alcohol use (54% fewer drinkers in the past month, 73% fewer heavy drinkers, and 79% fewer getting drunk more than one time a month), and marijuana use (71% fewer users). A current study is evaluating the program's effectiveness in 56 New York state public schools, and another project is examining its suitability for urban minority populations.

Summary

The past decade of smoking and alcohol abuse prevention research provides an encouraging picture. By regarding substance use behaviors as social and functional and providing opportunities to learn and practice social skills, young adolescents appear to be less likely to smoke tobacco. An extension of these approaches also appears promising for delaying and minimizing alcohol and drug use. Although the preliminary evidence suggests some optimism for social influences and life skills models of prevention, the effects appear to decay over time. This suggests the need for more intensive interventions repeated across multiple grades, with adequate booster sessions.

Community-Level Substance Abuse Prevention

The school is only one enclave within a larger society. Its boundaries are permeable, and as the society affects the school, so does the school affect the society. A question that might be asked concerns the linkages between the school and the extraschool environment. How can school-based programs achieve changes in health-related behavior that are sustained outside the school setting, are enduring, and affect the larger community? The answer points to the involvement of families, as well as cooperation among schools, churches, and other organizations that influence community behavior. It points to the use of mass media, marketing, and larger environmental and economic changes to support and sustain the gains made within the schools.

Several smoking and drug abuse prevention programs have gone beyond the classroom into the larger school and community environments. Mass media have been used to disseminate social influences messages, attract audience attention, increase interpersonal communication, and augment school-based programs (Flay, 1986). The Midwestern Prevention Project (Pentz, Dwyer, MacKinnon, Flay, Hansen, Wang, & Johnson, 1989) is an ongoing community-wide drug abuse prevention program that includes (a) school-based education (using a peer-led social influences model); (b) parental education and organization; (c) mass media; (d) community organizations; (e) and changes in school and local government policy. By involving the community, the program is attempting to create environmental support for the changes made within the school-based component, thus changing the social norm of drug use. One-year results indicate that the prevalence rates for cigarette smoking, alcohol use, and marijuana use are significantly lower in the intervention communities (Pentz et al., 1989).

Two large community-based cardiovascular disease prevention trials, the Minnesota Heart Health Program and the Finland North Karalia Project, provide further support for the importance of community-level interventions (Blackburn et al., 1984; Perry, Klepp, & Schultz, 1988; Puska, 1984). Both of these studies included school-based, social influences smoking prevention programs embedded within a larger heart health program that emphasized smoking cessation, healthy eating, and physical fitness for all community members. Long-term results indicate prevention effects for smoking with youth that complement the results from school-alone prevention programs. The Minnesota study used peer leaders and 3 consecutive years of smoking prevention intervention including the MSPP (Perry, Kelder, Murray, & Klepp, 1992). The prevalence of smoking was 40% to 50% lower in the educated community 5 years following the MSPP. In North Karalia a teacher-led and peer-led social influences plus community intervention showed a significant reduction after 4 and 8 years in the proportion of smoking compared with a nonintervention reference group (Vartiainen, Pallonen, McAlister, Koskela, & Puska, 1986; Vartiainen, Pallonen, McAlister, & Puska, 1990). These results led the North Karalia researchers to conclude that community and school programs can influence youthful nonsmokers to avoid tobacco over the long term.

Summary

Social influences programs are most effective when the prevailing community norms reinforce the prevention message. Evaluation of social influences and life skills programs have found that most approaches appear to have a positive effect on knowledge (Rundell & Bruvold, 1988), but there has been little consistent evidence suggesting that specific approaches can delay the onset of alcohol use or have long-term smoking effects (Moscowitz, 1989). For example, the use of both tobacco and marijuana have found increasing societal disapproval, while the use of alcohol is still considered normative and a part of growing up. Substance abuse prevention programs appear to be more successful with socially unacceptable substances and less effective in preventing the use of adult- and media-approved substances such as alcohol. Perry (1986) has suggested that changes at multiple levels in the community are important to impact norms and optimize school-based prevention programs. These include (a) counteradvertising against substance use; (b) individual or self-help instruction such as direct messages given by physicians; (c) family involvement; (d) school environmental changes, such as explicit and enforced smoking policies for students and teachers; and (e) community-wide campaigns in which adolescents have an active role.

CASE EXAMPLE

As part of the authors' current work, the MSPP was designed to be implemented with sixth- and seventh-grade students. The MSPP addresses the prevention of tobacco use by influencing the social and psychological factors that encourage the onset of smoking. The six-session curriculum includes a review of the major social influences that encourage and support smoking among youth. These important initiating factors include peer pressure, advertising, models of smoking parents and siblings, a false belief that the majority of students smoke tobacco, and a lack of behavioral skills with which to resist many of these influences. The program is specifically designed to (a) help the students identify why people start to smoke; (b) teach them that nonsmoking is normative; (c) provide them with skills to resist peer pressure; (d) recognize the covert messages in tobacco advertisements; and (e) most important, give them practice at refusing offers to use tobacco and choosing nontobacco alternatives. Peer leaders implement most of the MSPP activities and have proved to be effective communicators for many of the social and psychological messages intrinsic to the program. Table 5.3 provides a summary of the MSPP activities and curriculum.

In Minnesota, dissemination of the MSPP received support after a bill passed the Minnesota Legislature in 1985 increasing the state cigarette excise tax. A half-cent per pack raised approximately $1.5 million per year that was directly earmarked for tobacco prevention (Griffin, Loeffler, & Kasell, 1988). Research demonstrating the efficacy of social influences-based tobacco prevention led to the MSPP becoming an endorsed program for the sixth and seventh grade by the Minnesota Department of Education. Before the availability of state money, proponents of the MSPP had to compete with traditional health programs and convince school districts of the value of a new and unfamiliar method. Introducing an innovative curriculum is a complex process and requires cooperation at all levels within the school structure, a structure that is often resistant to change. The presentation of positive research results assisted dissemination, but frequently it was

TABLE 5.3 Summary of the Minnesota Smoking Prevention Program

Session & Topic	Description
1. Negative Consequences of Smoking	Introduce program; introduce peer leaders and describe what they will do; brainstorm all the negative consequences of smoking; show and discuss video, "The Feminine Mistake," which focuses on the reasons for adolescent smoking.
2. Smokeless Tobacco; Reasons for Using Tobacco	Show and discuss video, "The Big Dipper," which examines the negative health and social consequences of smokeless tobacco; compare smokeless and smoking tobacco; brainstorm why people start to use tobacco; describe adult smoking assignment interview.
3. Alternatives to Peer Pressure	Review adult smoking interview; help students discover that tobacco is addictive; brainstorm alternatives to using tobacco; correct normative beliefs on the number of tobacco smokers; review pressures to use tobacco and methods of refusing.
4. Resisting Pressure	Discuss a variety of positive methods for resisting social pressures to smoke; role-play some of the "NO" techniques; summarize that students can control whether or not they choose to use tobacco.
5. Countering Advertising and Mass Media Influence	Discuss the techniques advertisers use to attract new smokers; show and discuss video, "Growing Up in Smoke," which reports on tobacco advertising; have students create advertising ideas for promoting the benefits of nonsmoking.
6. Public Commitment	Have students presentation their ad campaign promoting nonuse; review the negative consequences of tobacco use; have students create personal reasons not to use tobacco and individually read their reasons to the class; present awards and certificates of achievement.

Note. From *Minnesota Smoking Prevention Program: A Tobacco-Use Prevention Curriculum* by R. V. Luepker, D. M. Murray, & C. L. Perry, 1991. Center City, MN: Hazelden Promotional Services. Copyright 1991 by Hazelden Promotional Services. Reprinted by permission.

necessary to engender support by directly visiting the school, presenting at local and state conferences, and enlisting other community organizations, such as the 4-H, the American Lung Association, the American Cancer Association, and the American Heart Association.

Notwithstanding all of these efforts, the key to gaining acceptance of the program appears to be prepackaging a teacher-friendly curriculum and providing in-service training (Perry, Murray, & Griffin, 1991). Because the MSPP is taught in the sixth or seventh grades, where there frequently are no health instructors, the curriculum was specifically designed for those less familiar with health topics, such as teachers of social studies, science, math, or English. The curriculum is modular, with explicit goals and objectives for each teacher- and peer-led activity. Each session plan begins with a list of materials needed to conduct that session and an outline of topics to be presented. More important than the curriculum layout, however, is that the activities are entertaining and fun for both the instructor and student, in contrast to the information-only and scare tactics typical of prior health education efforts.

Teacher and peer-leader training are essential to ensure the MSPP's proper implementation. The teacher training lasts about 6 hours. Social influences curricula differ substantially from the lecture and discussion methods of traditional education and require mastery of a few new teaching strategies. Thus, it is important to begin teacher training by enthusiastically demonstrating the necessity of tobacco prevention and the effectiveness of social influences–based education. Given the great strides made during the last 25 years toward reducing the prevalence of smoking, many teachers may not realize that smoking is still the single greatest cause of premature death and disability in the United States (Schultz, 1991). Presenting the facts and figures of smoking's health-compromising effects, while sobering, should convince the instructors of the value of prevention.

In addition to engaging the teachers in the importance of smoking prevention, it is necessary to demonstrate and allow time for practicing a few innovative MSPP activities. Most teachers are familiar with student-led small group discussions but have not led a role-play session. After numerous teacher trainings it is evident to us that instructors who have never taught in a role-play situation will tend to eliminate that segment unless they have tried it during training. In fact, in a study of teacher training, Sobol et al. (1989) noted in a study of teacher training that skills needed to lead role plays are difficult for novice teachers to acquire. Adequate instruction and practice for teachers (with feedback and coaching) are essential, because behavioral skill acquisition is critical if students are to learn to resist the social pressures to smoke.

Peer leader training for MSPP usually lasts about 2 hours, or two class periods. As in teacher training, it is necessary to "sell" the peer leaders on the value of smoking prevention. It is also essential that they practice a few of the activities such as brainstorming and role playing so that they understand what is expected of them. In our experience, a designated time away from the classroom (morning sessions appear to work best), alone with the teacher, creates a special relationship between the students and the instructor that continues throughout the program.

FUTURE DIRECTIONS

The prevention efforts described thus far have focused on school- and community-based interventions. As reported by Johnston et al. (1990), there have been declines in the use of illicit drugs and tobacco (but not alcohol) during the last 15 years. In fact Johnston et al. (1990) have remarked that "the likelihood of a young person in high school or college today actively using illicit drugs is only half of what it was a decade ago" (p. 2). These changes may be due, in part, to school-based drug prevention interventions and to the gradual shifts in social attitudes and norms that control substance use behavior. Consequently, future research and action in this area must include (a) refinement and dissemination of social influences and life skills models of school and community interventions, and (b) continued study of the social-environmental antecedents and control of substance use.

Dissemination and Refinement

The risk-reduction programs described in this chapter have been developed, implemented, and evaluated through years of research programs. Unfortunately, the diffusion of programs beyond the demonstration site is often slow, with a loss in the potential for significant public health gains. Though many questions remain about the optimum prevention program, the available evidence suggests that social influences and life skills models succeed at least as well and frequently better than existing curricula. One survey on diffusion of tobacco prevention programs in Texas reported that receptivity from school administrators was high but that most school districts developed their own curriculum programs (Parcel et al., 1989). These in-house programs may or may not contain important elements of the successfully evaluated programs. Additionally, a Minnesota survey of ninth graders reported 65% of students having never been exposed to a social influences curriculum, and one quarter of students receiving no tobacco prevention during the seventh, eighth, or ninth grades (Murray, Jacobs, Perry, Pallonon, Harty, Griffin, Moen, & Hanson, 1988). From a public health view, the existing data on the efficacy of social influences programs and the current low level of exposure to these programs strongly suggest the desirability of increased efforts for implementation of the social influences and life skills models in schools across the country.

Several avenues for refining and enhancing substance abuse prevention remain to be explored. Best (1989) described the challenges for school health promotion as follows: (a) When should we intervene? All interventions must take into consideration the appropriate level of cognitive and behavioral development. (b) For how long should we intervene? Should interventions include booster sessions that span multiple age groups or just the age when the behavior is becoming established? (c) What mediates intervention effects? What are the effects of family- or community-based interventions that supplement school health promotion? and (d) What are the intervention targets? Should the focus be on individual motivation or on social norms and policies that regulate behavior? Are social influences models that focus on specific substance use behaviors more appropriate than models that focus on generic life skills? Should abstinence or responsible use be the goal?

Others have noted the white middle-class homogeneity of research populations that have received most substance prevention programs (Moscowitz, 1989; Orlandi, 1986; Rotheram-Borus & Tsemberis, 1989). Prevention policymakers and researchers need to modify and evaluate the existing prevention interventions in a culturally sensitive manner. The extent to which the current social influences and life skills models generalize to low-income and minority populations deserves additional research.

Finally, even though dissemination of the current models of social influences and life skills curricula has been recommended, methodological flaws of the studies on which we base our judgment prohibit taking a conclusive position. Several articles (Cook, 1985; Flay, 1985; Moscowitz, 1989) review shortcomings of substance use prevention research and offer recommendations calling for improvements in (a) reducing subject attrition and improved long-term tracking, (b) controlling for possible Hawthorne effects (i.e., novelty), (c) biochemical validating to increase honesty of reporting, (d) ensuring that the unit of statistical analysis is the same as the unit of assignment, (e) standardizing dependent measures across studies, and (f) enhancing implementation integrity and training quality.

Social-Environmental Strategies

School-based social influences and life skills curricula are designed to effect change at the students' most proximal level of social influence, that is, at the level of the individual, family, peers, and school. Community interventions create additional consistency between the proximal and distal community levels of influence. Changes in larger and more distally influential social systems may be necessary to achieve the desired prevention impact. As noted earlier, tobacco interventions appear more efficacious than alcohol programs. This relative success of tobacco interventions may be due to the consistency of messages adolescents receive from proximal and distal sources of influence. For example, most high school alcohol curricula are vague regarding adolescent alcohol use because school officials cannot endorse a program that assumes some adolescents drink because minimum drinking age laws prohibit alcohol use for this age group. Yet, most adolescents do drink and are encouraged to do so by mass media, advertising, and adult role models. This example illustrates the discrepancy among adolescents' actual behavior, official and unofficial community standards, and the school alcohol curriculum. Additionally, since 1964 the United States has mounted a sustained campaign against smoking, while no comparable social movement exists for preventing adolescent alcohol use and alcohol-related problems. Sustained success in preventing alcohol abuse may have to await changes in the social climate toward such a goal.

Attempts to modify large-scale social-structural systems are normally outside the practice of school-based health promotion. However, school health professionals should be aware of what offers potential success at this level to influence community, state, and federal decision makers persuasively. Even if such changes are expensive and difficult, and take years to achieve, prevention efforts should initiate action that would neutralize the social-structural influences facilitating the use of tobacco, alcohol, or drugs. This might be accomplished through measures that alter: (a) the price of tobacco and alcohol via excise taxes, (b) the availability of these substances to adolescents, (c) the promotion of use through the mass media, and (d) enforcement strategies.

Econometric studies have indicated that the number of cigarettes smoked varies inversely with changes in the price of cigarettes (Warner, 1986b). Using 1984 as the base year, Warner estimated that a $0.16-increase would annually discourage 800,000 teenagers and almost 1 million young adults ages 20 to 25 from beginning to smoke. Before the 1991 tax increase, the federal tax on alcohol had remained constant since 1951, and the tax on alcohol in distilled spirits increased in 1985 after having remained unchanged for nearly 35 years (U.S. Department of Health and Human Services, 1990). With respect to fatal automobile crashes, it is estimated that a doubling of the beer tax (approximately $1.50 increase per 24-unit case of 12 ounce cans) would reduce highway deaths 27% among 18- to 21-year-olds, 18% among 15- to 17-year-olds, and 19% among 21- to 24-year-olds (Saffer & Grossman, 1987). Considering that few people begin to smoke past age 25, and that most alcohol-related problems occur with teenagers and young adults, the federal and state excise tax on these two substances is a potent tool for public health policy.

Several mechanisms are available for altering the availability of substances to adolescents. It was recently demonstrated how easily adolescents can purchase tobacco in Minnesota, especially from vending machines (Forster, Klepp, & Jeffery, 1989). As a result, local ordinances to ban vending machines in several Minnesota cities and across the country have been enacted, thereby considerably reducing teenage access to a dangerous substance. Wagenaar & Farrell (1989) reviewed the evidence regarding minimum drinking age, concluding that decreases in the drinking age (which occurred during the 1970s) resulted in a significant increase in alcohol-related crashes and that the subsequent reversal, (i.e., increases in the drinking age) resulted in reductions in motor vehicle crashes. A separate review concluded that both the consumption of alcohol and the incidence of drinking after driving were reduced by raising the drinking age (U.S. Department of Health and Human Services, 1990). It was also reported that the number and type of outlets that sell alcoholic beverages, and the hours of sale, influence alcohol consumption (U.S. Department of Health and Human Services, 1990).

Cigarettes and alcohol are two of the nation's most heavily advertised consumer products. Research has not yet documented a strong relationship between tobacco and alcohol advertising and teenage onset and abuse (U.S. Department of Health and Human Services, 1990; Warner, 1986a). In fact, both industries consistently deny that advertising influences teenagers, claiming that advertising serves merely to influence brand selection. Yet, one has only to look at the frequency of advertising on televised sporting events, billboards, and magazines to see the intended appeal to young people. Attractive, youthful, or famous characters in advertisements serve as role models that glamorize the use of alcohol and tobacco. Mass media and advertising are significant sources of socialization and provide positive functional meanings for adolescents for substance use (Wallack, 1984). Alcohol and tobacco are frequently portrayed on television and movies as purely pleasurable activities associated with success, solving personal problems, or normative behaviors in which everyone engages. Even worse, dependence on tobacco and alcohol advertising revenues has caused editors, publishers, and writers to avoid articles on smoking and health, or to tone them down (Warner, 1986a). Public health policymakers have often noted that tobacco is the only consumer product that is harmful when used as intended and have called for a ban on all forms of advertising. In Norway, for example, the increase in tobacco use ceased immediately following a ban on advertising, and a pattern of declining consumption set in thereafter (Warner, 1986a). Regarding alcohol advertising, where many people safely use the substance, issues of regulation are less clear (although alcohol advertising is also banned in Norway). At a minimum, a cooperative effort with television writers and directors is needed to create a realistic representation of alcohol's harmful effects and to increase messages of responsible use. In addition, increased public service announcements targeted to a teenage audience are in order.

Finally, enforcement of existing laws would have a general deterrent effect on drinking and driving. A wide variety of deterrent and enforcement programs exist including enforcement crackdowns, sobriety checkpoints, mandatory jail, and "tough" laws that emphasize increased severity and swiftness of punishments (e.g., fines, imprisonment, and license revocation). These strategies have not been studied extensively with respect to adolescent populations. In adult populations, though, deterrent strategies increasing the perceived certainty of punishment (apprehension) have had short-term effects, but strategies increasing severity of punishment, or swiftness through administrative license suspension, have had little measurable effect (Klitzner, 1989).

The greatest net reduction of preventable public health problems requires population-level changes in behavior (Rose, 1981; 1985). Widespread reductions of substance abuse problems are likely to occur when interventions are directed toward large groups at moderate risk rather than only at small groups at high risk. This is true because alcohol and drug use, and the resultant problems, involves the majority of adolescents. Until now, most prevention research and intervention programs in our country have been conducted with those at moderate risk, that is, the white middle class. However, a great need exists for primary prevention in this country with people of color and in poorer populations. We cannot ignore research suggesting that higher vulnerability to alcohol problems may be largely a reflection of such social and economic problems as unemployment, adverse living conditions, poor health care, and racial discrimination (Herd, 1987). Given their often-pleasurable and stress-reducing effects, mood-altering drugs may be naturally attractive to the distressed and deprived. In a high-stress environment, with few sources of socially acceptable stimulation, individuals who are unable (or unwilling) to delay gratification and are lacking sufficient self-control skills could be particularly vulnerable to the use and abuse of tobacco, alcohol, and drugs. And although communities at higher risk have not been silent in their prevention efforts, they have, perhaps wisely, chosen to place far greater resources in other areas of basic human need.

It may be that issues of employment, housing, access to health care, the stress of daily living, and feelings of powerlessness loom larger in some populations than do concerns with tobacco and alcohol abuse. Yet all of these factors, including substance abuse, form a complex web of cause and effect; it is difficult to deal with one of these issues without considering the others. The promotion of opportunities for improvement in each of these areas should be considered a salutary development, and one consistent with more global aims of promoting overall adolescent health and substance abuse prevention.

REFERENCES

Bandura, A. (1986). *social foundations of thought and action*. Englewood Cliffs, NJ: Prentice Hall.
Best, J. A. (1989). Intervention perspectives on school health promotion research. *Health Education Quarterly, 16*, 299–306.
Blackburn, H., Luepker, R. V., Kline, F. G., Bracht, N., Carlaw, R., Jacobs, D., Mittelmark, M., Stauffer, L., & Taylor, H. L. (1984). The Minnesota Heart Health Program: A research and demonstration project in cardiovascular disease prevention. In J. D. Matarazzo, S. M. Weiss, J. A. Herd, N. E. Miller, & S. M. Weiss (Eds.), *Behavioral health: A handbook for health enhancement and disease prevention* (pp. 1171–1178). Silver Springs, MD: John Wiley.
Blum, R. (1987). Contemporary threats to adolescent health in the United States. *Journal of American Medical Association, 257*, 3390–3395.
Botvin, G. J. (1986). Substance abuse prevention research: Recent developments and future directions. *Journal of School Health, 56*, 369–374.
Botvin, G. J., & Dusenbury, L. (1989). substance abuse prevention and the promotion of

competence. In G. W. Albee & J. M. Joffe (Eds.), *Primary prevention of psychopathology* (Vol. 12, pp. 146–178). Newberry Park, CA: Sage.

Botvin, G. J., Renick, N. L., & Baker, E. (1983). The effects of scheduling format and booster sessions on a broad spectrum psychosocial models to smoking prevention. *Journal of Behavioral Medicine, 6,* 359–379.

Cook, T. D. (1985). Priorities in research in smoking prevention. In C. S. Bell & R. Battjes (Eds.), *Prevention research: Deterring drug abuse among children and adolescents* (Research Monograph No. 47, pp. 196–220). Rockville, MD: National Institute on Drug Abuse.

Ellickson, P. L., & Bell, R. M. (1990). *Prospects for preventing drug abuse among young adolescents,* Santa Monica, CA: Rand Corporation.

Flay, B. R. (1985). Psychosocial approaches to smoking prevention: A review of the findings. *Health Psychology, 4,* 449–488.

Flay, B. R. (1986). Mass media linkages with school-based programs for drug abuse prevention. *Journal of School Health, 56,* 402–406.

Flay, B. R. Koepke, D., Thompson, S. J., Santi, S., Best, J. A., & Brown, K. S. (1989). Six-year follow-up of the first Waterloo School Smoking Prevention Trial. *American Journal of Public Health, 79,* 1371–1375.

Forster, J. L., Klepp, K. I., & Jeffery, R. J. (1989). Sources of cigarettes for 19th graders in two Minnesota cities. *Health Education Research, 4,* 25–31.

Glynn, T. J. (1989). Essential elements of school-based smoking prevention programs. *Journal of School Health, 5,* 181–188.

Griffin, G. A., Loeffler, H. J., & Kasell, P. (1988). Tobacco-free schools in Minnesota. *Journal of School Health, 58,* 236–239.

Hansen, W. B., Johnson, C. A., Flay, B. R., Graham, J. W., & Sobel, J. (1988). Affective and social influences approaches to the prevention of multiple substance abuse among seventh grade students: Results from project SMART. *Preventive Medicine, 17,* 135–154.

Herd, D. (1987). Rethinking black drinking. *British Journal of Addictions, 82,* 219–223.

Jessor, R. (1984). Adolescent development and behavioral health. In J. D. Matarazzo, S. M. Weiss, J. A. Herd, N. E. Miller, & S. M. Weiss (Eds.), *Behavioral health: A handbook for health enhancement and disease prevention* (pp. 69–90). Silver Springs, MD: John Wiley.

Jessor, R., & Jessor, S. L. (1977). *Problem behavior and psychosocial development: A longitudinal study of youth.* Orlando, FL: Academic Press.

Johnston, L. D., O'Mally, P. M., & Bachman, J. G. (1987). *National trends in drug use and related factors among American high school students and young adults, 1975–1986.* Rockville, MD: National Institute on Drug Abuse.

Johnston, L. D., O'Mally, P. M., & Bachman, J. G. (1990). *Press release of the 1989 national high school senior survey.* Ann Arbor, MI: University of Michigan, Institute for Social Research.

Kandel, D. B. (1977). Stages in adolescent involvement in drug use. *Science, 190,* 912–914.

Kandel, D. B., & Davies, M. (1986). The consequences in young adulthood of adolescent drug involvement. *Archives of General Psychiatry, 43,* 746–754.

Kandel, D. B., & Logan, S. A. (1984). Problems of drug use from adolescence to young adulthood: Periods of risk initiation, continued use, and discontinuation. *American Journal of Public Health, 74,* 660–666.

Klepp, K., Halper, A., & Perry, C. L. (1986). The efficacy of peer leaders in drug abuse prevention. *Journal of School Health, 56,* 407–411.

Klitzner, M. (1989). Youth impaired driving: Causes and countermeasures. In United

States Department of Health and Human Services, *Surgeon General's Workshop on Drunk Driving* (pp. 192–206). Washington, DC: United States Government Printing Office.

Kohn, P. M., Goodstadt, M. S., Cook, G. M., Sheppard, M., & Chan, G. (1982). Ineffectiveness of threat appeals about drinking and driving. *Accident Analysis and Prevention, 14*, 457–464.

Luepker, R. V., Murray, D. M., & Perry, C. L. (1991). *Minnesota Smoking Prevention Program: A tobacco-use prevention curriculum.* Center City, MN: Hazelden Promotional Services.

Moskowitz, J. M. (1989). The primary prevention of alcohol problems: A critical review of the research literature. *Journal of Studies on Alcohol, 50*, 54–88.

Murray, D. M., Davis-Hearn, M., Goldman, A. E., Pirie, P., & Luepker, R. V. (1988). Four- and five-year follow-up results from four seventh-grade smoking prevention strategies. *Journal of Behavioral Medicine, 11*, 395–405.

Murray, D. M., Jacobs, D. R., Perry, C. P., Pallonon, U., Harty, K. C., Griffin, G., Moen, M., & Hanson, G. (1988). A statewide approach to adolescent tobacco-use prevention: The Minnesota-Wisconsin adolescent tobacco-use research project. *Preventive Medicine, 17*, 461–474.

Newcomb, M. D., & Bentler, P. M. (1988a). *Consequences of adolescent drug use: impact on the lives of young adults.* Newberry Park, CA: Sage.

Newcomb, M. D., & Bentler, P. M. (1988b). Impact of adolescent drug use and social support on problems of young adults: A longitudinal study. *Journal of Abnormal Psychology, 97*, 64–75.

Newcomb, M. D., & Bentler, P. M. (1989). Substance use and abuse among children and teenagers. *American Psychologist, 44*, 242–248.

Orlandi, M. A. (1986). Community-based substance abuse prevention: A multicultural perspective. *Journal of School Health, 56*, 394–401.

Parcel, G. S., Eriksen, M. P., Lovato, C. Y., Gottlieb, N. H., Brink, S. G., & Green, L. W. (1989). The diffusion of school-based tobacco-use prevention programs: Project description and baseline data. *Health Education Research, 4*, 111–124.

Pentz, M. A. (1983). Prevention of adolescent substance abuse through social skill development. In T. J. Glynn, C. G. Luekefeld, & J. P. Ludford (Eds.), *Preventing adolescent drug abuse: Intervention strategies* (Research Monograph No. 47, pp. 195–232). Rockville, MD: National Institute on Drug Abuse.

Pentz, M. A., Dwyer, J. H., MacKinnon, D. P., Flay, B. R., Hansen, W. B., Wang, E. Y., & Johnson, C. A. (1989). A multicommunity trial for primary prevention of adolescent drug abuse: Effects on drug use prevalence. *Journal of American Medical Association, 261*, 3259–3266.

Pentz, M. A., MacKinnon, D. P., Flay, B. R., Hansen, W. B., Johnson, C. A., & Dwyer, J. H. (1989). Primary prevention of chronic diseases in adolescence: Effects of the Midwestern Prevention Project on tobacco use. *American Journal of Epidemiology, 130*, 713–724.

Perry, C. L. (1986). Community-wide health promotion and drug abuse prevention. *Journal of School Health, 56*, 359–363.

Perry, C. L., & Grant, M. (1988). Comparing peer-led to teacher-led youth alcohol education in four countries. *Alcohol Health & Research World, 12*, 322–326.

Perry, C. L., & Jessor, R. (1985). The concept of health promotion and the prevention of adolescent drug abuse. *Health Education Quarterly, 12*, 169–184.

Perry, C. L., Kelder, S. H., Klepp, K., & Murray, D. M. (1992). Communitywide smoking prevention: Long-term outcomes of the Minnesota Heart Health Program and the class of 1989 study. *American Journal of Public Health, 82*, 1210–1216.

Perry, C. L., Klepp, K., & Schultz, J. M. (1988). Primary prevention of cardiovascular disease: Community-wide strategies for youth. *Journal of Consulting and Clinical Psychology, 56,* 358–364.

Perry, C. L., Klepp, K., & Sillers, C. (1989). Community-wide strategies for cardiovascular health: The Minnesota Heart Health Program Youth Program. *Health Education Research, 4,* 87–101.

Perry, C. L., & Murray, D. M. (1985). The prevention of adolescent drug abuse: Implications from etiological, developmental, behavioral, and environmental models. *Journal of Primary Prevention, 6,* 31–52.

Perry, C. L., Murray, D. M., & Griffin, G. (1991). Evaluating the statewide dissemination of smoking prevention curricula: Factors in teacher compliance. *Journal of School Health, 60,* 501–505.

Polich, J. M., Ellickson, P. L., Reuter, P., & Kahan, J. P. (1984). *Strategies for controlling adolescent drug use,* Santa Monica, CA: Rand Corporation.

Puska, P. (1984). Community-based prevention of cardiovascular disease: The North Karalia Project. In J. D. Matarazzo, S. M. Weiss, J. A. Herd, N. E. Miller, & S. M. Weiss (Eds.), *Behavioral health: A handbook for health enhancement and disease prevention* (pp. 1140–1148). Silver Springs, MD: John Wiley.

Rose, G. (1981). Strategy of prevention: Lessons from cardiovascular disease. *British Medical Journal, 282,* 1847–1851.

Rose, G. (1985). Sick individuals and sick populations. *International Journal of Epidemiology, 14,* 32–38.

Rosen, D. S., Xiangdong, M., & Blum, R. W. (1990). Adolescent health: Current trends and critical issues. *Adolescent Medicine: State of the Art Reviews, 1,* 15–31.

Rotheram-Borus, M. J., & Tsemberis, S. J. (1989). Social competency training programs in ethnically diverse communities. In G. W. Albee & J. M. Joffe (Eds.), *Primary prevention of psychopathology* (Vol. 12, pp. 297–318). Newberry Park, CA: Sage.

Rundell, T. G., & Bruvold, W. H. (1988). A meta-analysis of school-based smoking and alcohol use prevention programs. *Health Education Quarterly, 15,* 317–334.

Saffer, H., & Grossman, M. (1987). Drinking age laws on highway mortality rates: Cause and effect. *Economic Inquiry, 25,* 403–417.

Schultz, J. M. (1991). Smoking-attributable mortality and years of potential life lost—United States, 1988. *Morbidity and Mortality Weekly Report, 40,* 62–71.

Silvis, G. L., & Perry, C. L. (1987). Understanding and deterring tobacco use among adolescents. *Pediatric Clinics of North America, 34,* 363–379.

Sobol, D. F., Rohrbach, L. A., Dent, C. W., Gleason, L., Brannon, B. R., Johnson, C. A., & Flay, B. R. (1989). The integrity of smoking prevention curriculum delivery. *Health Education Research, 4,* 59–68.

Sussman, S. (1989). Two social influence perspectives on tobacco use development and prevention. *Health Education Research, 4,* 213–223.

Temple, M., & Ladouceur, P. (1985). The alcohol-crime relationship as an age-specific phenomenon: A longitudinal study. *Contemporary Drug Problems, 13,* 89–116.

Tobler, N. (1988). Meta-analysis of 143 adolescent drug prevention programs: Quantitative outcome results of program participants compared to a control or comparison group. *Journal of Drug Issues, 16,* 537–567.

Wagenaar, A. C., & Farrell, S. (1989). Alcohol beverages control policies: Their role in preventing alcohol-impaired driving. In *Surgeon General's workshop on drunk driving* (pp. 1–14). Washington, DC: United States Department of Health and Human Services, United States Government Printing Office.

Wallack, L. (1984). Drinking and driving: Toward a broader understanding of the role of mass media. *Journal of Public Health Policy, 12,* 471–498.

Warner, K. E. (1986a). Public policy on smoking and health: Toward a smoke-free generation by the year 2000. *Circulation, 73*, 381a–394a.
Warner, K. E. (1986b). Smoking and health implications of a change in the federal cigarette excise tax. *Journal of American Medical Association, 255*, 1028–1032.
United States Department of Health and Human Services. (1990). *Alcohol and Health* (DHHS Publication No. ADM 90-1656). Washington, DC: United States Government Printing Office.
Vartiainen, E., Pallonen, U., McAlister, A., Koskela, K., & Puska, P. (1986). Four-year follow-up results of the smoking prevention program in the North Karalia Youth Project. *Preventive Medicine, 15*, 692–698.
Vartiainen, E., Pallonen, U., McAlister, A., & Puska, P. (1990). Eight-year follow-up results of an adolescent smoking prevention program: The North Karalia Youth Project. *American Journal of Public Health, 80*, 78–79.

CHAPTER 6

Preventing Teenage Pregnancy

W. LaVome Robinson, Peggy Watkins-Ferrell, Patricia Davis-Scott, and Holly S. Ruch-Ross

"What shall I do here, Mother, and when?"
"You'll dream in a waking sleep,
Then sow your dreams in the minds of men
Till the time shall come to reap."
(Yvonne Gregory, *Christmas Lullaby for a New-Born Child*)

... love moderately; long love doth so:
Too swift arrives as tardy as too slow.
(William Shakespeare, *Romeo and Juliet*)

DESCRIPTION OF THE PROBLEM

Adolescence has long been recognized as a critical developmental period, characterized by tremendous cognitive, biological, and social transformations. Changing, and often murky, legal status also marks this developmental stage. Today, adolescent adjustment is further challenged by the accelerated developmental demands of American society and undermined by the so-called social morbidities (Bearinger & Blum, 1987). The social morbidities include homicide, suicide, substance abuse, sexually transmitted diseases (STDs), unintended pregnancy, and infection with the human immunodeficiency virus (HIV) that can lead to AIDS. Intimately linked to preventable social, environmental, and behavioral factors, the social morbidities have emerged as the leading contemporary threat to adolescent well-being (Bearinger & Blum, 1987; Gans, Blyth, Elster, & Gaveras, 1990).

The alarming rate of risk behavior among American adolescents supports the contention that today's adolescents are experiencing a developmental crisis and are seriously threatened by the social morbidities. These risk behaviors include, either singularly or synchronously, substance use and abuse (Shedler & Block, 1990), gang membership (Huff, 1989), school failure and dropout (Dryfoos, 1990), violence (Fingerhut & Kleinman, 1989), and early and unprotected sexual activity (Hayes, 1987b). The ultimate price of adolescent risk taking can be overwhelming. For example, the potential consequences of unprotected sexual intercourse include early pregnancy and parenting, HIV infection, and other STDs. Each of these outcomes is associated with enormous physical, psychological, social, and economic costs.[1]

This chapter's focus is adolescent pregnancy, an all-too-frequent and costly outcome of teenage sexual activity. The chapter begins with a contextual examination of the problem, reviewing what is known about adolescent sexual activity and the consequences of early parenthood. Interventions designed to prevent teenage pregnancy are then critiqued, followed by an actual intervention. The case example details the development, implementation, and evaluation of a pregnancy prevention intervention developed by the first and second authors. Lastly, future directions are discussed, particularly in view of systemic societal variables. A foundation to spur continued and refined efforts to curtail unprotected adolescent sexual activity is provided.

Accepting adolescent sexual activity as normal may be difficult; nonetheless, teenagers, in astonishing numbers, are sexually active. It is estimated that at least one half of the 15- to 19-year old population is sexually active (Hayes, 1987b), with age, ethnicity, and gender differences evident. In the 1983 National Longitudinal Survey of Youth (Hayes, 1987b), 60% of the adolescent white males in the sample reported having had sexual intercourse by age 18, and 60% of the white females reported having had sexual intercourse by age 19. In comparison, 60% of the African-American male adolescents reported having had sexual intercourse by age 16, and 60% of the African-American females reported having had sexual intercourse by age 18 (Hayes, 1987b). Although the ethnic differences for adolescent sexual activity are less pronounced when socioeconomic differences are controlled (Hayes, 1987b), the available research documents the overall pervasiveness of this phenomenon and consistently points to higher rates of adolescent sexual activity among African-Americans, males, the economically disadvantaged, and those adolescents served by schools with high dropout rates (Clark, Zabin, & Hardy, 1984; Hayes, 1987b; Moore, Simms, & Betsey, 1986). The young age of America's youth at initiation of sexual intercourse, coupled with an age-associated failure to use contraception (Hayes, 1987b), renders them particularly at risk for early child bearing.

Although adolescents represent only 18% of the sexually active women capable of becoming pregnant in the United States, they account for almost 46% of all out-of-wedlock births and 31% of all abortions (Alan Guttmacher Institute, 1981). Each year, approximately 1,000,000 teenagers become pregnant. Of the estimated 1,051,370 teenage pregnancies in 1983, 499,038 babies were born, an estimated 411,390 abortions were performed, and about 140,942 miscarriages occurred (Pittman & Adams, 1988). A comparative study of adolescent pregnancy found that American females between the ages of 15 to 19 years became pregnant, gave birth, and had abortions significantly more often than did adolescents with similar patterns of sexual activity in comparable industrialized countries (Jones et al., 1985). The contrast was most striking for females younger than 15 years; the United States' rate of 5 births per 1,000 for girls 14 years or younger was 4 times that of Canada, the only comparable developed country with as much as 1 birth per 1,000 girls at age 14 years or younger (Jones et al., 1985). Within the United States, African-American and Hispanic young women have higher birth rates than their white, non-Hispanic counterparts. In 1985, the estimated birth rate among African-American adolescents was 97 per 1,000; the comparable rate among Hispanic young women was 82 per 1,000; among white non-Hispanic adolescents, it was 43 per 1,000 (Pittman & Adams, 1988). Still, the disproportionately high pregnancy rates among African-American and Hispanic adolescents do not account for the significantly higher overall pregnancy rate in the United States; the pregnancy rate for white teenagers in the United States (83 per 1,000) is almost twice that of Great Britain (45 per 1,000), the next ranking country comparable with the United States (Jones et al., 1985). Although current adolescent pregnancy rates are disconcerting, future projections are even more perturbing. It is projected that 40% of today's 14-year-old females will be pregnant by age 20 (Alan Guttmacher Institute, 1985). In addition, it is estimated that as many as 50% of all adolescent mothers will have a repeat pregnancy within 2 years (Mosena, 1986; Trussell, & Menken, 1978).

Adolescent pregnancy and parenthood are all too frequently associated with both short- and long-term unfavorable consequences for the young mother and her baby. Many of these ill effects are due to poverty and poor medical care rather than the age of conception per se (Chilman, 1979). For example, recent studies show that when low-income pregnant women and adolescents receive quality prenatal care, the adverse health effects of child bearing are significantly reduced (Institute of Medicine, 1985). Nonetheless, the economic and health care status of many pregnant adolescents (Geronimus, 1986) renders this group at risk for prenatal problems associated with premature labor and delivery, intrauterine growth retardation, low birthweight, spontaneous abortion, fetal death, and maternal mortality (Klein, Hack, & Breslau, 1989; Moore & Burt, 1982; Zuckerman, Walker, Frank, & Chase, 1986). In addition to the pernicious impact of poor medical care, adolescent mothers are at increased risk for single parenthood, unstable marriage and divorce, repeat births that are unintended and close together, reduced educational achievement and attainment, low-status employment, low income, and long-term welfare dependency (Furstenberg, 1976; Furstenberg, Brooks-Gunn, & Morgan, 1987; Moore & Burt, 1982). Furthermore, the negative effects of early child bearing extend downward to include the children of adolescent parents who are at increased risk for low educational achievement, behavioral and emotional problems, developmental delays, adolescent pregnancy and parenthood, and poverty (Furstenberg et al., 1987; Furstenberg, Levine, & Brooks-Gunn, 1990).

As with any phenomenon, the effects of adolescent parenthood are variable, with not all young mothers and their children experiencing prolonged harmful consequences. A 17-year follow-up of African-American teenage mothers revealed that a substantial number of these young women did eventually complete high school, and some went beyond high school; many also successfully entered the work force and eventually ended their dependence on the welfare system (Furstenberg et al., 1987). The long-term prognostic indicators for adolescent mothers likely involve differential individual- and system-level competencies and resources, such as existing familial supports and the teenager's own prior academic history (Furstenberg et al., 1987); a richer understanding of these and other predictive factors is needed. In general, however, adolescent pregnancy and parenthood are associated with spiraling adverse consequences that affect not only the young mothers and their children, but also the fathers (Card & Wise, 1978), the families involved, and society at large. According to the Center for Population Options, the direct and indirect annual dollar cost of adolescent pregnancy in the United States amounts to roughly $17 billion (Burt, 1986).

All available indicators suggest that parenting is a frequently chosen option among today's pregnant adolescents, across all ethnic groups (Rickel, 1989). Only about 10% of adolescent mothers in this country choose the adoption alternative; teenagers who carry their pregnancies to term typically intend to raise their infants (Chilman, 1979; Klerman, Bracken, Jekel, & Bracken, 1982). Although prevention would appear to be both the most cost-effective and compassionate course, the problem's complexity, including its association with other behavioral and socioeconomic factors, renders the prescription for prevention less than clear.

REVIEW AND CRITIQUE OF THE LITERATURE

A multitude of pregnancy prevention programs have been introduced in myriad settings and communities during the last two decades. Most have been based on either explicit or implicit theories regarding the etiology of adolescent pregnancy. Although many programs appear promising, most have not been evaluated adequately. As a result, strategies for reducing this country's alarming adolescent pregnancy rate are still largely untested.

Programs designed to prevent teenage pregnancy can generally be categorized into five groups: (a) traditional didactic sexuality education programs with the primary focus on increased knowledge, (b) skill-based programs that focus on clarifying values and enhancing behavioral competencies (e.g., assertiveness and decision-making skills), (c) programs that provide access to contraceptives (e.g., adolescent family planning clinics and comprehensive school-based clinics), (d) programs that aim to increase life options (e.g., job-training programs), and (e) multicomponent community-wide programs. Programs may fall into two or more of the preceding categories, with, for example, some job-training programs also including information about sexuality.

This section selectively reviews some representative programs that have been developed to deter adolescent pregnancy as well as their theoretical underpinnings. Particular attention will be given to programs that have included an evaluation component. Readers interested in a more comprehensive review are urged to consult Dryfoos (1990) and Hayes (1987a). As this review highlights, there is still a dearth of rigorous research and considerable disagreement regarding the best strategy for preventing early unintended pregnancy.

Sexuality Education Programs

Traditional sexuality education programs, conducted in schools, are one primary strategy employed in the effort to prevent teenage pregnancy. These programs typically impart knowledge regarding human sexuality and reproduction. The rationale for this approach is the belief that adolescents who are knowledgeable about sexuality will demonstrate responsible sexual behavior. This reasoning grew out of studies that found that teens lacked the necessary information required to prevent unintended pregnancies. For example, one study found that 41% of a sample of unmarried pregnant teenagers believed that they could not become pregnant when they conceived. Most reported that they thought it was the wrong time of the month for conception (Zelnik & Kanter, 1979).

The literature indicates that traditional sexuality education approaches have been successful in increasing participants' knowledge of multiple aspects of sexuality including male and female anatomy and physiology, birth control methods, probability of pregnancy, and sexually transmitted diseases (Darabi, Jones, Varga, & House, 1982; Gumerman, Jacknik, & Sipko, 1980; Kapp, Taylor, & Edwards, 1980; Kirby, 1984; Parcel & Luttman, 1981). However, the assessment of these programs' potential to influence values, change participants' behavior, and actually decrease unwanted adolescent pregnancies has varied tremendously. Regrettably, too few studies evaluating high school sexuality education programs have actually measured behavioral impact, and the results to date have been inconsistent across studies. One study found that teenagers who participated in a sexuality education course at a young age were more likely to initiate sexual activity at ages 15 and 16, but not at older ages (Marsiglio & Mott, 1986). In contrast, another study found that African-American females, along with white males and females, who participated in sex education classes were less likely to report having had sexual intercourse (Moore, Peterson, & Furstenberg, 1986). Nonetheless, most available studies indicate that an adolescent's participation in a sexuality education course does not influence the decision to engage in sexual intercourse, the age of first intercourse, or the actual rate of sexual activity (Dawson, 1986; Kirby, 1984; Zelnik & Kim, 1982).

Similarly, researchers have generally found traditional sexuality education programs to have no measurable impact on participants' contraceptive behaviors or their likelihood of becoming teenage parents (Dawson, 1986; Kirby, 1984; Marsiglio & Mott, 1986). However, in their analysis of survey data, Zelnik and Kim (1982) found that adolescents who participated in sexuality education programs were more likely to use some method of birth control during first intercourse, were more likely to have used some method of birth control at some point in their lives, and were less likely to become pregnant.

Overall, it appears that traditional sexuality education programs are able to achieve their goal of increasing participants' knowledge, but their impact on participants' attitudes and behaviors is more variable. There is no conclusive evidence that such programs reduce the rates of unintended adolescent pregnancy (Hayes, 1987a). Thus, additional and more refined evaluation research is required to determine whether and under what circumstances they are effective.

Skill-Based Programs

Prevention research in many areas has demonstrated that knowledge is generally an insufficient catalyst for behavior change. Among adolescents, there appears to be a large gap between knowledge and the use of this relevant information to prevent a pregnancy. Thus, in light of the discouraging results achieved by traditional sex education programs, researchers have begun to explore the preventive potential of skills-training approaches. The rationale for this type of intervention comes from studies showing that specific skill deficits (i.e., poor interpersonal problem-solving and communication skills) predispose adolescents to be at high risk for unplanned pregnancy (Flaherty, Marecek, Olsen, & Wilcove, 1983; Steinlauf, 1979). For example, research has suggested that successful use of birth control is linked to effective communication between sexual partners (Cvetkovich & Grote, 1981; Jorgenson, King, & Torrey, 1980).

Depending on a program's specific focus, various theoretical models may be used in the development of an actual intervention. Research suggests that critical cognitive abilities, such as moral reasoning and the ability to plan for the future, are still developing between the ages of 14 and 15 years, thereby rendering sexually active young adolescents at very high risk for pregnancy (Gruber & Chambers, 1987). Thus, some programs have attempted to help teenagers increase their ability to plan for the future and more accurately assess their level of risk. Elkind's

(1967) developmental theory of adolescent egocentricism asserts that teenagers believe themselves to be invulnerable to harm; this reasoning may serve as the catalyst for a high level of risk taking because adolescents do not perceive their true level of susceptibility.

Others point out that the many confusing messages teenagers receive regarding sexual morality may influence and interfere with their ability to make effective contraceptive decisions, even after the decision to become sexually active (Reppucci, 1987). For example, teenagers are often told by adults that having sex is wrong; this may cause sexually active young people to feel distressed by their sexual behavior. At the same time, adolescents are bombarded by media messages that portray sex as glamorous. Such conflictual messages may impede adolescents' ability to acknowledge and, thus, plan ahead for their sexual encounters.

Two highly correlated theoretical constructs, sex guilt (Mosher, 1966, 1968) and erotophobia (Fisher, Byrne, & White, 1983), support the preceding speculation that the emotional aspect of sexual behavior is germane to active contraception. Sex guilt is a cognitive predisposition that inhibits some types of sexual behavior and promotes negative affect when internalized sexual mores are violated (Mosher, 1968). Erotophobia/erotophilia, conversely, refers to a continuum along which people may be assigned, depending on their emotional orientation toward sex and sexuality (Fisher, Byrne, & White, 1983). Schwartz (1973) found that college students who were high on the measured dimension of sex guilt retained less information from a lecture on contraception than those students who experienced low sex guilt. In addition, sex guilt and erotophobia have been associated with inhibited sexual knowledge (Fisher et al., 1983) and greater discomfort for the acquisition of condoms, in addition to the use of a campus contraception clinic (Fisher et al., 1979; Fisher, Fisher, & Byrne, 1977).

Byrne (1983) proposed that contraception involves the following five behavioral steps, each of which must be successfully performed to achieve successful contraception: (a) acquiring, processing, and retaining accurate information about contraception; (b) acknowledging the likelihood of engaging in sexual intercourse; (c) obtaining a contraceptive; (d) communicating with one's partner about contraception; and (e) using the chosen method. Based on Byrne's model, successful contraception clearly involves the use of many skills. Byrne argues that sex guilt may critically inhibit the behavioral performance of these skills. Although adolescents are likely to have difficulty at each step, acknowledging the likelihood of engaging in sexual intercourse (i.e., the second step) appears to be particularly troublesome. In a large survey of adolescents, unexpected participation in sexual intercourse was the most frequent reason given for contraceptive nonuse (Zelnik & Kantner, 1979). Sexually active teenagers may need help in accepting their own sexuality and acknowledging their sexual behavior to be able to plan ahead for the successful acquisition and use of contraceptives. As a coping strategy for the adverse behavioral impact of sex guilt and erotophobia, behavioral techniques such as modeling, desensitization, cognitive restructuring, and assertiveness training have been recommended (Frost, McCluskey-Fawcett, & Sharp, 1989).

Schinke, Blythe, and Gilchrist (1981) developed and evaluated a program that taught high school sophomores to apply problem-solving models to decisions about dating, sexuality, birth control, abortion, pregnancy, child bearing, and parenthood. Students were also taught verbal and nonverbal communication skills via modeling, role playing, and rehearsal. Training techniques were based on a cognitive-behavioral approach. Compared with control students, experimental students more skillfully solved interpersonal problems, used eye contact in role plays, said "no" to sexual risk taking, and demanded shared responsibility for using birth control. Furthermore, the researchers found a positive relationship between participation in the program and self-reported contraceptive behavior. At a 6-month follow-up, students who participated in training groups used contraception more habitually, had greater protection at last intercourse, and relied less on inadequate methods of birth control. Although promising, these results must be interpreted with caution because of the very small sample size employed ($N = 36$ experimental students). Furthermore, some students were not sexually active and were eliminated from this part of the analysis.

The Schinke et al. program did not explicitly promote a value orientation toward sexual activity or contraceptive behavior. Others, however, have developed skill-based programs with the specific aim of delaying the initiation of sexual activity. One program that has been widely implemented is the 10-session Postponing Sexual Involvement curriculum (Howard & McCabe, 1990). An evaluation of the program that targets eighth-grade males and females indicated that only 17% of the participating females had initiated sexual intercourse by the end of the ninth grade, compared with 27% of the control group. Likewise, 39% of the participating males had initiated sexual intercourse by the end of the ninth grade compared with 61% of the control group (Howard & McCabe, 1990).

Programs Providing Access to Contraceptives

Providing adolescents with access to family planning services has been viewed as a promising, albeit controversial, approach to reducing the incidence of teenage pregnancy. Many contend that the most serious barrier to adolescent contraception in this country is accessibility (Morrison, 1985). In other industrialized countries, such as Sweden, the Netherlands, and Great Britain, contraceptives are much more readily available to teenagers (Jones et al., 1986). Lower pregnancy rates, birth rates, and abortion rates in these countries support the contention that barriers to obtaining contraceptives are putting adolescents in the United States at high risk.

Statistics indicate that in 1983, about one third of the patients (i.e., 1.6 million) served by U.S. family planning clinics were under age 20. Of this group of patients, 57% were ages 18 to 19 years, and 43% were under the age 18 years (Torres & Forrest, 1985). Research indicates that adolescents who are enrolled in family planning programs are more likely to use a reliable method of contraception and less likely to use no method at all compared with nonenrolled adolescents (Forrest, Hermalin, & Henshaw, 1981). Researchers have also found that adolescents living in communities with more subsidized family planning programs are significantly less likely to become pregnant than those living in communities with fewer services of this type (Moore & Caldwell, 1977).

Although family planning programs appear to improve participants' contraceptive behaviors, it appears that nearly half of America's adolescent females delay clinic use (i.e., family planning services) until 9 or more months after a first coital experience (Zabin & Clark, 1981). Furthermore, more than one third of all female adolescent family planning clinic patients make their first visit to a clinic because they suspect pregnancy, and only 14% come to a family planning clinic before their first coital experience (Zabin & Clark, 1981). Data indicate that nearly half of all initial premarital teenage pregnancies occur in the first 6 months of sexual activity, with more than one fifth occurring in the first month (Zabin, Kantner, & Zelnik, 1979). Many teenagers may not use family planning services in time to avoid an unwanted pregnancy.

A unique approach to providing adolescents with access to contraceptives has been the establishment of school-based health clinics. The number of comprehensive school-based health clinics has proliferated in recent years. As of early 1991, there were 306 school-based health clinics, with more in the planning stages (Waszak & Neidell, 1991). Comprehensive clinics provide a wide range of health services including family planning counseling. On the average, only 10% to 25% of all clinic visits are for family planning services (Dryfoos, 1988). Although most clinics offer some type of family planning counseling, a smaller percentage prescribe contraceptives and according to a recent survey, less than 20% dispense contraceptives on site (Waszak & Neidell, 1991). Importantly, most clinics require parental permission to participate.

One of the first comprehensive school-based health clinics was established by the St. Paul Maternal and Infant Care Project (Edwards, Steinman, Arnold, & Hakanson, 1981). The first St. Paul clinic was opened in a junior-senior high school in 1973. Even though this school closed 3 years later, the fertility rates dropped significantly from 79 to 35 births per 1,000 between 1973 and 1976. Based on 1,002 students, this represented a decline of 56% (Edwards, Steinman, Arnold, & Hakanson, 1981). Unfortunately, it is not known how this decrease compared with the area population as a whole nor what the rates of abortion were.

Today, there are four St. Paul high schools that house comprehensive health clinics. These clinics, which are operated by Healthstart, Inc., also report a decline in fertility rates. Healthstart (cited in Dryfoos, 1988) reported that between 1976 and 1985, the birth rates declined from 59 to 37 births per 1,000 female students. Additionally, data from 1982 indicated that for those students who began using contraception, the 12-month continuation rate was 93%, whereas the 24-month continuation rate was 90%. These rates were much higher than the rates for adolescents elsewhere (Lovick & Wesson, 1986). Importantly, 18% of the female adolescent clinic patients requested family planning services before they became sexually active; this compared favorably with a rate of 8% of comparable female adolescents who were using a local hospital clinic.

A pregnancy prevention program sponsored and evaluated by the Johns Hopkins School of Medicine has also produced promising results (Zabin, Hirsch, Smith, Streett, & Hardy, 1986). This program was established in a junior high school and a senior high school in Baltimore, providing students with sexuality and contraceptive education, individual and group counseling, and medical and contraceptive services. Although clinic staff provided educational and counseling services in the schools, the actual clinic (i.e., where medical and contraceptive services were rendered) was located adjacent to the schools.

The evaluation was conducted over a 3-year period and included two comparison schools matched for ethnicity and socioeconomic status. Students at the two intervention schools demonstrated significantly higher levels of sexual and contraceptive knowledge than comparison students (Zabin et al., 1986). This finding was particularly strong among the younger students. In contrast, the program appeared to have little or no impact on the students' attitudes about teenage pregnancy or their perceptions regarding the ideal age for child bearing. For students who were exposed to the program for 3 years, some delay in the initiation of first intercourse was demonstrated. The most striking finding was that attendance at the clinic increased dramatically among students of both sexes and all grade levels. Unexpectedly, adolescent males from the junior high school used the clinic as frequently as adolescent girls of the same age. In addition, the data indicated that students visited the clinic sooner after first engaging in sexual intercourse as compared with student use of family planning clinics before the establishment of the program. Most important, for students who were exposed to the program for 3 years, the pregnancy rate decreased by 30%. This was in sharp contrast to the pregnancy rate at the comparison schools, which increased by 58% during the same time period. Overall, the evaluation of this program indicated that the students at participating schools did significantly better in many areas. However, precisely which component(s) (i.e., counseling, access to contraceptives, education) was most crucial to this success has not been explored (Zabin et al., 1986).

A recent nationwide evaluation of six school-based clinics examined the impact of these clinics on a wide range of behaviors including use of health care, alcohol and drug use, contraceptive behavior, students' absenteeism, and pregnancy (Kirby, Waszak, & Ziegler, 1989). Results were generally encouraging and suggested that school-based clinics can increase students' contraceptive use and reduce students' consumption of alcohol and tobacco. However, unlike the two preceding studies, this evaluation found no difference in pregnancy rates between clinic and comparison schools.

Life Options Approaches

Programs in this category typically focus on increasing self-esteem and educational and career aspirations, with the ultimate aim of preventing adolescent pregnancies. Their rationale is based on research suggesting that adolescents with better grades and higher aspirations are more likely than adolescents with lower school achievement and aspirations to postpone sexual involvement (Hayes, 1987b). Dryfoos (1983) emphasized that there is a distinct difference between an adolescent's ability to contracept (i.e., knowledge, access to contraceptives), and his or her motivation to do so. One study of pregnant teens found that two-thirds had wanted to become pregnant (Lindemann & Scott, 1981). Ladner (1987) noted that adolescents, particularly those who experience a severe void in their academic and economic opportunities, may not necessarily regard early child bearing as a negative life event. In fact, recent data illuminate the contributive influence of social and environmental factors to avoiding pregnancy. For example, a survey of sexually active African-American females in Chicago revealed that living in a ghetto, coming from a low socioeconomic background, having one or more sisters who were teenage mothers, and growing up in a single-parent family with many children were all risk factors for adolescent pregnancy (Hogan, Astone, & Kitagawa, 1985). Furthermore, Hogan and Kitagawa (1985) found that African-American adolescents from this type of high-risk environment were 8.3 times more likely to become pregnant than were African-American girls from lower-risk environments. Thus, although some teenagers may possess knowledge regarding contraceptives and where to obtain them, as well as the necessary skills and level of comfort to avoid pregnancy, they may not be sufficiently motivated to delay parenthood. Maracek (1987) proposed that societal change that provides more meaningful and rewarding educational and employment opportunities is needed to delay child bearing, particularly among disenfranchised adolescents.

One life options intervention that has been evaluated is the Teen Outreach program, sponsored by local schools and Junior Leagues in several American cities (Philliber, 1988). The program's goals include reducing school suspensions, dropout rates, and unintended pregnancies. The program's after-school format involves having students participate in small-group discussions that deal with life planning and goal setting as well as volunteering in the community. Initial findings suggested that the program was successful in reducing both pregnancy rates and school failure. However, follow-up data indicated that, over time, the lower pregnancy rates were no longer evident. Although this program appears to hold some promise, it should be noted that the evaluation contained substantial methodological weaknesses (e.g., lack of random assignment to experimental and control groups).

Multicomponent Community-Wide Programs

As noted earlier, there appears to be a need for more comprehensive programming that reaches larger and more heterogeneous groups in the community at large. Illustratively, a community-wide demonstration program using the mass media was initiated in 1982 by the University of South Carolina School of Public Health (Vincent, Clearie, & Schluchter, 1987). The program's overall goal was to determine whether high pregnancy rates could be reduced by an intensive program using the mass media in conjunction with programming in the schools. Targets of the radio and newspaper campaign included parents, teachers, ministers, community leaders, and children. The program targeted one half of a county and employed the other half as a comparison group. Three similar counties were also used as comparison populations. The program appeared to reduce pregnancy rates in the targeted area significantly, with the estimated pregnancy rate for teenagers in the target area dropping from 61 to 25 per 1,000 over the 4-year project period. There was a nonsignificant decline in the comparison portion of the county, and increased adolescent pregnancy rates in the comparison counties for this same period.

Summary

In summary, several diverse teen pregnancy prevention strategies have been developed, implemented, and evaluated, yielding some encouraging directions (e.g., cognitive-behavioral skills training, school-based health clinics). Further research is needed to determine optimal methods to prevent this multifaceted problem, particularly in high-risk populations outside the mainstream. Outcome evaluation studies have not always resulted in consistent findings owing, in part, to methodological weaknesses. In addition, cultural considerations have scarcely been examined by the literature to date. The role of males in the contraceptive process and in the general prevention of adolescent pregnancies has also been severely neglected. These three issues will be addressed in more detail in the chapter's final section.

CASE EXAMPLE

The Teens Learning to Cope Program

The available research points to numerous factors contributive to teenage pregnancy. In view of this, multidimensional strategies seem to be needed to understand and prevent this outcome successfully. Multicomponent interventions would (a) impart knowledge, (b) enhance cognitive and behavioral competencies (e.g., decision making, assertiveness), (c) reduce emotional discomfort, (d) explore the problem's motivational aspect, and (e) provide teens who choose to be sexually active with access to contraceptives. The development of the Teens Learning to Cope Program (popularly known as the TLC Program) was based on the recognition that all of the preceding components are important to the successful prevention of unplanned adolescent pregnancy.

The TLC Program is a comprehensive school-based, psychosocial intervention that aims to promote responsible sexual behavior in adolescence. It adheres to an information dissemination and competency-building model, grounded in both developmental and cognitive-behavioral theory. The program spans thirteen 40-minute sessions of regular classroom time and primarily targets 10 knowledge and skill areas of prime importance for promoting responsible adolescent sexuality: (a) self-esteem enhancement, (b) the diversity of human relationships and sexual-social values clarification, (c) sexual-social decision making, (d) reproductive-sexual anatomy and physiology, (e) birth control methods, (f) STDs, (g) sexual assault, (h) sexual assertiveness, (i) social support development, and (j) future options.

A needs assessment of an urban all-female parochial high school marked the start of the TLC Program. The needs assessment identified adolescent pregnancy as the most pressing problem facing the students. The school administrators requested assistance at two levels: (a) consultation regarding issues of cultural and socioeconomic diversity, and (b) intervention to prevent pregnancy within the school's student population. Both requests were granted, with the development of the TLC Program as the eventual product. Program development occurred in five pivotal and somewhat overlapping phases: (a) community entry, (b) goal identification and program design, (c) implementation, (d) evaluation, and (e) community feedback and data dissemination.

Community Entry

The TLC Program has now been implemented in two high schools, one parochial and one public. It is remarkable, but reflective of the level of concern within the school, that a Roman Catholic parochial school would permit this intervention, as it includes the presentation of the full range of contraceptive options. It is equally noteworthy that the program passed the bureaucracy of the public school system.

Entry into the parochial school system was aided by a colleague who had established a working relationship with the school; this colleague had earned the system's trust and respect. The subsequent entry into the public school was facilitated by the TLC Program's success in the parochial school; in other words, a track record was established and provided a vehicle of approach. In both cases, it was important to connect with at least one key person within the system.

The identification of the initial within-system collaborator is a judicious undertaking. This person must share the vision; in the case of instituting programs, this person must sincerely embrace the program. Second, as this person plays a major role in infusing the program into the system, he or she must be a power broker within the system. In addition, the initial within-system collaborator must have the interpersonal savvy, energy, and fortitude to make it all happen. The talents and abilities of the initial within-system collaborator, however, will not be enough to institute and sustain the program; the program developer(s) must also have the fortitude, energy, and savvy to persist. For example, it took 2 years of painstaking effort to initiate the TLC Program in the public school system.

Community entry is typically more difficult for controversial programs such as the TLC Program. The United States has not yet unanimously reconciled to the reality that its youth are sexually active in vast numbers; moreover, a consensus has not been reached as to the appropriateness of sex education within educational systems. The unique liberalness and vision of the parochial school permitted the genesis of the TLC program; however, entry into the public school was more complex and time intensive. Values and the potential for litigation are pivotal concerns surrounding programs such as TLC. Recognizing that community entry is often smoother for less controversial programs (e.g., substance abuse prevention programs), entry is still likely the most challenging aspect of community programming, especially for programs that include an evaluation component.

Goal Identification and Program Design

Early problem identification and goal clarification typically involve the input of those high in the system's hierarchy. However, this process should soon expand to include the entire system to help ensure accuracy and completeness for meaningful program design. In the TLC Program's early developmental phase, school administrators and officials were relied on for problem and goal identification. This input was informative, but the direct input of the students within the schools, their parents, and community advisory boards was also sought. Several strategies were employed to obtain input including staff meetings with school officials at the schools, group meetings within the communities, and one-to-one interviews with the students and other key players. A process of constant communication and feedback was used to narrow and clarify the problem's definition, the intervention's goals, and the program's design. Although this was a slow process, the project was committed to "doing it right" rather than "doing it quick." "Doing it right" was a value. Because values always influence program development, it is important to clarify them within the project team up front.

Adolescent pregnancy prevention efforts are torn by a multitude of conflicting values. For example, many argue ardently that pregnancy prevention programs should focus exclusively on the promotion of total sexual abstinence. Others argue with equal fervor that although pregnancy prevention programs need to emphasize abstinence as the only sure way to prevent a pregnancy, they should simultaneously promote the consistent use of contraception for teens who are sexually active. Values regarding elective abortion have also been a minefield for pregnancy prevention programs. Pregnancy prevention program planning must include decisions regarding the presentation of abortion issues. For example, will the program include this controversial topic? If so, should abortion be presented as a method of contraception—should the abortion alternative be presented as one resolution to an unwanted pregnancy? Values were central to the development of the TLC Program. During the program's development, all parties were encouraged to put their values on the table to design a program that reflected community and staff values. A program cannot be robust if it conflicts with community values. Similarly, staff cannot effectively deliver an intervention that conflicts with personal and professional values.

A commitment to a program is critical to its development and survival. Collaborative and horizontal relationships encourage commitment and program bonding; program developers from outside the system often initially guide a program's development, but the program is owned by the many who ultimately share in its construction. A collaborative spirit helps to ensure that the needs and goals of those served are truly met, as they too contribute to goal identification and program design. Collaboration clarifies that the working relationship is one of sharing, parity, and respect.

Implementation

The TLC Program's conceptual philosophy steered its implementation. The intent was to create a pragmatic, low-cost, and effective intervention that would be feasible for most school systems, as school systems are one of the oldest and most potent social institutions serving this country's youth.

The reported successes of school-based clinics argued for an intervention that was experiential, intimate, and accessible. Thus, the TLC Program employed a participatory small-group format, infused into the class schedules of its participants. In addition to the provision of information, behavioral competency was emphasized and fostered via behavioral rehearsal of the various skills (e.g., decision making, communication). Students were assigned to stable, gender-homogenous groups of 8 to 10 members. Each group was assigned a permanent facilitator; the group facilitators were gender- and ethnically diverse doctoral students in psychology. Each group was conducted in a separate area of the school (such as a classroom or chapel) to facilitate intimacy and privacy. With the exception of holidays and conflicting school activities, each group met at a set time weekly for 13 weeks.

The group facilitators participated in training sessions before each intervention session to maximize the consistency of implementation of the TLC curriculum across facilitators and groups. As a further assurance of fidelity to intervention procedural reliability data were obtained for all group facilitators for 20% of their total group sessions. Procedural reliability was excellent, ranging from 87.5% to 100%, with a median of 95.3%. Group rapport, group stability, and an atmosphere of trust, along with student attendance and participation, were essential to the program's success; group rules were paramount in achieving this end. These rules, particularly those governing privacy and respect, were negotiated among group members at the start of the program. To date, the participating schools have honored the students' right to privacy. Incentives were provided to promote group stability, attendance, and participation further. For instance, students received one raffle ticket each time they were present at a group session. At the end of the program there was a raffle of prizes, with the odds of winning the raffle increasing with each ticket entered.

Logistical management was another cornerstone of the program's success. Before implementing the program, logistical arrangements were negotiated. These included the specification of group meeting times (i.e., days and class periods), students and teachers to be involved, roles and responsibilities, the assignment of space to groups and groups to facilitators, procedures for resolving schedule changes and unforeseen crises, among other issues. In addition to the project director, it was essential to have a logistics overseer based within the school. For both the TLC parochial and the public schools, this person was a school counselor.

For solid program operations, it was imperative that the system, as a unit, endorse the program. The fundamental roles of the program developer(s) and the initial within-system person(s) did not obviate the importance of others within the system or other program staff. Program tasks were carefully matched to the various and complementary talents and roles of the program implementors. The program depended on the support of the participants' parents, the schools' principals, counselors and teachers, and the school-based clinic staff as well as the approval and support of the Chicago Board of Education. Most crucial was the interest and involvement of its participants—the students.

Evaluation

The TLC Program evolved out of a service need. To enhance the efficacy of service, an evaluation component was intertwined with service delivery. A pretest-posttest, wait-list control evaluation design was employed. Because of the overriding commitment to service and ethics, this design was deemed the design of choice, although wait-list controls compromise future follow-up efforts. Students were randomly assigned to the TLC and wait-list control conditions. A paper-and-pencil evaluation measure (i.e., the TLC Questionnaire) was used, with assessment sessions occurring during regular class periods; these sessions were conducted by psychology doctoral students. The TLC questionnaire was divided into two sections and administered in a counterbalanced fashion on two consecutive days. Class incentives were offered to increase attendance at the assessment sessions. For example, the male and female class with the best attendance during the pretesting sessions won a pizza party; similar incentives were employed at posttesting.

An evaluation of the program conducted at the public school during the 1989–90 school year yielded promising findings, particularly for the male participants (Watkins-Ferrell & Robinson, 1993). The evaluation indicated that the program was extremely effective in increasing male participants' reported use of condoms. Furthermore, at posttesting, male TLC participants were significantly more likely to report using an effective method of birth control than were the male wait-list control participants. The findings also revealed that the program effectively enhanced the male TLC participants' problem-solving skills in sexual situations. Finally, the evaluation found that male TLC participants increased their knowledge of contraception significantly more than that of the male wait-list control participants.

The findings for the female TLC participants were not as significant. Although the female TLC participants also increased their knowledge of contraception significantly more than that of the wait-list control participants, significance on other variables (e.g., condom usage, problem-solving skills) was not reached. The female participants, however, did show a slight trend in the expected direction. As significantly more males than females reported having intercourse during the 4 weeks preceding posttesting, the analyses regarding use of birth control were much more powerful for the male sample; this difference may explain some of the gender differences found. Generally, the TLC evaluation produced promising findings that can further inform interventions with inner-city youth. Importantly, these findings demonstrate that it is imperative to intervene with males regarding issues of sexuality.

Community Feedback and Data Dissemination

Feedback and communication nuances were operative at all phases of TLC programming, from community entry to program evaluation, and included process and outcome factors. At its inception, the TLC program assumed a posture of participatory community programming, acknowledging community members as equal contributors to the social constitution of knowledge (Serrano-García, 1990). To this end, issues pertaining to data ownership and dissemination were negotiated rather than prescribed; feedback channels were created and nurtured to advance horizontal relationships and constant information flow.

Communities initially may be somewhat resistant to the process of sharing data and offering feedback. To counter resistance to the TLC Program and promote community receptivity, several steps were taken. First, a Community Advisory Board (composed of clergy, teachers, parents, etc.) was established to guide and advise the intervention process. From the start, the community enjoyed input and monitoring authority, thereby fostering a shared ownership of the program. This core group of community members helped to clarify the community's needs, which enabled the development of an intervention strategy that was community relevant. Because communication was prized, care was taken to use concise, jargon-free language. Also, multiple channels of communication were employed (e.g., graphs and figures, pamphlets). Every effort was given to the immediacy of feedback rather than the customary debriefing approach to providing feedback. Ongoing community input and feedback was valued and incorporated into the modifications and refinements of the TLC intervention; dissemination decisions were joint ones. Thus, the TLC Program was conducted in a collaborative and nonexploitive manner. It is believed that this approach contributed significantly to the program's success. Although this approach appears optimal for successful community programming, it is also reflective of good ethical practice.

FUTURE DIRECTIONS

Social and political factors have historically influenced the development of human problems as well as their solutions. The problem of teenage pregnancy is no different in this regard. The higher adolescent pregnancy rate in the United States, relative to that of other industrialized countries (Jones et al., 1986), along with the disproportionate representation of certain segments of the American population, demonstrates that adolescent pregnancy is a social phenomenon.

The extent of poverty in a country has been shown to correlate significantly with teenage fertility (Jones et al., 1986). A recent study revealed that American females with low basic skills from improverished families are 5 to 7 times more likely to give birth during their adolescent years than females with average or better basic skills and from relatively advantaged families, regardless of ethnicity (Pittman & Adams, 1988). Other data, however, suggest that ethnic minority youth in the United States are disproportionately at risk for early parenthood (Moore, Simms, & Betsey, 1986; Pittman & Adams, 1988). The overrepresentation of ethnic minorities within the United States' poverty ranks may be a factor in their greater risk for early parenthood (Hayes, 1987b; Moore et al., 1986). Nevertheless, both ethnicity and socioeconomic status appear to influence early parenthood independently. One study found that about 1 in 100 high-ability, affluent African-American women from intact families became single teenage parents; for comparable white women, the birth rate was 1 in 1,000 (Abrahamse, Morrison, & Waite, 1988). Furthermore, African-American women from poor single-parent families who scored low on standardized tests had a 1 in 4 chance of becoming a single adolescent parent, whereas comparable white women had a 1 in 12 chance (Abrahamse et al., 1988). The relationship between ethnic-minority status and teenage pregnancy and parenthood needs to be better understood. It may be that ethnic minorities, particularly African-Americans and Hispanics, feel alienated from mainstream American society and its values; their future expectations for favorable employment and economic prosperity may be realistically daunted. Conceivably, these and other societal biases inhibit minority youth from delaying parenthood.

In addition to ethnic and socioeconomic status, affordable and accessible adolescent family planning services are also critical to curtailing teenage pregnancy. The 37-country comparative study sponsored by the Guttmacher Institute found lower pregnancy, birth, and abortion rates in countries where contraceptive services were most accessible (Jones et al., 1986). For adolescents in the United States, these services are extremely limited, as adolescent family planning programs and school-based clinics with reproductive components continue to be quite controversial. In addition to economic constraints, attitudes in this country regarding adolescent sexuality are, in all likelihood, exacerbating teenage pregnancy.

It is quite common to hear a young woman express concern about what her parents will think if they discover that she is sexually active or if she becomes pregnant. It is less common to hear a young man express the same concern regarding what will happen if he has a child; in fact, young males in American society are subtly, and not so subtly, encouraged to be sexually active (Dryfoos, 1988). Moreover, male domination continues to be a factor in many relationships; young women frequently state that they became sexually active or pregnant to satisfy their male partners. The age-old value that females must bear the bulk of the responsibility for postponing sexual involvement, avoiding pregnancy, and child bearing must be modified.

Findings from the Guttmacher Institute's comparative survey suggest that a society's openness and consistency of message about sex may be critical in the determination of adolescent pregnancy and child bearing (Jones et al., 1986). Although most religious doctrines teach that premarital sex is unacceptable and the federal government often funds programs that encourage teenagers to "just say no" (Jones et al., 1986), elements of contemporary culture (e.g., song lyrics, television programming, movies) portray premarital sex as exciting and acceptable. In these portrayals, little emphasis is placed on the responsibility that accompanies the decision to engage in sexual intercourse. A study that examined the soap opera depictions of sex, contraception, and STDs revealed strong messages that sex is primarily for unmarried partners. Contraception was rarely mentioned, pregnancy was almost nonexistent, and STDs were unheard of (Lowry & Towles, 1989).

Clearly, a sensitivity to the special stressors of youth in this country is required to ameliorate the teenage pregnancy epidemic. Many youth must cope with very real material deprivation; others must also cope with the effects of both historical and contemporary racism. Our nation's youth face the perplexing task of sorting through inconsistent and contradictory messages regarding normal and appropriate sexual expression. The fact that many youth's decision-making abilities are compromised is not surprising. Thus, the question of whether existing interventions have been most sensitive and far reaching arises.

Society may be viewed as consisting of four levels—the individual, the small group, the organizational, and the institutional (Rappaport, 1977). To date, however, pregnancy prevention efforts have been restricted to the individual, small group, and organizational level(s). The failure of intervention strategies to focus on institutional change risks a "blame the victim" orientation (Ryan, 1971). The field of behavioral community psychology, as well as the field of community psychology in general, have much to offer in this area. Systems-level and environmentally focused projects are emerging, along with methodologies and the technology for studying environments, conducting well-designed interventions, and systematically evaluating outcomes (Jason & Glenwick, 1984).

Institutional-level intervention, in its attempt to be all-inclusive, is sometimes abstract and elusive. Thus, it is difficult to discern when, where, how, and for whom intervention ought best to begin. Nonetheless, prime areas for societal change can be targeted. For example, fewer than half of 1% of all family planning clinic patients in the United States are male (Dryfoos, 1985). Most adolescent pregnancy research and programming has focused on adolescent females and virtually ignored males. This is a serious omission, particularly in view of the growing AIDS crisis. Currently, the best method of AIDS prevention for sexually active individuals is the use of condoms in combination with the spermicide nonoxynol-9. Unlike the pill, using a condom takes the direct agreement and involvement of the male partner. Therefore, it is obvious that intervention with males is critical to ensuring that couples use condoms consistently. Furthermore, interventions should target both males and females to increase their level of knowledge regarding contraceptives, to dispel myths surrounding contraceptives, and to develop skills for the successful acquisition and use of contraceptives. Increasing young couples' ability to communicate openly with each other on the topic of sexuality and birth control also needs to be emphasized. Both males and females need to have a sense that they have a choice about becoming and remaining sexually active, along with protecting themselves from disease and pregnancy within a sexual relationship. Moreover, both males and females need alternatives to early child bearing.

The AIDS pandemic adds a new sense of urgency to unprotected adolescent sexual activity. Additional government funding for alternative programs, such as school-based health centers and condom distribution programs, is essential. The United States can no longer afford pretentious values; the prevention of unprotected adolescent sexual activity is a public responsibility. The relationship between poverty and early parenthood must be brought home to policy makers to ensure that adequate resources are deployed to provide opportunities for all youngsters. The success of the Perry Preschool Program, a 2-year intervention designed to compensate for cognitive delays in economically disadvantaged children, supports the claim that the provision of high-quality, early educational opportunities for all youngsters is an important factor in preventing adolescent pregnancy. The results of that study found significantly lower pregnancy rates for participants at age 19 (64 per 1,000) than for the control group (117 per 1,000) (Schweinhart, Berruta-Clement, Barnett, & Weikart, 1985).

Helping teenagers increase their future orientation may be doomed to failure when nothing or little is being done actually to alter the future that they can expect. Failure to address cultural and environmental issues may result in an ineffective and often irrelevant program for youths who are most in need of intervention. For example, acceptable assertive responses in one culture may be inappropriate within another culture. These realities highlight the importance of system-level intervention and change.

In recent years, there has been a discernible shift in perspective in the adolescent pregnancy literature, away from viewing adolescent child bearing as the central issue and toward perceiving it as one of a range of outcomes associated with serious underlying social problems (Dryfoos, 1990). This perspective does not reduce the importance of pregnancy prevention interventions; rather, by emphasizing the shared roots of multiple problems, it illuminates the societal context of the problem and the need for institutional-level change. The individual and social consequences of these problems are great; the current dearth of resources directed toward these issues is unconscionable. The need for further theoretical and applied research is clear. The future of American youth and, indeed, of the country, is dependent on our ability to develop and use fully the capabilities of all young people to achieve, in the words of former Surgeon General C. Everett Koop (Burton, 1990), "a future not of risk, but of promise."

NOTE

1. The potential costs of other adolescent risk behaviors are similarly mammoth and far-reaching. However, it is beyond the scope of this chapter to explore the full range of adolescent risk taking. For a more complete review of adolescent risk taking, see J. Dryfoos, *Adolescents at Risk: Prevalence and Prevention* (New York: Oxford University Press, 1990); J. Gans, D. Blyth, A. Elster, & L. Gaveras (Eds.), *American Adolescents: How Healthy Are They?*, Vol. 1 (Chicago: American Medical Association, 1990); and J. Gibbs, *Young, Black and Male in America: An Endangered Species* (Done, MA: Auburn House Publishing Co., 1988).

ACKNOWLEDGMENT

We thank Marie Austria, Peter Bishop, Amy Davies, and Deborah Marotta for their invaluable assistance in preparing this chapter.

REFERENCES

Abrahamse, A. F., Morrison, P. A., & Waite, L. J. (1988). *Beyond stereotypes: Who becomes a single teenage mother?* (R-3489-HHS/NICHD). Santa Monica, CA: The RAND Corporation.
Alan Guttmacher Institute (1981). *Teenage pregnancy: The problem that hasn't gone away.* New York: Alan Guttmacher Institute.
Alan Guttmacher Institute (1985). *Report on adolescent pregnancy.* New York: Alan Guttmacher Institute.
Bearinger, L., & Blum, R. (1987). Adolescent medicine and psychiatry: Trends, issues and needs. *Psychiatric Annals, 17,* 775–779.
Burt, M. (1986). *Public Costs of teenage childbearing.* Washington, DC: Center for Population Options.
Burton, P. (Producer). (1990). *Listening to teenagers* [Film]. New York: MacNeil/Lehrer Productions.
Byrne, D. (1983). Sex without contraception. In D. Byrne & W. S. Fisher (Eds.), *Adolescents, sex and contraception* (pp. 3–31). Hillsdale, NJ: Erlbaum.
Card, J. J., & Wise, L. L. (1978). Teenage mothers and teenage fathers: The impact of early childbearing on the parents' personal and professional lives. *Family Planning Perspectives, 10,* 199–210.
Chilman, C. S. (1979a). *Adolescent sexuality in a changing American society: Social and psychological perspectives.* Washington, DC: U.S. Government Printing Office.
Chilman, C. S. (1979b). Teenage pregnancy: A research review. *Social Work, 43,* 492–498.
Clark, S. D., Zabin, L. S., & Hardy, J. B. (1984). Sex, contraception and parenthood: Experience and attitudes among urban black young men. *Family Planning Perspectives, 16,* 77–82.
Cvetkovich, G., & Grote, B. (1981). Psychosocial maturity and teenage contraceptive use: An investigation of decision-making and communication skills. *Population and Environment Behavioral and Social Issues, 4,* 211–226.
Darabi, K. F., Jones, J., Varga, P., & House, M. (1982). Evaluation of sex education outreach. *Adolescence, 17,* 57–64.
Dawson, D. A. (1986). The effects of sex education on adolescent behavior. *Family Planning Perspectives, 18,* 162–170.
Dryfoos, J. G. (1983). A new strategy for preventing unintended teenage childbearing. *Family Planning Perspectives, 16,* 193–195.
Dryfoos, J. G. (1985). School-based health clinics. A new approach to preventing adolescent pregnancy. *Family Planning Perspectives, 7,* 70–75.
Dryfoos, J. G. (1988). *Putting the boys in the picture: A review of programs to promote sexual responsibility among young males.* Santa Cruz, CA: Network Publications.
Dryfoos, J. G. (1988). School-based health clinics: Three years of experience. *Family Planning Perspectives, 20,* 193–200.

Dryfoos, J. G. (1990). *Adolescents at risk: Prevalence and prevention.* Oxford: Oxford University Press.

Edwards, L. E., Steinman, M. E., Arnold, K. A., & Hakanson, E. Y. (1981). Adolescent pregnancy prevention services in high school clinics. In F. F. Furstenberg, R. Lincoln, & J. Menken (Eds.), *Teenage sexuality, pregnancy, and childbearing* (pp. 372–381). Philadelphia: University of Pennsylvania Press.

Elkind, D. (1967). Egocentrism in adolescence. *Child Development, 38,* 1025–1034.

Fingerhut, L. A., & Kleinman, J. C. (1989). *Trends and current status in childhood mortality, United States, 1900–85.* Vital and Health Statistics, Series 3, No. 26 (DHHS Publication No. PHS 89-1410). Hyattsville, MD: National Center for Health Statistics.

Fisher, W. A., Byrne, D., Edmunds, M., Miller, C. T., Kelley, K., & White, L. A. (1979). Psychological and situation-specific correlates of contraceptive behavior among university women. *Journal of Sex Research, 15,* 38–55.

Fisher, W. A., Byrne, D., & White, L. A. (1983). Emotional barriers to contraception. In D. Byrne & W. A. Fisher (Eds.), *Adolescents, sex, and contraception* (pp. 207–239). Hillsdale, NJ: Erlbaum.

Fisher, W. A., Fisher, J. D., & Byrne, D. (1977). Consumer reactions to contraceptive purchasing. *Personality and Social Psychology Bulletin, 3,* 293–296.

Flaherty, E. W., Marecek, J., Olsen, K., & Wilcove, G. (1983). Preventing adolescent pregnancy: An interpersonal problem-solving approach. *Prevention in Human Services, 2,* 49–64.

Forrest, J. D., Hermalin, A., & Henshaw, S. (1981). The impact of family planning clinic programs on adolescent pregnancy. *Family Planning Perspectives, 13,* 109–116.

Frost, H. L., McCluskey-Fawcett, K., & Sharp, J. A. (1989). Adolescent sexual behavior: A model for behavioral strategies. *The Behavior Therapist, 12,* 239–242.

Furstenberg, F. F. (1976). *Unplanned parenthood: The social consequences of teenage parenthood.* New York: Free Press.

Furstenberg, F. F., Brooks-Gunn, J., & Morgan, S. (1987). Adolescent mothers and their children in later life. *Family Planning Perspectives, 19,* 142–151.

Furstenberg, F. F., Levine, J. A., & Brooks-Gunn, J. (1990). The children of teenage mothers: Patterns of early childbearing in two generations. *Family Planning Perspectives, 22,* 54–61.

Gans, J., Blyth, D., Elster, A., & Gaveras, L. (1990). *America's adolescents: How healthy are they?* Chicago: American Medical Association.

Geronimus, A. T. (1986). The effects of race, residence, and prenatal care on the relationship of maternal age to neonatal mortality. *American Journal of Public Health, 76,* 1416–1421.

Gregory, Y. (1963). Christmas lullaby for a new-born child. In A. Bontemps (Ed.), *American Negro poetry* (p. 153). New York: Hill & Wang.

Gruber, E., & Chambers, C. V. (1987). Cognitive development and adolescent contraception: Integrating theory and practice. *Adolescence, 22,* 661–670.

Gumerman, S., Jacknik, M., & Sipko, R. (1980). Sex education in a rural high school. *Journal of School Health, 50,* 478–480.

Hayes, C. (1987a). Preventive interventions. In C. Hayes (Ed.), *Risking the future* (Vol. 1, pp. 141–188). Washington, DC: National Academy Press.

Hayes, C. (1987b). Trends in adolescent sexuality and fertility. In C. Hayes (Ed.), *Risking the future* (Vol. 1, pp. 33–74). Washington, DC: National Academy Press.

Hogan, D. P., Astone, N. M., & Kitagawa, E. M. (1985). Social and environmental factors influencing contraceptive use among black adolescents. *Family Planning Perspectives, 17,* 165–169.

Hogan, D. P., & Kitagawa, E. M. (1985). The impact of social status, family structure, and

neighborhood on the fertility of black adolescents. *American Journal of Sociology, 90,* 825–853.
Howard, M., & McCabe, J. B. (1990). Helping teenagers postpone sexual involvement. *Family Planning Perspectives, 22,* 21–26.
Huff, C. R. (1989). Youth gangs and public policy. *Crime & Delinquency, 35,* 524–537.
Institute of Medicine (1985). *Preventing low birth weight.* Washington, DC: National Academy Press.
Jason, L. A., & Glenwick, D. S. (1984). Behavioral community psychology: A review of recent research and applications. In M. Hersen, R. M. Eisler, & P. M. Miller (Eds.), *Progress in behavior modification* (Vol. 18, pp. 85–121). Orlando, FL: Academic Press.
Jones, E. F., Forrest, J. D., Goldman, N., Henshaw, S., Lincoln, R., Rosoff, J. I., Westoff, C. F., & Wulf, D. (1985). Teenage pregnancy in developed countries: Determinants and policy implications. *Family Planning Perspectives, 17,* 53–63.
Jones, E. F., Forrest, J. D., Goldman, N., Henshaw, S., Lincoln, R., Rosoff, J. I., Westoff, C. F., & Wulf, D. (1986). *Teenage pregnancy in industrialized countries.* New Haven, CT: Yale University Press.
Jorgensen, S. R., King, S. L., & Torrey, B. A. (1980). Dyadic and social network influences on adolescent exposure to pregnancy risk. *Journal of Marriage and the Family, 42,* 141–155.
Kapp, L., Taylor, B., B. A., & Edwards, L. E. (1980). Teaching human sexuality in junior high school: An interdisciplinary approach. *Journal of School Health, 50,* 80–83.
Kirby, D. (1984). *Sexuality education: An evaluation of programs and their effects.* Santa Cruz, CA: Network Publications.
Kirby, D., Waszak, C. S., & Ziegler, J. (1989). *An assessment of six school-based clinics: Services, impact, and potential.* Washington, DC: Center for Population Options.
Klein, N. K., Hack, M., & Breslau, N. (1989). Children who were very low birth weight: Development and academic achievement at nine years age. *Journal of Developmental and Behavioral Pediatrics, 10,* 32–37.
Klerman, L., Bracken, M., Jekel, J., & Bracken, M. (1982). The delivery-abortion decision among adolescents. In I. Stuart & C. Wells (Eds.), *Pregnancy in adolescence.* (pp. 219–235). New York: Van Nostrand Reinhold.
Ladner, J. A. (1987). Black teenage pregnancy: A challenge for educators. *Journal of Negro Education, 56,* 53–63.
Lindemann, C., & Scott, W. J. (1981). Wanted and unwanted pregnancy in early adolescence: Evidence from a clinic population. *Journal of Early Adolescence, 1,* 185–193.
Lovick, S., & Wesson, W. (1986). *School-based clinics: Update.* Washington, DC: Center for Population Options.
Lowry, D. T., & Towles, D. E. (1989). Soap opera portrayals of sex, contraception, and sexually transmitted diseases. *Journal of Communication, 39,* 76–83.
Marecek, J. (1987). Counseling adolescents with problem pregnancies. *American Psychologist, 42,* 89–93.
Marsiglio, W., & Mott, F. L. (1986). The impact of sex education on sexual activity, contraceptive use and premarital pregnancy among American teenagers. *Family Planning Perspectives, 18,* 151–161.
Moore, K. A., & Burt, M. R. (1982). *Private crisis, public cost: Policy perspectives on teenage childbearing.* Washington, DC: Urban Institute Press.
Moore, K. A., & Caldwell, S. (1977). *Out of wedlock childbearing.* Washington, DC: The Urban Institute.
Moore, K. A., Peterson, J. L., & Furstenberg, F. F. (1986). Parental attitudes and the occurrence of early sexual activity. *Journal of Marriage and the Family, 48,* 777–782.

Moore, K. A., Simms, M. C., & Betsey, C. L. (1986). *Choice and circumstance: Racial differences in adolescent sexuality and fertility*. New Brunswick, NJ: Transaction Publisher.

Morrison, D. M. (1985). Adolescent contraceptive behavior: A review. *Psychological Bulletin, 98*, 538–568.

Mosena, P. W. (1986). *Adolescent parent outreach follow-up survey*. Children's Policy Research Project, University of Chicago, Illinois Department of Public Aid.

Mosher, D. L. (1966). The development and multitrait-multimethod matrix analysis of three measures of three aspects of guilt. *Journal of Consulting Psychology, 30*, 25–29.

Mosher, D. L. (1968). Measurement of guilt in females by self-report inventories. *Journal of Consulting and Clinical Psychology, 32*, 690–695.

Parcel, G. S., & Luttman, D. (1981). Evaluation of a sex education course for young adolescents. *Family Relations, 30*, 55–60.

Philliber, S. (1988). *Teen outreach: Data from the third year of the national replication*. Accord, NY: Philliber Research Associates.

Pittman, K., & Adams, G. (1988). *Teenage pregnancy: An advocate's guide to the numbers*. Washington, DC: Children's Defense Fund.

Rappaport, J. (1977). *Community psychology: Values, research, and action*. New York: Holt, Rinehart & Winston.

Reppucci, N. D. (1987). Prevention and ecology: Teenage pregnancy, child sexual abuse, and organized youth sports. *American Journal of Community Psychology, 15*, 1–22.

Rickel, A. U. (1989). Teen pregnancy and parenting. New York: Hemisphere.

Ryan, W. (1971). *Blaming the victim*. New York: Random House.

Schinke, S. P., Blythe, B. J., & Gilchrist, L. D. (1981). Cognitive-behavioral prevention of adolescent pregnancy. *Journal of Counseling Psychology, 28*, 451–454.

Schwartz, S. (1973). Effects of sex guilt and sexual arousal on the retention of birth control information. *Journal of Consulting and Clinical Psychology, 43*, 61–64.

Schweinhart, L. J., Berruta-Clement, J. R., Barnett, W. S., & Weikart, D. P. (1985). Effects of the Perry Preschool Program on youths through age 19: A summary. *Topics in Early Childhood Special Education, 5*, 26–35.

Seranno-García, I. (1990). Implementing research: Putting our values to work. In P. Tolan, C. Keys, F. Chertok, & L. Jason (Eds.), *Researching community psychology: Issues of theory and methods* (pp. 171–182). Washington, DC: American Psychological Association.

Shakespeare, W. (1916). Romeo and Juliet. In R. A. Law (Ed.), *Five tragedies* (pp. 1–235). London: D. C. Heath & Company.

Shedler, J., & Block, J. (1990). Adolescent drug use and psychological health: A longitudinal inquiry. *American Psychologist, 45*, 612–630.

Steinlauf, B. (1979). Problem-solving skills, locus of control, and the contraceptive effectiveness of young women. *Child Development, 50*, 268–271.

Torres, A., & Forrest, J. D. (1985). Family planning clinic services in the United States, 1983. *Family Planning Perspectives, 17*, 32.

Trussell, J., & Menken, J. (1978). Early childbearing and subsequent fertility. *Family Planning Perspectives, 10*, 209–218.

Vincent, M. L., Clearie, A. F., & Schluchter, M. D. (1987). Reducing adolescent pregnancy through school and community-based education. *Journal of the American Medical Association, 257*, 3382–3386.

Waszak, C., & Neidell, S. (1991). *School-based and school-linked clinics: Update 1991*. Washington, DC: Center for Population Options.

Watkins-Ferrell, P., & Robinson, W. L. (1993). *Preventing sexual risk-behavior in Afri-*

can-American adolescents: A cognitive-behavioral approach. Manuscript submitted for publication.

Zabin, L. S., & Clark, S. D. (1981). Why they delay: A study of teenage family planning clinic patients. *Family Planning Perspectives, 13,* 205–217.

Zabin, L. S., Hirsch, M. B., Smith, E. A., Streett, R., & Hardy, J. B. (1986). Evaluation of a pregnancy prevention program for urban teenagers. *Family Planning Perspectives, 18,* 119–126.

Zabin, L. S., Kantner, J. F., & Zelnik, M. (1979). The risk of adolescent pregnancy in the first months of intercourse. *Family Planning Perspectives, 11,* 215–222.

Zelnik, M., & Kantner, J. F. (1979). Reasons for nonuse of contraception by sexually active women aged 15–19. *Family Planning Perspectives, 11,* 289–294.

Zelnik, M., & Kim, Y. J. (1982). Sex education and its association with teenage sexual activity, pregnancy, and contraceptive use. *Family Planning Perspectives, 14,* 117–126.

Zuckerman, B., Walker, D. K., Frank, D. A., & Chase, C. (1986). Adolescent pregnancy and parenthood. In M. Wolraich & D. K. Routh (Eds.), *Advances in developmental and behavioral pediatrics* (Vol. 7, pp. 275–311). Greenwich, CT: JAI Press.

CHAPTER 7

Prevention of AIDS

Jeffrey A. Kelly and Debra A. Murphy

DESCRIPTION OF THE PROBLEM

The first cases of acquired immune deficiency syndrome (AIDS) were identified in 1979. In that year there were 14 known cases of AIDS. In 1982, approximately 238 AIDS cases were diagnosed in the United States. Just 8 years later, 160,000 Americans had been diagnosed with the disease, and the number of AIDS cases reached nearly 300,000 by 1993 (Centers for Disease Control, 1993). AIDS is presently one of the leading causes of death among men and women under age 45 in the United States; in some large cities, infection with the human immunodeficiency virus (HIV), which causes AIDS, is now the most common life-threatening illness affecting newborn infants (Buehler, Devine, Berkelman, & Chevarly, 1990; Chu, Buehler, & Berkelman, 1990). In contrast to illnesses such as heart disease, cancer, and stroke, which have relatively stable incidence from year to year, AIDS incidence has increased sharply each year since it was first identified. For that reason, and because the AIDS/HIV epidemic is worldwide in scope, AIDS has been designated as one of the highest research and health priorities of the World Health Organization, the American Medical Association, the American Psychological Association, the United States Public Health Service, and most other health organizations.

Although AIDS is usually the identified target for prevention, efforts to prevent AIDS are more accurately primary prevention efforts to curb the spread of HIV infection. Most individuals who contract HIV infection remain asymptomatic and in good clinical health for a number of years before the onset of illnesses. The latency period between *minimal* infection and AIDS diagnosis, made when a patient develops a life-threatening illness, is generally between 7 and 10 years (Schechter et al., 1988), and this period may gradually lengthen given recent advances in medical regimens that delay the onset of some serious illness in persons with HIV infection. Because AIDS is an end consequence of HIV infection, limiting future AIDS cases requires curtailing the incidence of new HIV infections.

Throughout its short history in world health, it has been apparent that AIDS and HIV infection are associated with certain identifiable risk characteristics. In the United States and in most Western countries, most AIDS cases in adults have occurred among gay men (56% of AIDS cases in the United States to date), intravenous drug users (IVDUs) (23% of cases), men who are *both* homosexual and users of injected drugs (7% of cases), heterosexual persons (7% of cases), and transfusion recipients and hemophiliacs (2% of cases), with the remaining cases being of undetermined risk history (Centers for Disease Control, 1993). This HIV epidemiology is considered "Pattern 1" and reflects early introduction and high prevalence of the virus among gay men and IVDUs. In other areas of the world, especially in Africa and Third World nations, a different epidemiology ("Pattern 2") is present, with most AIDS cases being diagnosed in heterosexual adults of both sexes and in young children, unrelated to either male homosexual behavior or drug use. Pattern 2 epidemiology reflects transmission of HIV in much the same fashion as other heterosexually transmitted diseases.

Because currently diagnosed AIDS cases reflect the epidemiology and demography of HIV infections occurring 7 to 10 years ago, AIDS case surveillance tracks where the HIV epidemic has been and not necessarily where it is going. Unfortunately, data on population HIV infection prevalence are much less reliable than AIDS case reporting. It is believed that approximately 1.5 million Americans and from 5 to 10 million persons worldwide presently have HIV infection, and most have not yet developed AIDS (Curran et al., 1988). HIV prevalence is very high in some populations. Approximately 40% of gay men in New York City and 50% of gay men in San Francisco already have HIV infection (Anderson & Levy, 1985; Carlson et al., 1985; Curran et al., 1988), with prevalence lower among gay men in smaller communities. More than half of intravenous drug users in New York City and New Jersey have HIV, although the virus is still less common in drug users in most other regions of the country (Magura et al., 1989). Although the prevalence of HIV infection in the general population (excluding gay men and IVDUs) remains at much less than 1%, risk for heterosexual transmission is increasing, especially in urban areas, in populations with high rates of other STDs and for individuals whose heterosexual partners may have HIV infection (Robbins, Spence, Marks, Armstrong, & Lauver, 1990). As the HIV epidemic enters this "second wave," Pattern 1 risk (chiefly in gay men and IVDUs) will coexist with growing Pattern 2 risk (increased heterosexual transmission). How quickly this will occur is a matter of considerable speculation and debate.

Risk Behavior for HIV Infection

Although classification of AIDS cases based on "risk group" status has served a useful public health surveillance purpose, it may also contribute to the incorrect perception that risk is related to an individual's identity (e.g., as a gay male or an intravenous drug user), when in fact it is confirmed by specific behavioral practices. Among gay or bisexual men, HIV infection risk is most strongly associated with engaging in unprotected anal intercourse with an infected partner and, to a lesser degree, with other practices that permit the exchange and entry of sexual fluids that carry HIV (Detels et al., 1989; Kingsley et al., 1987). Gay men who do not engage in higher risk practices or those who are in exclusive relationships where both partners are uninfected are not at risk for HIV. In a similar sense, HIV risk to IVDUs is conferred by exchanging or sharing needles that carry blood traces and that were used by an infected IVDU. While drug abuse is, and always has been dangerous for a multitude of other reasons, HIV risk is specifically related to the sharing or reuse of contaminated injection apparatus. Just as overreliance on "high-risk group" membership may lead to overgeneralization about risk for some groups, it leads to underestimation of risk for others. This is especially true with respect to the heterosexual population, where an individual's sexual contact with large numbers of partners will be increasingly likely to result in exposure to infected partners and the potential for contracting HIV from them. Women, particularly women of color in impoverished urban areas, who contract HIV from infected heterosexual partners constitute a population where risk is now growing steadily (Bakeman, McCray, Lumb, Jackson, & Whitley, 1987). At this stage in the HIV epidemic, it is more useful to define risk in terms of an individual's behavior practices than in relation to identity or "risk group membership" per se, which neither intrinsically conveys risk nor protects from it.

Table 7.1 summarizes behavior practices most strongly associated with risk for contracting (or transmitting) HIV infection as well as risk reduction steps. From a perspective of HIV primary prevention, the objective of intervention is to discourage the initiation, or reduce the occurrence, of high-risk behaviors among persons who engage in them and to encourage the consistent adoption of relevant precautionary behavior changes. Several aspects of risk behavior change objectives require elaboration. First, not all sexual practices are equally efficient in potential for viral transmission if one person is infected. Anal intercourse affords a highly efficient opportunity for HIV transmission, probably greater than vaginal intercourse in most circumstances (Chmiel et al., 1987; Kingsley et al., 1987). Oral-genital sex is not as strongly associated with risk, although case reports indicate that HIV transmission is at least possible during this activity. Second, risk and protection from risk are relative rather than absolute. For example, inter-

TABLE 7.1 Risk Behavior for HIV Infection and Risk-Reduction Steps

Gay or bisexual men	*High-risk behavior*: Unprotected anal intercourse. Risk level is lower for oral sex, although cases of HIV transmission have been associated with this practice. *Risk-reduction steps*: Consistently refraining from anal intercourse and other activities that permit entry of sexual fluids. Adopting condom use during sex or engaging in nonpenetrative activities that prevent entry and minimize contact with sexual fluids.
Intravenous drug uses	*High-risk behavior*: Sharing or reusing needles that may have blood traces from a previous user. *Risk-reduction steps*: Cessation of drug use. If using IV drugs, using clean needles and not sharing needles. If needles have been used, fully cleaning with bleach solution. Using condoms and following safer sex practices.
Heterosexual and adolescent men and women	*High-risk behavior*: Unprotected vaginal or anal intercourse with any nonmonogamous partner and any partner who may be at risk. *Risk-reduction steps:* Using condoms for sexual activity other than in monogamous relationships with an uninfected partner.

course protected by latex condoms greatly reduces risk but, because of occasional condom failures, does not entirely eliminate risk. Low rates of risk behavior among persons who are not likely to be infected carries lower probability of threat than the same rates of risk behavior in an environment where HIV infection is more prevalent. Thus, unprotected intercourse by nonmonogamous gay men or by heterosexual persons whose partners may be drug users carries an unusually great level of risk because HIV prevalence is already high in those populations. Finally, effective protection must consider not only the health "ideal" (that individuals will not engage in risk-producing behavior) but also the life-styles of individuals at risk, and the extent of change people are really likely to make on a practical basis. Thus, although it might be ideal to urge that individuals refrain from casual or nonmonogamous sex, a more practical and reliable objective is to encourage those who are sexually active to adopt safer sex practices consistently to lessen risk within the context of life-styles that are unlikely to support monogamy or abstinence. Similarly, although few would argue with the desirability of engaging IVDUs in drug treatment programs, most drug users are not in treatment, and HIV prevention efforts must promote behavior changes even in those IVDUs who continue to remain addicted and do not seek out drug treatment.

REVIEW AND CRITIQUE OF THE LITERATURE

The urgency of the HIV epidemic required that community-level prevention programs be quickly mobilized. Because of this urgency, most AIDS primary prevention efforts were implemented without strong evaluation components and, even when evidence of behavior change has been found (such as among gay men in San Francisco, New York, and other large cities), it remains difficult to establish what characteristics have made various prevention efforts successful. Further, evaluation of AIDS prevention approaches is complicated because the risk behavior's importance occur privately and are difficult to assess, because change in AIDS case incidence is a distant and uncertain outcome measure, because populations most vulnerable to AIDS are often difficult to identify and reach in program evaluation studies, and because there remains some lack of consensus in the research literature concerning how best to measure behavior change and even what specific behavior practices carry high risk.[1] Nonetheless, despite these difficulties, a research base has evolved in the areas of AIDS primary prevention, and some conclusions can now be reached concerning prevention approaches with these key populations: gay men, IVDUs, and heterosexual adults and adolescents.

HIV Prevention Programs for Gay Men

AIDS cases were first diagnosed among homosexually active men, and the greatest number of American AIDS cases continue to occur in gay men. For these reasons, and because most AIDS prevention campaigns first emerged in the gay community, homosexually active men remain the population most widely studied in the AIDS literature.

Numerous surveys have revealed that gay men, especially in large-city AIDS epicenters, have made substantial behavior changes in response to the HIV epidemic including reductions in high-risk behavior practices, decreased rates of sexual activity with multiple partners, and increased adoption of safer sex practices (Martin, 1987; McKusick et al., 1985). In the mid-1980s these reported behavior changes were corroborated by declining incidence of sexually transmitted diseases (STDs), reduced patronage at bathhouses, and a leveling of HIV infection prevalence—albeit at very high levels—among gay men in cities such as San Francisco and New York (Golubjatnikov, Pfister, & Tillotson, 1983; Winkelstein, Samuel, & Padian, 1987). These changes coincided with several events including extensive and multifaceted community AIDS education programs, campaigns to promote safer sex practices as a gay community norm, a sharp increase in number of AIDS cases and deaths owing to AIDS in large cities, availability and encouragement of HIV antibody testing, and public health efforts to discourage high-risk conduct in bathhouses and settings associated with frequent casual sex. It remains unclear which of these factors—education, norm changes, fear resulting from the social immediacy of AIDS, serostatus testing and self-knowledge, or public health policy—most contributed to behavior changes exhibited by many gay men in large cities hard hit by AIDS or whether all added incrementally to produce change. This question is of importance, because the delineation of community prevention elements effective with gay men in large cities can guide prevention efforts with other populations that have shown less change in risk behavior.

Several correlational studies have explored factors that predict risk behavior change or maintenance among homosexual men. In general, maintained high-risk behavior or lapses to unsafe sex were associated with younger age, lower education level, frequency and high "reinforcement value" of risk behavior practices in the past, low perceived self-efficacy for implementing behavior changes, low perceived personal vulnerability for AIDS, and beliefs that safer sex practices are not an accepted norm within one's peer group (Ekstrand & Coates, 1990; Joseph et al., 1987; Kelly, St. Lawrence, Brasfield, Lemke, Amide, Roffman, Hood, Smith, Kilgore, & McNeill, 1990; Kelly, St. Lawrence, & Brasfield, 1991). In addition, continued high-risk behavior was associated with intoxicant overuse or recreational drug use preceding sex (Stall, McKusick, Wiley, Coates, & Ostrow, 1986) and with the presence of affectionate feelings toward one's sexual partner (Kelly, Kalichman et al., in press). Several studies have found that gay men who knew their HIV antibody status were more likely to adopt precautionary behavior changes than men who had not been tested, although this finding was not consistent across studies and may reflect that those men who sought testing were the same men who were motivated to make risk-reduction behavior changes regardless of their test result (Farthing, Jesson, Taylor, Lawrence, & Gazzard, 1987).

Experimental outcome studies on AIDS risk-reduction intervention for gay men are still uncommon in the literature. However, two general types of intervention strategies have been evaluated in controlled fashion. In one line of outcome research, groups of gay men have been engaged in intervention intended to change high-risk behavior patterns. For example, Valdisseri and colleagues compared involvement in a workshop that trained safer sex skills with a comparison program that focused only on AIDS risk education (Valdisseri et al., 1989). Men who received skills training exhibited greater evidence of skill competence for implementing safer sex practices and reported lower rates of risk behavior in a short-term follow-up. Methods of risk reduction information prevention also appear to influence later behavior. Gay men exposed to, and taught, methods to "eroticize" safer sex are more likely to adopt those practices than men simply given factual information alone on risk reduction (D'Eramo, Quadland, Shattls, Shumann, & Jacobs, 1988). In a series of studies, we have found that gay men with histories of multiple partners greatly reduced risk behavior, increased precautionary changes, and showed improved skill for handling high-risk coercion following participation in a multiple-session behavioral intervention that provided AIDS education and trained self-management, sexual assertiveness, problem solving, and cognitive-modification skills pertinent to risk reduction (Kelly & St. Lawrence, 1990; Kelly, St. Lawrence, Betts, Brasfield, & Hood, 1990; Kelly, St. Lawrence, & Brasfield, in press; Kelly, St. Lawrence, Hood, & Brasfield, 1989). (This intervention model will be described in detail later in the chapter.)

Community-level campaigns (including dissemination of educational materials, media messages, presentations, peer education programs, and condom distribution) have long been underway in the gay communities of most cities and represent a second type of intervention strategy. Some campaigns, such as the "Stop AIDS" program originated in San Francisco and now adopted elsewhere, focus strongly on peer education through the conduct of AIDS prevention presentations in people's homes and other small-group social settings. Although widely regarded as beneficial in changing social norms to encourage risk reduction, the impact of most of these grassroots campaigns has not been well evaluated. In one recent study, Kelly, St. Lawrence, Diaz, Stevenson, Hauth, Brasfield, Kalichman, Smith, and Andrew (1991) experimentally evaluated a community-level intervention. This study assessed AIDS risk behavior patterns by administering surveys to men patronizing gay bars in several geographically isolated small cities. Following baseline population assessment, an intervention was introduced that identified popular opinion leaders in one city's gay population and trained these popular people to disseminate health promotion messages to their peers that emphasized how to implement behavior changes and that endorsed the social acceptability of precaution taking. This intervention produced substantial reductions in high-risk behavior among men in the intervention city relative to comparison city populations assessed at the same points in time, suggesting the viability of peer norm intervention for effecting population-wide behavior change (Kelly, St. Lawrence, Diaz, Stevenson, Hauth, Brasfield, Kalichman, Smith, & Andrew, 1991).

Although research findings have demonstrated behavior change among gay men in response to AIDS, and a limited number of studies identified interventions to promote change, there is growing evidence that more effective primary prevention efforts are still needed with this population. Risk behavior reductions observed in cohorts of homosexual men in San Francisco and New York often have not been found among gay men in smaller cities outside major AIDS epicenters (Fleming et al., 1987; Kelly, St. Lawrence, Brasfield, Stevenson, Diaz, & Hauth, 1990; Kelly, St. Lawrence, Diaz, Stevenson, Hauth, Brasfield, Kalichman, Smith, & Andrew, 1991; St. Lawrence, Hood, Brasfield, & Kelly, 1989), suggesting the need for better prevention efforts in these areas. Even in large cities, there is now evidence that a substantial proportion of gay men have difficulty maintaining behavior changes and experience "relapse" to unsafe sex on an occasional or frequent basis (Ekstrand & Coates, 1990; Kelly, Kalichman et al., 1991), and, although the incidence of homosexually transmitted STDs decreased in the mid-1980s, it is beginning to rebound in some areas (Handsfield & Schwebke, 1990). HIV primary prevention efforts continue to be needed for homosexual men, especially those who have not yet changed risk behavior and who have difficulty consistently maintaining behavior change.

HIV Prevention Program for IVDUs

Efforts toward primary prevention of HIV infection among IVDUs have had three major objectives: (a) preventing the initiation of drug injection practices in groups not yet addicted and engaging current addicts in treatment programs to curb their drug dependence; (b) reducing HIV drug use risk behaviors among IVDUs who continue to inject by teaching "safer injection" practices; and (c) encouraging the adoption of safer sex practices by IVDUs to prevent transmission of HIV from drug use to their sexual partners. Just as AIDS prevention efforts in the gay community relied primarily on grassroots educational campaigns with an applied rather than evaluative focus, research on HIV risk behavior with drug users has been primarily descriptive and only very rarely has sought to evaluate in controlled fashion the effectiveness of specific prevention approaches. As a result, more is known about IVDUs' risk behavior patterns than why they occur or how they can be changed.

Risk for HIV infection among IVDUs is associated with the sharing and reuse of syringes that carry HIV-contaminated blood traces from previous users of the needles. Several studies have shown that needle sharing and reuse is influenced by strength and chronicity of addition, frequency of injection, type of drug injected, and setting where drug injection occurs. Long-term frequent injectors, those who inject cocaine, and those who inject in shooting galleries and in closely knit social networks are more likely to share syringes with one another (Chitwood et al., 1990; Magura et al., 1989). However, several other situational factors also influence needle-sharing behavior including local norms, which may either discourage sharing or sanction needle sharing as an accepted trust-related ritual within the IVDU social network; the availability of new, clean syringes in the community; and criminal statutes for carrying drug paraphernalia. Somewhat paradoxically, laws intended to discourage drug abuse (such as syringe availability only by prescription and strong penalties for carrying new syringes) may create shortages of injection apparatus and inadvertently contribute to HIV risk by encouraging needle reuse.

Although it is popular to stereotype drug addicts as unresponsive to health issues, numerous surveys indicate that AIDS is a high-level concern to most IVDUs, that greater numbers of addicts than ever before are seeking drug withdrawal treatment or methadone maintenance to reduce their risk for HIV, and that self-reported "safer injection" practices (such as syringe cleaning with bleach and avoiding syringe sharing) have increased considerably during the past several years (Des Jarlais et al., 1987; Harris, 1990; Sorensen, Guydish, Costantini, & Batki, 1989). The aim of promoting risk-reduction changes among street addicts is essential for HIV prevention, given limited availability of drug treatment services and the limited success of most programs in achieving permanent long-term treatment success.

In the United States, community-level HIV prevention efforts with IVDUs have focused primarily on educating about HIV risk and teaching procedures for needle cleaning. Several interventions combining education, skills training in needle-cleaning techniques, and availability of HIV antibody testing have been conducted in both drug withdrawal treatment and methadone maintenance settings. These efforts have generally produced evidence of increased risk knowledge, threat sensitization, and reported behavior change (Des Jarlais, Friedman, & Hopkins, 1985; Sorensen, Gibson, Heitzman, Dumonet, & Acampora, 1988). Unfortunately, most IVDUs are not in treatment or methadone programs and therefore are not reached through such structured program-based behavior change interventions. Many large cities now conduct community outreach AIDS education programs to encourage precautionary behavior changes by addicts not presently in treatment. Although there have been few controlled evaluations of these outreach models owing to the enormous methodological difficulties in assessing them, prevention efforts credibly delivered in the IVDU community are widely regarded as critical to both risk reduction and encouragement to enter drug treatment. One study (Jackson & Rotkiewicz, 1987) found that distribution of vouchers offering drug treatment at no charge and with no waiting period as a component of an AIDS outreach education program produced substantial increases in persons entering treatment.

In several European countries, AIDS prevention efforts rely strongly on needle distribution and exchanges as well as outreach education and treatment. In its most common form, clean syringes are made available to addicts in a one-for-one exchange for used syringes. Compelling data from several countries show a rapid leveling of new HIV infections among IVDUs when clean needles are made available in exchange programs, and there has been no evidence that such programs result in an increase in the size of the drug addict population (Van den Hoek, Coutinho, Van Zadelhoff, Van hass Trecht, & Goudsmit, 1987). Nonetheless, needle exchange and distribution programs remain extremely controversial in the United States for fear that they might tacitly encourage drug abuse. Demonstration programs are needed to evaluate the benefits of needle exchanges and to address scientifically political and community concerns about their benefits and cost in conjunction with outreach education and improved availability of drug treatment services.

HIV prevention directed toward IVDUs entails both reduction in needle-use risks as well as risk reduction in sexual practices. Although changes in needle use have been well documented among drug users in areas with active outreach prevention programs, adoption of safer sex practices by IVDUs has been demonstrated much less consistently. Several surveys have indicated that, although intentions to use condoms are high and many IVDUs report occasional use of condoms during intercourse, only a small minority of drug users consistently practice safer sex (Des Jarlais, Tross, Abdul-Quader, & Friedman, 1988). As we will next discuss, this is disturbing because most cases of HIV infection among non-IVDU heterosexuals in the United State are due to sexual contact with an infected drug-user partner (Chiasson et al., 1990; Lewis et al., 1990).

HIV Prevention Programs for Heterosexual Populations

Because AIDS cases historically have been categorized by "risk group" and because using nondrug heterosexuals have accounted for only a small proportion of diagnosed American cases of AIDS to date, there remains a perception that HIV is an insignificant threat to heterosexual persons who do not use injected drugs. However, because AIDS cases lag years behind initial HIV infection, current trends in new HIV infection—the critical factor in predicting the AIDS epidemic—cannot be reliably determined only by present AIDS case incidence. It is now clear that HIV can be transmitted during vaginal intercourse with an infected heterosexual partner (Holmes, Karon, & Kreiss, 1990; Padian et al., 1987), and, indeed, this is the most predominant form of transmission in most of the Third World. Populations most vulnerable to heterosexually transmitted HIV are the same as those also most vulnerable to other STDs. For example, HIV prevalence ranging from 10% to 50% has been reported for female prostitutes (Fischl, Dickinson, Flanagan, & Fletcher, 1988). Because of the high prevalence of HIV infection among intravenous drug users, urban and minority populations and other persons whose sexual partners are in closer geographical proximity to the drug-user cultures are at greater risk. Elevated HIV infection prevalence is found among inner-city populations, STD clinic attendees, and persons reporting heterosexual contact with partners either known or at potential risk for HIV infection (Krueger, Wood, Diehr, & Maxwell, 1990; Robbins et al., 1990). However, it is also important to note that as HIV enters a "second wave" of increased prevalence in some non-IVDU heterosexual populations, HIV transmission patterns are likely to resemble those of other STDs and not require direct sexual contact only with IVDUs (Calabrese & Gopalakrishna, 1986). Whether the prevalence of HIV within vulnerable heterosexual populations will increase gradually or rapidly is still a matter of speculation and debate.

As a result of public education campaigns, knowledge about AIDS has increased dramatically over the past several years among both adults and adolescents (Kegeles, Allen, & Irwin, 1988; Klonoff, Cargill, & Gayle, 1988; Strunin &

Hingson, 1987). Unfortunately, the picture of actual change observed in most heterosexual populations is much less sanguine. Condom use among sexually active and nonmonogamous heterosexual adolescents and adults remains inconsistent and low, even among persons who report having multiple and multiple serial sexual partners. (Research and Decisions Corporation, 1986; Strunin & Hingson). Reasons for the relative lack of precaution taking among heterosexuals have not yet been well studied, but they are likely to involve low perceived personal vulnerability for AIDS, negative attributions concerning condom use, inadequate social norms to promote precautionary behavior changes, associations between licit or illicit substance use and sexual activity, and perceived inconsistency between safer sex practices and feelings of affection toward one's sexual partner (Hatchett, 1990; Stoneburner, Chiasson, Weisfuse, & Thomas, 1990). Among inner-city populations, barriers related to socioeconomic disadvantage and cultural factors also influence risk vulnerability. For example, we recently found that urban women, although concerned about AIDS, reported greater immediacy of concern about other "social survival" stressors including lack of housing, employment, food, transportation, and availability of child care (Kelly, St. Lawrence, Banks, Stevenson, Diaz, Powers, & Brasfield, 1991). Earlier debut of sexual activity, higher rates of sexual activity, and reduced access to health care, family planning, and contraception services are patterns more common in the inner city and contribute to risk for HIV infection (Elder-Tabrizy, Wolitski, Rhodes, & Baker, 1990; Mays, 1989).

To date, experimental evaluations of AIDS prevention interventions with heterosexual populations are still uncommon; controlled outcome; controlled outcome evaluations with urban and minority populations are even more rare. Indeed, although it is possible to speak of prevention approaches with "heterosexual populations," there are many *different* heterosexual populations—including heterosexual men, women, adolescents, prostitutes, minority, nonminority, and so on—for which risk occurs in different social and cultural contexts. Because most HIV prevention efforts have focused on gay men and IVDUs, there has still been little prevention research with many of these heterosexual populations. Most prevention programs that have been studied involve brief educational workshops that demonstrated increases in AIDS knowledge, attitudes, and (less frequently) behavior changes to reduce HIV risk. For example, McDonald, Kleppel, and Jenssen (1990) have described AIDS education programs for low-income women who attend Women, Infants, and Children clinics, and Cargill (1989) has undertaken large-scale school-based AIDS awareness and peer education programs with inner-city young adolescents that attempt to establish social norms discouraging high-risk sexual and drug use practices. Media programs have also shown promise as a vehicle for encouraging parent and adolescent communication about AIDS and sexual issues (Crawford et al., 1990). Cochran, Keidan, and Kalechstein (1990) found that more than one half of college students attending

AIDS education and skills training sessions reported a subsequent reduction in high-risk behavior at follow-up. In one of the few well-controlled intervention outcome studies, Rotheran-Borus, Koopman, and Haignere (1990) offered minority and primarily minority male and female adolescents a multiple-session group behavioral skills training program accompanied by risk education and enhanced health care service access. Six months following intervention, adolescents in the experimental program exhibited substantial reductions in sexual risk behavior relative to a comparison group that had not received the intervention.

CASE EXAMPLE

A distinction can be made between "clinical" behavior change interventions (those that involve direct face-to-face contact with individuals to assist in risk behavior reduction) and broad population-based "community" interventions (those that, through media or other channels, seek to influence a population). Both approaches are relevant to HIV primary prevention. An analogy can be drawn to cigarette smoking, where population-level interventions are used to prevent or discourage smoking but where individual smokers often require face-to-face assistance to implement smoking cessation effectively. In the case of AIDS prevention, there are groups of persons at sufficiently high risk that direct involvement in risk behavior reduction interventions is warranted, cost-effective (in relation to the costs that would occur if even a small proportion developed HIV infection), practical, and necessary for successful risk behavior change. Examples of populations for which behavioral assistance may be needed are gay men who still engage in unsafe sex; IVDUs in treatment or in the community; STD clinic patients; and heterosexual adolescents and adults with multiple sexual partners, especially in inner-city areas where HIV infection is increasing.

Although the problems of AIDS and HIV infection are new, behavior change interventions have long been used to help individuals change other health-threat behavior patterns, such as smoking, obesity, substance abuse, and cardiovascular risk. Although HIV risk behaviors are considerably different from risk behaviors in other health-related areas, they are also considerably similar in some ways and may be amenable (as are other health-risk behaviors) to change using such procedures as risk education, problem-solving and self-management approaches tailored to risk-producing situations, assertiveness and cognitive modification intervention, and reinforcement of behavior change efforts. In a series of studies, members of our AIDS/HIV behavior research team have explored the impact of group intervention to assist persons in changing high-risk patterns (Kelly et al., 1989; Kelly et al., 1990; Kelly, St Lawrence, Betts, Brasfield, & Hood, 1990; Kelly, St. Lawrence, & Brasfield, in press).[2] In the following section, we summarize this intervention approach, with particular emphasis on practical aspects of its conduct.

Recruiting and Assessing Participants for AIDS Prevention Project

Few persons spontaneously seek out assistance to change HIV risk behaviors, presumably because of the stigma associated with AIDS; reluctance to acknowledge engaging in risk behaviors; fear of identifying oneself as gay, a drug user, or sexually active; lack of comfort, motivation, or resources for traditional help seeking; and the inaccessibility of mental health services to constituent populations most at risk for AIDS. For these reasons, HIV prevention programs are most effective when closely integrated into community, social, or health resources that already reach, and are already credible to, the intended community population. For example, AIDS prevention interventions can be offered in conjunction with the services of primary urban health clinics, STD clinics, HIV testing and counseling programs, schools, gay community organizations, and drug treatment centers. The focus of the research to be described here was gay men. To recruit these participants, brochures and posters were placed in gay bars; videos describing the program were produced and played over the dance floors of those clubs; meetings were held with members of local gay and AIDS organizations to solicit endorsements and recommendations for the content of the intervention; and program staff actively "outreached" by speaking to both formal and informal social groups to describe the program, seek participants, and alleviate concerns, especially those involving confidentiality. All research program activities, including intervention group sessions, were conducted in an office setting selected for its community accessibility, privacy, and comfort to participants. Most recently, we have taken community access a step further and actually conduct sessions within bars because these are natural settings pertinent and familiar to the intended population.

Evaluation of AIDS prevention programs requires detailed and specific assessment of behaviors that are both private and sensitive. This argues in favor of assessment using multiple measures that, taken together, provide convergent evidence of change. As we have described elsewhere (Kelly et al., 1989), it seems prudent to approach assessment using a comprehensive battery of measures sensitive to different aspects of change, such as risk behavior knowledge, attitudes concerning risk, behavioral and cognitive skills needed to implement behavior change (including, for example, sexual assertiveness exhibited in role plays, problem-solving skill when confronted with simulated risk pressures, or skill in correctly using condoms), self-reported risk behavior practices, ongoing self-monitored risk behavior, behavioral intentions, and history of STDs. If such a set of related measures shift consistently in the direction of reduced risk following intervention, confidence in the interventions' impact is heightened.

In the Kelly et al. (1989) project used here for illustrative purposes, each participant entering the study was individually administered an objective test of HIV risk behavior knowledge; measures assessing substance use and number of sexual partners and behavior practices over the preceding 2 weeks, 3 months, and 12 months; and role-play assessments in which the participant responded to situations describing and simulating coercion to engage in high-risk sexual practices. In addition, participants were provided with, and shown how to complete, forms for self-monitoring risk behavior over successive 2-week intervals. To ensure clarity and appropriateness, all measures had been pilot-tested before use. A total of 104 participants who met criteria for high-risk behavior were entered in the study.

Collection of accurate data on AIDS risk requires that research participants be candid in their reports of behavior that is sensitive, personal, and sometimes illegal. It is essential that participants are convinced that data will be treated confidentially and with strict privacy safeguards. This can be accomplished by explanation of safeguards, by arranging measure administration so that responses are not immediately seen by research staff, by allowing participants to use numeric codes rather than their own names on measures, and otherwise assuring the protection of sensitive data. Protection of the participants' identity, beyond protection of the information they provide, is also of paramount importance both for research ethics and to encourage the provision of valid behavior reports.

Behavior Change Intervention

In the Kelly et al. (1989) study, the sample of participants was randomly divided into immediate intervention and waiting-list comparison groups. Participants in the immediate intervention condition attended a 12-session series of weekly groups. Each session lasted about 90 minutes. Because most behavioral intervention procedures require practice and individualization, participants were subdivided into smaller groups of 8 to 12 persons for training purposes. Each group session was led by one male and one female leader experienced in behavioral intervention procedures, knowledgeable about HIV risk reduction, and comfortable discussing life-style issues affecting gay men. The intervention itself included four major components: (a) risk behavior education, (b) self-management training applied to personal behavior patterns related to HIV risk; (c) sexual awareness training; and (d) attention to life-style, pride, and relationship issues pertinent to HIV risk.

Risk Behavior Education

Detailed information was presented by the session leaders (and supplemented with handouts, brochures, and audiovisual materials) on prevalence and basic epidemiology of HIV infection and AIDS, mechanisms by which the virus is transmitted, high-risk behavior practices, risk-reduction changes and their rationales, and common myths and misconceptions about risk. The intent of these group discussions was to assure that participants understood not only risk-reduction precautions but also the broader framework concerning *reasons why* behavior changes reduce risk. The risk level of various sexual practices was presented along a continuum from highest to least risk, and participants were encouraged to identify where on that continuum they were presently and where they would like to be to establish personal behavior change goals.

Self-Management Training

Several group exercises were used to teach participants to manage better situations that served to "trigger" high-risk behavior. For example, each participant wrote scenarios describing circumstances surrounding three past occasions when he engaged in high-risk behavior including the setting; partner characteristics; the participant's mood or intoxicant use, thoughts, and feelings; and other circumstances at the time of each risk episode. Members identified and described common themes across their own risk episodes, and the leaders encouraged group problem solving to help each member identify alternative ways to handle risk triggers.

In another self-management session, participants were taught cognitive-behavioral modification procedures applied to risk reduction including generation of self-statements to guide avoidance of high-risk behavior, adoption of precautionary steps, and cognitive self-reinforcement of efforts to implement changes. This training was accomplished by instruction, in-session practice exercises, and at-home practice assignments. At the start of each group session, all participants discussed the success of, and problems encountered in, their practice efforts. Finally, participants were encouraged to make other changes to support risk-reduction efforts including buying and practicing at home the use of condoms, avoiding sexual fantasies about high-risk behavior and "replacing" them with fantasies concerning safer sex practices, avoiding situations conducive to high-risk behavior, and cognitively identifying and rehearsing statements that reinforce the benefits of maintaining precautionary changes.

Sexual Assertiveness Training

All HIV risk behaviors are interpersonal in nature and require, in essence, that two persons assent to engage in some high-risk practice. Because of its interpersonal nature, individuals can lessen their risk by developing and using effective assertiveness skills to "negotiate" understandings concerning AIDS precautions in advance with a sexual partner, and, if necessary, assertively refuse coercions to engage in high-risk practices. Over several group sessions, participants were taught assertiveness skills in both of these contexts. Training was conducted by instruction and group discussion of assertive handling of potential risk situations, modeling by group leaders of examples of assertive responses, and participant role play behavioral rehearsal of how they would handle coercions or pressures to engage in risky activities. Rehearsal was accomplished by dividing the group into triads, providing each with vignettes describing risk situations, and asking one triad member to play the part of a coercive partner and another to practice assertive responses to the coercions. Feedback, suggestions, and reinforcement were provided following each role-play effort, and training continued using vignettes developed by the leaders and by the participants, based on their past experiences. The objective was to help participants become skilled and comfortable initiating the subject of safety and refusing pressures to engage in unsafe practices. Homework assignments involved using these skills in real life if situations occurred requiring assertiveness.

Life-Style, Pride, and Relationship Issues as Contexts for Change

Populations presently most affected by AIDS—gay men, drug users, minorities, and the urban poor—are groups for which lack of pride, empowerment, and personal efficacy are significant life issues. Although there is no evidence that improved pride and self-esteem alone change risk behavior, it does seem likely that self-pride, a feeling of concern for oneself and others, and a belief that one deserves quality relationships form a social context in which change efforts are easier to achieve and maintain.

Considerable group discussion involved themes related to these topics. For example, although participants entering the study had very high levels of sexual activity (a participant mean of 12 different partners in the past year and 18 occurrences of unprotected anal intercourse with them), most reported a desire to meet "someone special," and develop a stable and safe monogamous relationship with that person. The group leaders encouraged group problem solving to explore how these goals could be achieved, barriers to relationship stability, and ways to rearrange life activities to promote relationship development. Many members expressed interest in learning how to "date" rather than seek casual partners, and others raised the problem of how to maintain safer sex practices in the context of affectionate stable relationships. There are few "templates" in the behavior change literature for how to teach these skills, and the leaders relied on group problem solving and, occasionally, role-play rehearsal to generate strategies. Finally, participants were encouraged to evaluate their current social activities and networks, and to replace social patterns conducive to risk vulnerability with activities affirming, and supportive of, risk-reduction maintenance. Examples included involvement in local AIDS prevention and service organizations, community service programs, or simply informal networks of friends who would be supportive of risk-reduction behavior changes.

Study Outcomes

As described in detail previously (Kelly et al., 1989), this intervention was evaluated by repeating the same assessment battery used as baseline after the intervention participants had completed the program and comparing change shown by participants with that of the comparison group. For ethical reasons, all persons who had been in the comparison group were then immediately offered the same intervention, and original intervention participants continued to be followed for a 24-month period to assess long-term change maintenance. These evaluations revealed that, relative to the comparison group, intervention participants showed significant preintervention to postintervention increases in AIDS risk behavior knowledge scores and improved ratings of sexual assertiveness skill during assessment role plays. Frequency of unprotected anal intercourse decreased to near-zero levels, as assessed by both self-monitoring and 3-month retrospective behavior self-reports, whereas condom use increased from 25% to almost 90% of intercourse occasions. These changes were well maintained at long-term follow-up (Kelly et al., 1989). The program also was favorably evaluated by participants. In fact, it was so well received that additional cycles of the intervention continued to be offered to additional persons who later sought to enter it (Kelly & St. Lawrence, 1990; Kelly, St. Lawrence, Betts, Brasfield, & Hood, 1990).

Logistical and Other Application Issues

The prevention challenges posed by AIDS call for the application of established behavior change principles in unconventional contexts. Most of the intervention components used in the research program just described—self-management, assertiveness, and problem-solving skills, for example—are well established in the behavioral literature. However, applying them to AIDS prevention requires special knowledge of life-style and behavioral realities of the intended population, comfort and nonjudgmentalism dealing with topics and behaviors pertinent to HIV risk, credibility to the community in which one hopes to intervene, and an affirmative stance toward the needs of individuals and communities most affected by AIDS.

As suggested earlier, programs of this kind are most successful when they grow out of a community's own perception of need and when they are integrated into social, health, or service networks already serving the constituent community. For example, we are now developing and testing a similar research intervention model for urban women at risk for HIV. There are very different social and cultural contexts influencing risk behavior among inner-city women compared with gay men. For example, our women's program is conducted in community health primary care clinics serving urban neighborhoods because these are settings accessible and credible to this population. With some change in target risk behaviors and careful attention to cultural differences, behavioral interventions of this general kind might also be adapted for AIDS prevention efforts in drug treatment centers, schools, STD clinics, and similar settings.

The program described here is not expensive to conduct, although collection of research outcome data adds to its cost. The most critical contributors to program success involve staffing, staff training, developing of intervention content that is culturally relevant to the population being served or studied, soliciting input and involvement from relevant parties in the constituent community, and taking intervention activities into community settings rather than expecting persons to seek out the intervention. Because trust is a key aspect of program acceptance and because groups most affected by AIDS may be distrustful of behavioral scientists and establishments (often with reason), it is also important to listen closely to the priorities, needs, and concerns of the constituent community and to address these issues in intervention planning. For example, in the Kelly et al. (1989) project, consideration was initially given to the use of pre- and follow-up HIV antibody testing as a dependent research measure to assess behavior change impact. However, the conservative southern state in which that study was conducted required reporting of the identity of persons with HIV infection and had defeated state laws to protect HIV-infected individuals from discrimination. Members of the gay community suggested to the research team that under those circumstances, HIV testing would frighten and deter individuals most at risk from participating in the project. We concurred and believe the project was more successful as a result. Soliciting community input early in project planning is important in all applied research but is especially critical in AIDS prevention behavioral studies.

FUTURE DIRECTIONS

Although the problem of AIDS itself is new, efforts to prevent HIV infection can be based on behavior change principles and models already used in other health promotion areas if they are carefully adapted to HIV risk behaviors, sensitive to the unique social and community contexts affecting populations most vulnerable to AIDS, and accessible to the intended populations. Perhaps because AIDS is still a recent crisis, first identified in 1979, there has been a paucity of controlled evaluative research on HIV risk behavior change interventions; innovative community prevention programs are being widely undertaken in field settings but rarely with strong evaluation components. It will be of immense value to test behavior change models better experimentally so that those that are most promising can be widely implemented and disseminated. This requires closer collaboration between health behavior researchers and community organizations interested in AIDS prevention.

AIDS itself is a changing epidemic. Although gay men and IVDUs remain the populations most affected by AIDS, every indication points toward an increase in HIV infection in inner-city, minority, and socially disadvantaged communities. Little research has yet been directed toward the evaluation of HIV primary prevention approaches in the inner city except with drug users, and the historical track record of other health promotion efforts in central cities and with disadvantaged populations is not good. AIDS challenges us to develop intervention models that can curtail the incidence of new HIV infections within urban areas. The same models will prevent HIV infection also may help to address many other urgent social health problems affecting inner cities, such as drug use, STDs, teenage pregnancy, and infant mortality. In addition, we still know very little about the types of intervention that are needed to make HIV prevention efforts effective and salient to women and adolescents.

Finally, the scope of effort needed to prevent HIV infection in any population requires multiple levels, types, and intensities of intervention. The research example described in this chapter illustrates one model for face-to-face intervention with persons of high-risk behavior appropriate for settings where clients are seen directly and when they seek behavior change assistance. However, there is a concurrent need to develop, field test, and evaluate broader and mass-level community instructions that can educate, support behavior change skill development, and foster social norms that encourage risk-reduction efforts (Coates, 1988; Kelly et al., 1991). Population-level interventions are needed both to help individuals avoid the initiation of risk patterns and to assist persons in their efforts to change existing high-risk behavior. The challenges here are many, the tasks formidable, and the time short.

NOTES

1. For example, there is current debate and conflicting recommendations concerning the risk level associated with oral sex or the risk level associated with anal intercourse using condoms, given the potential for condom failure and the high probability for viral transmission if condoms fail during the activity. Similarly, some researchers define only *receptive* anal intercourse as a high-risk behavior, because the receptive partner is at greater risk, while others define any unprotected anal intercourse as high-risk, because this practice always places one partner at risk.
2. The intervention research studies described here were originally conducted by Jeffrey A. Kelly, Janet S. St. Lawrence, Ted L. Brasfield, and Harold V. Hood. These studies were supported by grant #ROI–MH–41800 from the National Institute of Mental Health.

REFERENCES

Anderson, R. E., & Levy, J. S. (1985). Prevalence of antibodies to AIDS-associated retrovirus. *Lancet, 1*, 217.
Bakeman, R., McCray, E., Lumb, J. R., Jackson, R. E., & Whitley, P. N. (1987). The

incidence of AIDS among blacks and Hispanics. *Journal of the National Medical Association, 79*, 921–928.

Buehler, J. W., Devine, O. J., Berkelman, R. L., & Chevarley, F. M. (1990). Impact of the human immunodeficiency virus epidemic on mortality trends in young men, United States. *American Journal of Public Health, 80*, 1080–1086.

Calabrese, C. H., & Gopalakrishna, K. V. (1986). Transmission of HTLV–III infection from man to woman to man. *New England Journal of Medicine, 314*, 987.

Cargill, V. A. (1989, October). *SAMM: An innovative approach to AIDS education for black adolescents.* Paper presented to the annual meeting of the American Public Health Association, Chicago, IL.

Carlson, J. R., Bryant, M. L., Hinrichs, S. H., Yamamoto, J. K., Levy, N. B., Yee, J., Levine, A. M., Holland, P., Gardner, M. B., & Pedersen, N. C. (1985). AIDS serology testing in low and high risk groups. *Journal of the American Medical Association, 253*, 3405–3408.

Centers for Disease Control (1993, May). *HIV/AIDS surveillance.* Atlanta, GA: Centers for Disease Control, United States Public Health Service.

Chiasson, M. A., Stoneburner, R. L., Lifson, A. R., Hildebrandt, D. S., Ewing, W. E., Schultz, S., & Jaffe, H. W. (1990). Risk factors for human immunodeficiency virus type 1 (HIV-1) infection in patients at a sexually transmitted disease clinic in New York City. *American Journal of Epidemiology, 131*, 208–220.

Chitwood, D. D., McCoy, C. B., Inciardi, J. A., McBride, D. C., Comerford, M., Trapido, E., McCoy, V., Page, B., Griffin, J., Fletcher, M. A., & Ashman, M. A. (1990). HIV seropositivity of needles from shooting galleries in south Florida. *American Journal of Public Health, 80*, 150–152.

Chmiel, J. S., Detels, R., Kaslow, R. A., Van Raden, M., Kingsley, L. A., Brookmeyer, R., & the Multicenter AIDS Cohort Study Group. (1987). Factors associated with prevalent human immunodeficiency virus (AIDS) infection in the Multicenter AIDS Cohort Study. *American Journal of Epidemiology, 126*, 568–577.

Chu, S. Y., Buehler, J. W., & Berkelman, R. L. (1990). Impact of the human immunodeficiency virus epidemic on mortality in women of reproductive age, United States. *Journal of the American Medical Association, 264*, 225–229.

Cochran, S. D., Keidan, J., & Kalechstein, A. (1990, April–June). Sexually transmitted diseases and acquired immune deficiency syndrome: Changes in risk reduction behaviors among young adults. *Sexually Transmitted Diseases*, 80–86.

Crawford, I., Jason, L. A., Riordan, N., Kaufman, J., Salina, D., Sawalski, L., Ho, F. C., & Zolik, E. (1990). A multimedia-based approach to increasing communication and the level of AIDS knowledge within families. *Journal of Community Psychology, 18*, 361–373.

D'Eramo, J. E., Quadland, M. E., Shattls, W., Shumann, R., & Jacobs, R. (1988, June). *The 800 Men Project: A systematic evaluation of AIDS prevention programs demonstrating the efficacy of erotic, sexually explicit safer sex education on gay and bisexual men at risk for AIDS.* Paper presented at the IV International Conference on AIDS, Stockholm.

Des Jarlais, D. C., Friedman, S. R., & Hopkins, W. (1985). Risk reduction for the acquired immunodeficiency syndrome among intravenous drug users. *Annals of Internal Medicine, 103*, 755–759.

Des Jarlais, D. C., Wish, E., Friedman, S. R., Stoneburner, R., Yancovitz, S. R., Mildvan, D., El-Sadr, W., Brady, E., & Cuadrado, M. (1987). Intravenous drug use and the heterosexual transmission of the human immunodeficiency virus: Current trends in New York City. *New York State Journal of Medicine, 87*, 283–286.

Detels, R., English, P., Visscher, B. R., Jacobson, L., Kingsley, L. A., Chmiel, J. S., Dudley, J. P., Eldred, L. J., & Ginzburg, H. M. (1989). Seroconversion, sexual activity, and condom use among 2915 HIV seronegative men followed for up to 2 years. *Journal of Acquired Immune Deficiency Syndromes, 2*, 77–83.

Ekstrand, M. L., & Coates, T. J. (1990). Maintenance of safer sexual behaviors and predictors of risky sex: The San Francisco Men's Health Study. *American Journal of Public Health, 80*, 973–977.

Elder–Tabrizy, K. A., Wolitski, R. J., Rhodes, F., & Baker, J. G. (1990, June). *AIDS and competing health concerns of blacks, hispanics, and whites.* Paper presented at the VI International Conference on AIDS, San Francisco, CA.

Farthing, C. F., Jesson, W., Taylor, H. -L, Lawrence, A. G., & Gazzard, B. G. (1987, June). *The HIV antibody test: Influence on sexual behavior of homosexual men.* Paper presented to the III International Conference on AIDS, Washington, DC.

Fischl, M. A., Dickinson, G. M., Flanagan, S., & Fletcher, M. A. (1987, June). *Human immunodeficiency virus (HIV) among female prostitutes in south Florida.* Paper presented at the III International Conference on AIDS, Washington, DC.

Fleming, D. W., Cochi, S. L., Steece, R. S., & Hull, H. F. (1987). Acquired immunodeficiency syndrome in low-incidence areas: How safe is unsafe sex? *Journal of the American Medical Association, 258*, 785–787.

Golubjatnikov, R., Pfister, J., & Tillotson, T. (1983). Homosexual promiscuity and the fear of AIDS. *Lancet, 2*, 681.

Handsfield, H. H., & Schwebke, J. (1990). Trends in sexually transmitted diseases in homosexually active men in King County, Washington, 1980–1990. *Sexually Transmitted Diseases, 17*, 211–215.

Harris, R. E., Langrod, J., Hebert, J. R., Lowinson, J., Zang, E., & Wynder, E. L. (1990). Changes in AIDS risk behavior among intravenous drug abusers in New York City. *New York State Journal of Medicine, 90*, 123–126.

Hatchett, D. (1990). The impact of AIDS on the Black community. *Crisis, 97*, 28–30.

Holmes, K. K., Karon, J. M., & Kreiss, J. (1990). The increasing frequency of heterosexually acquired AIDS in the United States, 1983–88. *American Journal of Public Health, 80*, 858–863.

Jackson, J., & Rotkiewicz, L. (1987, June). *A coupon program: AIDS education and drug treatment.* Paper presented at the III International Conference on AIDS, Washington, DC.

Joseph, J. G., Montgomery, S. B., Emmons, C. -A., Kirscht, J. P., Kessler, R. C., Ostrow, D. G., Wortman, C. B., O'Brian, K., Eller, M. & Eshleman, S. (1987). Perceived risk of AIDS: Assessing the behavioral and psychosocial consequences in a cohort of gay men. *Journal of Applied Social Psychology, 17*, 231–250.

Kegeles, S. M., Allen, N. E., & Irwin, C. E. (1988). Sexually active adolescents and condoms: Changes over one year in knowledge, attitudes, and use. *American Journal of Public Health, 78*, 460–461.

Kelly, J. A., Kalichman, S. C., Kauth, M. R., Kilgore, H. G., Hood, H. V., Campos, P. E., Rao, S. M., Brasfield, T. L., & St. Lawrence, J. S. (1991). Situational factors associated with AIDS risk behavior lapses and coping strategies used by gay men who successfully avoid lapses. *American Journal of Public Health, 81*, 1335–1338.

Kelly, J. A., & St. Lawrence, J. S. (1990). The impact of community–based groups to help persons reduce HIV infection risk behaviors. *AIDS Care, 2*, 25–36.

Kelly, J. A., St. Lawrence, J. S., Banks, P. G., Stevenson, L. Y., Diaz, Y. E., Powers, A., & Brasfield, T. L. (1991). *AIDS risk knowledge, perceptions, and behavior among socially disadvantaged women.* Unpublished manuscript, Medical College of Wisconsin.

Kelly, J. A., St. Lawrence, J. S., Betts, R., Brasfield, T. L., & Hood, H. V. (1990). A skills-training group intervention model to assist persons in reducing risk behaviors for HIV infection. *AIDS Education and Prevention, 2,* 24–35.

Kelly, J. A., St. Lawrence, J. S., & Brasfield, T. L. (1991). Predictors of vulnerability to AIDS risk behavior. *Journal of Consulting and Clinical Psychology, 59,* 163–166.

Kelly, J. A., St. Lawrence, J. S., & Brasfield, T. L. (in press). Group intervention to promote HIV risk reduction: Procedures and impact on high-risk behavior. In R. Berkvens & M. de Bruyn (Eds.), *AIDS prevention through health promotion: Changing behavior* (World Health Organization Monograph). Geneva: World Health Organization.

Kelly, J. A., St Lawrence, J. S., Brasfield, T. L., Lemke, A., Amidei, T., Roffman, R. E., Hood, H. V., Smith, J. E., Kilgore, H., & McNeill, C. (1990). Psychological factors which predict AIDS high-risk and AIDS precautionary behavior. *Journal of Consulting and Clinical Psychology, 58,* 117–120.

Kelly, J. A., St. Lawrence, J. S., Brasfield, T. L., Stevenson, L. Y., Diaz, Y. Y., & Hauth, A. C. (1990). AIDS risk behavior patterns among gay men in small southern cities. *American Journal of Public Health, 80,* 416–418.

Kelly, J. A., St. Lawrence, J. S., Diaz, . E., Stevenson, L. Y., Hauth, A. C., Brasfield, T. L., Kalichman, S. C., Smith, J. E., & Andrew, M. E. (1991). HIV risk behavior reduction following intervention with key opinion leaders of population: An experimental analysis. *American Journal of Public Health, 81,* 168–171.

Kelly, J. A., St. Lawrence, J. S., Hood, H. V., & Brasfield, T. L. (1989). Behavioral intervention to reduce AIDS risk activities. *Journal of Consulting and Clinical Psychology, 57,* 60–67.

Kingsley, L. A., Detels, R., Kaslow, R., Polk, B. F., Rinaldo Jr., C. R., Chmiel, J., Detre, K., Kelsey, S. F., Odaka, N., Ostrow, D., Van Raden, M., & Visscher, B. (1987). Risk factors for seroconversion to human immunodeficiency virus among male homosexuals. *Lancet, 1,* 345–349.

Klonoff, E. A., Cargill, V. A., & Gayle, J. (August, 1988). AIDS education and prevention in an urban minority population. In J. A. Kelly (Chair), *Outcomes of AIDS prevention programs: What works best with whom.* Symposium presented at the annual meeting of the American Psychological Association, Atlanta, GA.

Krueger, L. E., Wood, R. W., Diehr, P. H., & Maxwell, C. L. (1990). Poverty and HIV seropositivity: The poor are more likely to be infected. *AIDS, 4,* 811–814.

Lewis, D. K., Watters, J. K., & Case, P. (1990). The prevalence of high-risk sexual behavior in male intravenous drug users with steady female partners. *American Journal of Public Health, 80,* 465–466.

Magura, S., Grossman, J. I., Lipton, D. S., Siddiqi, Q., Shapiro, J., Marion, I., & Amann, K. R. (1989). Determinants of needle sharing among intravenous drug users. *American Journal of Public Health, 79,* 459–462.

Martin, J. L. (1987). Impact of AIDS on gay male sexual behavior patterns in New York City. *American Journal of Public Health, 77,* 578–581.

Mays, V. M. (1989). AIDS prevention in black populations: Methods of a safer kind. In V. M. Mays, G. W. Alber, & S. F. Schneider (Eds.), *Primary prevention of AIDS: Psychological approaches.* Newbury Park, CA: Sage.

McDonald, M., Kleppel, L., & Jenssen, D. (1990). Developing AIDS education for women in county WIC clinics. *American Journal of Public Health, 80,* 1391–1392.

McKusick, L., Wiley, J. A., Coates, T. J., Stall, R., Saika, G., Morin, S., Charles, K., Horstman, W., & Conant, M. A. (1985). Reported changes in the sexual behavior of men at risk for AIDS, San Francisco, 1982–1984: The AIDS Behavioral Research Project. *Public Health Reports, 100,* 622–629.

Padian, N., Marquis, L., Francis, D. P., Anderson, R. E. Rutherford, G. W., O'Malley, P.

M., & Winkelstein, W. (1987). Male-to-female transmission of human immunodeficiency virus. *Journal of the American Medical Association, 258,* 788-790.
Research and Decisions Corporation. (1986). Designing an effective AIDS risk reduction program for San Francisco: Results from the first probability sample of multiple/high-risk partner heterosexual adults. San Francisco: Author.
Robbins, S., Spence, M., Marks, S., Armstrong, K. A., & Lauver, D. (1990, June). *A description of HIV risk factors among 17,619 women.* Paper presented at the VI International Conference on AIDS, San Francisco, CA.
Rotheram-Borus, M. J., Koopman, C., & Haignere, C. (1990, June). *Reducing HIV sexual risk behaviors among runaway adolescents.* Paper presented at the VI International Conference on AIDS, San Francisco, CA.
Schechter, M. T., Craib, K. J. P., Willoughby, B., Douglas, B., McLeod, W. A., Maynard, M., Constance, P., & O'Shaughnessy, M. (1988). Patterns of sexual behavior and condom use in a cohort of homosexual men. *American Journal of Public Health, 78,* 1535-1538.
Sorensen, J. L., Gibson, D. R., Heitzmann, C., Dumonet, R., & Acampora, A. (1988, August). *AIDS prevention with drug abusers in residential treatment: Preliminary report.* Paper presented at the annual meeting of the American Psychological Association, Atlanta, GA.
Sorensen, J. L., Guydish, J., Costantini, M., & Batki, S. L. (1989). Changes in needle sharing and syringe cleaning among San Francisco drug abusers. *new England Journal of Medicine, 320,* 807.
St. Lawrence, J. S., Hood, H. V., Brasfield, T., & Kelly, J. A. (1989). Differences in gay men's AIDS risk knowledge and behavior patterns in high and low AIDS prevalence cities. *Public Health Reports, 104,* 391-395.
Stall, R., McKusick, L., Wiley, J., Coates, T. J. & Ostrow, D. G. (1986). Alcohol and drug use during sexual activity and compliance with safe sex guidelines for AIDS: The AIDS Behavioral Research Project. *Health Education Quarterly, 13,* 359-371.
Stoneburner, R. L., Chiasson, M. A., Weisfuse, I. B., & Thomas, P. A. (1990). The epidemic of AIDS and HIV-I infection among heterosexuals in New York City. *AIDS, 4,* 99-106.
Strunin, L., & Hingson, R. (1987). Acquired immunodeficiency syndrome and adolescents: Knowledge, beliefs, attitudes and behaviors. *Pediatrics, 79,* 825-828.
Valdiserri, R. O., Lyter, D. W., Leviton, L. C., Callahan, C. M., Kingsley, L. A., & Rinaldo, C. R. (1989). AIDS prevention in homosexual and bisexual men: Results of a randomized trial evaluating two risk reduction interventions. *AIDS, 3,* 21-26.
Van den Hoek, J. A. R., Coutinho, R. A., Van Zadelhoff, A. W., Van Hass Trecht, H. J., & Goudsmit, J. (1987, June). *Prevalence, incidence, and risk factors for HIV infection among drug addicts in Amsterdam.* Paper presented at the IV International Conference on AIDS, Stockholm.
Winkelstein, W., Lyman, D. M., Padian, N., Grant, R., Samuel, M., Wiley, J. A., Anderson, R. E., Long, W., Riggs, J., Levy, J. A. (1987). Sexual practices and risk of infection by the human immunodeficiency virus: The San Francisco Men's Health Study. *Journal of the American Medical Association, 257,* 321-325.

CHAPTER 8

Increasing Road Safety Behaviors
E. Scott Geller

DESCRIPTION OF THE PROBLEM

Unintentional injury kills about 140,000 Americans per year and costs our country more than $100 billion annually (Graham, 1988). Of these injury deaths, motor vehicle crashes are responsible for approximately 46,000 per year, at a cost of $69.5 billion (National Highway Traffic Safety Administration, 1985). Although the highway fatality rate in 1990 reached a historic low of 2.1 deaths per 100 million miles of travel, that year there still were more than 44,000 fatalities and 400,000 serious injuries from vehicle crashes (Curry, 1991).

Two basic intervention approaches have been applied in an attempt to reduce the number of fatal and nonfatal injuries caused by vehicle collisions: engineering (or high-technology strategies) and behavior change (or low-technology strategies). Typically, the engineering approach changes the driving environment (e.g., vehicles, roads, traffic signals) to prevent crashes (e.g., antilock brakes, improved steering systems, increased road traction) or to reduce the severity of an injury in the event of a collision (e.g., airbags, impact-absorbing chasses, collapsible steering wheels, shatter-proof windshields). The behavior change approach targets a particular driving behavior that can either prevent a vehicle crash (e.g., maintaining a safe driving speed or vehicle following distance, eliminating drinking before driving) or reduce the probability of injury or death following a vehicle crash (e.g., increasing the use of vehicle safety belts and child safety seats). By far the most popular approach to changing target behaviors relevant to road safety has been the passage and enforcement of laws (e.g., to control vehicle speeds, increase safety belt use, and reduce alcohol-impaired driving). The legal approach is also used to maintain and increase vehicle safety standards (e.g., by requiring automobile manufacturers to install safety devices or requiring vehicles to meet certain safety standards at regular vehicle inspections).

Besides laws and police enforcement, education procedures (e.g., through driver training courses, public service announcements, community posters, flyers, or pamphlets) represent the other traditional procedure to improve behavior related to road safety. The general impression in the traffic safety community, based on empirical studies, is that educational efforts to improve driver behavior are ineffective, whether implemented as high school driver education (Conger, Miller, & Rainey, 1966; Lund, Williams, & Zador, 1986), applied in employee safety programs (Geller, 1982; Phillips, 1980), broadcasted on home television (Robertson, 1976; Robertson et al., 1974), or disseminated throughout an entire community in varied formats (Cunliffe et al., 1975). In fact, many traffic safety professionals (backed by much of the insurance industry and large-scale group statistics) are convinced that driver education in high school actually adds to traffic casualties, primarily because it puts teenagers behind the wheel sooner (O'Neill, 1990).

Thus, the history of failures to improve driving behavior through education and standard communication techniques has resulted in increased emphasis on attempts to automate safety (e.g., through environmental engineering); and when behavior change is necessary, safety professionals (from government officials to local traffic engineers and police officers) rely on the implementation of "quick-fix" legal mandates. Indeed, this author's 15 years of experience with research grant and contract agencies at the federal and state levels (e.g., the U.S. Department of Transportation, the National Highway Traffic Safety Administration, the Virginia Department of Transportation, the Centers for Disease Control) has shown a steady decline in appreciation for behavioral science approaches to improving road safety (see also Strategic Transportation Research Study Committee, 1990). Most, if not all, of the limited funds for researching the human element in traffic injuries and fatalities have recently focused on finding ways to increase compliance with traffic safety laws, in addition to standard support for categorizing traffic injuries and fatalities according to specific demographic, behavioral, and environmental factors (Roberts, 1987). This latter epidemiological research is typically done to define areas for increasing road safety through environmental engineering or legislation rather than providing behavioral scientists with target behaviors and information relevant to maximizing intervention impact (e.g., by matching behavior change techniques with characteristics of target populations or environments (Geller, 1989a; Winett, Altman, & King, 1990).

This chapter illustrates the behavioral science approach to improving road safety and, in the process, reviews a number of behavior change techniques that can be used to increase the impact of standard legal and educational approaches to preventing or reducing injuries from vehicles crashes. In the 1980s, substantial research was accomplished in the domain of safety belt promotion (see reviews by Geller, 1988, 1989b, 1992a; Thyer & Geller, 1990), and effective intervention strategies resulting from this research (as reviewed here) can be adapted to other domains of community health promotion. Applications of behavioral science to reduce alcohol-impaired driving have not been nearly as effective as the safety-belt research (see reviews by Geller, 1990a, 1992a; Geller, Elder, Hovell, & Sleet, 1991; Geller & Lehman, 1989), partly because the behaviors in this problem domain are much more complex. However, reviewing some of the behavior analysis research in this aspect of traffic safety illustrates an approach and preliminary findings with substantial promise in helping to alleviate a most serious societal problem.

REVIEW AND CRITIQUE OF THE LITERATURE

As mentioned earlier, it appears the human behavior aspect of road safety has been receiving relatively little research attention, especially compared with engineering technology (see also Geller, 1992a; Parsons, 1992). However, much engineering technology for road safety can only be effective with concomitant changes in human behavior. For example, the vehicle airbag is only maximally effective if the vehicle occupant is also buckled up; this ensures the occupant is behind the air cushion when it deploys. In fact, drivers who stop using their lap/shoulder belt because they have an airbag increase their risk of fatality by 41% (Evans, 1991). Similarly, the automatic shoulder belts found in several contemporary vehicles manufactured since 1989 are only optimally protective if the manual lap belt is also worn. Yet, field observations have suggested that some vehicle occupants have stopped using their manual lap belts when they became automatically protected with a shoulder belt (Williams, Wells, Lund, & Teed, 1989).

When designing the 1991 Saturn, General Motors (GM) engineers considered the problems of lowered lap-belt use with high-technology shoulder-belt systems. Specifically, they consulted behavioral science research that studied drivers' safety-belt use behaviors regarding the standard buzzer-light reminder system (Berry & Geller, 1991; Geller, Casali, & Johnson, 1980; von Buseck & Geller, 1984), and they installed an innovative buzzer-light reminder system to encourage use of the manual lap belts in the 1991 Saturn. Specifically, on starting the Saturn, a lap-belt icon begins to flash for 6 seconds, and if the driver does not buckle the lap belt within 6 seconds after starting the vehicle, the icon stops flashing, and a 6-second tone sounds. The lap-belt icon remains lit until the driver's lap belt is buckled. Because the average front-seat occupant takes 4 to 5 seconds to buckle a combination lap and should belt (von Buseck & Geller, 1984), occupants can easily avoid the reminder tone by buckling their lap belts before or immediately after starting the Saturn. In all other vehicles, drivers who buckle up after starting their vehicle cannot avoid the 4 to 8 second "reminder buzzer," which begins as soon as the ignition key is turned on. Thus, through collaboration between engineers and behavioral scientists, an engineering device that has been quite ineffective at prompting safety-belt use (Geller et al., 1980; Robertson, 1975) was perhaps made more effective at increasing an injury-preventive behavior. Of course, behavioral studies are now needed to determine whether this engineering innovation based on behavioral principles and research is, in fact, cost effective.

Designing Behavior Change Interventions to Improve Road Safety

The basic three-term contingency, activator-behavior-consequence framework, or ABC model, defines the basic behavior analysis approach to intervention development. In other words, conditions or events preceding (i.e., activators) or following (e.g., consequences) designated target behaviors are arranged systematically to increase or decrease the target behavior's frequency of occurrence.

The behavior analysis and intervention process is readily remembered by the acronym "DO RITE," which represents the sequence of (1) define the target behavior to be changed; (2) observe the target behavior; (3) record occurrences of the target behavior; (4) intervene with a program to change the target behavior; (5) test the impact of the behavior change intervention by comparing records of behavior before and after the intervention; and (6) evaluate whether the program was cost-effective, whether a more potent intervention program is needed, whether the program should be implemented on a larger scale, or whether it is advisable to start the DO RITE process all over again (Geller, Lehman, & Kalsher, 1989). To do this process right for road safety is not as straightforward as it seems, as is realized by considering only the first step of DO RITE—defining a target behavior to change.

Defining Target Behaviors for Road Safety Intervention

As indicated earlier, the use of the shoulder and lap belt is the single most protective behavior that can be conveniently taken to reduce the risk of death or injury in a vehicle crash. It has been estimated, in fact, that 55% of all fatalities and 65% of all injuries from vehicle crashes would be prevented if combination lap and shoulder belts were used (Federal Register, 1984); yet large-scale observational surveys by the National Traffic Safety Administration indicate that safety-belt use is only 50% in states with safety-belt use laws and 33% in states without safety-belt use laws (R. M. Schweitz, personal communication, January 17, 1990). It has been estimated that a mere 10% increase in vehicle safety belt use would prevent as many as 30,000 injuries and save 1,500 lives and $800 million in direct costs (Sleet, 1987). Consequently, the rationale for selecting safety belt use as a prime target behavior to increase with behavioral technology is clear. Not only is the buckle-up response a priority from a practical injury-control perspective, it is also optimal from a DO RITE perspective. Vehicle safety-belt use is readily observable in naturalistic settings, making intervention studies practical. By recording license-plate numbers, individual drivers can be tracked over repeated occasions, thus enabling single-subject studies of a community health behavior (Geller, 1983; Ludwig & Geller, 1991). Moreover, because using a vehicle safety belt requires minimal response cost (i.e., safety belts are convenient to use and comfortable when used) and because buckling up readily becomes a habit for some individuals, a behavior change intervention to increase safety-belt use is apt to be successful, even over the long term, thereby reinforcing and increasing research and application in this domain of road safety.

Some behaviors that reduce the risk of personal injury from a vehicle crash require only a one-time behavior change (e.g., purchasing a larger vehicle or a vehicle with particular safety features), but most behaviors for risk reduction on the road require repetitive action (e.g., safety-belt use, speed reduction, turn-signal use, and avoidance of alcohol consumption before driving). For the "one-time" behaviors, the user usually pays a one-time, relatively high monetary cost for the subsequent convenience of not having to make continued response input. It is important to emphasize, however, that the purchase of a vehicle safety device does not obviate the need for repetitive safe-driving behaviors, even though safety promotion campaigns have often treated engineering innovations independently from human behaviors, thereby implying that engineering technology (e.g., airbags) substitutes for certain safe behaviors (e.g., safety-belt use).

Recently, a research team at the University of Michigan Transportation Research Institute systematically examined police crash reports from 11 states to determine those behavioral factors most frequently reported by police to have caused the vehicle collisions (Streff, 1991; Streff, Schultz, & Molnar, 1990). The eventual data set documented 1,868,142 crashes, involving a total of 3,421,258 motor vehicles and resulting in all levels of injury severity (from only property damage to a fatality). This data set was the largest and most comprehensive ever examined for driving behaviors related to crashes. For 55.7% of the vehicles, the police had identified specific driving behaviors as contributing to the crash, and in more than 79% of these cases only one crash-related behavior was reported. The behaviors included in this data set, and the percentage of collisions caused by each behavior in those crashes where only one unsafe behavior had been designated as contributing, were as follows: failure to yield (19.3%), speeding (16.9%), following too closely (10.3%), driver inattention (6.6%), traffic signal disregarded (5.0%), alcohol/drugs (3.2%), improper turn (3.0%), failure to control vehicle (2.8%), improper backing (2.2%), improper passing (1.6%), improper lane use (1.6%), improper lane change (1.5%), driving left of center (1.2%), improper lookout (0.5%), wrong way (0.2%), and improper signal (0.2%).

An obvious weakness in the Streff et al. data set is that it relied completely on police reports of unsafe driving behaviors inferred from physical evidence and interviews at the crash site rather than direct observation by the police officer. Thus, in addition to identifying priority behaviors to address in behavior change interventions (i.e., failure to yield, speeding, and following too closely accounted for 46.5% of the total), this research pointed out significant directions for behavioral science involvement in the road safety domain. For example, behavioral scientists could work directly with police officers in completing crash reports and determining human behavior factors. Behavioral scientists could also teach police officers to define, observe, and record crash-related behaviors more precisely and objectively, thus contributing to defining more reliably the priorities for behavior change intervention. This could result in objective measurement of the prevalence of unsafe driving behaviors during normal driving, leading to a determination of the relative riskiness of various unsafe behaviors (i.e., the proportion of crashes per occurrence of unsafe driving in the general population). In other words, if the relative frequencies of the unsafe behaviors listed previously vary substantially among the driving public, such that a significantly higher proportion of a low-ranking behavior (e.g., alcohol use or improper lane change) results in a vehicle crash than a higher ranking behavior (e.g., speeding), it would be inappropriate to determine behavior change priorities from the hierarchy defined by Streff et al. and given earlier. In addition, the combination of more than one unsafe driving behavior requires careful study. The frequently cited estimate, for example, that alcohol contributes to 50% to 55% of fatal vehicle accidents and 18% to 25% of injury-producing crashes (Fell, 1982) suggests that several of the unsafe behaviors listed previously occurred concomitantly with alcohol impairment.

Collaboration between police officers and behavioral scientists regarding the identification of unsafe driving behaviors could also provide information useful for the development and implementation of crash-avoidance interventions. For example, if certain unsafe driving behaviors are found to covary, then interventions to reduce the frequency of one unsafe behavior could have beneficial effects on other unsafe behaviors. For example, Fricker and Larsen (1990) observed a positive correlation between the use of safety belts and turn signals before and after the enforcement of Indiana's mandatory belt use law (BUL), and Ludwig and Geller (1991) found a significant increase in pizza deliverers' use of turn signals after implementing a successful behavior change intervention that targeted only safety-belt use.

Activators for Road Safety

Activators (often referred to as stimulus control, prompting, response priming, or antecedent techniques) are environmental manipulations occurring before the target behavior in an attempt to increase the frequency of desired target behaviors or decrease occurrences of undesired target responses. Activators for road safety can take several forms, and, in fact, Geller et al. (1990) identified 18 different activator strategies used in the road safety field. These were categorized as (a) passive communication/education (i.e., lecture, demonstration, and policy); (b) active communication/education (i.e., commitment, consensus building, and becoming an intervention agent); (c) individual activators (i.e., written and oral messages, assigned and personal goals, competition, individual incentives and disincentives); and (d) group activators (i.e., group or team goals, competition, group incentives and disincentives). Comprehensive reviews of this research are available (e.g., Geller, 1984, 1988, 1990a, 1992a) and most of the activator formats defined by Geller et al. (1990) have not been adequately researched. The following review highlights only those behavior change strategies that have been evaluated objectively with regard to improving road safety; most of these targeted safety-belt use but are applicable to many of the behaviors discussed in the preceding section.

Policy

A policy is a written document defining (or mandating) the standards, norms, or rules for appropriate behavior within a particular environmental context. Safety-belt use has increased substantially in virtually every state of the United States that has passed a BUL. During the last 6 months of 1985, for example, observations of front-seat occupants in 17 states without a BUL revealed 21.6% using safety belts (Zeigler, 1986), whereas means post-BUL belt use across states with BULs was 48% in 1986 (Campbell, Stewart, & Campbell, 1987) and 47% in 1987 (Campbell, Stewart, & Campbell, 1988). It is generally believed that those drivers most apt to comply with speed limits and traffic laws are the first to comply with a BUL; therefore, the most prominent decreases in injuries from vehicle crashes won't occur until risky drivers buckle up (Campbell et al., 1987). In other words, "those segments of the driving population who are least likely to comply with safe driving laws are precisely those groups that are at highest risk of serious injury" (Waller, 1987, p. 43). This presumed direct relationship between risky behavior and noncompliance with behavior change policy has empirical support in that young males (Preusser, Williams, & Lund, 1985), persons with elevated blood alcohol consumption (Wagenaar, 1984), and drivers with shorter headway distances between their vehicles and the vehicles they are following (Evans, Wasielewski, & von Buseck, 1982) were least likely to comply with a BUL.

Those actively caring about reducing DUI (driving under the influence of alcohol) have relied almost exclusively on policy or legal intervention. Stricter penalties for DUI, liability legislation for servers of alcoholic beverages, and increased enforcement of DUI legislation (including police roadblocks for DUI checks) have been on the increase throughout the United States during the past decade. In addition, 41 states have increased the minimum legal drinking age to 21 (Steed, 1988). Unfortunately, the deterrence effects of stricter DUI laws and increased enforcement have been mild and transitory, primarily because of the low probability of punishment—about one DUI per 5,000 miles of alcohol-impaired driving (Ross, 1987). Raising the legal drinking age has reduced significantly the vehicle-crash injuries and fatalities in the affected age group (Wagenaar, 1983), but this impact is minuscule when considering the overall DUI problem (Ross, 1982, 1985; Russ & Geller, 1985).

Education

As discussed earlier in this chapter, traditional education strategies have been insufficient in changing driving behaviors. However, adding certain behavior change strategies to the education format (i.e., consensus-building discussion and involvement exercises) has resulted in substantial increases in vehicle safety-belt use. Geller and Hahn (1984), for example, implemented a 20-minute educational program in a corporate setting that tripled safety-belt use among blue-collar workers. Following a 3-minute film, the author led an informal group discussion about the value of safety belts and factors that inhibit people from buckling up. It is likely that the success of this educational program was due to the active involvement of the workers in the group discussion (i.e., a consensus-building exercise). A similar interactive educational approach to promoting safety-belt use was successful with different discussion leaders at two large North Carolina industries—at Burroughs Wellcome in Greenville (Cope, Grossnickle, & Geller, 1986) and at the Reeves Brothers Curon Plant in Cornelius (Kello, Geller, Rice, & Bryant, 1988).

Geller (1989b) and Lehman and Geller (1990a, 1990b) applied a participatory education approach in school and recreation settings for children (from ages 4 to 10) and found prominent increases in children's safety-belt use as a result. We also observed significant increases in parents' safety-belt use after their children received the participatory education (Lehman & Geller, 1990a, 1990b). Consequently, this research has supported earlier research by Lewin (1958), which can be summarized by the instructive phrase, "Tell them, and they'll forget; demonstrate, and they'll remember; involve them, and they'll understand!"

Teaching the servers of alcoholic beverages techniques for reducing the risk of DUI is a promising approach to road safety if effective education procedures are applied, and if the ongoing contingencies in the drinking environment (e.g., the tavern or bar) support the server intervention techniques taught during the training. The concept of "server intervention training" developed as a result of "Dram Shop" laws that hold tavern owners liable if they serve alcohol to an intoxicated patron who is later involved in an injury-producing crash (Mosher, 1979). Thus, many bar owners have been motivated to provide server intervention training to their wait personnel, and over the last few years several different agencies in the private and public sectors have been providing server intervention training throughout the United States. In the state of Oregon, server intervention training for wait personnel is required for an establishment to obtain a liquor license.

Most server intervention training programs teach trainees to identify the specific warning signs of alcohol impairment. They also teach servers how to use a variety of impairment-reduction tactics including offering food, delaying alcohol drink service, serving nonalcoholic beverages, and suggesting that the patron not drive. Some programs include the use of video vignettes and role playing to help servers evaluate customers' behaviors and to practice intervention skills. More recently, increased attention has been given to changing management and serving policies, as well as the bar environment, to be consistent with the server intervention strategies (Saltz, 1989).

A few field studies have evaluated the overall impact of server intervention training (Geller, Russ, & Delphos, 1987; McKnight, 1987; Russ & Geller, 1987; Saltz, 1986), but no published studies have conducted a component analysis of server intervention programs nor compared two or more approaches to server intervention. Although each of the evaluation studies supported the potential of server intervention training as a practical and cost-effective approach to reduce DUI risk, the results were equivocal because of indirect (nonbehavioral) dependent variables (McKnight, 1987; Saltz, 1986), nonconvincing behavioral data (McKnight, 1987), or a small-scale intervention and short-term evaluation period (Geller et al., 1987; Russ & Geller, 1987). However, the health and road safety potential of this approach is clear, as well as the need for additional research and development. Not only are comparison evaluations of different intervention training programs needed, but behavior change techniques (many like those described in this chapter) must be added to server intervention programs to motivate servers to practice the intervention procedures they learn. These could include the application of on-the-job reminders, performance feedback, commitment and goal setting, incentives/rewards, and implementation of techniques for encouraging peer support and teamwork among employees.

Reminder Strategies

The beneficial effects of education can be extended over the long term by implementing oral or written activators to remind trainees or learners of the behavioral responsibilities specified (or implied) by the educational program. Simple response-specific messages, for example, have been effective in increasing safety-belt use including a dashboard sticker with the message "Safety Belt Use Required in This Vehicle" (Rogers, 1984; Thyer & Geller, 1987) and a large flash card with the message "Please Buckle-Up—I Care." The flash card increased safety-belt use of observers when the message was displayed by the occupant of one vehicle to an occupant of another vehicle (Geller, Bruff, & Nimmer, 1985), when the flash card was held by an individual at the entrance/exit of a parking lot (Thyer, Geller, Williams, & Purcell, 1987), and when groups of young children held up flash cards to their parents as they were arriving to pick them up at a summer recreation center (Geller, 1989b). It is noteworthy that the effective behavior change messages in these studies requested a specific, convenient-to-emit response, and made the request at the time and place for the response to occur (as in point-of-purchase advertising, Tillman & Kirkpatrick, 1972). As applied by Geller et al., (1985), the flash-card reminder also included modeling of the desired behavior by the "flasher."

In a recent field study, Nocks and Howell (1993) manipulated the presence versus absence of the dashboard buckle-up sticker with compliance versus noncompliance by the vehicle driver, and found a provocative interaction. Specifically, passenger safety-belt use was highest when the driver buckled up and the reminder was present (100%) and was lowest when the driver did not buckle up and the reminder was present (43%). This finding has broad implications in the realm of safety and health promotion, suggesting that when corporate or community leaders (e.g., supervisors, police officers, or teachers) do not comply with posted safety or health rules, they are influencing others to disregard the health or safety message.

Commitment and Goal Setting

An evaluation program can also be supported by requests of oral or written statements from learners or trainees that they will perform certain target behaviors. Geller and Lehman (1991), for example, developed and evaluated a "buckle-up promise" technique for safety-belt promotion. Target individuals were simply asked to sign a statement specifying personal commitment to buckle up for a designated period. Buckle-up promise cards have been distributed after a lecture or group discussion at industrial sites (Cope, Grossnickle, & Geller, 1986; Geller & Bigelow, 1984; Kello et al., 1988), during church services (Talton, 1984), and throughout a large university campus (Geller, Kalsher, Rudd, & Lehman, 1989) and naval base (Kalsher, Geller, Clarke, & Lehman, 1989). In every case, many pledge-card signers increased their use of safety belts following their "commitment" behavior.

Environmental Factors

Safety-Belt Reminder Systems

As discussed earlier, engineering and design interventions have been invaluable in improving road safety by making the driving environment more protective or easier to use safely. Modifications in the environment can also facilitate (or encourage) the occurrence of safe driving behaviors. The safety-belt reminder system, discussed earlier, is an example of an engineering device to activate safety-belt use. Over the years, a variety of buzzer-light reminder systems have been included in motor vehicles. Most intrusive was the buzzer that continued to sound until front-seat belts were buckled. Another intrusive environmental manipulation to encourage safety-belt use was the "ignition interlock system" in 1974 vehicles that required front-seat belts to be buckled before a vehicle could be started. Most vehicle owners undermined the unlimited buzzer and ignition interlock systems by disconnecting them or sitting on a buckled belt (Geller, Casali, & Johnson, 1980; Robertson, 1975). Hence, these intrusive engineering activators lasted only 1 year.

Buzzer-light reminders in contemporary vehicles consist of only a panel light and a buzzer or chime that initiates when the ignition key is turned on if the driver is unbuckled and terminates in 4 to 8 seconds. As discussed earlier, drivers who start their vehicles before buckling up cannot avoid the reminder tone. However, the reminder tone is barely noticed anyway, given that it is not very loud and initiates simultaneously with several other sounds (e.g., the "roar" of the engine, the fan for the heater or air conditioner, and perhaps the radio). For these reasons, and our observations that 50% of 1,492 drivers buckled up after starting their vehicles (von Buseck & Geller, 1984), the author recommended to engineers at the GM Research Laboratories that the safety-belt reminder be delayed several seconds after the ignition key was turned. This would enable the negative reinforcement of safety-belt use (i.e., the reminder tone could be avoided by the buckle-up response). In addition, the delayed buzzer would be more readily noticed, because its initiation would not be masked by the initiation of other vehicle sounds. As discussed earlier, this behavioral science rationale, along with the results of field research including the study of various reminder systems in an experimental vehicle (Berry & Geller, 1991), lead to the innovative safety-belt reminder system in the 1991 Saturn.

Drinking Environment

The environmental context where alcohol consumption occurs can determine whether or not alcohol consumption results in DUI risk. Geller, Russ, and Altomari (1986), for example, offered convincing evidence from their bar observations of 243 college students that the sale of beer in pitchers could contribute to excessive beer consumption and subsequent risk for DUI. Although the most beer was consumed per person when it was ordered in a pitcher (i.e., mean per capita beer consumption was 35.2 ounces from pitchers, 15.1 ounces from bottles, and 10.0 ounces from cups), the rate of drinking did not vary significantly as a function of drink container, because those who ordered their beer in a pitcher stayed in the bar significantly longer (mean of 66 minutes) than those ordering beer in a bottle (mean of 34 minutes) or a cup (mean of 23 minutes).

In a series of naturalistic observation studies of alcohol consumption at university parties, the author and his colleagues found several intriguing environment-behavior relationships that have direct relevance for DUI prevention. In two studies (Kalsher & Geller, 1991; Russ & Geller, 1988), we found dramatic effects of the labels placed on beer kegs. Specifically, students' beer consumption matched the results of their taste preference tests only when the beer kegs were unlabeled. When beer kegs were labeled according to the three types of beer available (i.e., regular, light, and low-alcohol beer), the beer drinkers rarely chose the low-alcohol beer, suggesting a desire to get drunk. Only with unlabeled kegs was the low-alcohol beer consumed in large quantity. Interestingly, when the kegs were labeled according to brand, the light beer was preferred over the regular beer by both males and females, suggesting that the light beer was perceived as having fewer calories and not less alcohol.

Geller and Kalsher (1990) demonstrated intriguing effects of the method used to dispense alcoholic beverages at a party. In this study, 94 males and 84 females at a fraternity party chose to drink beer or mixed drinks throughout the evening, and were assigned randomly to one of two available serving modalities—bartender or self-serve. Our analysis of drink type and quantity per serving mode revealed that partiers (especially males) consumed significantly more beer from the self-serve station than from the bar; however, those who chose mixed drinks (especially males) obtained more beverages from the bar than from the self-serve table. We interpreted these results with straightforward response-cost notions, presuming that partiers drank more beer when they could serve themselves, because pouring beer from a pitcher to a mug is faster and more convenient than requesting and receiving a beer from a bartender. Conversely, preparing a mixed drink requires some knowledge and inconvenience, and therefore the bartender decreased this response cost and increased the consumption of mixed drinks.

The degree of blood alcohol concentration (BAC) measured in students when they exited parties varied considerably across the various fraternity parties studied by Geller and his colleagues; and examining environmental differences across the parties suggested that certain environmental factors contributed to excessive alcohol consumption and DUI risk. Most obvious was the finding that the party (studied by Geller & Kalsher, 1990) with the highest BAC per partier (i.e., mean exit BAC was .115% for males and .077% for females) was substantially more crowded than the other parties. The amount of floor space (i.e., space for dancing and drink acquisition) was about 5.6 square feet per person at this party (mean BAC=.097) compared with 10.1 square feet per person (mean BAC = .069) at the two parties studied by Kalsher and Geller (1991), 17.8 square feet per person (mean BAC = .045) for Experiment 1 in Geller, Kalsher, and Clarke (1991), and 21.3 square feet per person (mean BAC=.052) for Experiment 2 in Geller et al. (1991). In fact, the acquisition of alcoholic beverages appeared more inconvenient at the crowded party where exit BAC was highest. At the crowded party, there was also minimal space to dance (on a 12 feet × 16 feet dance area) compared with the other parties with much larger dance floors (i.e., 20 × 20 feet for Kalsher and Geller (1991) and 20 × 30 feet for Geller et al. (1991). In addition, dancing was promoted to a greater degree at the parties with less alcohol impairment, because only those parties employed a professional disc jockey to play music and announce "dance contests." Furthermore, the sound quality of the dance music was clearly the worst at the party with highest BACs.

Another environmental factor that may have contributed to differential alcohol consumption across the parties we studied was the attire of the partiers. The attire at the party with the highest exit BACs was the most informal, with casual dress (mostly jeans, shirts/blouses) being the norm. In fact, no male at this party wore a tie, and very few females wore a dress or skirt. In contrast, at the parties studied by Kalsher and Geller (1991) the students wore semiformal clothes (i.e., the men wore slacks, and sweater or tie, and women wore dresses or blouses and skirts); and the party-goers studied by Geller et al. (1991) wore costumes according to a particular theme (i.e., "western" and "20,000 leagues under the sea"). Additional research is certainly warranted to determine more systematically the degree to which certain milieu factors (e.g., spatial density, music quality, dancing frequency, attire) contribute to drinking rates and alcohol impairment in bars and party settings.

Incentives and Disincentives

An incentive is an announcement to an individual or group, in written or oral form, of the availability of a reward (i.e., a pleasant consequence) contingent on the occurrence of a certain behavior or an outcome of one or more behaviors. In contrast, a disincentive is an activator announcing the possibility of receiving a penalty (i.e., an unpleasant consequence) contingent on the occurrence of a particular undesirable behavior. Research has shown quite clearly that the impact of a legal mandate (e.g., a safety-belt use or DUI law) varies directly with the amount of media promotion of disincentive (cf. Ross, 1982). Similarly, the success of a reward program depends on making the target population aware of the possible rewards for emitting a certain behavior or meeting a certain outcome contingency (Geller et al., 1990).

Drink promotions, such as "happy hour," "ladies night," and Monday Night Football," are incentive programs that increase alcohol consumption and DUI risk. Babor, Mendelson, Uhly, and Souza (1980) studied the impact of reduced drink prices on individual drinking patterns by monitoring the same persons as they drank in experimental and natural settings. In each setting, reduced prices during a "happy hour" increased significantly the frequency of drinking episodes and amount of alcohol consumed among both casual and heavy drinkers. Such findings, as well as negative public reaction to high drinking/driving mortality rates, have led Boston and other cities, as well as 16 states, to ban special drink prices and similar promotions (Waller, 1986).

Consequences for Road Safety

Geller et al. (1990) defined six different consequence techniques for improving road safety by considering that feedback, reward, and penalty consequences can be given to an individual (e.g., individual feedback) or a group (e.g., group feedback). Rewards include pleasing items or events as well as opportunities to escape or avoid unpleasant items or events. In contrast, a penalty can be the presentation of an unpleasant item or event (e.g., a jail term or requirement to do community service) or the removal of a pleasant item or privilege (e.g., money or a driver's license).

During the past decade, several different types of reward programs have been implemented in an attempt to increase the use of vehicle safety belts and child safety seats. This is partly because the use of these safety devices is readily observable in the community; and individuals can be rewarded on the spot for using these safety behaviors, or the vehicle license-plate numbers can be recorded for later delivery of a reward. Indeed, it is likely that more reward programs have been applied to this aspect of road safety than to any other community-based behavior.

Direct and Immediate Rewards

As reviewed by Geller (1984), "on-the-spot" consequences for safety-belt promotion programs have usually been inexpensive and have varied widely (e.g., flowers, candy, balloons, trinkets, lottery tickets, coupons exchangeable for money or food). It has been particularly worthwhile to solicit donations for prizes from community businesses. This has reduced program expense while involving the local community in a worthwhile safety effort. Most community merchants appreciated the goodwill advertising available for their support of a local safety-belt program. Direct rewards for safety-belt use have at least doubled the baseline percentage of those buckled up in target vehicles, whether implemented at industrial sites (Geller, 1983; Geller, Davis, & Spicer, 1983; Spoonhour, 1981; Stutts, Hunter, & Campbell, 1984), shopping malls (Elman & Killebrew, 1978), bank exchange windows (Geller, Johnson, & Pelton, 1982), high schools (Campbell, Hunter, & Stutts, 1984), or universities (Geller, Paterson, & Talbott, 1982). Although belt use dropped substantially after removal of every incentive/reward program, in most cases the postintervention follow-up percentages of belt use remained significantly higher than the preintervention baseline levels.

None of the direct and immediate reward programs cited previously targeted young children, a critical age group for developing a "buckle-up" habit. Roberts and his colleagues applied direct and immediate rewards successfully to protect children in vehicles by (a) rewarding parents with lottery tickets redeemable for prizes if their children (ages 0.5–6 years) were buckled up appropriately when arriving at day care centers (Roberts & Turner, 1986); (b) rewarding preschool children with colorful stickers when they were buckled up appropriately in child safety seats on arriving at day care centers (Roberts & Layfield, 1987); and (c) teaching PTA volunteers to reward elementary school children with lapel stickers, lottery tickets for pizzas, bumper stickers, and coloring books if all vehicle occupants were buckled up when arriving at school (Roberts & Fanurick, 1986; Roberts, Fanurick, & Wilson, 1988). In all of these child-directed studies, the use of safety belts or child safety seats increased dramatically, from baseline buckle-up averages as low as 5% (Roberts & Fanurick, 1986) and 11% (Roberts & Turner, 1986) to usage levels of 70% and 64%, respectively. When these rewards were withdrawn, safety-belt use declined prominently but remained higher than the initial baseline levels, as with the reward programs that targeted adults.

Direct and Delayed Rewards

Because vehicles cannot always be stopped conveniently and safely, rewards for safety-belt use must sometimes be delayed. For delayed reward programs, shoulder-belt use was observed as vehicles entered or existed the program site; and without stopping the vehicles, the license plate numbers of vehicles were recorded for a subsequent prize drawing. Winning license plates numbers were publicly posted, and the owners of the identified vehicles claimed prizes at announced locations.

This procedure was applied on a large university campus with 21,000 registered vehicles by having the university police record license numbers for weekly raffles (Rudd & Geller, 1985). Kalsher et al. (1989) adapted this delayed-reward strategy for the Norfolk Navy Base (with approximately 75,000 vehicles entering the base each day) by using the navy base police to collect license plate numbers for weekly prize lotteries. Even though 22 officers recorded a total of 6,859 entries for the 9 intervention weeks of the campus program, and 20 officers recorded more than 16,000 raffle entries during the 4-week navy base program, none of the officers reported disruption in their daily duties. This suggests that a police-administered, delayed-reward program for safety belt promotion is feasible for community-wide or even statewide application. It is likely that such a program would make the enforcement of a state BUL more palatable for both the public and the police and would thus increase the use of vehicle safety belts beyond levels attained with BULs alone.

Indirect Rewards

Some reward programs have combined the "buckle-up promise card" strategy described earlier (Geller & Lehman, 1991) with rewarding consequences (Geller et al., 1989; Horne & Terry, 1983; Nimmer & Geller, 1988). The author has labeled this an "indirect reward" technique (Geller, 1984) because rewards were not given directly for individual safety-belt use; rather individuals signed buckle-up promise cards to enter a raffle drawing. Hence, the behavior of making an explicit commitment to buckle up was rewarded. For example, because it was impossible to develop an equitable system for choosing winners among the 6,000 potential safety-belt users entering or exiting the six gates across two work shifts at the GM Technical Center in Warren, Michigan, an indirect-reward strategy was applied. That is, all employees were given a chance to enter the GM "Seatbelt Sweepstakes" if they signed buckle-up promise cards committing them to use vehicular safety belts for 1 year. This program increased safety-belt use from 36% mean belt use during baseline to an average belt-use percentage of 60% 2 years after the program was terminated (Horne, 1984).

Group Rewards

In addition to the individual promise-card contingency, the GM "Seatbelt Sweepstakes" included a group reward contingency. The entire work force of 6,000 employees had to reach a certain percentage of safety-belt use (i.e., the group goal) before each of three successive prize drawings was held in which a new automobile was the first prize. Employees reported incidents of peer pressure to buckle up to achieve each goal, and the successively increasing belt-use goals per raffle of 55%, 65%, and 70% were reached.

Another group-based reward contingency was implemented by Geller and Hahn (1984) to increase the impact of their corporate-based safety-belt program. For this direct and delayed reward program, a single cash prize was raffled off each week from the pool of license-plate numbers collected from daily observations of safety-belt use. The amount of the cash reward for weekly raffle was determined by the average percentage of safety-belt use by the work group during the preceding week (i.e., the cash prize amounted to $1 per percentage point). A feedback chart displayed the mean safety-belt use daily and reminded workers of their group-based reward contingency. This public posting of daily group progress probably had motivating properties of its own, as found in a variety of community-based feedback programs for motivating behavior change (Geller, Winett, & Everett, 1982).

Feedback

Feedback is essentially the presentation of either oral or written information to an individual or a group concerning performance levels related to particular desired or undesired behavior. Road safety researchers have demonstrated beneficial behavior change effects of posting information that displayed performance levels of the community of vehicle drivers. For example, Van Houten and his colleagues (e.g., Van Houten & Nau, 1983; Van Houten, Nau, & Marini, 1980) found that community signs posting the daily percentage of drivers exceeding the speed limit increased the percentage of drivers who subsequently complied with the speed limit. Ragnarsson and Bjorgvinsson (1991) replicated this feedback effect in a residential area in Iceland, showing feedback signs to reduce significantly both mean vehicle speed (from 42.9 mph to 39.4 mph) and the percentage of drivers exceeding the posted speed limit (from 41.0%–20.5%). Furthermore, Jonah (1989) reported significant increases in safety-belt use following the posting of roadway feedback signs that displayed the "percentage of drivers wearing seat belts yesterday."

Because drinkers may often be unaware of the degree of their alcohol impairment, personal feedback about one's BAC may reduce the probability of DUI (e.g., Geller, Altomari, & Russ, 1984; Geller & Lehman, 1988; Geller & Russ, 1986). Feedback regarding a drinker's level of alcohol impairment can be furnished imprecisely in the natural environment in the form of (a) a breath alcohol test that can be self-administered, (b) a chart estimating BAC from one's body weight and rate of alcohol consumption, and (c) performance on a "field sobriety test."

Measurements of BAC are readily obtainable with portable and inexpensive breath analyzers. These BAC meters have been made available in some drinking establishments for providing immediate, individualized BAC feedback to guide individuals in their drinking/driving decisions. Unfortunately, research assessing the utility of BAC meters has not been entirely favorable (see review by Russ, Geller, & Leland, 1989). For example, Oates (1976) found that bar patrons who received BAC feedback were no more likely to use the available public transportation services (i.e., bus or taxi) than were nonparticipants. Calvert-Boyanowsky and Boyanowsky (1980) placed BAC monitors in several bars in British Columbia and concluded that although breath testing was popular, knowledge of BAC did not deter most alcohol-impaired subjects from driving.

Drinkers can use a special BAC chart or "nomogram" to estimate their BAC from body weight and the number of drinks consumed in 2 hours. For example, a 120-pound person consuming four 12-ounce beers in 2 hours could be legally drunk with a BAC of .10% (U.S. Department of Transportation, 1979). Nomograms have been printed on keys chains, bar napkins, and used as mail stuffers; and they have been distributed nationwide in campaigns against alcohol-impaired driving. Although nomogram scales were derived from carefully controlled laboratory studies, O'Neill, Williams, and Dubowski (1983) found the range of actual BACs to vary widely for a given weight and time period. Consequently, nomograms can lead drinkers to underestimate or overestimate their BACs (Waller, 1986).

Because alcohol adversely affects performance along several dimensions, including reaction time and standing steadiness (Carpenter, 1962), behavioral tests of alcohol impairment might be useful in social contexts to determine a person's level of impairment or ability to drive a vehicle. In fact, field sobriety tests may be more valid than BAC as indicators of performance deficits related to driving (Johnson, 1983). Thus, this author and his colleagues tested a variety of simple performance tasks that could be readily administered in party and tavern settings and were significantly predictive of alcohol impairment. The tasks with the most predictive validity were a ruler-drop reaction time task, a body balance task, a one-leg stand (Geller & Russ, 1986; Russ & Geller, 1986; Streff, Geller, & Russ, 1989), and a simple handwriting task (Geller, Clarke, & Kalsher, 1991). Several drinkers reported that poor performance on these tasks would dissuade them from driving; however, such favorable reaction to the field sobriety tests decreased as the participants' BACs increased (Russ & Geller, 1986). Thus, further research is needed to increase the utility and social validity (Schwartz & Baer, 1991) of performance-feedback procedures as interventions to reduce excessive alcohol consumption or DUI.

Consequences for DUI

In an attempt to deter alcohol-impaired driving, states have legislated a variety of penalties for DUI including (a) suspension of a driver's license on arrest for an alcohol-involved driving violation; (b) "illegal per se," which makes driving a motor vehicle above a specified BAC level illegal and punishable by license suspension or jail; (c) mandatory jail sentence or performance of community service for convicted drunk drivers; and (d) suspension of one's driver's license on conviction of alcohol-related driving offense. A comprehensive analysis of fatal crash statistics across states with different penalties for DUI (Klein, 1989) led to the conclusion that some form of licensing sanction was most promising as a DUI deterrent.Given that administrative license suspension is much more certain and swift than other severer penalties, which typically involve the criminal justice system, the conclusion by Klein is consistent with the opinion by most experts in the road safety domain that the perceived probability and immediacy of punishment has greater control over driver behavior than the severity of punishment (Evans, 1991). Indeed, Ross (1991) made a convincing case for decriminalizing drunk driving to remove the administration of DUI penalties from the criminal justice system, and thereby increase the certainty and swiftness of a penalty (i.e., suspension of a driver's license) for DUI. This perspective is certainly consistent with behavior-change principles developed from experimental behavior analysis. It is unfortunate that those responsible for developing and administering contingencies for controlling DUI have not paid more attention to research and theory in the behavioral sciences. This is partly due to behavioral scientists' insufficient attention to dissemination issues and challenges (Geller, 1991; Redmon, 1991).

CASE EXAMPLE

As reviewed in this chapter, there are numerous ways to apply the DO RITE process for road safety. There are many target behaviors to address, and there are varieties of intervention techniques available. In fact, the choice of a target behavior to change and an intervention strategy for changing a selected behavior in the road safety domain can seem overwhelming. The author recommends starting with safety-belt use as the target behavior to increase in frequency, for the following reasons, which are probably already obvious from the preceding review: (a) the use of a shoulder belt is easy to observe and record unobtrusively (thus the "define," "observe," "record," "test," and "evaluate" components of the DO RITE process are readily accomplished); (b) the behavior change research is substantial and unequivocal in this road safety domain; (c) increasing safety-belt use among a large group of drivers is one of the surest ways to reduce losses from injury; (d) the success stories in this area of applied behavioral science are numerous, large scale, and readily modeled; and (e) the effective behavior change techniques in this domain are often applicable to other injury-control and health-promotion targets.

One can choose any one of a number of environmental settings at which to apply a behavior change program to increase vehicle safety-belt use (e.g., schools, day care centers, banks, armed forces installations, shopping centers, parking lots, fast-food restaurants), and examples of successful safety-belt programs at each of these settings were highlighted in this chapter. Indeed, any place where vehicles can be conveniently and safely stopped can be the site for implementing activators and consequences to promote safety-belt use. The present case study focuses on the corporate setting because business profits vary directly with employee safety and health, and employees are a "captive" audience for cost-effective promotional campaigns. In addition, the DO RITE approach to safety-belt promotion can be applied successfully to increase on-the-job safety (Geller, Lehman, & Kalsher, 1989), and an effective corporate-based safety-belt program can establish the rationale, experience, and confidence for applying a behavior management approach to other safety and health concerns at the work site.

Eight years ago, this author was the only outside consultant on a special training team that gave a series of daylong workshops on the DO RITE process for safety-belt promotion to safety representatives from every Ford Motor Company plant in the United States. This training resulted in the initiation of effective safety-belt intervention programs at more than 110 Ford plants. An overall employee belt use of 12% during baseline (in the days before BULs) was increased to 54% company-wide. In less than a year it was estimated that safety-belt interventions (resulting from our DO RITE training) saved the lives of at least eight Ford employees, prevented serious injury among 400 others, and reduced the company cost of vehicle accidents by nearly $10 million (Gray, Geller, & Bohan, 1985). By the end of the following year, the cumulative cost savings to Ford had reached $22 million (Gray, 1988). Following this success with employee safety-belt promotions, Ford Motor Company supported the preparation of a comprehensive DO RITE process for on-the-job safety and health (Geller et al., 1989) and subsequently financed a series of 2-day training seminars to teach DO RITE principles to their corporate executives, safety engineers, plant managers, hourly workers, and union leaders (see Geller, 1990b, for a description of these workshops).

The components of a successful safety-belt program are analogous to those of most any health or safety program that requires behavioral input. According to the author's firsthand experience and to corporate surveys by the National Safety Council (Richardson & Race, 1984) and the National Highway Traffic Safety Administration (1984), the most successful corporate-based programs to increase and maintain employee safety-belt use have the following components: (a) an active and visible commitment on the part of management to a long-term safety-belt program; (b) a clearly defined and well-enforced policy of mandatory, on-the-job belt use; (c) an incentive/reward program (as discussed earlier) to initiate belt use and maintain a buckle-up habit; (d) a comprehensive safety-belt education program; (e) systematic record keeping of motor vehicle crashes that includes the use or nonuse of safety belts; (f) ongoing safety-belt promotion campaigns (i.e., activators) within the company; (g) periodic audits of employee safety-belt use to demonstrate successive progress toward attaining and maintaining belt-use goals; and (h) community outreach efforts to spread safety belt promotion beyond the workplace—especially to employee's families.

Throughout this chapter, several strategies have been described for accomplishing these components of an effective safety-belt program (e.g., from increasing the impact of an education program with consensus-building discussions, buckle-up promise cards, and reminder strategies to maintaining compliance to a belt-use policy with direct, delayed, or indirect reward strategies). The author has not found an easier intervention program to evaluate than a corporate safety-belt program, because all that are required are a few random, unannounced days of 15-minute observation sessions at the company's parking-lot exits before, during, and after an intervention program.

In 1985, when Ford implemented its company-wide program to increase employees' use of safety belts, the intervention agents (i.e., members of the plants' safety committees) initially complained about the requirement to obtain baseline, treatment, and follow-up measures of vehicle safety-belt use. However, after completing a few observation sessions and graphing belt-use percentages, many employees actually looked forward to collecting evaluation data. Peak levels of excitement and program involvement were reached when the intervention agents observed increases in safety-belt use percentages as a result of their intervention programs (see examples in Geller, 1985). Consequently, employees learned the DO RITE approach to health and safety by implementing and evaluating their own corporate safety-belt programs. This author knows of no better way to develop experience and commitment toward a behavioral science approach to safety and health promotion, with employees preventing injuries or fatalities in the process.

FUTURE DIRECTIONS

Although there are numerous success stories regarding the application of behavioral science principles to increase safety-belt use, there are many important questions yet to be answered with empirical research. And with regard to influencing the human element in other aspects of road safety (e.g., from increasing safe driving to reducing risks of DUI), the behavioral science approach has been severely neglected. The need for much more behavioral science research in the road safety domain will not be fulfilled, however, unless behavioral scientists get more involved in dissemination. Currently, the research funding agencies are listening to the "quick-fix" promises of high-technology engineers and appear to have given up on the potential of behavioral science to produce and maintain more beneficial impact than the traditional prevention education. Indeed, epidemiologists, who only categorize health and safety problems according to various personal, behavioral, and environmental factors (usually with relatively weak self-report data,), are obtaining substantially more research support than behavioral scientists who often use more convincing measurement techniques (i.e., actual behavioral observation instead of self report), study cause-and-effect relationships (rather than only correlations), and have a technology for actually preventing injuries and increasing health behaviors (rather than for only finding correlations). Thus, from this author's perspective, the most essential future direction in the domain of road safety (as well as in other health areas) is to convince others (from those in funding agencies to the general public) that behavioral scientists can make beneficial differences in health and safety, often by collaborating with engineers and epidemiologists.

When research funding is increased for the application of behavioral science to road safety, the author proposes the following questions or areas of concerns as an initial listing. For the critical problem of DUI prevention, behavioral science applications are clearly in their infancy, but there is clear prevention potential in applying behavioral science principles to (a) study naturalistic relationships between environmental factors and DUI risk (e.g., in bars and at parties where alcoholic beverages are served); (b) improve the long-term impact of programs to reduce DUI risk (e.g., server intervention, designator driver, low-alcohol drink alternatives); and (c) develop techniques for increasing the probability that individuals will become informal intervention agents and interact with others (e.g., family members, friends, acquaintances) to reduce excessive alcohol consumption or DUI risk.

With respect to the promotion of relatively simple and convenient road safety behaviors (e.g., the use of safety belts, turn signals, and child safety seats), there is actually an arsenal of behavior change techniques available (along with support from published empirical evaluations), but there has been little attempt to categorize these procedures in terms of relative effectiveness. As a result, intervention agents for health and safety are faced with the formidable task of selecting an intervention program from an incomplete and disorganized list of potential behavior change procedures. This author and his colleagues have begun to develop a taxonomy of behavior change techniques and a scoring system for selecting one technique over another in a particular situation (Geller, 1992a; Geller et al., 1990), but much more needs to be done before a cogent, comprehensive, empirically and socially valid system is available for guiding the development of optimal intervention programs. Moreover, our attempt to derive such a system has revealed several critically important questions requiring behavioral science research including (a) when (if ever) should an incentive/reward program program be based on outcomes (e.g., vehicle crashes or injuries) rather than behaviors (e.g., fastening a safety belt, selecting a low-alcohol alternative, becoming a designated driver); (b) under what situations will intervention effects spread to nontargeted behaviors (e.g., when an increase in safety-belt use leads to an increase in turn-signal use or safe stopping at intersections); (c) should intervention agents be concerned with a possibility of risk compensation (e.g., an increase in speeding following an increase in safety-belt use or driving a vehicle with an airbag); (d) how do milieu and culture variables moderate the impact of an intervention program; (e) how can behavior change techniques be matched with population characteristics to increase their impact; (f) how can behavioral scientists be more effective at convincing others of the need, utility, and validity of their approach to addressing public health issues; and (g) how can we get more governments, industries, community agencies, and individuals to apply behavior change interventions to health problems?

Several years ago, this author proposed to several administrators and researchers at the U.S. Department of Transportation a framework for coordinating the principles and technology reviewed in this chapter into a community-wide system (Geller, 1992b). What should be done next to get those who can influence large-scale applications of public health initiatives to appreciate the real-world utility of behavioral science? Approximating answers to these questions is clearly an overwhelming challenge, but given that answers could prevent thousands of deaths and millions of serious injuries, a call for immediate action is imperative.

REFERENCES

Babor, T. F., Mendelson, J. H., Uhly, B., & Souza, E. (1980). Drinking patterns in experimental and barroom settings. *Journal of Studies on Alcohol, 41,* 634–651.

Berry, T. D., & Geller, E. S. (1991). Evaluating vehcile safety belt reminders with experimental behavioral analysis: Back to basics. *Journal of Applied Behavior Analysis, 24,* 13–22.

Calvert-Boyanowsky, J., & Boyanowsky, E. O. (1980). *Tavern breath testing as an alcohol countermeasure* (Tech. Rep.). Ottawa, Ontario: Ministry of Transport.

Campbell, R. J., Hunter, W. W., & Stutts, J. C. (1984). The use of economic incentives and education to modify safety belt use of high school students. *Health Education, 15,* 30–33.

Campbell, R. J., Stewart, J. R., & Campbell, F. A. (1987). *1985–1986 experiences with belt laws in the United States.* Chapel Hill, NC: UNC Highway Safety Research Center.

Campbell, R. J., Stewart, J. R., & Campbell, F. A. (1988, December). *Chnages in death and injury associated wirth safety belt laws: 1985–1987.* Chapel Hill, NC: UNC Highway Safety Research Center.

Carpenter, J. A. (1962). Effects of alcohol on some psychological processes: A critical review with special reference to automobile driving skill. *Quarterly Journal of Studies on Alcohol, 23,* 274–314.

Conger, J. J., Miller, W. C., & Rainey, R. V. (1966). Effects of driver education: The role of motivation intelligence, social class, and exposure. *Traffic Safety Research Review, 10,* 67–71.

Cope, J. G., Grossnickle, W. F., & Geller, E. S. (1986). An evaluation of three corporate strategies for safety belt use promotion. *Accident Analysis and Prevention, 18,* 243–251.

Cunliffe, A. P., DeAngelis, F., Foley, C., Lonero, L. P., Pierce, J. A., Siegel, C., Smutylo, T., & Stephen, K. M. (1975, September). *The design and implementation of a seat-belt education program in Ontario.* Paper presented at the annual conference of the Roads and Transportation Association of Canada, Calgary.

Curry, J. R. (1991). Safety achievement—prelude to progress. *Auto & Traffic Safety,* Summer, *1,* 1.

Elman, D., & Killebrew, T. J. (1978). Incentives and seat belts: Changing a resistant behavior through extrinsic motivation. *Journal of Applied Social Psychology, 8,* 72–83.

Evans, L. (1991). *Traffic safety and the driver.* New York: Van Nostrand Reinhold.

Evans, L., Wasielewski, P., & vonBuseck, C. R. (1982). Compulsory seat belt usage and driver risk-takinbg behavior. *Human Factors, 24,* 41–48.

Federal Register. (1984, July). *Federal motor vehcile standards: Occupant crash protection* (Final Rule, 48, No. 138). Washington, DC: Department of Transportation.

Fell, J. C. (1982). Alcohol involvement in traffic crashes. *American Association for Automobile Medicine Quarterly Journal, 4,* 23–42.

Fricker, J. D., & Larson, R. J. (1990). Safety belts and turn signals: Driver disposition and the law. *Transportation Research Record, 1210,* 47–52.

Geller, E. S. (1982). *Development of industry-based strategies for motivating seat-belt usage: Phase II* (Quarterly Report for DOT Contract DTRS5681–0032). Blacksburg, VA: Virginia Polytechnic Institute and State University.

Geller, E. S. (1983). Rewarding safety belt use at an industrial setting: Tests of treatment generality and reponse maintenance. *Journal of Applied Behavior Analysis, 16,* 43–56.

Geller, E. S. (1984). *Motivating safety belt use with incentives: A critical review of the past and a look to the future* (SAE Technical Paper Series, No. 840326). Warrendale, PA: Society of Automotive Engineers.

Geller, E. S. (1985). *Corporate safety belts programs*. Blacksburg, VA: Virginia Polytechnic Institute and State University.

Geller, E. S. (1988). A behavioral science approach to transportation safety. *Bulletin of the New York Academy of Medicine, 65,* 632–661.

Geller, E. S. (1989a). Applied behavior analysis and social marketing: An integration to preserve the enironment. *Journal of Social Issues, 45,* 17–36.

Geller, E. S. (1989b). Intervening to increase children's use of safety belts. *Alcohol, Drugs and Driving, 5,* 37–59.

Geller, E. S. (1990a). Performance management and occupational safety: Start with a safety belt program. *Journal of Organizational Behavior Management, 11,* 149–174.

Geller, E. S. (1990b). Preventing injuries and deaths from vehicle crashes: Encouraging belts and discouraging booze: In J. Edwards, R. S. Tindale, L. Heath, & E. Posavac (Eds.), *Social influence processes and prevention* (pp. 249–277). New York: Plenum.

Geller, E. S. (1991). Are applied behavior analysts technological to a fault? *Journal of Applied Behavior Analysis, 24,* 401–406.

Geller, E. S. (1992a). Applications of behavior analysis to prevent injuries from vehicle crashes. In S. Glenn (Ed.), *Progress in behavioral studies* (Vol. 3). Cambridge, MA: Cambridge Center for Behavioral Studies.

Geller, E. S. (1992b). Follow-up commentary: With a little help from my friends. In S. Glenn (Ed.), *Program in behavioral studies* (Vol. 3). Cambridge, MA: Cambridge Center for Behavioral Studies.

Geller, E. S., Altomari, M. G., & Russ, N. W. (1984, November). *Innovative approaches to drunk driving prevention: Special seminar on alcohol and driving*. Warren, MI: Societal Analysis Department, General Motors Research Laboratories.

Geller, E. S., Berry, T. D., Ludwig, T. D., Evans, R. E., Gilmore, M. R., & Clarke, S. W. (1990). A conceptual framework for developing and evaluationg behavior change interventions for injury control. *Health Education Research: Theory and Practice, 5,* 125–137.

Geller, E. S. & Bigelow, B. E. (1984). Developmnet of corporate incentive programs for motivating safety belt use: A review. *Traffic Safety Evaluation Research Review, 3,* 21–38.

Geller, E. S., Bruff, C. D., & Nimmer, J. G. (1985). "Flash for Life": Community-based prompting for safety belt promotion. *Journal of Applied Behavior Analysis, 18,* 145–159.

Geller, E. S., Casali, J. G., & Johnson, R. P. (1980). Seat-belt usage: A potential target for applied behavior analysis. *Journal of Applied Behavior Analysis, 13,* 94–100.

Geller, E. S., Clarke, S. W., & Kalsher, M. J. (1991). Knowing when to say when: A simple assessment of alcohol impairment. *Journal of Applied Behavior Analysis, 24,* 65–72.

Geller, E. S., Davis, L., & Spicer, K. (1983). Industry-based incentives to promote seat belt usage: Differential impact on salary vs. hourly employees. *Journal of Organizational Behavior Management, 5,* 17–29.

Geller, E. S., Elder, J. P., Hovell, M. F., & Sleet, D. A. (1991). Behavior change approaches to deterring alcohol-impaired driving. In W. B. Ward, & F. M. Lewis (Eds), *Advances in health education and promotion* (Vol. 3, pp. 45–68). London: Jessica Kingsley.

Geller, E. S., & Hahn, H. A. (1984). Promoting safety belt use at industrial sites: An effective program for blue collar employees. *Professional Psychology: Research and Practice, 15,* 553–564.

Geller, E. S., Johnson, R. P., & Pelton, S. L. (1982). Community-based interventions for encouraging safety belt use. *American Journal of Community Psychology, 10,* 183–195.

Geller, E. S., & Kalsher, M. J. (1990). Environmental determinants of party drinking: Bartenders vs. self-service. *Environment and Behavior, 22,* 74–90.

Geller, E. S., Kalsher, M. J., & Clarke, S. W. (1991). Beer vs. mixed drink consumption at university parties: A time and place for low-alcohol alternatives. *Journal of Studies on Alcohol, 52,* 197–204.

Geller, E. S., Kalsher, M. J., Rudd, J. R., & Lehman, G. R. (1989). Promoting safety-belt use on a university campus: An integration of commitment and incentive strategies. *Journal of Applied Social Psychology, 19,* 3–19.

Geller, E. S., & Lehman, G. R. (1988). Drinking-driving intervention strategies: A person-situation framework. In M. D. Laurence, J. R. Snortum, & F. E. Zimring (Eds.), *The social control of drinking and driving* (pp. 297–320). Chicago, IL: University of Chicago Press.

Geller, E. S., & Lehman, G. R. (1991). The Buckle-Up Promise Card: A versatile intervention for large-scale behavior change. *Journal of Applied Behavior Analysis, 24,* 91–94.

Geller, E. S., Lehman, G. R., & Kalsher, M. J. (1989). *Behavior analysis training for occupational safety.* Newport, VA: Make-A-Difference, Inc.

Geller, E. S., Paterson, L., & Talbott, E. (1982). A behavioral analysis of incentive prompts for motivating seat belt use. *Journal of Applied Behavior Analysis, 15,* 403–415.

Geller, E. S., & Russ, N. W. (1986). Drunk driving prevention: Knowing when to say when. In *Alcohol, accidents, and injuries* (Ms. No. P-173). Warrendale, PA: Society of Automotive Engineers.

Geller, E. S., Russ, N. W., & Altomari, M. G. (1986). Naturalistic observations of beer drinking among college students. *Journal of Applied Behavior Analysis, 19,* 391–396.

Geller, E. S., Russ, N. W., & Delphos, W. A. (1987). Does server intervention training make a difference? An empirical field evaluation. *Alcohol, Health and Research World, 11,* 64–69.

Geller, E. S., Winett, R. A., & Everett, P. B. (1982). *Preserving the environment: New strategies for behavior change.* Elmsford, NY: Pergamon.

Graham, J. D. (1988). Injury control, traffic safety, and evaluation research. In J. D. Graham (Ed.), *Preventing automobile injury* (pp. 1–23). Dover, MA: Auburn House.

Gray, D. A. (1988, October). Introduction to invited address by E. S. Geller at the annual National Safety Council Congress and Exposition, Orlando, FL.

Gray, D. A., Geller, E. S., & Bohan, W. (1985, April). *How to implement an effective employee seat belt program.* Workshop presented at the 24th Annual ASSE Professional Development Conference & Exposition, San Diego, CA.

Horne, T. D. (1984, November). *Incentives and corporate safety belt promotion.* Workshop presentation at the Michigan Life Savers Conference, Boyne, Mountain, MI.

Horne, T. D., & Terry, T. (1983). *Seat belt sweepstakes—an incentive program* (SAE Technical Paper Series, No 830474). Warrendale, PA: Society of Automotive Engineers.

Johnson, D. (1983). *Drunkeness may not be accurately measured by blood-alcohol levels: UCB researchers report* (Public Information Office News). Boulder, CO: University of Colorado.

Jonah, B. A. (1989, November). *Occupant restraint use in Canada: Past, present, and*

future. Invited address to the SWOV Institute for Road Safety Research, Leidschendam, The Netherlands.
Kalsher, M. J., & Geller, E. S. (1991). *Beer consumption at university parties: Stimulus control of brand labels.* Unpublished manuscript, Virginia Polytechnic Institute and State University, Blacksburg, VA.
Kalsher, M. J., Geller, E. S., Clarke, S. W., & Lehman, G. R. (1989). Safety belt promotion on a naval base: A comparison of incentives vs. disincentives. *Journal of Safety Research, 20,* 103–113.
Kello, J. E., Geller, E. S., Rice, J. C., & Bryant, S. L. (1988). Motivating auto safety belt wearing in industrial settings: From awareness to behavior change. *Journal of Organizational Behavior Management, 9,* 7–21.
Klein, T. M. (1989, July). *Changes in alcohol-involved fatal crashes associated with tougher state alcohol legislation* (Technical Report DOT HS 807–511 available from the National Technical Information Service, 5285 Port Royal Road, Springfield, VA 22161).
Lehman, G. R., & Geller, E. S. (1990a). Educational strategies to increase children's use of safety belts: Are extrinsic rewards necessary? *Health Education Research: Theory and Practice, 5,* 187–196.
Lehman, G. R., & Geller, E. S. (1990b). Participative education for children: An effective approach to increase safety belt use. *Journal of Applied Behavior Analysis, 23,* 219–225.
Lewin, K. (1958). Group decision and social change. In E. E. Maccoby, T. M. Newcomb, & E. L. Hartley (Eds.), *Readings in social psychology* (pp. 197–211). New York: Holt, Rinehart & Winston.
Ludwig, T. D., & Geller, E. S. (1991). Improving the driving practices of pizza deliverers: Response generalization and moderating effects of driving history. *Journal of Applied Behavior Analysis, 24,* 31–44.
Lund, A. K., Williams, A. F., & Zador, P. (1986). High school driver education: Further evaluation of the De Kalb County study. *Accident, Analysis, & Prevention, 18,* 349–357.
McKnight, A. J. (1987). *Development and field test of a responsible alcohol service program, Vol. 1: Research findings* (Report No. DOT HS 807 221). National Highway Traffic Safety Administration, U.S. Department of Transportation, Washington, DC.
Mosher, J. F. (1979). Dram shop liability and the prevention of alcohol-related problems. *Journal of Studies on Alcohol, 40,* 773–798.
National Highway Traffic Safety Administration (1984). *The profit in safety belts: A handbook for employees* (DOT HS 806 443). Washington, DC: U.S. Department of Transportation.
National Highway Traffic Safety Administration (1985, September). *The economic costs to society of motor vehicle accidents* (1984 update, Memorandum). Washington, DC: Office of Plans and Policy, National Highway Traffic Safety Administration, U.S. Department of Transportation.
Nimmer, J. G., & Geller, E. S. (1988). Motivating safety belt use at a community hospital: An effective integration of incentive and commitment strategies. *American Journal of Community Psychology, 16,* 381–394.
Nocks, E. S., & Howell, R. H. (1993). Effect of modeling and compliance with directional cue on car safety belt use. Submitted for publication.
Oates, J. F. (1976). *Study of self tests for drivers* (Final Report DOT–HS–5–01241). Washington, DC: National Highway Traffic Safety Administration.
O'Neill, B. (1990, September-October). ANTI high school driver education: It causes crashes by putting 16-years-olds on the road. *Traffic Safety,* 10–12.

O'Neill, B., Williams, A. F., & Dubowski, K. M. (1983). Variability in blood alcohol concentrations: Implications for estimating individual results. *Journal of Studies on Alcohol, 44*, 222–230.

Parsons, H. M. (1992). Commentary on "Application of behavior analysis to prevent injuries from vehicle crashes" by E. Scott Geller. In S. Glenn (Ed.), *Progress in behavioral studies* (Vol. 3). Cambridge, MA: Cambridge Center for Behavioral Studies.

Phillips, B. M. (1980, June). *Safety belt education program for employees: An evaluation study* (Opinion Research Corp. Final Report for Contract DOT–HS–01707). Washington, DC: U.S. Department of Transportation.

Preusser, D. F., Williams, A. F., & Lund, A. K. (1985). *The effect of New York's seat belt use law on teenage drivers*. Washington, DC: Insurance Institute for Highway Safety.

Ragnarsson, R. S., & Bjorgvinsson, T. (1991). Effects of public posting on driving speed in Icelandic traffic. *Journal of Applied Behavior Analysis, 24*, 53–58.

Redmon, W. K. (1991). Pinpointing the technological fault in applied behavior analysis. *Journal of Applied Behavior Analysis, 24*, 441–448.

Richardson, B., & Race, K. E. H. (1984). *Development of nontraditional constituencies of highway safety: A focus on the workplace*. Chicago, IL: National Safety Council.

Roberts, M. C. (1987). Public health and health psychology: Two cats of Kilkenny? *Professional Psychology, 18*, 145–149.

Roberts, M. C., & Fanurik, D. (1986). Rewarding elementary school children for their use of safety belts. *Health Psychology, 5*, 185–196.

Roberts, M. C., Fanurik, D., & Wilson, D. (1988). A community program to reward children's use of seat belts. *American Journal of Community Psychology, 16*, 395–407.

Roberts, M. C., & Layfield, D. A. (1987). Promoting child passenger safety: A comparison of two positive methods. *Journal of Pediatric Psychology, 12*, 257–271.

Roberts, M. C., & Turner, D. S. (1986). Rewarding parents for their children's use of safety seats. *Journal of Pediatric Psychology, 11*, 25–36.

Robertson, L. S. (1975). Safety belt use in automobiles with starter-interlock and buzzer-light reminder systems. *American Journal of Public Health, 65*, 1319–1325.

Robertson, L. S. (1976). The great seat belt campaign flop. *Journal of Communication, 26*, 41–46.

Robertson, L. S., Kelly, A. B., O'Neill, B., Wilson, C. W., Eiswirth, R. S., & Haddon, W. (1974). A controlled study of the effect of television messages on safety belt use. *American Journal of Public Health, 64*, 1071–1080.

Rogers, R. W. (1984). *Promoting safety belt use among state employees: The effects of prompting, stimulus control and a response-cost intervention*. Unpublished doctoral dissertation, Florida State University, Tallahassee, FL.

Ross, H. L. (1982). *Deterring the drinking driver: Legal policy and social control*. Lexington, MA: D. C. Heath Lexington Books.

Ross, H. L. (1985). Deterring drunken driving: Analysis of current efforts. *Journal of Studies on Alcohol* (Suppl. 10), 122–128.

Ross, H. L. (1987). Reflection on doing policy-relevant sociology: How to cope with MADD mothers. *American Sociologist, 18*, 173–178.

Ross, H. L. (1991). Decriminalizing drunk driving: A means to effective punishment. *Journal of Applied Behavior Analysis, 24*, 89–90.

Rudd, J. R., & Geller, E. S. (1985). A university-based incentive program to increase safety belt use: Toward cost-effective institutionalization. *Journal of Applied Behavior Analysis, 18*, 215–226.

Russ, N. W., & Geller, E. S. (1985, December). changing the behavior of the drunk driver: Current status and future directions. *Psychological Documents*, 1–30.

Russ, N. W., & Geller, E. S. (1986). Using sobriety tests to increase awareness of alcohol impairment. *Health Education Research: Theory and Practice, 1,* 255–261.

Russ, N. W., & Geller, E. S. (1987). Training bar personnel to prevent drunken driving: A field evaluation. *American Journal of Public Health, 77,* 952–954.

Russ, N. W., & Geller, E. S. (1988). Exploring low alcohol beer consumption among college students: Implications for drunk driving. *Journal of Alcohol and Drug Education, 33,* 1–5.

Russ, N. W., Geller, E. S., & Leland, L. S. (1989). Blood-alcohol level feedback: A failure to deter impaired driving. *Psychology of Addictive Behavior, 2,* 124–130.

Saltz, R. F. (1986). Server intervention: Will it work? Alcohol, Health, and Research World, 10, pp. 12–19, 35.

Saltz, R. F. (1989). Research needs and opportunities in server intervention programs. *Health Education Quarterly, 16,* 429–438.

Schwartz, I. S., & Baer, D. M. (1991). Social validity assessments: Is current practice state of the art? *Journal of Applied Behavior Analysis, 24,* 189–204.

Sleet, D. S. (1987). Motor vehicle trauma and safety belt use in the context of public health priorities. *The Journal of Trauma, 27,* 695–702.

Spoonhour, K. A. (1981, September-October). Company snap-it up campaign achieves 90 percent belt use. *Traffic Safety,* pp. 18–19, 31–32.

Steed, D. K. (1988, February). *The administrator.* Washington, DC: National Highway Traffic Safety Administration, U.S. Department of Transportation.

Strategic Transportation Research Study Committee. (1990, November). *Special Report 229: Safety research in a changing highway environment.* Washington, DC: Transportation Research Board.

Streff, F. M. (1991). Crash avoidance: New opportunities for behavior analysis. *Journal of Applied Behavior Analysis, 24,* 77–79.

Streff, F. M., Geller, E. S., & Russ, N. W. (1989, November). Evaluation of sobriety tests for use by social hosts. *Proceedings of the 11th Annual Conference on Alcohol, Drugs and Traffic Safety.* Chicago, IL.

Streff, F. M., Schultz, R. H., & Molnar, L. J. (1990). *Analysis of speed and other unsafe driving acts* (Report No. UMTRI-90-11). Ann Arbor, MI: University of Michigan Transportation Research Institute.

Stutts, J. C., Hunter, W. W., & Campbell, B. J. (1984). Three studies evaluating the effectiveness of incentives for increasing safety belt use. *Traffic Safety Evaluation Research Review, 3,* 9–20.

Talton, A. (1984). *Increasing safety belt usage through personal commitment: A church-based pledge card program.* Unpublished master's thesis, Virginia Polytechnic Institute and State University, Blacksburg, VA.

Thyer, B. A., & Geller, E. S. (1987). Dashboard stickers: An effective strategy for promoting safety belt use. *Environment and Behavior, 19,* 484–494.

Thyer, B. A., & Geller, E. S. (1990). Behavior analysis in the promotion of safety belt use: A review. In M. Hersen, R. M. Eisler, & P. M. Miller (Eds.), *Progress in behavior modification* (Vol. 26, pp. 150–172). Newbury Park, CA: Sage.

Thyer, B. A., Geller, E. S., Williams, M., & Purcell, S. (1987). Community-based "flashing" to increase safety belt use. *Journal of Experimental Education, 53,* 155–159.

Tillman, R., & Kirkpatrick, C. A. (1972). *Promotion: Persuasive communication in marketing.* Homewood, IL: Richard D. Irwin.

U.S. Department of Transportation (1979). *A message to my patients* (DOT-HS-804-089). Washington, DC: National Highway Traffic Safety Administration.

Van Houten, R., & Nau, P. A. (1983). Feedback interventions and driving speed: A parametric and comparative analysis. *Journal of Applied Behavior Analysis, 16*, 253–281.

Van Houten, R., Nau, P. A., & Marini, Z. (1980). An analysis of public posting in reducing speeding behavior on an urban highway. *Journal of Applied Behavior Analysis, 13*, 383–396.

von Buseck, C. R., & Geller, E. S. (1984). *The vehicle safety belt reminder: Can refinements increase safety belt use?* (Tech. Rep. for General Motors Research Laboratories). Warren, MI. General Motors Research Laboratories.

Wagenaar, A. C. (1983). *Alcohol, young drivers, and traffic accidents.* Lexington, MA: D. C. Heath Lexington Books.

Wagenaar, A. C. (1984). *Restraint usage among crash-involved motor vehicle occupants* (Report UMTRI-84-2). Ann Arbor, MI: University of Michigan Transportation Research Institute.

Waller, J. A. (1986). State liquor laws as enablers for impaired driving and other impaired behaviors. *American Journal of Public Health, 76*, 787–792.

Waller, J. A. (1987). Injury: Conceptual shifts and prevention implications. *Annual Review of Public Health, 8*, 21–49.

Williams, A. F., Wells, J. D., Lund, A. K., & Teed, N. (1989). Observed use of seat belts in 1987 cars. *Accident Analysis and Prevention, 19*, 243–249.

Winett, R. A., Altman, D. G., & King, A. C. (1990). Conceptual and strategic foundation for effective media campaigns for preventing the spread of HIV infection. *Evaluation and Program Planning, 13*, 91–104.

Zeigler, P. (1986, January). Observed safety belt and child safety seat usage at road intersections: 19-city survey results. *Research Notes.* Washington, DC: Office of Driver and Pedestrian Research, National Highway Traffic Safety Administration, U.S. Department of Transportation.

PART III

Innovative Strategies for Promoting Health

CHAPTER 9

Media-Based Behavior Change Approaches for Prevention

Richard A. Winett

DESCRIPTION OF THE PROBLEM

The critical part of most prevention efforts is individual behavior change. Population-based primary prevention programs often must include interventions at the organizational, community, and institutional levels to be effective (Jeffrey, 1989; Winett, King, & Altman, 1989), but these environmental changes typically guide, facilitate, and support mass individual changes (e.g., Farquhar et al., 1990). Even when a primary prevention effort seeks to eliminate substances, or modify laws and regulations or situations detrimental to health, change must focus on some influential people such as legislators, opinion leaders in the community, and business persons (e.g., Altman, Foster, Rosenick-Douss, & Tye, 1989).

Secondary prevention efforts generally follow case-finding, clinical intervention strategies. Individuals at high risk for a problem or disorder, or those individuals showing early or mild signs of the problem or disorder, are identified and offered intervention. Most frequently these interventions entail adopting new health behaviors, learning social and other skills, or following medical regimens.

A consistent dilemma in primary and secondary prevention efforts has been how to deliver individual interventions that reach many people yet retain most of the conceptual and strategic elements that appear essential for behavior change. For example, effective individual programs often require some tailoring of a basic program and opportunities to practice new behaviors and receive feedback. How can programs with these elements be delivered reliably to large population groups?

When the discussion turns to delivering individual behavior change programs to many people reliably, a variety of media-based methods usually are considered. Media-based methods are differentiated from methods typically relying on interpersonal contact, although media and interpersonal methods are frequently used in concert (Rogers, 1983). However, once the goal is to reach thousands, if not millions, of people, media methods become prominent. Although there can be exceptions to the rule, there simply are not enough resources for employing armies of personal change agents.

By definition, media encompass different forms and delivery systems. For example, self-help brochures and books use the same medium but are different forms and often are obtained from different delivery systems (e.g., brochures obtained from a physician's office as part of treatment; self-help books obtained on one's own for self-assistance). Radio and television have different forms, costs, and potentials. Computer technology has spawned a host of versatile, potentially personalized media that vary from hand-held microcomputers to large computer systems housed in public-access kiosks. VCRs have so saturated the market that they can be thought of as a household utility capable of providing a wide range of behavior change programming.

Thus, the possibilities for media-based preventive interventions seem endless in combinations and capabilities. It actuality, though, this is *not* the real state of affairs. To be effective, media-based interventions must adhere to well-researched concepts and strategies for behavior change (Bandura, 1986). However, the history of media-based behavior change efforts is, unfortunately, replete with projects violating basic behavior change guidelines. In addition, few media-based efforts have used systematic formative and pilot research and prototype testing to develop programs. Consequently, it is not surprising that many media-based behavior change efforts have been disappointingly ineffective. In fact, until recently, an axiom in communication studies was that "media can change knowledge and attitudes but not behavior."

This chapter briefly reviews essential elements for behavior change that must be encapsulated within media programs. A discussion follows that highlights some of the controversy in the field from historical and contemporary perspectives. Most of the examples and discussion will revolve around mass media. The series of radio or television spots can be thought of as a prototype for the discussion. Clearly, recent technological changes (e.g., interactive media) create more intriguing, individualized, and potentially effective interventions. However, most of the literature is based on mass media, and it is likely many contemporary and near-future media-based prevention efforts will rely on mass media and somewhat more specialized videotape programs. Further, it is a mistake to believe the new media automatically will result in "appropriate" behavior changes. New media *may* have greater potential for behavior change, but only if new media interventions also adhere to essential elements of behavior change (Winett, 1986).

Underscoring the need to attend to behavior change concepts and strategies, this chapter also provides a framework for designing, developing, and evaluating media-based behavior change programs. These concepts and strategies are brought together in a description of our AIDS prevention project for parents and young teens, which revolves around an instructional video program for home use by the family.

REVIEW AND CRITIQUE OF THE LITERATURE

Objectives and Stages of a Media-Based Behavior Change Prevention Program

It is instructive to delineate the objectives and stages of a media-based behavior change prevention program. AIDS prevention is used as the example to illustrate typical objectives, stages, and essential behavior change elements (Brownell, Marlatt, Lichtenstein, & Wilson, 1986; Catania, Kaegeles, & Coates, 1990).

The objectives and stages of a media-based AIDS prevention program include the following:

1. Attracting and holding the attention of appropriate target groups through salient media content and formats about HIV infection
2. Increasing the awareness of appropriate target groups of the importance of preventing HIV infection
3. Increasing, if appropriate, the perceived saliency and personal vulnerability of target groups to contracting a HIV infection
4. Fully informing target groups about the origins and nature of HIV infection, means of transmission, means of prevention, procedures for testing, and procedures and outcomes for treatment
5. Increasing the initial motivation to change specific behaviors through the culmination of the prior awareness, saliency, vulnerability, and information steps
6. Fully convincing target groups that appropriate actions can be effective in preventing or (to some extent) treating HIV infection (i.e., increase outcome expectancies)
7. Facilitating the decision to take specific actions through the foregoing steps and an initial commitment to change

8. Providing appropriate mechanisms (i.e., modeling, practice exercises, feedback, social support) so that effective preventive behaviors can be performed in both practice situations and real-life settings (i.e., behavioral rehearsal)
9. Providing additional mechanisms so that preventive behaviors and strategies are performed repeatedly in diverse real-life settings over longer periods (i.e., behavioral maintenance)

These objectives, stages, and change strategies, with some differential emphasis and variation, are the key ones in virtually any intervention focusing on individual behavior change. For simplicity, the objectives, stages, and strategies are presented as linear in their sequence. Many readers will recognize all these elements as directly derived from Bandura's (1986) social cognitive theory.

There are at least six compelling points about media-based interventions', objectives, stages, and strategies: (a) By the early 1990s, most theoreticians and practitioners specifically interested in media-based behavior change agreed about the importance of all these elements. (b) A good part of the science of media-based behavior change efforts involves the careful design of each stage to fit specific target groups (audiences) using social marketing, formative research, and several frameworks. (c) Included in the design process is the selection of appropriate media and distribution systems to fit together behavioral requirements for change, situational constraints, and special interests and patterns of target groups. (d) Every objective, stage, and strategy, as well as the entire effort, can be evaluated with data feedback used as an ongoing process to refine media-based behavior change efforts. (e) The conceptual and technical bases to perform all the necessary steps are identifiable. (f) These stages are not simple, and emphasizing each element can be complicated; yet the process appears rational and doable.

Why Are Media-Based Efforts Often Not Effective?

The preceding six points indicate that media-based behavior change efforts can be systematized. Even today, though, very few media-based behavior change efforts thoroughly follow systematic conceptual and strategic frameworks and document successful outcomes.

There are several contemporary and historical reasons why media-based behavior change efforts are usually ineffective. These reasons can be placed in the following overlapping categories.

Undervaluation of Conceptual and Strategic Bases

This category includes several different manifestations. Large federal or state programs, for example, often assign a campaign to an advertising agency. Once a campaign to change complex behaviors is reduced to a series of spots and ads, it makes the funding agency appear very naïve. Ads and sports apparently are not understood as only one part (i.e., promotion) of an intricate marketing approach. Conversely, advertising agencies may believe that preventive behavior changes may be instituted in a manner similar to promoting any other product. They may be unmindful of their own company's involved, orchestrated marketing programs, the difficulty of instituting preventive behavior changes, or both.

Examples of this approach have included various ads and songs (frequently produced by the Ad Council) on drug and alcohol abuse that are most noteworthy for being virtually indistinguishable from the ongoing programming and failing to identify properly any preventive behavior. A more expensive version of the failure to use sound conceptual and strategic bases was the first televised "America Responds to AIDS" campaign. Apparently, this hastily conceived and expensive campaign only resulted in limited changes in AIDS knowledge and awareness (Winett, Altman, & King, 1990).

Another way sound conceptual and strategic bases become undervalued is when the entire enterprise is reduced to an "art form," not subject to much, if any, scientific input. This is not to suggest that no art is involved in successful efforts. Clearly, story lines, production qualities, staging of scenes (e.g., acting, visual qualities), and formative features (i.e., the "syntax and grammar" of media) do have an important artistic component. However, media-based efforts must use art to enhance particular objectives, stages, and other behavior change elements and not have the art alone become the central focus. For example, from the perspective of behavior change, a scene with reasonable production qualities and acting that clearly and explicitly demonstrates desired behavior is much preferred to a scene with the best acting and production qualities, but where the desired behavior is less than clearly and explicitly demonstrated. Furthermore, many of these "artistic elements" *do* revolve around science and technology (Moore, 1990; Wright & Huston, 1983). For example, the pace of a presentation and the integration of particular audio and visual components have predictable effects on attention and memory.

Self-fulfilling Prophecy

A persistent belief held by many behavioral scientists is that "media cannot effect behavior change." In part, this belief is the result of a reaction to a very early "hypodermic needle" communication model of the 1930s (Laswell, 1948). In totalitarian societies, where virtually all sources of information were controlled centrally and dissension was punishable by death, it was not surprising that media seemed to have a profound impact on a passive audience. "Media content was seen as injected in the veins of the audience that was supposed to act in foreseeable ways" (McQuail & Windhal, 1981, p. 41). When this very strong media effects model was tested in more open societies, the model was found to be wanting (McLeod & Reeves, 1981). Unfortunately, this led to the "weak effects" model. Behavioral scientists became committed to proving that media cannot affect behavior (McLeod & Reeves, 1981), in contrast to finding out what qualities of media can affect which behaviors under which conditions. As a result of some minimal experimentation, the weak effects model gained currency. What these behavioral scientists were saying is that an entire class of stimuli, delivered in a particular way, has no behavioral influence. This was true even though at the same time other behavioral scientists (e.g., Liebert, Sprafkin, & Davidson, 1982) were decrying the strong and negative influence on youth from violence in television programs (i.e., a strong effects model).

One result of the weak effects model has been a marvelous self-fulfilling prophecy. If media-based interventions are at best minimally effective, then only minimal resources should be devoted to their design, pretesting, delivery, and evaluation. The outcomes of these endeavors are poorly conceived, executed, and evaluated campaigns, with the negative results supporting the original belief and subsequent minimal efforts.

Faulty Hierarchy of Effects Model

The series of objectives, stages, and strategies described previously starts with more cognitive ones (e.g., attention, awareness, knowledge) and progresses to more behavioral ones (e.g., behavioral rehearsal, behavioral maintenance). These elements can be seen as a series in a "hierarchy of effects" model. There often must be a reasonable effect in one step if there is to be an effect in the next step.

However, for at least two major reasons, a persistent shortcoming of many media-based efforts has been to focus only on the initial cognitive elements. The first reason is to make the media-based program resemble an ad campaign, which is thought to be good (see earlier discussion). The first cognitive elements in a campaign are seen as not only essential but necessarily influencing later (behavioral) elements. However, it is now more widely accepted that such cognitive elements as awareness and knowledge may be influenced by strategies and procedures quite different from those needed for behavioral influence. Also, cognitive change often does not result in sustained behavior change (Bandura, 1986).

Figure 9.1 presents a schema of the processes and influences in a simplified hierarchy of effects model and a more complex model. In the simplified model, the same processes and influences are assumed to effect all the important objectives and stages in a media-based intervention. Additionally, a unidirectional, linear linkage between objectives or stages is assumed. In the more complex model, conversely, multiple and diverse processes and influences are postulated. Also, relationships are viewed as interactive, with any objective or stage potentially influencing at any time any other objective or stage. For example, attentional and

Simplified	Complex
• Attention	• Attention 　• Presentation Format 　• Design 　• Differentiation
• Saliency	• Saliency 　• Models 　• Social Comparisons
• Vulnerability	• Vulnerability 　• Models 　• Information Framing 　• Vividness of Information
• Knowledge	• Knowledge 　• Specific to Audience 　• Presentation Format 　• Interaction
• Motivation	• Motivation 　• Step-by-step Process 　• Benefits of Change
• Outcome Expectancy	• Outcome Expectancy 　• Costs and Benefits 　• Framing 　• Models
• Decision/Commitment	• Decision/Commitment 　• Framing 　• Persausion 　• Strategies
• Skills	• Skills 　• Modeling 　• Practice/Feedback 　• Contextual Accuracy
• Maintenance	• Maintenance 　• Modeling 　• Generalization 　• Practice/Feedback

FIGURE 9.1 Different assumptions, processes, and influences in a simplified hierarchy of effects model and a more complex effects model.

saliency factors can influence skill development, whereas increased self-efficacy and skill development may sharpen attention.

Relatively specific processes and influences may be required for different objectives and stages. For example, certain formats hold attention, and differentiating messages from ongoing programs is important; saliency can be increased with appropriate models and social comparisons; knowledge increments can be facilitated by careful assessments of the target groups and formats allowing for repetition, elaboration, and interaction; outcome expectancies and motivation for behavior change may be increased by proper framing of the costs and benefits of different actions; a decision to change behavior may be helped by the framing of information, whereas commitment to change may require a coaxed but public step; self-efficacy and skill development are highly interactive steps that depend on proper modeling sequences in appropriate contexts, as well as step-by-step approaches to behavior change and practice-feedback sequences; behavioral maintenance requires modeling, skill, contextual, and practice-feedback elaborations. Thus, the complex model of behavior change is, indeed, quite complex.

There is, however, further conceptual and design complexity important to most media-based efforts. A sine qua non of marketing is the designing and targeting of programs for the interests and needs of specific audiences (Kotler & Roberts, 1989; Manoff, 1985). Many programs seem to violate this dictum. Early objectives and stages, as noted, are emphasized at the expense of later behavioral ones. But, most significantly, there often has not been an assessment of specific target audiences to determine what stage of change should be emphasized (Catania et al., 1990). For example, a program for well-informed and highly motivated female prostitutes could most effectively focus on how to eroticize lower HIV-risk behaviors, *not* on the basic facts about protection from HIV.

There is a second reason many media-based efforts focus only on cognitive and not specific behavior changes. Supporters and practitioners may believe that such programs will be less controversial and more acceptable. This is probably true, but a program that only increases awareness and knowledge, unless setting the stage for a subsequent behavioral influence effort (i.e., a second program or campaign), will be a disappointment on measures of real concern (e.g., number of alcohol-related automobile accidents). Thus, at least some programs offend no one by influencing no one.

Myth of the Sanctity of Interpersonal Influence

When media efforts, for a variety of reasons, have failed to show convincing evidence of behavior change, negative data often have been used to reinforce the sanctity of interpersonal influences. That is, "Media cannot effect behavior change. Only interpersonal processes result in behavior change." Quite obviously, interpersonal influence, when used appropriately, can have marked effects on behavior. Interpersonal contact, however, can have positive, negative, or no effects on behavior (e.g., the inconsistent results of studies with "social support").

The belief in the efficacy of interpersonal influence and nonefficacy of media has had several predictable results that have been noted earlier (i.e., the ad agency mentality, the self-fulfilling prophecy, the faulty simplified hierarchy of effects model, and the use of inappropriate stages of change). It has also led in some circles to an almost cultlike reverence for several models of interpersonal influence which tend to denigrate the potential of media-based efforts.

The most prominent of the interpersonal influence approaches has been the diffusion of innovation model (Rogers, 1983). Until recently, this model was tested largely in undeveloped countries having limited modern media capabilities. In these countries, interpersonal influence remained central for spreading new ideas and behaviors. However, as Bandura (1986) has noted, modern media, with their visual qualities and ability to depict behaviors in exquisite detail, constitute an excellent behavioral influence channel. Further, in a reinterpretation of data in Rogers (1983) by this author (Winett, 1986), it appeared that even in a study of birth control conducted in the 1970s in a relatively undeveloped part of China, media appeared to have a much greater influence than suggested by Rogers (1983) or other diffusion researchers.

Unrealistic Goals

Though media can be effective for behavioral influence, on balance some caveats are required. Media, as perhaps any other behavioral influence intervention, can be particularly effective when behaviors are relatively easy to perform, the behavior does not run counter to prevailing norms, there are minimal countermessages, and the behavior is likely to be reinforced frequently and, preferably, immediately. These requirements for a high probability of behavior change best fit inexpensive purchases, such as a soft drink, readily promoted by various media. However, even in the special case of a "simple purchase," a promotional ad is but one part of an orchestrated marketing plan (e.g., the product is readily available, relatively inexpensive, satisfying, and fits into current customs and settings).

Moreover, with few exceptions, most of the health behavior changes that purposeful media-based campaigns attempt to promote are *complex* behaviors, with those behaviors at times contradicting *subcultural norms* and subject to countermessages, with the behavior changes unlikely to be reinforced frequently and immediately. For example, assume for the moment that it was possible to present graphic, well-crafted, and targeted "safer sex" spots on network television that appeared at optimal times with repeated presentations over several months. The safer sex spots would be a major breakthrough for national health promotion/disease prevention media. Should it be assumed that, as reflected in self-reports and sexually transmitted disease statistics, the behavioral impacts of this television campaign would be profound?

Performing safer sexual practices, such as using condoms or removing oneself from unsafe situations, involves complex and sensitive behaviors. In some subcultures, such safer behaviors are considered at best irrelevant (Flora & Thoresen, 1988) and at worst an admission of sinfulness (Mays & Cochran, 1988). Thus, the behaviors run counter to strong norms. Innumerable other message sources (e.g., popular movies, some television soap operas, MTV) frequently portray or suggest unsafe sexual practices with few or any negative consequences. Therefore, it is unlikely that individuals opting to try safer sexual practices will be reinforced immediately or frequently. More likely, they may be subject to social and even physical punishment.

Under these circumstances, which are not atypical for some other health behaviors as well, it would be unrealistic to expect more than a small impact from the media-based program. If goals were set unrealistically high, then by most goal-related measures the effort would be a failure. With more modest, realistic goals, the program could appear reasonably effective.

The major point is that any media-based program needs to do considerable formative research and a priori analysis not only to formulate and target programs appropriately but also to develop realistic goals. With severe constraints, the best that may be done is to reach some cognitive goals (e.g., knowledge) and the beginning stages of behavior change. With fewer constraints, behavioral goals still need to be realistic but may be reasonably high. For example, given the greater availability of lower fat and higher fiber products in most supermarkets, it may be realistic to expect 70% of the viewers who saw at least 70% of televised cancer prevention nutrition spots to have at least tried one new lower fat or high fiber product.

Methodological Problems

This category includes an array of methodological problems, *any one* of which can undermine an effort substantially, if not totally. A traditional problem of media-based interventions that has been receiving more recent attention is the failure to conduct adequate formative research and other marketing research to design and refine the interventions for particular population segments properly (Winett et al., 1990). In the absence of extensive and ongoing formative and marketing research, followed by a series of pilot studies actually to pretest for behavior change, an intervention is usually a "best guess" of what will work. The history of media-based interventions indicates that, in the absence of careful behavior change and pilot research, best guesses are often incorrect guesses (Robertson et al., 1974). This point will be illustrated in the case example that follows.

Another set of problems pertains to design sensitivity (Lipsey, 1990). Included in this set are issues concerning the experimental rigor of an evaluation study; adequate differences between treatment and comparison conditions; the reliability and validity of process and outcome measures, and the ability of such measures to detect change; study participants' characteristics (particularly where the study is testing a prototype and where effects are likely to be meaningful but small); the number of study participants (traditionally thought of as the power issue, although all these issues relate to power); and the type of data analyses performed. Suffice it to say that many media-based intervention evaluations have had problems in *all* these areas. Therefore, it is often not surprising that the bottom-line verdict is "no effect."

Summary. It is apparent that there are several overlapping reasons why media-based behavioral influence interventions are frequently not very effective. Interestingly, and in contrast, about 20 years ago Mendelsohn (1973) noted many similar reasons why media programs *can* succeed. He indicated that media campaigns can succeed if middle-range and reasonable goals are picked and if a social marketing approach is taken to design different campaigns for different target population segments. As a final point (perhaps still applicable today), Mendelsohn (1973) concluded:

> very little of our mass communications research has really tested the effectiveness of the application of empirically grounded mass communications principles simply because most communications practitioners do not consciously utilize these principles. (p. 51)

Effective Media-Based Behavior Change

The chapter to this juncture and Mendelsohn's (1973) quote suggest that there are few examples in the published literature of media-based behavior change efforts that meet minimal methodological guidelines to demonstrate efficacy. Indeed, in a review conducted seven years ago, this author could identify only about 15 published studies (Winett, 1986). This number is expanded appreciably if self-help books and video programs are included under the rubric of media-based behavior change. A major caveat is that although some of these materials have been evaluated in methodologically sound studies, these materials often are used as a component or adjunct to therapy (Gould, 1991). Thus, it is not clear how effective many books and video programs are when they are used alone.

However, the prior review of effective media-based studies (Winett, 1986) and more recent work (Farquhar et al., 1990; Winett et al., 1991) all point to the importance of the objectives, steps, concepts, and procedures shown in Figure 9.1 plus several other critical elements based on communication models and social psychological research (McGuire, 1981). These elements include increasing the impact of the "message" through media with high production qualities; relying on trustworthy, expert, or competent sources to deliver the message; and using persuasive tactics such as acknowledging and then countering competing messages or arguments.

Farquhar et al. (1990) reported on the results of Stanford University's Five-City Project, perhaps the largest community health-promotion, disease-prevention, research and demonstration effort in this country. The key health behavior targets for this multilevel program involved dietary change, activity promotion, and smoking cessation, with both primary and secondary prevention emphasized. Diverse media (e.g., pamphlets, self-help booklets, TV spots) were targeted to different audiences and were used for all the objectives and steps in Figure 9.1. Because the media component of the program is only part of a multilevel intervention, with institutional, community, organizational, group, and individual components working in concert, the efficacy of media alone cannot be determined. However, Stanford's forerunner Three-Community Study suggested that media alone could have some lasting health behavior impacts; the project served as a seminal proving ground for the design, implementation, and evaluation of media-based behavior change materials and tactics (Solomon & Maccoby, 1984).

Winett et al. (1991) demonstrated that all the objectives and steps shown in Figure 9.1 could be encapsulated within an interactive information system used to promote the purchase of lower-fat and higher-fiber food items within the supermarket. Customers individually entered the system, which provided a weekly series of interactive programs guiding system users through information and awareness steps (i.e., dietary cancer links) to initial food purchase changes, and then to more extensive purchase and meal changes. The system also tracked an individual user's purchases and was able to provide individualized feedback and goals for changes in food purchases and attainment of nutritional guidelines (e.g., less than 30% calories from fat). Several other psychological strategies (e.g., commitment) were used, and the interactive system without any other intervention components demonstrated the capability of promoting appropriate changes in food purchases.

These two examples of effective media-based behavior change may appear daunting rather than encouraging because media were part of a very extensive overall program or were the substance of a complex interactive system. As the example at the end of this chapter shows, though, media can be effective for behavior change when used alone in conventional delivery modalities, i.e., videotape. However, besides attending to the sequencing of objectives and steps shown in Figure 9.1, the design, testing, and evaluation of effective media needs to follow an iterative, generative framework.

Behavioral Systems Framework

Figure 9.2 presents a representation of the behavioral systems framework used to conceptualize, plan, design, implement, and evaluate primarily media-based behavior change interventions. The framework borrows freely from health education, social marketing, and public health approaches (Green & Anderson, 1986; Manoff, 1985; Winett et al., 1989) but emphasizes more formative and pilot research than those approaches.

Note that on the left-hand side the framework has more conceptual steps, whereas the right-hand side has more strategic steps. On both sides, the steps progress from more general considerations to specific considerations germane to a particular intervention. Note also that steps are linked to each other using bidirectional arrows to suggest an iterative process between steps. The most basic notions of the framework are the following:

1. Theoretical and conceptual considerations will suggest how to define a problem; multilevel analyses will examine facilitators and barriers to change, and the relative costs and benefits of intervention at different levels; and a decision will be reached on the level(s) of intervention. Because this chapter's focus is media-based interventions, it is assumed for illustrative purposes that a decision is made to use media but perhaps in concert with another level of intervention (e.g., social cognitive theory and a public health model strongly suggest the addition of an environmental component to an individually based intervention). Notice also at this early stage of intervention, development ideas pertinent to social marketing and stages of change need to be addressed.

2. Once a problem has been defined and the level of intervention determined, the more specific principles to guide intervention design are examined. These principles are ones derived from the theories, concepts, and frameworks, and more than likely several principles will be used together. The steps in the behavioral systems framework between principles and intervention design require considerable formative research. For example, characteristics of models important to particular population groups can be identified by using focus groups, face-to-face interview, and surveys. Of course, similar methods can be used to identify subgroups, approaches and materials pertinent to subgroups, and how ready subgroups are to change. Concepts related to perceived vulnerability and other health benefits also may guide the formative research.

3. The principles and formative research suggest a particular intervention design, with specific goals, requiring particular personnel and settings, with the intervention promoted to particular audiences. The process of intervention design also becomes more specific because this step is guided by ideas about specific procedures. For example, particular ideas about effective behavioral modeling, market segmentation, intervention tailoring, and movement from cognitive change to behavioral enactment would be considered carefully. These steps re-

Conceptual Steps

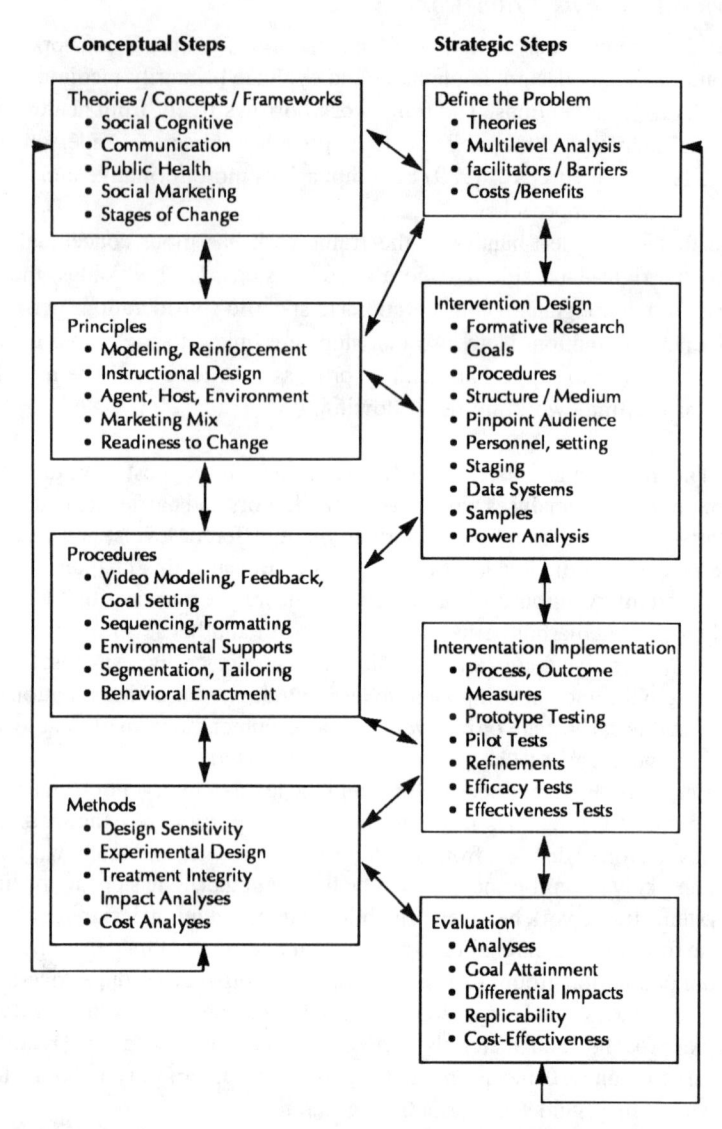

Theories / Concepts / Frameworks
- Social Cognitive
- Communication
- Public Health
- Social Marketing
- Stages of Change

Principles
- Modeling, Reinforcement
- Instructional Design
- Agent, Host, Environment
- Marketing Mix
- Readiness to Change

Procedures
- Video Modeling, Feedback, Goal Setting
- Sequencing, Formatting
- Environmental Supports
- Segmentation, Tailoring
- Behavioral Enactment

Methods
- Design Sensitivity
- Experimental Design
- Treatment Integrity
- Impact Analyses
- Cost Analyses

Strategic Steps

Define the Problem
- Theories
- Multilevel Analysis
- facilitators / Barriers
- Costs /Benefits

Intervention Design
- Formative Research
- Goals
- Procedures
- Structure / Medium
- Pinpoint Audience
- Personnel, setting
- Staging
- Data Systems
- Samples
- Power Analysis

Intervention Implementation
- Process, Outcome Measures
- Prototype Testing
- Pilot Tests
- Refinements
- Efficacy Tests
- Effectiveness Tests

Evaluation
- Analyses
- Goal Attainment
- Differential Impacts
- Replicability
- Cost-Effectiveness

Note: From "Effective Media Campaigns to Prevent the Spread of HIV Infection" by R. A. Winett, D. G. Altman, and A. C. King, 1990, *Evaluation and Program Planning*, *13*, p. 100. Copyright 1990 by Prentice Hall. Adapted by permission.

FIGURE 9.2 A representation of the behavioral systems framework.

quire additional formative research, with this stage of development culminating in a facsimile of the intervention. For example, at this stage a very brief, rough version of a video program may be tried out for feedback. The facsimile is inexpensive and may be altered in a series of brief trials to fit specific audiences better. Thus, there can be a series of facsimile tests. Not surprisingly, the intervention design steps require attention to potential data systems and samples of people for evaluation. Feedback from facsimile tests provide information about the viability of measures, effect sizes, and power considerations.

4. Next, the methodological steps are solidified with a series of considerations grouped under the term *design sensitivity* (Lipsey, 1990). A sensitive design will include a strong intervention, typically only one or two comparison conditions, analyses to reduce statistical variability (i.e., analyses of covariance [ANCOVA], repeated measures analyses), and methods to assure treatment integrity (Lipsey, 1990). Various cost analyses can also be conducted. Obviously, all these points and steps entail careful planning (West, 1985).

5. Within this framework (intervention implementation), there is a series of prototype tests, pilot tests, and efficacy and effectiveness tests. Most significantly, the early testing of an intervention is called for, where the early tests focus on behavior change and where the series of tests allows sufficient feedback and time for program refinements to result in an effective intervention. Unfortunately, these crucial tests *focusing on behavior change* are the ones most *in*frequently used in the development of media-based interventions. The idea here is to continue to refine and fine-tune an intervention through prototype tests (i.e., a close approximation of the intervention, more advanced than a facsimile), a series of pilot tests, efficacy tests (a test under ideal conditions), and effectiveness tests (a test under real-world conditions).

6. The evaluation step emphasizes how the intervention worked, with whom, what goals were reached or not reached, and the replicability of the intervention in practical terms (costs).

7. The framework in a sense is recursive, because the insights and specific results obtained from the intervention's evaluation inform future conceptual and strategic considerations for additional and related efforts.

The particular uses and methods of formative research, facsimile, prototype and pilot tests, and efficacy and effectiveness tests have been detailed in Winett, Moore, and Anderson (1991) and used in two recent media-based health behavior change projects (Winett & Moore, 1991a; Winett & Moore, 1991b). It is emphasized again that the careful attention to a series of steps focusing on behavior change is critical. Sufficient time must be allowed in the overall process of intervention conceptualization, design, implementation, and evaluation for changes and refinements to be made to produce an intervention capable of yielding meaningful behavioral changes.

In the next section, some of the steps from the framework are illustrated together with practical and logistical considerations for developing and implementing an effective intervention.

CASE EXAMPLE

Background

Although the various steps in the framework, particularly the methodological ones, follow routine guidelines for applied research, the many facets of formative research are probably less well-known and are far from standardized. The different facets of formative research will be illustrated by our "Family/Media AIDS Prevention Project" (Winett et al., 1991a). Several conceptual and strategic issues (that are part of the behavioral systems framework) were clarified or settled by formative research occurring *before* the project and by prior research by the author on media-based behavior change programs.

In the formative research (interviews) preceding the project, we found that for parents the home was an acceptable place for a sensitive, frank intervention. Parents wanted a program to help them talk with their teens about topics such as sexual behavior, but there were few programs available for use in the home by parents and teens *together.* Parents highly endorsed the notion of a home-based video program. Virtually all lower middle- to upper middle-class families we interviewed owned a video cassette recorder, (VCR), and a home-based video could reduce the time and effort involved for parents and teens to gain information and learn and practice new skills. Finally, the use of modeling, with story lines, repetition, and practice segments, appeared to be a relatively standard and effective format for skill training using a video program (Bandura, 1986; Winett, 1986). We have employed *all* the behavior change principles, strategies, and procedures discussed earlier in the chapter, with perhaps one important exception (to be discussed later).

The choice of intervening with the family and at home was further based on the limitations on the explicitness of content in many school-based programs covering the same or similar topics, the possibility of parent and teen discussions of information, and parental guidance of teen practice and use of skills. Younger teens were the focus of this *preventive* intervention because younger teens are often not yet sexually active.

There are two important points to emphasize concerning the early decisions we made. Two obvious modes and points of intervention were rejected, namely, schools and television. Although there are many school-based prevention programs (e.g., concerning substance use) in many other areas of the country (including our own), highly explicit programs dealing with sexual behavior are difficult to place in schools. In fact, to further confirm this notion, as the project started we wanted to see if we could just *recruit* families from public schools to be involved in the project. It quickly became apparent that the project staff would have to spend countless days and nights in meetings *possibly* to be granted permission to recruit through the public schools.

It was also doubtful that network affiliates or even local cable television stations would show an explicit program. Moreover, the one-time viewing of a television program was inconsistent with the idea of using of using a video program as a vehicle for the modeling *and practice* of skills over time. Thus, the choice of a video program was an attempt at the outset to bypass barriers to the program's content and training approach.

Additionally, a videotape program could be disseminated because about 75% of U.S. homes have VCRs. Clearly, a more preferred modality for skill development is an interactive video program. However, few homes in the next 10 years will have videodisc players, thus limiting the dissemination potential of interactive programs. Moreover, if our program is effective and mass produced, it could be available for only $10 to $15 per copy.

Teens are an important target audience for HIV prevention. They are at risk for HIV because: (a) by their middle to late teens most teens are sexually active, (b) only a small percentage of teens regularly use adequate protection during sexual activity, (c) many teens experiment sexually with multiple partners, (d) the rates of some other STDs (e.g., syphilis) have increased for teens during the last decade, and (e) experimentation with alcohol and drugs increases the probability of engagement in other risk behaviors (Miller, Turner, & Moses, 1990).

Current data on persons who are AIDS-diagnosed indicate that fewer than 1% of these cases are adolescents (Centers for Disease Control, 1991). However, these same data reveal that about 20% of these cases are persons in their early 20s (Centers for Disease Control, 1991). Because the incubation period from first infection to AIDS diagnosis can be 8 to 10 years, it is likely that AIDS-diagnosed persons in that age range contracted HIV as adolescents (Miller et al., 1990).

The present state of the epidemic perhaps is represented best by persons who are currently HIV infected but not AIDS diagnosed, and by those persons at high risk for contracting HIV. A recent National Academy of Science Report (Miller et al., 1990) has stated that HIV infection is no longer restricted geographically or demographically, and that the adolescent population has been "seeded" with HIV.

A primary objective of the video program ("Cartwheels to Carwheels") is to provide parents and teens with up-to-date information about HIV infection, other STDs, and risk behaviors (alcohol and drug use) that are often antecedents to engagement by teens in nonprotected sexual behaviors. Other objectives of the program are to teach parents and teens how to use problem-solving skills within family interactions and to teach teens how to use problem-solving and assertiveness skills in ordinary everyday situations and high-risk situations. A final objective is more general. It entails conveying the major conceptualization of the video program, that parents can markedly reduce their teenager's risk of contracting HIV and other STDs, as well as reduce the probability of other problems (e.g., drug use), by discussing these topics explicitly, by keeping teens involved in constructive activities (e.g., school, community, sports), and by learning and using specific skills offered in the program.

This program is best seen as a primary prevention program for the general population. The program attempts to impact information and skills useful for many parents and teens. Its goal also appear to be modest (although in some ways, as will be discussed shortly, they actually may be quite ambitious). Because the program is *not* aimed at identifiable high-risk families and teens, the project has received some criticism. Why are we wasting the taxpayers' money on low-risk families? One answer to this question is that as HIV spreads to various population segments, the relative risk of some groups now at low risk will probably rise. A second answer is that there *are* needs for preventive interventions for the general population, and moreover, the content and skills addressed in the program are important for other highly prevalent teen problems (i.e., early pregnancy and substance abuse).

Social Marketing/Formative Research

An extensive series of social marketing and formative research steps was undertaken. These steps fully involved our team of psychologists, educational technologists, professional assessors, script writers, television production staff and, of course, narrators, actors, and actresses. The purposes of these steps were to (a) develop methods to recruit participants into the project effectively, (b) reliably measure important cognitive and behavioral variables, (c) develop content acceptable to both parents and teens, and (d) determine whether the content could result in appropriate cognitive and behavior change.

As we have detailed elsewhere (Winett et al., 1991), this has been a challenging and, at times, daunting task. More than 250 families have participated in a 12-part series of formative research, pilot test, and prototype studies during a 3-year period. For example, we initially conducted 3-hour home interviews with teens and parents to find out about topics discussed (e.g., sexual behavior), how (and where, when, and by whom) these topics were discussed, appropriate words, and communication styles. All of these interviews were videotaped and studied by project staff.

Role plays were tested with families in their homes to see, for example, how problem-solving strategies could be enacted. Initial role plays also were used to test assessment measures. These initial forays led to (a) a brief 10-minute program (facsimile) to test the basic program ideas with families and to receive feedback from them; (b) an extended four-tape, 2.5-hour video program (prototype) with high-level language, terms, and involved training content; (c) a simplified four-type, 2-hour program with a story line, (d) a one-tape, 1-hour teen-only program; (e) a simplified but "hard-hitting" two-tape 1.5-hour parent and teen program.

Our assessment approach also has been much revised. Extensive, less structured role plays were replaced by simple, standard role plays presented on our assessment videotape and scored by pairs of highly trained assessors rating independently in the home. These role plays then were expanded to require a much higher level of skill. We have, however, retained the home assessor's high degree of reliability in assessing skills. Additionally, we also assess knowledge using a questionnaire we developed, with the questionnaire also evolving over time.

Original program and assessment goals involved increasing parent and teen conversations about HIV and related topics, and *reliably tracking* these conversations. Various logs and telephone contacts were used. All of our attempts yielded *un*reliable (i.e., low parent-teen agreement) data.

The most important point about the development of the program and assessment techniques is that both evolved from the continual interaction of our project products with the target audience, the families. If we had used only the conceptual parts of the framework to produce one program, and not followed the many formative research, pilot, and prototype steps (as has so often been the case in media-based behavior change efforts), this project would have been a failure. Our first extended video program was *not* well received and simply did not work. Through the many steps we have taken we have found: (a) We can produce a program that is very appealing to parents and moderately appealing to teens. (b) Parents and teens can increase relevant knowledge and skills, with gains maintained at a 6-month follow-up; these overall program effects have been replicated with two sets of families. (c) To be effective, parents must be actively involved as a "coach" for their teen. (d) A teen-only program did not work (although it was liked by teens). This last finding called into question the efficacy of other programs available for teens alone in the home or with limited guidance in schools.

We have also found an excellent way to recruit families into the project. Specifically, we have worked directly with family physicians who identify eligible families in their practice and then send a letter about the project to each family. Project staff either call the family or wait for the family to call our 800 number. Using this procedure, we have enrolled about 50% of eligible families in the project. Notice, moreover, that working with individual physicians and group practices may be our dissemination channel for a final version of our program.

There is a humbling side of our work. It has taken many steps to reach what are realistically *proximal* goals—knowledge and skill enhancement. We have *not* demonstrated use of these skills in high-risk situations as the teens get older, much less reduction of rates of STDs and HIV. Furthermore, at times it has been frustrating to deal firsthand with some families' lack of interest and motivation for a primary prevention program (see Jeffrey, 1989). In part, this problem may represent our failure to have different program segments highlighted for families at different stages of change or to segment the market of "interested families with young teens" more rationally. These are conceptual and marketing shortcomings of our efforts. Conversely, we have kept ourselves motivated by the promise of our program and other primary prevention efforts. The impact of modest individual changes can be greatly magnified when *well-tested* programs become widely available to the public.

FUTURE DIRECTIONS

This chapter began by describing a major problem for preventive efforts. Regardless of the type of problem or even level of intervention, a critical part of any preventive effort involves modifying individual behavior. Indeed, with the exception of structural interventions that do not require mass individual change (although the behavior of politicians, key community people, and health professionals must be influenced to enact structural interventions), virtually every prevention program's effectiveness rests on its ability to change human behavior.

Once the focus is on mass individual change, attention usually is directed to media-based interventions so that many people can be reached. However, there are few well-documented examples in the literature of effective media-based interventions. Several conceptual, strategic, and methodological shortcomings of many media-based programs were noted. This chapter has, though, strongly emphasized that the conceptual, strategic, and methodological foundations for effective media-based behavior change programs are known; the steps and processes for the design and implementation of media-based programs can be systematized within a framework. Following all the steps and processes of the framework does *not* assure that a media-based program will be overwhelmingly successful. Rather, the case example in this chapter suggests that careful attention to the framework (particularly the use of formative and pilot research) increases the likelihood of achieving (albeit modest) success.

There is seemingly a great range of important day-to-day health and mental health problems that may be approached with preventive interventions using media. As was shown in this chapter, even conventional, inexpensive media may have an important role to play in such national concerns as AIDS prevention. With more conceptual creativity, the greater availability of new media with interactive capabilities, and the willingness to test, refine, and carefully evaluate interventions, media-based interventions may, in fact, become a major vehicle for promoting preventive health behavior changes.

ACKNOWLEDGMENTS

The writing of this chapter was supported by grants from the National Cancer Institute and National Institute of Mental Health. John Moore, Eileen Anderson, David Taylor, Richard Hook, Deborah Webster, Kathy Sikkema, and Tamara Neubauer have contributed to the Family/Media AIDS Prevention Project discussed in this chapter.

REFERENCES

Altman, D. G., Foster, V., Rosenick-Douss, L., & Tye, J. B. (1989). Reducing the sale of illegal cigarette to minors. *Journal of the American Medical Association, 261*, 80–83.

Bandura, A. (1986). *Social Foundations of thought and action: A social cognitive theory*. Englewood Cliffs, NJ: Prentice Hall.

Brownell, K. D., Marlatt, A., Lichtenstein, E., & Wilson, G. T. (1986). Understanding and preventing relapse. *American Psychologist, 41*, 765–782.

Catania, J. A., Kegeles, S. M., & Coates, T. J. (1990). Towards an understanding of risk behavior: An AIDS risk reduction model (ARRM). *Health Education Quarterly, 17*, 53–72.

Centers for Disease Control (1991). *HIV/AIDS surveillance data*. Washington, DC: National Center for Health Statistics.

Farquhar, J. W., Fortmann, S. P., Flora, J. A., Taylor, C. B., Haskell, W. L., Williams, P. T., Maccoby, N., & Wood, P. D. (1990). Effects of community-wide education on cardiovascular risk factors. *Journal of the American Medical Association, 264*, 359–365.

Flora, J. A., & Thoresen, C. E. (1988). Reducing the risk of AIDS in adolescents. *American Psychologist, 43*, 965–970.

Gould, R. A. (1991). *A meta-analysis of self-help, media-based programs*. Unpublished manuscript, Virginia Polytechnic Institute and State University, Blacksburg, VA.

Green, L. W., & Anderson, C. L. (1986). *Community health*. St. Louis, MO: Mosby.

Hanlon, J. J., & Pickett, G. E. (1984). *Public health: Administration and practice* (8th ed.). St. Louis, MO: Mosby.

Jeffrey, R. W. (1989). Risk behaviors and health: Contrasting individual and population perspectives. *American Psychologist, 44*, 1194–1202.

Kotler, P., & Roberts, E. L. (1989). *Social marketing: Strategies for changing public behavior*. New York: Free Press.

Laswell, H. D. (1948). The structure and function of communication in society. In A. Bryson (Ed.), *The communication of ideas* (pp. 57–79). New York: Harper & Row.

Levin, H. M. (1983). *Cost effectiveness: A primer.* Beverly Hills, CA: Sage.
Liebert, R. M., Sprafkin, I. N., & Davidson, E. S. (1982). *The early window: Effects of television on children and youth* (2nd ed.). Elmsford, NY: Pergamon.
Lipsey, M. W. (1990). *Design sensitivity.* Beverly Hills, CA: Sage.
Manoff, R. K. (1985). *Social marketing: Imperative for public health.* New York: Praeger.
Mays, V. M., & Cochran, S. D. (1988). Issues in the perception of AIDS risk and risk reduction activities by black and Hispanic/Latin women. *American Psychologist, 43,* 949–457.
McGuire, W. J. (1981). Theoretical foundations of campaigns. In R. E. Rice & W. J. Paisley (Eds.), *Public communication campaigns* (pp. 67–83). Beverly Hills, CA: Sage.
McLeod, J. M., & Reeves, B. (1981). On the nature of mass media effects. In G. C. Wilhoit (Ed.), *Mass communication review yearbook* (Vol. 2, pp. 245–282). Beverly Hills, CA: Sage.
McQuail, D., & Windahl, S. (1981). *Communication models for the study of mass communication.* New York: Longman.
Mendelsohn, H. (1973). Some reasons why information campaigns can succeed. *Public Opinion Quarterly, 37,* 50–60.
Miller, H. G., Turner, C. F., & Moses, L. E. (1990). *AIDS: The second decade.* Washington, DC: National Academy Press.
Moore, J. F. (1990, August). Instructional design technology and health behavior change. In R. A. Winett (Chair), *Dissemination of health behavior change information in the mass media.* Symposium presented at the annual convention of the American Psychological Association, Boston.
Robertson, L. S., Kelley, A. B., O'Neill, B., Wixom, C. W., Eiswirth, R. S., & Haddon, Jr., W. (1974). A controlled study of the effect of television messages on safety belt usage. *American Journal of Public Health, 64,* 1071–1080.
Rogers, E. M. (1983). *Diffusion of innovation* (3rd ed.). New York: Free Press.
Solomon, D. S., & Maccoby, N. (1984). Communication as a model for health enhancement. In J. D. Matarazzo, S. M., Weiss, J. A. Herd, N. E. Miller, & S. M. Weiss (Eds.), *Behavioral health: A handbook for health enhancement* (pp. 209–221). New York: Wiley.
West, S. G. (1985). Beyond the laboratory experiment: Experimental and quasi-experimental designs for interventions in naturalistic settings. In P. Karoly (Ed.), *Measurement strategies in health psychology* (pp. 183–233). New York: Wiley.
Winett, R. A. (1986). *Information and behavior: Systems of influence.* Hillsdale, NJ: Lawrence Erlbaum.
Winett, R. A., Altman, D. G., & King, A.C. (1990). Effective media campaigns to prevent the spread of HIV infection. *Evaluation and Program Planning, 13,* 91–104.
Winett, R. A., King, A. C., & Altman, D. G. (1989). *Health Psychology and public health: An integrative approach.* Elmsford, NY: Pergamon.
Winett, R. A., & Moore, J. F. (1991a). *Family/media approach to AIDS prevention.* Ongoing National Institute of Mental Health project, Virginia Polytechnic Institute and State University, Blacksburg, VA.
Winett, R. A., & Moore, J. F. (1991b). *Feedback/video systems to promote nutritious purchases.* Ongoing National Cancer Institute project, Virginia Polytechnic and State University, Blacksburg, VA.
Winett, R. A., Moore, J. F., & Anderson, E. S. (1991). Extending the concept of social validity: Behavior analysis for disease prevention and health promotion. *Journal of Applied Behavior Analysis, 24,* 215–230.

Winett, R. A., Moore, J. F., Wagner, J. L., Hite, L. A., Leahy, M., Neubauer, T. E., Walberg, J. L., Walker, W. B., Lombard, D., Geller, E. S., & Mundy, L. L. (1991). Altering shoppers' supermarket purchases to fit nutritional guidelines: An interactive information system. *Journal of Applied Behavior Analysis, 24,* 95–105.

Wright, J. C., & Huston, A. C. (1983). A matter of form: Potentials of television for young viewers. *American Psychologist, 38,* 835–844.

CHAPTER 10

Applications of Social Support to Preventive Interventions

*G. Anne Bogat, Linda A. Sullivan,
and Jacqueline Grober*

DESCRIPTION OF THE PROBLEM

Almost 20 years ago, Caplan (1974), Cassel (1976), and Cobb (1976) published influential review papers documenting associations between psychiatric disorder and the absence or disruption of social support. An enormous body of work has since substantiated that social support is positively related to both physical and mental health (e.g., Dohrenwend & Dohrenwend, 1974, 1981; House, 1981; Leavy, 1983; Mitchell, Billings, & Moos, 1982; Mueller, 1980). The beneficial aspects of support have captured the imagination of researchers, practitioners, policymakers, and the public. Gottlieb (1988) noted that mobilizing support is more cost-effective and culturally valid than traditional mental health services delivered by professionals, political conservatives appreciate the volunteerism aspect of support as well as its implied self-help ethos, political liberals prize the empowerment values of support, and laypersons appreciate the chance to learn skills that may make a difference in their lives and their communities. Unfortunately, the actual results of support interventions tend to be less exciting than the hypothetical ideal of support that fires our imaginations. This chapter examines why most current interventions fall short of our scientific standards and ideological values, and suggests how they might be improved. In the next section, we briefly summarize the theoretical literature on social support; this serves as a prelude to our discussion of findings from interventions that have either created or enhanced social support. These social support interventions are critiqued, and the literature is examined for its theoretical and methodological sophistication. We then, in the chapter's case example, examine one prototypical social support intervention to demonstrate the strengths and weaknesses of the extant literature. And, finally, in the last section, we suggest future directions that social support intervention research might usefully take.

REVIEW AND CRITIQUE OF THE LITERATURE

Social Support Theory

Models of Support

Two models have been advanced to explain the positive relationship between social support and adjustment: stress-buffering and main effect. The stress-buffering model suggests that persons experiencing high levels of life stress will evidence better adjustment when they receive adequate social support. The main effect model states that regardless of experienced stress, individuals benefit because of the perception or the actuality that they are part of a supportive network; this is believed to result in higher self-esteem and self-efficacy.

Much evidence has accumulated to substantiate the validity of both models. For example, Kessler and McLeod (1985) summarized 23 studies that examined social support in the context of general stress. Subjects in these studies were not students or victims of specific life crises. The authors concluded that social network structure variables and social involvement variables ("membership in affiliative networks") did not show buffering effects but did exhibit statistically small main effects. Emotional support and perceived adequacy of support variables demonstrated buffering effects but no main effects. Similar conclusions have been reached by other authors (e.g., Cohen & Wills, 1984), but further research is needed before these results can be considered definitive.

Measurement of Support

Theoretical notions of support are intimately related to its measurement. First, studies rarely measure more than one dimension of social support. "The separate buffer effects of emotional support and perceived availability of support might turn out to be a single effect if they were examined simultaneously" (Kessler & McLeod, 1985, p. 236). Second, although authors habitually clamor that research should specify the process and behaviors by which support is transmitted, measurement of support has relied almost solely on self-report data. This bias is so entrenched that researchers routinely assert, without justification, that questionnaire data can generate both objective and subjective aspects of support.

To move away from a reliance on questionnaire measures, some researchers have begun to investigate behavioral manifestations of supportive interactions. One self-report measure that examines supportive behaviors is a support diary or a social contract record (Cutrona, 1986; Sullivan, 1989). Subjects record every instance of social interaction during a specified period, whom they interacted with, and the nature of the interaction. Also, a few truly objective measurements of supportive behavior have been conducted. Liotta, Jason, Robinson, and LaVigne (1985) reliably rated five types of social support in a field setting. In a laboratory setting, Procidano and Heller (1983) showed that interaction rates among close friend or sibling dyads were influenced by whether subjects rated themselves high or low in perceived family and perceived friend support. Heller and Lakey (1985), in another laboratory study, were unable to identify specific interactional behaviors that distinguished high and low perceived support dyads. Subjects did not exhibit the supportive behaviors that psychologists have come to regard as important (e.g., "interpretations or reflections of feeling," p. 296).

Methodological Criticisms

Current research on social support is mainly correlational, which makes it vulnerable to alternative explanations. Kessler and McLeod (1985) observed that there is "little evidence that support is consequential for mental health. It might be that mental health is the causal variable and support the outcome or, more likely, that mental health and social support are connected in a complex web of mutual influence" (p. 236). And Kiesler (1985) noted that even if the buffering hypothesis were proved unequivocally true (which it has not been), there is simply no evidence that "an artificially or experimentally induced increase in social support would produce an increase in the defense against negative life events" (p. 351). As the reader will soon see, a central thesis of this chapter is that interventions seeking to manipulate social support could complement the cross-sectional correlational studies on which much of the theoretical literature is based. Experimental manipulation of social support could yield a more accurate understanding of the causal relationship between support and adjustment as well as elucidate the potency of social support in these relationships (e.g., Rook & Dooley, 1985).

From Theory to Practice: A Review of Social Support Literatures

Many previous writers have reviewed the literature on social support interventions, and some have outlined demonstration projects attempting to translate theory into action (e.g., Brody, 1985; Gottlieb, 1981a,b, 1983b, 1985; Halpern & Larner, 1987; Heller, Price, & Hogg, 1990; Hobfoll & Stephens, 1990; Vaux, 1988). One can only be impressed at the wide variety of problems that social support interventions have begun to address: for example, bereavement, divorce, child abuse and neglect, and health issues such as smoking cessation and weight loss. The method of service delivery includes group interventions (i.e., self-help groups and professionally led groups) as well as one-on-one supportive interventions provided by professionals and paraprofessionals. Interventions modify or enhance support in diverse ways. Some interventions provide one or more aspects of *functional support*. This includes (a) emotional support—expressions of empathy and caring, (b) informational support—the communication of information or skills, and (c) instrumental support—helping behaviors and the lending of money. Other interventions focus on modifying *structural support* by enhancing social networks—the number of persons with whom the participant can enter into meaningful social exchange (functional/structural taxonomy based on House, 1981).

The following review of the intervention literature is based on studies that met the following criteria. First, the interventions were based, in substantial part, on the provision of social support; that is, the authors had to state a minimum operational description of the type of support provided. It was not sufficient if the authors noted in passing that the service providers were encouraged to be supportive to the service recipients, or if the intervention was reconceptualized, post hoc, as supportive, or if *we* construed the intervention as providing or modifying social support, but the researchers did not. Furthermore, a study was not included if the intervention was a professional therapy service (e.g., group therapy), even if increased social support was an outcome of the intervention. We did not include research studies on those self-help groups where the social support provided could not be differentiated from the life philosophy of the intervention or could not be considered the dominant focus of the intervention (e.g., Alcoholics Anonymous). Second, the studies were all data-based evaluations. Studies with no statistical data, data on consumer satisfaction only, or data that were too vaguely summarized were not included. Third, all interventions were field studies. Laboratory interventions were not included.

The remainder of this section discusses the models of support tested (implicitly and explicitly) by researchers conducting interventions, describes and critiques the interventions, and offers a general methodological critique of the intervention literature.

Testing the Models of Support

Our review indicated that most applied researchers do not articulate models for social support. In the following paragraphs, we discuss how the two models of social support could be tested and how the approaches taken by intervention researchers fit these prototypes.

Figure 10.1 outlines how one might test for the main effect and the stress-buffering models of social support in a multiple-regression analysis without an intervention. Path A is a test of the main effect model; social support would directly

```
                    Social Support
                         |     \
                         |      \  A
                       B |       \
                         |        \
                         v         v
  Stress  - - - - - - - - - - - - - - - - - - - - - - > Adjustment
```

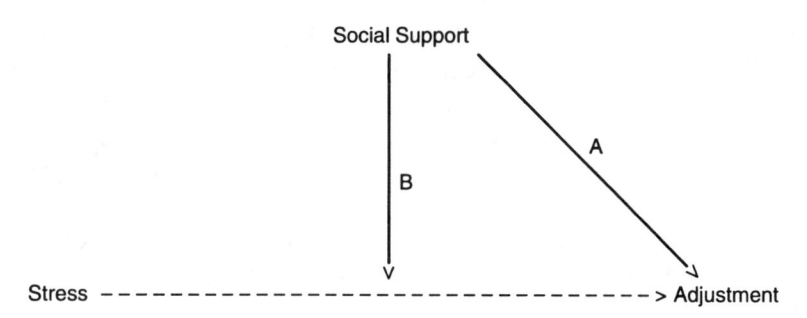

FIGURE 10.1   Testing for main effect and stress-buffering models of social support.

predict adjustment, regardless of level of stress. Path B is a test of the stress-buffering hypothesis. Only a social support × stress interaction term (and not social support by itself) would predict adjustment.

To test these models through intervention research, the same variables must be measured—social support, stress, and adjustment. Most intervention researchers employ repeated measures analysis of variance (ANOVA) statistical techniques when analyzing their data. Therefore, to verify a main effect model, researchers would need to determine that increased social support leads to better adjustment. In a simple 2 × 2 design, where subjects are randomly assigned to a control group or social support intervention group and tested before and after the intervention, one would expect to find a significant time × group interaction for adjustment, with experimental subjects demonstrating better postintervention adjustment than control subjects. The stress-buffering hypothesis could be tested with the administration of a stress scale before the intervention. Then, in a 2 × 2 × 2 design (time, group, and stress—high and low), one would expect a significant three-way interaction showing that only experimental subjects with high stress scores at preintervention would have better adjustment at postintervention when compared to control subjects.

Obviously, other statistical techniques can be employed. Multiple-regression techniques would offer greater power than ANOVA models, and Newcomb (1990) argues for the merits of structural equation modeling (SEM) to test the effects of social support. The advantages of using SEM include the extraction of latent variables from measured variables and the capability to study several dependent variables simultaneously, a need that arises often in social support research.

To date, *most* intervention research does not provide an adequate test of either model. Researchers often (a) assume a social support model is operative for a particular life problem, without testing it, (b) incorrectly conceptualize the key variables, or (c) provide an incomplete analysis of the key variables.

An example of the first point is a study by Barnett and Parker (1985). These researchers did not measure stress per se, but they did assess women's anxiety levels before the intervention. (It is not clear whether stress can be equated with anxiety in this study or in the Greene and Monahan [1987, 1989] studies discussed later.) High-anxiety women were assigned to a professional treatment condition, a nonprofessional treatment condition, or a control group. Moderate- and low-anxiety women were assigned to control groups. Thus, the researchers assumed that an intervention group would provide benefits only for high-anxiety women. Random assignment of all women to treatment groups would have gone further toward determining whether the stress-buffering model was, in fact, operative with this population.

Examples of the second point are quite common. For example, Abramowitz and Coursey (1989) evaluated a support group for family caretakers of schizophrenics. Subjects were assigned to control and experimental groups, and variables such as stress, anxiety, and self-efficacy were measured at preintervention and postintervention. To provide a test of the stress-buffering hypothesis, stress must be treated as an independent variable that interacts with support to produce better adjustment. These authors treated stress as a dependent variable.

Examples of the third point also occur frequently; that is, the appropriate data were collected to test for a main effect or stress-buffering model, but the authors did not perform the necessary statistical analyses. For instance, Greene and Monahan (1987, 1989) implemented "professionally guided support groups" for caretakers of frail elderly persons. The authors proposed that provision of support would result in less stress for the caretaker and, thus, in better caretaking of the elderly person. Variables including the caretaker's anxiety and depression, and his/her hostility to and perception of burden of the frail elderly person were measured before the program, after the program, and at a 6-month follow-up. In the 1989 study, four separate multiple-regression analyses were employed to predict the effect of the program on the caretakers. One analysis showed that reductions in anxiety were predicted by membership in the intervention group as well as by preintervention anxiety, hostility, and perceived burden. This statistical analysis tests the main effect model of support. That is, social support (as measured by membership in the intervention group) was a strong predictor of later adjustment (reduced anxiety). The authors could have tested the stress-buffering model by including an interaction term (group × anxiety) in the regression analysis, but they did not.

In summary, most interventions did not implement the research designs or statistical analyses necessary to test the models of support proposed by the theoretical literature. In all fairness, the earlier interventions we reviewed were not likely to have intentionally addressed such theoretical concerns; their implementation preceded, by some years, the literature on the nature of social support and the mechanisms by which it works (e.g., Cohen & McKay, 1984; Cohen & Wills, 1985; Heller & Swindle, 1983).

Social support interventions have addressed myriad social and individual problems. We have grouped these interventions into two broad categories: life-transition interventions and health-promotion interventions.

Life-Transition Interventions

Life-transition interventions include those directed toward parenting, bereavement, divorce/separation, and school transitions.[1] These interventions develop support in the context of a stressful life event, and thus follow either an implicit or explicit stress-buffering model. This approach corresponds to community psychology's stance of targeting at-risk populations to prevent problems before they start or become deeply entrenched. The ecological focus of most of these interventions is the individual, although Felner, Ginter, and Primavera's (1982) study is striking for its manipulation of the school environment. Finally, the type of social support provided in life-transition interventions is primarily informational and secondarily emotional.

Parenting. The typical parent support program was targeted toward "high-risk" mothers and infants. High-risk factors varied according to the individual study but included maternal variables such as youth, single parenthood, low SES, previous psychiatric disturbance, and previous substance abuse, as well as infant variables such as low birthweight. The characteristic program provided these mothers with one-on-one support rather than a support group. The service providers were mainly professionals. All of the studies increased the amount of informational support available to the mother (facts regarding proper diet, normal pregnancy and labor, new baby care, child development, etc.). In most studies, emotional support was also provided. More intensive programs also attempted to enhance the mother's social network by connecting her with community resources (Barrera, Rosenbaum, & Cunningham, 1986; Booth, Barnard, Mitchell, & Spieker, 1987; Booth, Mitchell, Barnard, & Spieker, 1989; Dawson, van Doorninck, & Robinson, 1989; Minde, Shosenberg, Thompson, & Marton, 1983; Olds, Henderson, Chamberlin, & Tatelbaum, 1986a; Olds, Henderson, Tatelbaum, & Chamberlin, 1986b), encouraging her to identify and engage already existing supports (Booth et al., 1989; Larson, 1980; Lee, 1988; Olds et al., 1986a, 1986b), structuring home visits to include persons in her support network (Olds et al., 1986a, 1986b), or providing her with better social skills (Booth et al., 1987, 1989). The duration of these interventions ranged from 6 weekly meetings (McGuire & Gottlieb, 1979) to about 33 visits over 2.5 years (Olds et al., 1986a, 1986b). Most interventions were approximately 1 year long, beginning before or at the child's birth and ending at 1 year of age.

Studies used a wide variety of outcome measures to assess the programs' effectiveness. Most studies were able to find some positive outcomes, regardless of whether the service providers were professional or nonprofessional. Interventions increased the mothers' social support (Booth et al., 1987; Larson, 1980; McGuire & Gottlieb, 1979; Olds et al., 1986b), improved the quality of mother-child interactions (Barrera et al., 1986; Boger, Richter, Kurnetz, & Haas, 1986; Booth et al., 1987, 1989; Larson, 1980; Minde et al., 1983), enhanced infants' cognitive functioning (Barrera et al., 1986), reduced the incidence of minor infant and childhood accidents (Larson, 1980; Olds et al., 1986a), and reduced verified cases of child abuse for mothers at highest risk for abusing their children (Olds et al., 1986a).

The effects of social support on more distal intervention goals such as the infant's physical health and maternal emotional well-being are less clear. Mothers' use of health services for minor infant illnesses varied in different studies (Dawson et al., 1989; Olds, 1986a; Siegel, Bauman, Schaefer, Saunders, & Ingram, 1980). The effect of social support on parent psychological health is also equivocal (Barnett & Parker, 1985; Booth et al., 1987; Elliott, Sanjack, & Leverton, 1988; Lee, 1988).

The confidence with which all of these results can be attributed to the experimental manipulation of social support is attenuated by four factors. First, the integrity of the interventions was often compromised by the absence of (a) manipulation checks, to determine whether social support was actually enhanced or created, and (b) standardization of protocols for interactions with the mothers. Only one study assessed the extent to which home visitors implemented program procedures and whether the program successfully manipulated the mothers' perceived social support (Booth et al., 1987). In this study, mothers who improved in mother-child interactions, compared with those who did not, attained more program goals during the intervention and reported more satisfaction with their social support at posttesting.

Second, outcomes were often assessed using nonstandardized, self-report measures. Only two studies also verified outcomes through official records (Dawson et al., 1989; Olds et al., 1986a, 1986b), and only Booth et al. (1987) employed objective ratings of observational data. Third, when specified, participants in these interventions were generally of lower or lower middle SES; thus, the generalizability to other populations in unknown. And, finally, assignment to groups was not always random (Booth et al., 1987; Larson, 1980). In summary, the extant research suggests that social support can mitigate some of the stresses associated with parenthood. Such interventions seem particularly effective in reaching proximal goals (e.g., enhancing mother-infant interactions). However, both the method of implementation (i.e., individual home visitors) and the length of the interventions (i.e., average length of 1 year) distinguish these programs as more labor intensive than other social support interventions.

Bereavement. The widowed were the modal target of these interventions. A popular intervention is the Widow-to-Widow program initially begun in 1969. The reader is referred to Silverman (1974, 1981, 1986, 1988) for a complete description of the program and a rich accumulation of anecdotal evidence describing widows' experiences in the program over the years. Briefly, widows are contacted about 2 months after the death of their husband and are offered the emotional support of another widow. To date, the only data-based experimental evaluation of the Widow-to-Widow program has been conducted by Vachon, Lyall, Rogers, Freedman-Letofsky, and Freeman (1980). Barrett's (1978) study examined three different widow groups that were based, in part, on Silverman's philosophy. Lieberman and Videka-Sherman (1986) evaluated another popular widow support group, They Help Each Other Spiritually (THEOS), a nationwide self-help group that provides both informational and emotional support.

Overall, these studies found positive outcomes for participants in widow groups. Participants experienced reduced distress (Vachon et al., 1980), were less depressed and anxious (Lieberman & Videka-Sherman, 1986), and had greater self-esteem (Barrett, 1978; Lieberman & Videka-Sherman, 1986) than nonparticipants. Generalizability of results is tempered by the fact that most subjects were women (93%–100%) and middle class. Widowers and members of lower SES groups may experience different stressors following the death of a spouse, and, thus, may require different types of support.

Two articles evaluated an intervention to help parents cope with the death of a child (Videka-Sherman, 1982; Videka-Sherman & Lieberman, 1985). Participants in the 18 most durable chapters of Compassionate Friends were surveyed at two time points concerning their mental health status, social functioning, and attitudes about bereavement. Higher levels of participation in the group were related to increases in the parents' interpersonal growth (Videka-Sherman, 1982). No other benefits accrued as a result of participation (Videka-Sherman & Lieberman, 1985).

Divorce and Separation. Interventions have been conducted for both separated adults (Bloom, Hodges, & Caldwell, 1982; Bloom, Hodges, Kern, & McFadden, 1985; Stolberg & Garrison, 1985) and the children of divorced parents (Alpert-Gillis, Pedro-Carroll, & Cowen, 1989; Kalter, Pickar, & Lesowitz, 1984; Pedro-Carroll & Cowen, 1985; Pedro-Carroll, Cowen, Hightower, & Guare, 1986). The Bloom et al. studies were 6-month interventions with separated adults. Participants were provided with emotional support by female paraprofessional program representatives and had access to sources of informational support in the form of study groups for various life transition issues (e.g., legal, homemaking). On standardized self-report measures, program participants showed a significant increase in psychological adjustment as compared with controls; however, the match (or mismatch) between the sex of the participants (males and females) and the service providers (all females) was implicated in participant outcomes. Positive mental health outcomes favored females at 6 and 30 months postintervention (Bloom et al., 1982), but favored males at the 4-year follow-up (Bloom et al., 1985). Stolberg and Garrison's (1988) findings suggested that much shorter interventions may benefit divorced adults. The adjustment of individuals who participated in a 12-week support group did not deteriorate from pretesting to posttesting, whereas the adjustment of divorced controls did.

Children of divorce exhibited similar benefits after participating in interventions that varied in length from 10 to 16 weeks. These interventions, led by professionals at their school, enhanced children's emotional support and social problem-solving skills through group discussion on issues surrounding divorce and the expression of anger and other feelings. Participants showed improvement, from preintervention to postintervention, on teacher-rated competencies and problem behaviors, parent-rated adjustment, and self-reported anxiety and self-concept (Alpert-Gillis et al., 1989; Pedro-Carroll & Cowen, 1985; Stolberg & Garrison, 1985). In perhaps the only intervention to test the stress-buffering model, Pedro-Carroll et al. (1986) compared a group of children of divorce with a matched control group of children from intact families. Before the intervention, the children of divorce were less well adjusted than the control group. At postintervention, the children of divorce showed significant improvement on ratings from all sources (self-report, teachers, parents), whereas the control children remained the same. Social support interventions of less than 10 weeks' duration may not be beneficial. Kalter et al. (1984) reported that an 8-week intervention did not affect children's perceived competence or adjustment.

Divorce/separation interventions differ from those discussed earlier in that the target subjects are both male and female, and of middle or upper middle SES. Unfortunately, both studies sought to enhance specific competencies as well as provide social support, making it impossible to disentangle the specific effects of support (Pedro-Carroll & Cowen, 1985).

School Transitions. Five studies formally evaluated supportive programs for children experiencing a school transition (Bogat, Jones, & Jason, 1980; Felner et al., 1982; Jason & Bogat, 1983; Jason et al., in press; Sloan, Jason, & Bogat, 1984). In the studies by Bogat and colleagues, the subjects were children transferring schools because of family mobility. The interventions were brief and involved either groups that provided mainly informational support (Bogat et al., 1980; Sloan et al., 1984) or informational groups plus the assignment of a buddy for the target child (Jason & Bogat, 1983). Jason et al. (in press) compared two interventions (tutoring/orientation and tutoring/orientation/parent-involvement programs) with a control group. Many outcome measures (e.g., grades, sociometric ratings, self-esteem) showed that children in the more intensive intervention faired better at posttreatment when compared with the other two groups. Subjects in the Felner et al. (1982) study were ninth graders making the transition to high school. The intervention was an ecological modification: Students were placed in a specially organized school environment designed to increase the level of teacher emotional support and the support that fellow students could provide to one another.

Results of four of the five programs found that participants, as compared with control group members, had better mental health outcomes (e.g., less anxiety, better self-esteem/self-concept) and better school performance (attendance, grades, teachers conduct ratings) following the intervention. The studies by Bogat and colleagues (1980, 1983, 1984) found that knowledge about school rules and regulations increased for participating children.

The results of these studies are encouraging; however, certain methodological problems exist in many of them. First, no study measured whether increased social support actually resulted for the subjects who participated in the programs. Second, several studies did not randomly assign subjects to conditions (Bogat et al., 1980; Felner et al., 1982). Third, three of the five studies were very brief interventions; the potency of the support provided to these children may have been minimal (Bogat et al., 1980; Jason & Bogat, 1983; Sloan et al., 1984).

Health-Promotion Interventions

Health-promotion interventions include those directed toward (a) caregivers and persons suffering from chronic illness, and (b) persons desiring to improve their physical health. These two types of interventions follow different implied models of social support. Clearly, caregivers and persons suffering from chronic illness are under some degree of life stress; thus, interventions aimed at these populations would seem to imply a stress-buffering model of support. However, persons desiring to improve their physical health would seem to be under no greater stress than average; therefore, these interventions might be considered tests of the main effect model. This latter intervention approach corresponds to the values of community psychology that advocate life enhancement and empowerment as important strategies. The ecological framework of most health-promotion interventions moves beyond a focus on the individual, and includes family and friends as central to the solution to the problem. Finally, the type of support provided by the physical health enhancement interventions is mainly emotional, with some informational support included. For the caregiver/chronic illness interventions, informational support is the predominant type of support provided, and emotional support is always a secondary component.

Caregivers and Persons Suffering from Chronic Illness.[2] Studies that intervened with caregivers or persons with chronic illnesses involved support groups where informational support was usually provided by an expert who educated members on the medical aspects of the illness, medications, and, in the caregiver groups, caregiving techniques. Emotional support occurred in the unstructured segments of each group meeting where persons could discuss their problems and feelings. Among the six studies that reported characteristics of group leaders, half were professionally led, and half were led by group members. No clear pattern of outcome findings was related to the professional status of the leader. In a comparison of professionally versus nonprofessionally led social support groups,

Toseland, Rossiter, and Labrecque (1989) did not find significant outcome differences for participants in the two groups.

Psychological adjustment was the most commonly targeted outcome measure of these interventions. Seven of the eight studies measured such indices of psychological distress as anxiety, depression, and psychosomatic symptomatology (Abramowitz & Coursey, 1989; Greene & Monahan, 1989; Haley, Brown, & Levine, 1987; Hinrichsen, Revenson, & Shinn, 1985; Toseland et al., 1989; Vadasy, Meyer, Fewell, & Greenberg, 1985; Zarit, Anthony, & Boutselis, 1987). Two factors seemed to influence whether participants experienced psychological benefits from the groups: (a) the length of the intervention and (b) the participants' levels of stress before the interventions.

First, social support interventions ranged from six weekly sessions to bimonthly meetings over 3 years, and one study examined the effectiveness of an ongoing support group (Hinrichsen et al., 1985). Three of the five short-term interventions for caregivers did not find significant improvements in caregiver emotional well-being (Haley et al., 1987; Toseland et al., 1989; Zarit et al., 1987). Both of the long-term interventions reported mental health benefits for participants (Hinrichsen et al., 1985; Vadasy et al., 1985). Vadasy et al. (1985), in a caregiver study, noted that caregivers who had participated in the program for 1 to 3 years reported significantly lower levels of depression than caregivers just entering the program.

Second, the nature and severity of illnesses varied widely across both types of studies, and this may have influenced the potency of the support intervention for participants. Few studies actually quantified the amount of stress the illness caused either the caregiver or the patient. However, Greene and Monahan (1989) found that the perceived burden felt by caregivers before the intervention was a significant predictor of reduced anxiety and reduced burden at posttesting. Hinrichsen et al. (1985), in a study of a support group for scoliosis sufferers, reported findings that might lend support to a stress-buffering model of support. The effectiveness of the support group (for adults only) was related to the intensity of medical treatment; those with more intensive medical treatment reported lower levels of psychosomatic symptoms, fewer feelings of shame and estrangement, and higher self-esteem when compared with adults with less severe problems. However, it should be noted that the reduced symptoms may have resulted directly from the medical treatment and not from stress buffering.

In many ways, the methodology of this group of studies was fairly rigorous. However, only four of the nine studies described steps taken to ensure standardization of intervention procedures (Abramowitz & Coursey, 1989; Haley et al., 1987; Toseland et al., 1989; Zarit et al., 1987). Thus, the exact type and amount of support that led to the observed outcomes are in doubt for the majority of the studies reviewed. Furthermore, in two studies random assignment to groups was constrained by the subjects' schedules; thus, subjects self-selected into the treatment or control groups (Abramowitz & Coursey, 1989; Greene & Monahan, 1987, 1989). And, in one case, the design of the study necessitated a nonequivalent control group (Hinrichsen et al., 1985). Overall, results are difficult to generalize. Only two studies provided information about the participants' SES (Haley et al., 1987; Montgomery & Borgotta, 1989).

In summary, social support interventions emphasizing both informational and emotional social support can enhance psychological well-being for persons facing chronic illness or for their caregivers. However, the length of the intervention and the perceived stress associated with the illness or role may be critical factors in producing and maintaining these psychological benefits.

Physical Health. Social support interventions to enhance physical health are quite numerous, and not all are reviewed here. These interventions have targeted obesity, smoking, and fitness behaviors. Interventions to reduce smoking and overeating are usually led by professionals. The length of the interventions varies considerably. Social support is usually provided by pairing the target individual with a helpful buddy, either a relative or a fellow group participant. A typical example of these studies is the weight reduction intervention by Brownell, Heckerman, Westlake, Hayes, and Monti (1978). The average subject was 58% overweight. Participants attended 10 weekly meetings of 1.5 hours' duration and 6 subsequent monthly sessions. Subjects were assigned to three conditions: group meetings where members each had a cooperative spouse who attended, group meetings where members each had a cooperative spouse who did not attend, and group meetings where members each had a noncooperative spouse. Cooperation was operationalized as the spouse's attendance at all couples' training sessions, during which the techniques of behavior modification were stressed, and nutritional information was provided. Results showed no differences among groups at 10 weeks posttreatment. However, at the 3- and 6-month follow-ups, those subjects with a cooperative spouse who attended group meetings showed greater weight loss than those in the other two groups.

Overall, the results of the 17 weight reduction interventions we reviewed were equivocal. Eight studies showed beneficial effects of social support (Brownell et al., 1978; Freemouw & Zitter, 1980; Israel & Saccone, 1979; Murphy, Williamson, Buxton, Moody, Absher, & Warner, 1982; Perri, McAdoo, McAllister, Lauer, & Yancey, 1986; Perri, McAdoo, Spevak, & Newlin, 1984; Pierce, LeBow, & Orchard, 1981; Rosenthal, Allen, & Winter, 1980). Nine studies showed no effects of support (Baranowski, Nadar, Dunn, & Vanderpool, 1982; Brownell & Stunkard, 1981; Dubbert & Wilson, 1984; O'Neill et al., 1979; Perri et al., 1987; 1988; Weitz & Bucher, 1980; Wilson & Brownell, 1978; Zitter & Freemouw, 1979). Moreover, in her review of weight-reduction interventions conducted at the workplace, Cohen (1988) concluded that the results for weight loss maintenance were not encouraging.

Many of the smoking cessation interventions that employed social support demonstrated an initial positive impact, but their effects often dissipated over time. (It should be noted that some programs have shown long-term success [e.g., Janis, 1983; Jason et al. 1989]). The reader is referred to two excellent reviews and commentaries on this topic (Cohen et al., 1988; Lichtenstein, Glasgow, & Abrams, 1986). Cohen et al. (1988) outlined many reasons for these failures. Perhaps the most obvious reason is that because researchers did not conduct manipulation checks, it is not clear whether experimental group members actually received support from their buddies or whether control group members sought out buddies for support (cf. Malott, Glasgow, O'Neil, & Klesges, 1984).

We reviewed three studies that attempted to increase exercise behavior through class participation for 1 or more hours per week (Gillett, 1988; King & Frederiksen, 1984; Wankel, Yardley, & Graham, 1985). Interventions ranged in length from about 1 to 4 months and were conducted by professional instructors. Social support was usually operationalized by the development of group cohesion (Gillett, 1988) and the assignment of an exercise buddy (King et al., 1984; Wankel et al., 1985), and consisted of both emotional and informational support. For instance, Wankel et al. (1985) had their subjects attend a weekly dance class. Treatment subjects received an informational booklet describing how to structure their social environment to facilitate attendance at class, had the class leader work through these materials with them, and were assigned to work with an exercise buddy.

Overall, social support appears to facilitate adherence to exercise regimens. Indeed, an earlier review by Wankel (1984) concluded that the buddy system was quite effective; however, buddies who were already friends were more effective than those who were strangers. In light of the discouraging results from the weight and smoking studies, the apparent success of the exercise interventions should not be overestimated. These studies examined adherence over a relatively short period—a few weeks—a time-span perhaps too short to reveal relapse.

For the most part, all of the health promotion interventions we examined (exercising, dieting, and smoking) adhered to strict methodological criteria: Subjects were randomly assigned to groups; outcome data were usually objective rather than subjective; and the interventions were standardized, and thus easily replicable. However, these studies' ecological validity may be limited, as the samples are biased toward female subjects.

Summary of Social Support Interventions

Social support interventions have been applied to many important problems and stressors. Although not every study found positive effects for the targeted outcomes, at least several studies within each category examined in this chapter did so. Our confidence in the benefits of these interventions is tempered by certain methodological problems. First, results of most studies are based on self-report measures (the exception was research on physical health promotion). Self-reported benefits may accrue from placebo effects rather than social support per se. The use of attention placebo groups and more objective outcome measures should become a priority for social support program evaluations.

Second, most of the interventions either targeted women or attracted predominantly female participants. Interestingly, most research has shown that females receive more emotional support (Burda, Vaux, & Schill, 1984; Stokes & Wilson, 1984) and more support, in general, than do males (Butler, Giordano, & Neren, 1985; Caldwell, Pearson, & Chin, 1987). Women also ask for more support (Butler et al., 1985) and report more satisfaction with their support than do men (Caldwell et al., 1987; Rosenthal, Gesten, & Schiffman, 1986). Thus, support interventions seem to attract and target the very people who are most capable of forming supportive relationships on their own. Striking examples of this phenomenon are support programs for spouse bereavement. Research indicates that males have more serious physical and mental health consequences on losing a spouse than do females (Stroebe & Stroebe, 1983); however, more than 93% of the participants in the programs we reviewed were female. Interventions that focus on interpersonal disclosure may be more appealing to women than men, who prefer activity-focused interactions (Wheeler & Nezlek, 1977). This suggests that researchers must develop alternative interventions for men. For example, Pilisuk and Minkler (1980) described a program called "Senior Gleaners." The goal of the program was activity focused—elderly participants collected food for themselves and others—but an important byproduct was "the development of new [social] ties to the extent desired by the individual members" (p. 110).

Third, subjects in many of the interventions may have been a uniquely motivated group of participants. Many social support interventions recruited subjects through the media (newspaper advertisements in particular). Subjects responding to these recruitment techniques might be more highly motivated to change, more comfortable in group settings or meeting new people, and better able to learn new skills (cf. Lieberman & Videka-Sherman, 1986; Videka-Sherman & Lieberman, 1985).

A final characteristic of these studies (though not a methodological problem) is that most involved participants with existing problems; the focus was predominately secondary prevention. The exception was parent support programs, most of which attempted to involve parents before the birth of their child and thus before parenting problems began. Because of community psychology's preferred emphasis on primary prevention, as well as the enormous benefits that good parenting can have for children throughout their life-span, the next section uses parent support programs as a case example of implementing social support interventions.

CASE EXAMPLE

The senior author of this chapter has served as a consultant for the Children's Trust Fund of Michigan for the Prevention of Child Abuse and Neglect (CTF) for the last 6 years. In this role, she monitors and supervises the implementation of small-scale preventive programs throughout Michigan, some of which are parent support programs. Several evaluations of these projects have been implemented (e.g., Brookins, 1990). This author's experience, in conjunction with the studies of Olds and colleagues (1986a, 1986b, 1988), reviewed earlier, serves as the basis for this section.

Implementing Parent Support Programs

The formal application of social support as a means of solving many different problems in living, including parenting, meets with widespread community enthusiasm and little or no opposition. For example, CTF funded portions of 34 parent support programs in both 1989 and 1990. These programs included several types of supportive interventions: one-on-one support of parents by other, experienced parents; one-on-one support of parents by trained staff/professionals; parent support groups with an emphasis on support rather than education; and parent support groups with an emphasis on education rather than support. Most programs were a mixture of these four approaches. The settings for these programs were quite diverse. They included community mental health centers, child guidance clinics, adult education centers, minority mental health outreach organizations, YWCAs, public health facilities, and temporary shelters for abused women. The number of parents served (in the year funded) by these programs ranged from 8 to 197. Costs per program ranged from $5,508 to $105,725; per parent costs averaged $597 per year. The cost-effectiveness of such programs becomes apparent when one examines the costs for various forms of treatment that might be necessitated if a child actually suffered abuse. Immediate per child costs could include foster care ($450 per month), hospital costs (about $1690 per hospital stay), and special education services ($655 per year) (Daro, 1988). Long-term costs might include those related to court and detention, long-term foster care, and drug/alcohol rehabilitation programs, to name but a few (Daro, 1988).

Labor-Intensive Nature of the Intervention

The implementation of one-on-one parent support programs is labor intensive. It takes one full-time, committed employee to administer even the smallest program. Liaisons must be established with various client referral organizations, such as schools, public health clinics, and hospitals. Ongoing contact with these agencies is crucial because most parent support programs try to involve mothers before the birth of the children. Paraprofessional or professional service providers have to be recruited and trained. Again, liaisons with various community organizations such as service clubs are necessary to provide a steady supply of service providers. Because paraprofessionals often do not have the time to provide services to more than one or two mothers at any given time, recruitment and training are ongoing activities. Supervision to service providers is usually furnished on a weekly basis.

Professional Values

Professional Preciousness. Learning to provide social support or enhance social networks (or teach others to do so) is an unusual role for professionals. Olds et al. (1986a) emphasized that the activities of nurses in their study were quite different from those of traditional community health nurses, yet the intervention team adhered to many traditional, professional values. Olds (1988) raised concerns that the parenting program might have increased dependency on the nurses by the parents, and that a priori selection of home visitation nurses was important even though "it is possible to educate helping professionals in methods of forming effective therapeutic relationships" (p. 21).

The importance of understanding the service providers' behavior in social support interventions cannot be overemphasized. In the study by Heller and Lakey (1985) cited earlier, subjects did not exhibit the supportive behaviors that *psychologists* have come to regard as important. Professional biases concerning support must not blind us to the fact that, for laypersons, support might come wrapped in unlikely packages (perhaps dependency). The absence of data from both service providers and clients, detailing their interactions in parent support programs, means that we can only assume, but cannot be certain, that social support interventions are qualitatively different from supportive, *therapy* interactions. Furthermore, we can only guess at what actual behaviors clients regard as supportive. (We take up this problem in more detail in the final section.)

Clash of Cultures. Most parent support programs involve, at least in part, informational support about good parenting. To some extent, professionals' views of good parenting reflect mainstream, middle-class values or the dominant scientific model at a given point in time. Olds (1988) described some of these dilemmas. His program "was grounded in commonsense concepts, [thus] the content of the program was congruent with family members' ways of thinking about what constitutes the optimal conditions for pregnancy, birth, and early care of the child" (p. 12); however, the investigators were also influenced by current research, some of which ran counter to commonsense ideas. The solution reached by this research group was that the nurses were allowed to be insistent about their values when there was strong scientific evidence to support them (e.g., picking up a crying child to help mother and infant form a secure attachment); when the scientific evidence was less conclusive, the nurses accepted the parents' values (e.g., the introduction of solid foods to the infant). Of course, this posture speaks to a certain value about the credence of the scientific enterprise that may not be held by parents in the program. What we do not know is (a) how a clash of cultural values might influence the supportive relationship between the service provider and parent and (b) whether the parent's adoption of the service provider's values influences the parent's relationship with existing supporters.

Targeting At-Risk Populations

Most parent support programs target mothers or parents believed to be at-risk for poor parenting outcomes. Labeling a parent "at-risk" may become a self-fulfilling prophecy (Rosenthal, 1973; Rosenthal & Jacobson, 1968) with negative consequences (cf. Broskowski & Baker, 1974). We do not know whether parents participating in support programs, as compared with nonparticipants, are more likely to exhibit parenting deficiencies simply because their behavior is under greater scrutiny. Furthermore, Olds (1988) suggested that parent support programs, by setting high standards for parenting behavior, may have the unintended effect of raising the stress level of an already stressed mother.

Evaluation Issues

To date, none of the existing evaluations of parent support programs advance our theoretical understanding of how social support affects new mothers. Several factors may account for this. The number of parents served by a typical program is small ($N = 66$ in the average CTF-funded program). To obtain a reasonable sample size, including a randomly assigned control group (Campbell & Stanley, 1963), subjects must usually be recruited over the course of 2 to 3 years.

Furthermore, for many outcomes of interest, the base rates are low. For example, the annual incidence figures for child abuse and neglect are estimated at 1% to 3% (Helfer, 1982; National Committee for Prevention of Child Abuse, 1984); but the rates differ according to the age of the child, "largely due to the fact that 0–2 years old [are] significantly less likely to be abused than [are] older children" (United States Department of Health and Human Services, 1988, pp. 5–42). Most support programs target mothers prenatally and intervene during the first 1 to 2 years of the infants' lives. If these programs do, in fact, reduce parents' abusive behavior, the national incidence rates suggest that these effects are most likely to appear several years after the intervention is completed. Thus, detecting these lower rates of abuse would require expensive, longitudinal research with many subjects.

Finally, the financial cost of even the most minimal theoretically driven evaluation is considerable. Training and supervision must be monitored to ensure the intervention's integrity. Even if the investigator tests only the stress-buffering versus the main effect models, data collection needs to include measures of stress, adjustment, and social support. Adequate assessment of some outcomes (e.g., parent–child interactions) necessitates behavioral observation, a very labor-intensive and expensive procedure.

FUTURE DIRECTIONS

The most important question about social support interventions continues to remain unanswered: If support is beneficial, how do these benefits occur? Answering this question may mean examining support in different and innovative ways. Currently, measurement of social support or social networks focuses on end points of relationships (e.g., a supporter is perceived by the individual as providing emotional support, the individual feels very satisfied with the level of information and advice support in his or her life). We know little about what transpires within the relationship(s) that lead to these perceptions of support. It is particularly important for those researchers who develop interventions that create or enhance support to understand how the process of support occurs between two individuals. This process data is probably the most theoretically and programmatically useful information that applied researchers might collect, yet no efforts in this direction were found in the literature. Because such efforts would be quite time-consuming, we end this chapter by pointing to two theoretical frameworks about relationships that might provide useful avenues for exploration: referent power and social exchange theories.

Referent power is the potency one individual has to influence another. "A person with referent power is able to induce genuine internalized changes in [the] attitudes, values, and decisions [of another individual]" (Janis, 1983, p. 149). A relationship involving an individual with referent power has three hierarchical phases: establishment of the relationship, advice and help to change behavior, and specific actions that help retain behavior change. Janis has operationalized these phases with 12 specific behaviors. The study by Heller and Lakey (1985), cited earlier, provides a useful example of the application of referent theory. The reader may recall that these researchers were unable to find differential interactions (e.g., "differential amounts of advice, agreements, interpretations or reflections of feeling," p. 296) between high- and low-support dyads. Many of the interactions examined for analysis correspond to Phase 1 communications. In Janis's framework, Phase 1 behavior occurs at the beginning of a relationship. Individuals overcome their initial wariness because the referent person provides a trusting, supportive environment. If the phases are, in fact, hierarchical, the established high-support dyads, observed by Heller and Lakey, would have completed Phase 1. Perhaps once the Phase 1 framework is in place, friends place less emphasis on these behaviors. Or, alternatively, friends may revert to Phase 1 behaviors only during moments in the relationship when friends are engaged in behavior change.

Janis (1983) believes that referent power accounts for the potency of short-term helping relationships inducing individual change. If referent power explains how social support works, it suggests that theoretical researchers as well as practitioners must turn their attention to understanding what occurs in one-on-one, supportive relationships. Current support questionnaires focus on perceptions of support throughout the social network rather than the support present in any particular relationship, as is implied by referent theory. Furthermore, because measurement of social networks and social support usually occurs at one or two points in time, and usually not at the inception of a relationship, the types of support measured by these questionnaires are not assumed to exist in a hierarchical relationship to one another. Self-report questionnaires could be modified to test referent theory by asking questions of support about individual network members rather than the network as a whole and by testing whether different types of support are preconditions for others.

A second useful theoretical framework for conceptualizing support is social exchange theory (Brody, 1985). Social interactions are viewed as exchanges of both extrinsic ("rewarding services") and intrinsic ("interpersonal rewards") benefits between individuals (Blau, 1964). Social exchanges occur first, but the relationship is stabilized and reinforced by the reciprocal interactions between the participants; that is, the interactions tend toward equilibrium. In the language of social support, reciprocity is viewed as a characteristic of the social networks that deliver support (e.g., Pilisuk & Minkler, 1980). Brody (1985) summarized research showing that healthy networks are characterized by reciprocity and unhealthy ones by a lack of it. Individuals feel indebted and uneasy when interactions are not reciprocal (Schreiber & Glidewell, 1978), and this may result in the network becoming unstable (Gottlieb, 1983a).

Reciprocity may have both practical and theoretical importance in the relationship between service providers and recipients. For example, when describing one-on-one parent support programs in this chapter, we detailed the types of extrinsic and intrinsic benefits that *service providers* are encouraged to provide to parents. If positive relationships are, by definition, reciprocal, what types of exchanges might the *mother* provide to the service provider to maintain equilibrium? If there are no such exchanges, the mother might feel indebted and uncomfortable when interacting with the service provider. Furthermore, the intervention might not be best defined as the provision of social support.

Alternatively, the mother may recognize that she affords the service provider a chance to help others, that is, herself (Brody, 1985; Staub, 1978). Thus, both parties are aware of receiving equal benefits from the relationship. In this case, Brody (1985) suggests there may be problems "redistributing resources into a network from outside" (p. 341). The new resources obtained by the mother from her service provider may create an imbalance in her relationships with her original social network. Over time, the mother may have more to offer these network members than they have to offer her, and the relationships may become severed.

In sum, although there is an enormous body of published literature on the topic of social support, our understanding of how support works is in its infancy. Those researchers who evaluate supportive interventions can do much to contribute to this understanding, but only if their evaluations actually measure the support that is implemented. We hope we have provided some useful suggestions for these future evaluations.

NOTES

1. Three studies that met the criteria for inclusion were not included because they could not be conveniently categorized with other studies. Lieberman, Bond, Solow, and Reibstein (1979) examined the effectiveness of women's consciousness-raising groups. After 4 months of participation, members, as compared with nonmembers, had greater self-esteem; however, depression and anxiety were unaffected by group membership. Lieberman and Gourash (1979) and Bogat and Jason (1983) attempted to enhance support among elderly persons through growth groups and one-on-one support, respectively. In the first study, many outcome variables yielded statistically few significant results for the experimental group. The second study showed no real benefit to participants.
2. Taylor, Falke, Mazel, and Hilsberg (1988) reviewed the existing empirical studies on cancer support groups; thus, these studies will not be reviewed here. About one half of the studies cited by these authors found positive adjustment (usually to death and dying) among participants who took part in the support groups.

ACKNOWLEDGMENTS

The authors wish to thank Karen Kiemel, Diana Shoendorff, and Chris Gray for their help in locating references for this chapter, Tim Speth for compiling the raw data from the CTF programs, and Belle Liang for her suggestions concerning the social support diagram.

REFERENCES

Abramowitz, I. A., & Coursey, R. D. (1989). Impact of an educational support group on family participants who take care of their schizophrenic relatives. *Journal of Consulting and Clinical Psychology, 57*, 232–236.

Alpert-Gillis, L. J., Pedro-Carroll, J. L., & Cowen, E. L. (1989). The children of divorce intervention program: Development, implementation, and evaluation of a program for young urban children. *Journal of Consulting and Clinical Psychology, 57*, 583–589.

Baranowski, T., Nader, P. R., Dunn, K., & Vanderpool, N. A. (1982). Family self-help: Promoting changes in health behavior. *Journal of Communication, 32*, 161–172.

Barnard, K. E., Magyary, D., Sumner, G., Booth, C. L., Mitchell, S. K., & Spieker, S. J. (1988). Prevention of parenting alterations for women with low social support. *Psychiatry, 51*, 248–253.

Barnett, B., & Parker, G. (1985). Professional and non-professional intervention for highly anxious primiparous mothers. *British Journal of Psychiatry, 146*, 287–293.

Barrera, M. (1986). Distinctions between social support concepts, measures, and models. *American Journal of Community Psychology, 14*, 413–445.

Barrera, M. E., & Rosenbaum, P. L. (1986). The transactional model of early home intervention. *Infant Mental Health Journal, 7*, 112–131.

Barrera, M. E., Rosenbaum, P. L., & Cunningham, C. E. (1986). Early home intervention with low-birth-weight infants and their parents. *Child Development, 51*, 407–414.

Barrett, C. J. (1978). Effectiveness of widows' groups in facilitating change. *Journal of Consulting and Clinical Psychology, 46*, 20–31.

Blau, P. M. (1964). *Exchange and power in social life.* New York: John Wiley.

Bloom, B. L., Hodges, W. F., & Caldwell, R. A. (1982). A preventive program for the newly separated: Initial evaluation. *American Journal of Community Psychology, 10*, 251–264.

Bloom, B. L., Hodges, W. F., Kern, M. B., & McFaddin, S. C. (1985). A preventive intervention program for the newly separated: Final report. *American Journal of Orthopsychiatry, 55*, 9–26.

Bogat, G. A., & Jason, L. A. (1983). An evaluation of two visiting programs for elderly community residents. *International Journal of Aging & Human Development, 17*, 267–280.

Bogat, G. A., Jones, J. W., & Jason, L. A. (1980). School transitions: Preventive intervention following an elementary school closing. *Journal of Community Psychology, 8*, 343–352.

Boger, R. P., Richter, R., Kurnetz, R., & Ilass, B. (1986). Perinatal Positive Parenting: A follow-up evaluation. *Infant Mental Health Journal, 7*, 132–145.

Booth, C. L., Barnard, K. E., Mitchell, S. K., Spieker, S. J. (1987). Successful intervention with multi-problem mothers: Effects on the mother-infant relationship. *Infant Mental Health Journal, 8*, 288–306.

Booth, C. L., Mitchell, S. K., Barnard, K. E., & Spieker, S. J. (1989). Development of maternal social skills in multiproblem families: Effects on mother-child relationship. *Developmental Psychology, 25*, 403–412.

Brody, J. G. (1985). Informal social networks: Possibilities and limitations for their usefulness in social policy. *Journal of Community Psychology, 13*, 338–349.

Brookins, C. (1990). *An experimental evaluation of a volunteer parent aide program.* Unpublished doctoral dissertation, Michigan State University, East Lansing, MI.

Broskowski, A., & Baker, F. (1974). Professional, organizational, and social barriers to primary prevention. *American Journal of Orthopsychiatry, 44*, 707–719.

Brownell, K. D., Heckerman, C. L., Westlake, R. J., Hayes, S. C., & Monti, P. M. (1978). The effect of couples' training and partner co-operativeness in the behavioral treatment of obesity. *Behavior Research and Therapy, 16*, 323–333.

Brownell, K. D., & Stunkard, A. J. (1981). Couples' training, pharmacotherapy, and behavior therapy in the treatment of obesity. *Archives of General Psychiatry, 38,* 1224–1229.

Butler, T., Giordano, S., & Neren, S. (1985). Gender and sex-role attributes as predictors of utilization of natural support systems during personal stress events. *Sex Roles, 13,* 515–524.

Burda, P. C., Jr., Vaux, A., & Schill, T. (1984). Social support resources: Variations across sex and sex role. *Personality and Social Psychology Bulletin, 10,* 119–126.

Caldwell, R. A., Pearson, J. L., & Chin, R. J. (1987). Stress-moderating effects: Social support in the context of gender and locus of control. *Journal of Personality and Social Psychology Bulletin, 13,* 5–17.

Campbell, D. T., & Stanley, J. C. (1963). *Experimental and quasi-experimental designs for research.* Chicago: Rand McNally.

Caplan, G. (1974). *Support systems and community mental health: Lectures on concept development.* New York: Behavioral Publications.

Cassel, J. (1976). The contribution of the social environment to host resistance. *American Journal of Epidemiology, 104,* 107–123.

Cobb, S. (1976). Social support as a moderator of life stress. *Psychosomatic Medicine, 3,* 300–314.

Cohen, R. Y. (1988). Mobilizing support for weight loss through work-site competitions. In B. H. Gottlieb (Ed.), *Marshaling social support: Formats, processes, and effects* (pp. 241–264). Beverly Hills, CA: Sage.

Cohen, S., & Hoberman, H. (1983). Positive events and social support as buffers of life change stress. *Journal of Applied Social Psychology, 13,* 99–125.

Cohen, S., Lichtenstein, E., Mermelstein, R., Kingsolver, K., Baer, J. S., & Kamarck, T. W. (1988). Social support interventions for smoking cessation. In B. H. Gottlieb (Ed.), *Marshaling social support: Formats, processes, and effects* (pp. 211–240). Beverly Hills, CA: Sage.

Cohen, S., & McKay, G. (1984). Social support, stress, and the buffering hypothesis: A theoretical analysis. In A. Baum, J. E. Singer, & S. E. Taylor (Eds.), *Handbook of psychology and health* (Vol. 4, pp. 253–267). Hillsdale, NJ: Lawrence Erlbaum.

Cohen, S., & Syme, S. L. (1985). The study and application of social support. In S. Cohen & S. L. Syme (Eds.), *Social support and health* (pp. 3–22). New York: Academic Press.

Cohen, S., & Wills, T. A. (1985). Stress, social support, and the buffering hypothesis. *Psychological Bulletin, 98,* 310–357.

Cutrona, C. E. (1986). Behavioral manifestations of social support: A microanalytic investigation. *Journal of Personality and Social Psychology, 51,* 201–208.

Daro, D. (1988). *Confronting child abuse: Research for effective program design.* New York: The Free Press.

Dawson, P., van Doorninck, W. J., & Robinson, J. L. (1989). Effects of home-based, informal social support on child health. *Journal of Developmental and Behavioral Pediatrics, 10,* 63–67.

Dohrenwend, B. S., & Dohrenwend, B. P. (1974). *Stressful life events: Their nature and effects.* New York: John Wiley.

Dohrenwend, B. S., & Dohrenwend, B. P. (1981). *Stressful life events and their contexts.* New York: Prodist.

Dubbert, P. M., & Wilson, G. T. (1984). Goal-setting and spouse involvement in the treatment of obesity. *Behavior Research and Therapy, 22,* 227–242.

Elliott, S. A., Sanjack, M., & Leverton, T. J. (1988). Parents groups in pregnancy: A preventive intervention for postnatal depression? In B. H. Gottlieb (Ed.), *Marshaling social support: Formats, processes, and effects* (pp. 87–110). Beverly Hills: Sage.

Felner, R. D., Ginter, M., & Primavera, J. (1982). Primary preventions during school transition: Social support and environmental structure. *American Journal of Community Psychology, 10,* 277-290.

Fremouw, W. J., & Zitter, R. E. (1980). Individual and couple behavioral contracting for weight reduction and maintenance. *Behavior Therapist, 3,* 15-16.

Gillett, P. A. (1988). Self-reported factors influencing exercise adherence in overweight women. *Nursing Research, 37,* 25-29.

Gottlieb, B. H. (1981a). Preventive interventions involving social networks and social support. In B. H. Gottlieb (Ed.), *Sage studies in community mental health: Vol. 4. Social networks and social support* (pp. 201-232). Beverly Hills, CA: Sage.

Gottlieb, B. H. (1981b). *Social networks and social support.* Beverly Hills, CA: Sage.

Gottlieb, B. H. (1983a). Social support as a focus for integrative research in psychology. *American Psychologist, 38,* 278-287.

Gottlieb, B. H. (1983b). *Social support strategies: Guidelines for mental health practice.* Beverly Hills, CA: Sage.

Gottlieb, B. H. (1985). Social support and community mental health. In S. Cohen & S. L. Syme (Eds.), *Social support and health* (pp. 303-326). New York: Academic Press.

Gottlieb, B. H. (1988). *Marshaling social support: Formats, processes, and effects.* Beverly Hills, CA: Sage.

Greene, V. L., & Monahan, D. J. (1987). The effect of a professionally guided caregiver support and education group on institutionalization of care receivers. *The Gerontologist, 27,* 716-721.

Greene, V. L., & Monahan, D. J. (1989). The effect of a support and education program on stress and burden among family caregivers to frail elderly persons. *The Gerontologist, 29,* 472-477.

Haley, W., Brown, L., & Levine, E. (1987). Experimental evaluation of the effectiveness of group interventions for dementia caregivers. *The Gerontologist, 27,* 376-382.

Halpern, R., & Larner, M. (1987). Lay family support during pregnancy and infancy: The Child Survival/Fair Start Initiative. *Infant Mental Health Journal, 8,* 130-143.

Helfer, R. E. (1982). A review of the literature on the prevention of child abuse and neglect. *Child Abuse & Neglect, 6,* 251-261.

Heller, K., & Lakey, B. (1985). Perceived support and social interaction among friends and confidants. In I. G. Sarason & B. R. Sarason (Eds.), *Social support: Theory, research, and applications* (pp. 287-300). Boston: Martinus Nijhoff.

Heller, K., Price, R. H., & Hogg, J. R. (1990). The role of social support in community and clinical interventions. In B. R. Sarason, I. G. Sarason, & G. R. Pierce (Eds.), *Social support: An interactional view* (pp. 482-507). New York: John Wiley.

Heller, K., & Swindle, R. W. (1983). Social networks, perceived social support, and coping with stress. In R. D. Felner, L. A. Jason, J. N. Moritsugu, & S. S. Farber (Eds.), *Preventive psychology: Theory, research, and practice* (pp. 87-103). New York: Pergamon.

Hinrickson, G. A., Revenson, T. A., & Shinn, M. (1985). Does self-help help? An empirical investigation of scoliosis peer support groups. *Journal of Social Issues, 41,* 65-87.

Hobfoll, S. E., & Stephens, M. A. P. (1990). Social support during extreme stress: Consequences and intervention. In B. R. Sarason, I. G. Sarason, & G. R. Pierce (Eds.), *Social support: An interactional view* (pp. 454-481). New York: John Wiley.

House, J. S. (1981). *Work stress and social support.* Reading, MA: Addison-Wesley.

Israel, A. C., & Saccone, A. J. (1979). Follow-up effects of choice of mediator and target of reinforcement on weight loss. *Behavior Therapist, 10,* 260-265.

Janis, I. L. (1983). The role of social support in adherence to stressful decisions. *American Psychologist, 38*, 143–160.
Jason, L. A., & Bogat, G. A. (1983). Evaluating a preventive orientation program. *Journal of Social Service Research, 7*, 39–49.
Jason, L. A., Lesowitz, T., Michaels, M., Blitz, C., Victors, L., Dean, L., Yeager, E., & Kinball, P. (1989). A worksite smoking cessation intervention involving the media and incentives. *American Journal of Community Psychology, 17*, 785–799.
Jason, L. A., Weine, A., Johnson, J., Warren-Sohlberg, L., Filippelli, L., Lardon, C., & Yeager-Turner, E. (1992). *School transitions: A strategic time to help our children.* San Francisco, CA: Jossey-Bass.
Kalter, N., Pickar, J., & Lesowitz, M. (1984). School-based developmental facilitation groups for children of divorce: A preventive intervention. *American Journal of Orthopsychiatry, 54*, 613–623.
Kessler, R. C., & McLeod, J. D. (1985). Social support and mental health. In S. Cohen & S. L. Syme (Eds.), *Social support and health* (pp. 219–240). New York: Academic Press.
Kiesler, C. A. (1985). Policy implications of research on social support and health. In S. Cohen & S. L. Syme (Eds.), *Social support and health* (pp. 347–364). New York: Academic Press.
King, A. C., & Frederiksen, L. W. (1984). Low-cost strategies for increasing exercise behavior: Relapse preparation training and social support. *Behavior Modification, 8*, 3–21.
Larson, C. P. (1980). Efficacy of prenatal and postpartum home visits on child health and development. *Pediatrics, 66*, 191–197.
Leavy, R. L. (1983). Social support and psychological disorder: A review. *Journal of Community Psychology, 11*, 3–21.
Lee, D. L. (1988). The support group training project. In B. H. Gottlieb (Ed.), *Marshaling social support: Formats, processes, and effects* (pp. 135–164). Beverly Hills, CA: Sage.
Lieberman, M. A., Bond, G. R., Solow, N., & Reibstein, J. (1979). Effectiveness of women's consciousness raising. In M. A. Lieberman & L. D. Boorman (Eds.), *Self-help groups for coping with crisis* (pp. 341–361). San Francisco, CA: Jossey-Bass.
Lieberman, M. A., & Gourash, N. (1979). Effects of change groups on the elderly. In M. A. Lieberman and L. D. Boorman (Eds.), *Self-help groups for coping with crisis* (pp. 387–405). San Francisco, CA: Jossey-Bass.
Lieberman, M. A., & Videka-Sherman, L. (1986). The impact of self-help groups on the mental health of widows and widowers. *American Journal of Orthopsychiatry, 56*, 435–449.
Liotta, R. F., Jason, L. A., Robinson, L., & LaVigne, V. (1985). A behavioral approach for measuring social support. *Family Therapy, 12*, 285–295.
Malott, J. M., Glasgow, R. E., O'Neil, H. K., & Klesges, R. C. (1984). Co-worker social support in a worksite smoking control program. *Journal of Applied Behavior Analysis, 17*, 485–495.
McGuire, J. C., & Gottlieb, B. H. (1979). Social support groups among new parents: An experimental study in primary prevention. *Journal of Clinical Child Psychology, 8*, 111–116.
Minde, K., Shosenberg, N., Thompson, J., & Marton, P. (1983). Self-help groups in a premature nursery—follow-up at one year. In E. Galewon & J. Call (Eds.), *Frontiers of infant psychiatry* (pp. 264–271). New York: Basic Books.
Mitchell, R. E., Billings, A. G., & Moos, R. F. (1982). Social support and well-being: Implications for prevention programs. *Journal of Primary Prevention, 3*, 77–97.

Montgomery, R., & Borgatta, E. (1989). The effects of alternative support strategies on family caregiving. *The Gerontologist, 29,* 457–464.

Mueller, D. P. (1980). Social networks: A promising direction for research on the relationship of the social environment to psychiatric disorder. *Social Science and Medicine, 14,* 147–161.

Murphy, J. K., Williamson, D. A., Buxton, A. E., Moody, S. C., Absher, N., & Warner, M. (1982). The long-term effects of spouse involvement upon weight loss and maintenance. *Behavior Therapy, 13,* 681–693.

National Committee for Prevention of Child Abuse. (1984). *The size of the child abuse problem.* Chicago: Author.

Newcomb, M. D. (1990). What structural equation modeling can tell us about social support. In B. R. Sarason, I. G. Sarason, & G. R. Pierce (Eds.), *Social support: An interactional view* (pp. 26–63). New York: John Wiley.

Olds, D. L. (1988). The Prenatal/Early Infancy Project. In R. H. Price, E. L. Cowen, R. P. Lorion, & J. Ramos-McKay (Eds.), *14 ounces of prevention: A casebook for practitioners* (pp. 9–23). Washington, DC: American Psychological Association.

Olds, D. L., Henderson, C. R., Chamberlin, R., & Tatelbaum, R. (1986a). Preventing child abuse and neglect: A randomized trial of nurse home visitation. *Pediatrics, 78,* 65–78.

Olds, D. L., Henderson, C. R., Tatelbaum, R., & Chamberlin, R. (1986b). Improving the delivery of prenatal care and outcomes of pregnancy: A randomized trial of nurse home visitation. *Pediatrics, 77,* 16–28.

O'Neill, P. M., Currey, H. S., Hirsch, A. A., Riddle, F. E., Taylor, C. I., Malcolm, R. J., & Sexauer, J. D. (1979). Effects of sex of subject and spouse involvement on weight loss in a behavioral treatment program: A retrospective investigation. *Addictive Behaviours, 4,* 167–177.

Parker, G., & Barnett, B. (1987). A test of the social support hypothesis. *British Journal of Psychiatry, 150,* 72–77.

Pearce, J. W., LeBow, M. D., & Orchard, J. (1981). Role of spouse involvement in the behavioral treatment of overweight women. *Journal of Consulting and Clinical Psychology, 49,* 236–244.

Pedro-Carroll, J., & Cowen, E. L. (1985). The children of divorce intervention project: An investigation of the efficacy of a school-based prevention program. *Journal of Consulting and Clinical Psychology, 53,* 603–611.

Pedro-Carroll, J. L., Cowen, E. L., Hightower, D. A., & Guare, J. C. (1986). Preventive intervention with latency-age children of divorce: A replication study. *American Journal of Community Psychology, 14,* 277–290.

Perri, M. G., McAdoo, W. J., McAllister, D. A., Lauer, J. B., Jordan, R. C., Yancey, D. Z., & Nezu, A. M. (1987). Effects of peer support and therapist contact on long-term weight loss. *Journal of Consulting and Clinical Psychology, 55,* 615–617.

Perri, M. G., McAdoo, W. J., McAllister, D. A., Lauer, J. B., & Yancey, D. Z. (1986). Enhancing the efficacy of behavior therapy for obesity: Effects of aerobic exercise and a multicomponent maintenance program. *Journal of Consulting and Clinical Psychology, 54,* 670–675.

Perri, M. G., McAdoo, W. J., Spevak, P. A., & Newlin, D. B. (1984). Effect of a multicomponent maintenance program on long-term weight loss. *Journal of Consulting and Clinical Psychology, 52,* 480–481.

Perri, M. G., McAllister, D. A., Gange, J. J., Jordan, R. C., McAdoo, W. J., & Nezu, A. M. (1988). Effects of four maintenance programs on the longer-term management of obesity. *Journal of Consulting and Clinical Psychology, 56,* 529–534.

Pilisuk, M., & Minkler, M. (1980). Supportive networks: Life ties for the elderly. *Journal of Social Issues, 36*, 95-116.

Procidano, M. E., & Heller, K. (1983). Measures of perceived social support from friends and from family: Three validation studies. *American Journal of Community Psychology, 11*, 1-24.

Rook, K. S., & Dooley, D. (1985). Applying social support research: Theoretical problems and future directions. *Journal of Social Issues, 41*, 5-28.

Rosenthal, B., Allen, G. J., & Winter, C. (1980). Husband involvement in the behavioral treatment of overweight women: Initial effects and long-term follow-up. *International Journal of Obesity*, 165-173.

Rosenthal, K. R., Gesten, E. L., & Shiffman, S. (1986). Gender and sex role differences in the perception of social support. *Journal of Sex Roles, 14*, 481-699.

Rosenthal, R. (1973). On the social psychology of the self-fulfilling prophecy: Further evidence for pygmalion effects and their mediating mechanisms. *MSS Modular Publication, 53*, 1-28.

Rosenthal, R., & Jacobson, L. (1968). *Pygmalion in the classroom.* New York: Holt, Rinehart & Winston.

Schreiber, S. T., & Glidewell, J. C. (1978). Social norms and helping in a community limited liability. *American Journal of Community Psychology, 6*, 441-453.

Siegel, E. Bauman, K. E., Schaefer, E. S., Saunders, M. M., & Ingram, D. D. (1980). Hospital and home support during infancy: Impact on maternal attachment, child abuse and neglect, and health care utilization. *Pediatrics, 66*, 183-190.

Silverman, P. R. (1986). *Widow-to-widow.* New York: Springer.

Silverman, P. R. (1988). Widow-to-widow: A mutual help program for the widowed. In R. H. Price, E. L. Cowen, R. P. Lorion, & J. Ramos-McKay (Eds.), *14 ounces of prevention: A casebook for practitioners* (pp. 175-186). Washington, DC: American Psychological Association.

Silverman, P. R., MacKenzie, D., Pettipas, M., & Wilson, E. W. (Eds.). (1974). *Helping each other in widowhood.* New York: Health Sciences.

Sloan, V. J., Jason, L. A., & Bogat, G. A. (1984). A comparison of orientation methods for elementary school transfer students. *Child Study Journal, 14*, 47-60.

Staub, E. (1978). *Positive social behavior and morality: Social and personal influences.* New York: Academic Press.

Stokes, J. P., & Wilson, D. G. (1984). The Inventory of Socially Supportive Behaviors: Dimensionality, prediction, and gender differences. *American Journal of Community Psychology, 12*, 53-69.

Stolberg, A. L., & Garrison, K. M. (1985). Evaluating a primary prevention program for children of divorce. *American Journal of Community Psychology, 13*, 111-124.

Stroebe, M. S., & Stroebe, W. (1983). Who suffers more? Sex differences in health risks of the widowed. *Psychological Bulletin, 93*, 279-301.

Sullivan, L. A. (1989). *Social interaction: Sex differences in the exchange of emotional support.* Unpublished doctoral dissertation, Michigan State University, East Lansing, MI.

Taylor, S. E., Falke, R. L., Mazel, R. M., & Hilsberg, B. L. (1988). Sources of satisfaction and dissatisfaction among members of cancer support groups. In B. H. Gottlieb (Ed.), *Marshaling social support: Formats, processes, and effects* (pp. 187-208). Beverly Hills, CA: Sage.

Toseland, R. W., Rossiter, C. M., & Labrecque, M. S. (1989, September). The effectiveness of two kinds of support groups for caregivers. *Social Service Review*, 415-432.

United States Department of Health and Human Services. (1988). *Study of national inci-*

dence and prevalence of child abuse and neglect (Contract No. 105-85-1702). Washington, DC: United States Government Printing Office.

Vachon, M. L., Lyall, W. A., Rogers, J., Freedman-Letofsky, K., & Freeman, S. J. (1980). A controlled study of self-help intervention for widows. *American Journal of Psychiatry, 137*, 1380-1384.

Vaux, A. (1988). *Social support: Theory, research, and intervention.* New York: Praeger.

Videka-Sherman, L. (1982). Effects of participation in a self-help group for bereaved parents: Compassionate Friends. *Prevention in Human Services, 1*, 69-77.

Videka-Sherman, L., & Lieberman, M. (1985). The effects of self-help and psychotherapy on child loss: The limits of recovery. *American Journal of Orthopsychiatry, 55*, 70-82.

Wankel, L. M. (1984). Decision-making and social support strategies for increasing exercise involvement. *Journal of Cardiac Rehabilitation, 4*, 124-135.

Wankel, L. M., Yardley, J. K., & Graham, J. (1985). The effects of motivational interventions upon the exercise adherence of high and low self-motivated adults. *Canadian Journal of Applied Sport Sciences, 10*, 147-156.

Weisz, G., & Bucher, B. (1980). Involving husbands in treatment of obesity—effects on weight loss, depression, and marital satisfaction. *Behavior Therapy, 11*, 643-650.

Wheeler, L., & Nezlek, J. B. (1977). Sex differences in social participation. *Journal of Personality and Social Psychology, 35*, 742-754.

Wilson, G. T., & Brownell, K. (1978). Behavior therapy for obesity: Including family members in the treatment process. *Behavior Therapy, 9*, 943-945.

Vadasy, P. F., Meyer, D. J., Fewell, R. R., & Greenberg, M. T. (1985). Supporting fathers of handicapped young children: Preliminary findings of program effects. *Analysis and Intervention in Developmental Disabilities, 5*, 151-163.

Zarit, S., Anthony, C., & Boutselis, M. (1987). Interventions with caregivers of dementia patients: A comparison of two approaches. *Psychology and Aging, 2*, 225-234.

Zitter, R. E., & Fremouw, W. J. (1978). Individual versus partner consequation for weight loss. *Behavior Therapist, 9*, 808-813.

CHAPTER 11

Promoting Health Through Community Development

Stephen B. Fawcett, Adrienne L. Paine, Vincent T. Francisco, and Marni Vliet

DESCRIPTION OF THE PROBLEM

Cardiovascular disease, substance abuse, cancer, adolescent pregnancy, and accidents are major causes of death and disability in the United States (United States Department of Health and Human Services, 1989). Each of these health concerns is linked to clear, risk-increasing behaviors, such as tobacco use, poor nutrition, insufficient exercise, alcohol misuse, unprotected sexual activity, or riding in motor vehicles without a seat belt (United States Department of Health and Human Services, 1991). Accordingly, they are substantially preventable on both individual and community levels.

Health promotion is "the process of enabling people to increase control over, and improve, their health" (World Health Organization, 1986, p. iii; Green & Raeburn, 1988). Articulated in the Ottawa Charter for Health Promotion (Epp, 1986), this strategy emphasizes the importance of environmental influences on the behaviors associated with health promotion and injury prevention. In contrast to the disease-oriented medical treatment model, the health-promotion paradigm assumes that health is particularly affected by behavior or life-style (O'Donnell, 1986) and by the environmental conditions that support or impede health-promoting behavior.

Health promotion efforts attempt to change two types of factors: (a) personal factors, such as the knowledge and skill of individuals at risk for health impairment, and (b) environmental factors, such as smoking cessation programs or substance abuse policies, that might help protect health and prevent disease (Breslow, 1990; Minkler, 1989). In a community-oriented approach, responsibility for health is shared by individuals and by the systems that affect environmental supports for health and risks for disease and injury.

The World Health Organization endorsed a *community development* approach to health promotion in the Alma Ata declaration on primary health care (Green & Raeburn, 1988). This declaration emphasized community participation and self-reliance, with individuals, families, and communities assuming more responsibility for their own health (World Health Organization, 1978). These themes—self-help, citizen participation, and community control—are hallmarks of a community development approach to health promotion.

Rothman and Tropman (1987) discussed three approaches to community organization and development that are relevant to the challenge of health promotion: social planning, social action, and locality development. Social planning is a top-down approach that primarily involves expert planners in problem solving, building linkages, setting goals, and designing action plans related to such goals as reducing substance abuse or cardiovascular disease. The social action approach often relies on experienced community organizers and conflict tactics to redistribute resources and extend community control to disadvantaged, oppressed, or marginalized populations. The third approach—the locality development approach—involves broad citizen involvement in setting goals and taking action and is characterized by a bottom-up orientation, that is, the use of indigenous leadership to address local concerns including those related to health and injury.

The community development approach is consistent with a self-help and citizen participation paradigm for health promotion. It assumes that, to be successful, health promotion efforts require active citizen involvement in identifying health needs, setting priorities, controlling and implementing solutions, and evaluating progress toward health goals (Green, 1986). The community development approach is well suited to addressing the health promotion goals outlined by the Ottawa charter: creating healthy public policy and supportive environments, strengthening community action through citizen involvement and community development, developing personal skills and encouraging life-style changes, and reorienting health service to encourage community involvement (Green & Raeburn, 1988).

This chapter describes opportunities and challenges in promoting health through community development. First, it summarizes and critiques prominent models and programs that use elements of community development practice in health promotion. It next describes the case example of the Kansas Initiative, a statewide, comprehensive program of health promotion and disease prevention using a community development model. Finally, we conclude by suggesting future research and action issues related to understanding and improving community health initiatives.

REVIEW AND CRITIQUE OF THE LITERATURE

Prominent Models of Health Promotion and Community Development

There are several prominent models and programs that use community development strategies to promote health. These include the PRECEDE model, PATCH programs, large-scale community demonstration projects, Healthy Cities/Healthy Communities, and the social reconnaissance model. Each is described below.

PRECEDE Model. The PRECEDE model (Green, Krueter, Deeds, & Partridge, 1980), and its successor, the PRECEDE-PROCEED model (Green & Kreuter, 1991), are social planning strategies that rely heavily on the input and analysis of experts in health planning and program development. The PRECEDE model—referring to "predisposing, reinforcing, and enabling causes in educational diagnosis and evaluation" (Green et al., 1980, p. 11)—is the dominant model in health education. It uses an interdisciplinary conceptual framework drawing on knowledge in the fields of epidemiology, behavioral science, administration, and education.

Consistent with a behavior-analytic model of community change (Fawcett, 1990; 1991), the PRECEDE model starts with the ultimate health outcome, such as the mortality and morbidity associated with heart disease, and works backward to the environmental determinants of a given health problem in designing an effective solution. According to the PRECEDE model, the first step is to study a community's social problems and concerns. It uses epidemiological data to identify specific health problems, such as a disproportionate incidence of adolescent pregnancy, that contribute to social problems. Second, the specific behaviors linked to the health problem are identified, such as intake of dietary fat (heart disease) or unprotected sexual activity (adolescent pregnancy). Third, change agents identify the predisposing conditions, such as knowledge and attitudes, reinforcing events, such as social consequences, and enabling conditions, such as resources and skills, associated with the health problem. These factors are used to design an intervention. Finally, the intervention is implemented and evaluated with attention to the multiple factors that may be associated with health outcomes. Elements of the PRECEDE and behavior-analytic models of community change are incorporated into the featured approaches to health promotion and community development that follow.

PATCH Programs. The Planned Approach to Community Health (PATCH) is an adaptation of the PRECEDE model for use at the grassroots community level (M. Kreuter, personal communication, October 1990). Sponsored by the Centers for Disease Control, local coordinators of PATCH programs are provided with training and workbooks that help in identifying key community members, setting up lines of communication, generating monetary and human resources, and formulating an action plan. The PATCH handbook guides participants through the complicated process of identifying problem areas, collecting and summarizing epidemiological and other data related to those problem areas, and disseminating that information to members of the community who can make necessary changes. With support from CDC staff, the PATCH model has been adopted by more than 17 states and 50 communities (Research Triangle Institute, 1990). Results from local application suggest that PATCH is a promising means of developing relationships among communities, local health departments, and the Centers for Disease Control. Although the PATCH program has been effective in producing changes in awareness and interest in health issues, few changes in community conditions or health outcomes have been documented.

As with the PRECEDE model, the intended result of PATCH programs is that community members change predisposing and enabling conditions in the community such that the overall health of local people is improved. Although this approach uses carefully crafted technology and would appear to be replicable, its complexity demands a degree of sophistication seldom available at the grassroots level. To be implemented widely, it would appear to require extensive support from trained outside professionals.

Large-scale Community Demonstration Projects. Several important community health-promotion initiatives are distinctive in the large scale of the intervention and the degree of control over the project exerted by outside researchers. Four projects particularly exemplify this model: the North Karelia Project in Finland, the Stanford Five-City Project, the Pawtucket Heart-Health Program, and the Minnesota Heart-Health Program.

The North Karelia Project in Finland was one of the first major community-wide approaches to health promotion (Puska, 1984). This project began after a community petition requested that action be taken on the high incidence of deaths owing to cardiovascular disease. The North Karelia Project focused on the primary prevention of heart disease by reducing risk factors, such as smoking, serum cholesterol, and blood pressure, and promoting secondary prevention among people already affected by heart disease.

The main independent variables used in the North Karelia Project included preventive services, education, behavior change programs, skills training, social support, environmental change, and community organization. A 10-year evaluation of the project found, for men, a 36% reduction in smoking, an 11% reduction in mean serum cholesterol levels, and a 5% reduction in mean diastolic blood pressure compared with a much smaller change in risk factor levels found in the control community (Puska et al., 1985); similar changes were found with women. These findings suggested the efficacy of this community demonstration project designed and implemented by expert researchers.

The Stanford Five-City Project (Farquhar et al., 1985) was an outgrowth of the Three Community Study (Fortman, Williams, Hulley, Haskell, & Farquhar, 1981). Supported by large external grants, the Five-City Project was a 6-year, community demonstration project designed to reduce the risk of heart disease. It used a media approach and was conducted in two cities, with three other cities serving as control communities. Information about risk reduction was provided through community-wide use of media and community-based programs, such as classes and seminars (see chapter 10 by Winett, in this book, for additional details of the media component). Community involvement was encouraged, and training of indigenous leaders was provided by Stanford University staff. A 5-year evaluation found significant reductions in average cholesterol levels (2%), blood pressure (4%), resting pulse rate (3%), and smoking rate (13%) in the treatment cities when compared with the control cities (Farquhar et al., 1990).

The Pawtucket Heart-Health Program targeted individuals, groups, and organizations in this small Rhode Island city in an attempt to reduce risk factors associated with cardiovascular disease. Relying on massive and long-term federal grant support, project researchers provided support and training for a volunteer-based delivery system that emphasized citizen involvement in planning, implementation, evaluation, and administration. The program targeted various channels through which to reach residents including schools, supermarkets, restaurants, senior citizen groups, and community events. Although data on broad program impact are not yet available, preliminary results suggested the efficacy of specific interventions, such as a point-of-purchase nutrition program in supermarkets that increased (from 36–54%), during a 4-year period, the percentage of customers who reported purchasing targeted heart-healthy items (Hunt et al., 1990).

Also funded by large federal grants, the Minnesota Heart-Health Program (Blackburn et al., 1984) involved three Minnesota communities in a 9-year project designed to reduce risk factors—including blood pressure, cholesterol, smoking, and exercise—associated with cardiovascular disease. The project consisted of mass media, education through classes and workshops, youth education programs, incentive programs, and community activities implemented by local task forces. Although designed by researchers, the program was reported to be implemented collaboratively by project administrators, local staff, and community leaders. An evaluation of a peer-led information and skills training program designed to reduce cigarette smoking among youth found significantly lower levels of students who reported ever smoking (61% compared with 70%) and current smokers (13% compared with 22%) in the treatment group when compared with the control group (Perry, Klepp, & Sillers, 1989).

Healthy Cities/Healthy Communities. The Healthy Cities/Healthy Communities project grew out of the World Health Organization's initiative, "Health for All by the Year 2000" (Ashton, Grey, & Barnard, 1988). Sponsored in the United States by the U.S. Office of Disease Prevention and Health Promotion (ODPHP), the approach begins with a definition of what a model healthy city or community should include, such as adequate sanitation, clean air, and potable water. The organizers took a top-down approach, convincing city officials to collaborate with leaders from a variety of sectors to develop plans designed to improve public health. Early applications suggested that this model may rely heavily on the artistry of ODPHP staff and outside contractors to design and implement projects. The Healthy Cities program, rather than encouraging grassroots change within communities, suggests a broad policy adoption format designed to affect long-term community variables such as clean air, sanitation, and clean water supply. Preliminary results from early applications suggest that coordinators find this approach useful (World Health Organization, 1988). Interim and long-term evaluations of the impact of this approach on morbidity and mortality have yet to be conducted.

Social Reconnaissance Model. The social reconnaissance model (Williams, 1990) combines top-down (social planning) and bottom-up (locality development) approaches to health promotion. Initially, elected officials, potential funding agents, and interested community members are assembled to discuss health problems, resources and barriers, and to establish priorities for community health initiatives. Supported by the Henry J. Kaiser Family Foundation, this interactive approach was used to establish collaborative programs in Kansas (with the Kansas Health Foundation), Washington, D.C., and eight southern states (Tennessee, South Carolina, Georgia, West Virginia, Mississippi, Arkansas, Louisiana, and Texas). Although results are not yet available, potential limitations of the approach include its lack of specification of the intervention and limited monitoring information about community action and change related to health goals.

Critique of the Literature

Fawcett (1990, 1991) described several standards for community research and action that can be used to characterize the literature on health promotion and community development. The standards outline criteria for collaborative relationships, research goals and methodology, intervention and dissemination, and advocacy and community change. The health promotion models and projects vary in the extent to which they maximize these dimensions.

Collaborative Relationships. Collaborative relationships are characterized by maximal community influence on the goals of the initiative and the design, implementation, and evaluation of its specific preventive interventions. Larger field trials and community demonstration projects, such as the Stanford Five-City Project, permit less community involvement, because the health problems and major aspects of the intervention are determined by outside university researchers and the granting agencies from which they receive support. By contrast, smaller scale or generic development processes, such as programs using the PATCH or social reconnaissance methodologies, provide considerably more community involvement in selecting health goals and designing and implementing interventions.

Research Goals and Methodology. Health promotion initiatives should respond to community needs and provide information about their effectiveness. Some variations of the PRECEDE model, such as PATCH programs, stress the importance of using information about the community's concerns as a partial basis for setting goals for research and action. Similarly, the North Karelia Project started in response to a community petition calling for action to prevent heart disease. By contrast, many community demonstration projects, such as the Stanford Five-City Project, are supported by categorical funding that restricts potential goals to particular health concerns, such as cancer or heart disease, and even to specific types of intervention, such as mass media. The social reconnaissance and Healthy Cities/Healthy Communities models appear to maximize community involvement in the choice of health goals and the design of interventions.

Evidence of program effectiveness varies in its availability and quality. For example, a 10-year evaluation of the North Karelia Project suggested the program's efficacy in reducing risk factors for cardiovascular disease. Similar evaluations of specific interventions, such as those for the Pawtucket and Minnesota Heart-Health Programs, suggested that particular components of community health interventions were successful in reducing risk factors for heart disease. However, the impact of community health initiatives on community action and change related to health goals—critical aspects of this development and change process—have not been well documented.

Intervention and Dissemination. Community health initiatives might also be judged against criteria for the design, diffusion, and maintenance of community health innovations. Virtually all of the programs rely on external, potentially unsustainable resources to implement the interventions. It is unclear whether even those projects using local volunteers, such as some interventions of the Pawtucket and Minnesota Heart-Health Programs, would continue without external grant monies and the large support services they provide. Some of the more technological programs, such as PATCH, are potentially replicable because they provide rather complete descriptions of what is necessary to implement the program. Other more general approaches—such as the social reconnaissance and Healthy Cities/Healthy Communities models—appear to rely more on artistic leadership than well-specified methodology. The complexity of even the more technological programs suggests, however, that dissemination likely would require extensive and long-term technical assistance.

Advocacy and Community Change. Results of community health initiatives should be used to maximize the program's impact and to empower people affected by the health concern including those of marginal status. Although a few studies (e.g., Fawcett, Seekins, & Jason, 1987) suggested that research data could be used to bring about changes in health-related policy, case studies of the instrumental uses of research data have been rare. Similarly, with few exceptions (e.g., Braithwaite & Lythcott, 1989; Couto, 1990; Wolff & Huppert, 1987), empowerment of people affected by health concerns has not been a primary goal of community health initiatives. Yet, empowerment of people with marginalized status may be central to the development process at individual and community levels (Fawcett et al., in press–b).

Conclusion. The literature suggests a continuum of community control over the process of health promotion and community change: from maximum community influence, such as with the social reconnaissance process, to minimum community control, such as with the larger scale community demonstration projects. Experimental data suggest the effectiveness of specific interventions for risk factors related to heart disease, but such data are lacking for other health concerns. The critical aspects of community development processes are not well specified, making it difficult to draw conclusions about causal relationships and to replicate successful interventions. Finally, although community mobilization strategies help set agendas and provide impetus for change, the absence of a system for monitoring community action and change limits opportunities to maintain and enhance the effectiveness of local community health initiatives.

CASE EXAMPLE

The Kansas Initiative is an ongoing community development effort attempting to build a statewide, comprehensive program in health promotion and disease prevention. The initiative is designed to address the major health concerns in Kansas: cardiovascular disease, substance abuse, certain forms of cancer, and adolescent pregnancy. Programs are designed to fit the state's values and profile, improve health outcomes, and be sustained over the long term. Begun in 1989, this initiative is sponsored by the Kansas Health Foundation, a statewide health care foundation based in Wichita, Kansas, with the mission of improving the health of the people of Kansas.

Kansas, with its 2.5 million people, is a 200 × 400 mile rectangle located in the geographical center of the United States. Its current relatively stable economy is based on agriculture, oil and natural gas production, business, and aeronautical and other industry. The leading causes of death in Kansas are cardiovascular disease and cancer, with unintentional injuries the leading cause of years of potential life lost before age 65. A review of available survey data suggested that substance abuse, particularly of tobacco and alcohol, may be relatively prevalent among adolescents; use of illegal drugs, such as marijuana and cocaine, appears to be higher in urban areas. Adolescent pregnancy, a particular problem in urban areas, appears to be increasing.

Conducting the Kansas Initiative involves several integrated and somewhat overlapping activities: (a) preparing the environment for action; (b) planning and developing a model for change; (c) implementation; (d) evaluation; and (e) developing a support system for program maintenance, dissemination, and quality control.

Preparing the Environment for Action: The Social Reconnaissance Process

The social reconnaissance process was used to prepare communities for action on identified health concerns. This process was implemented as part of a philanthropic partnership between the Kansas Health Foundation and the Henry J. Kaiser Family Foundation. The process involved community leaders, health experts, health consumers, and others in discussions of health issues, and opportunities and barriers for grantmaking in health promotion and disease prevention. In a series of 40 meetings in urban and rural communities, participants were asked to identify specific health promotion issues, such as substance abuse or adolescent pregnancy, and opportunities and barriers in addressing those issues. The process examined the history of problem solving in their community and local experiences with public-private partnerships. These discussions helped identify community leaders and yielded information about other state and local resources. The reconnaissance also provided opportunities for funders to obtain advice about the grantmaking needs of local communities from the perspective of representatives of agencies involved in health, education, and welfare.

Results of the Kansas Initiative town meetings suggested the need to better coordinate services and other resources relevant to health promotion and disease prevention. Identified strengths included an eagerness to use expertise for planning and coordination, successful experiences with public-private partnerships, and history of social planning in rural areas, especially through religious organizations. Additionally, local health care facilities were generally considered innovative and were the most often-cited local resources for solving community health problems. Finally, there existed a variety of health and human service networks and a strong system of higher education.

The major barrier facing health promotion programming in Kansas surfaced as the lack of leadership in health care and comprehensive planning for health.

Epidemiological data and vital statistics were available for only some health concerns. Inadequate incidence and prevalence rates for several risk factors made impossible the establishment of baseline data useful in local decision making. Additional barriers included the lack of technical and support services for local communities; a shortage of health care professionals, especially in rural areas; the large numbers of medically uninsured and underinsured (it was estimated that of the 2,500,000 Kansans, a minimum of 500,000 fall into this category); the absence of a school of public health within the state; the failure of county commissioners and state legislators to be informed and educated properly on issues pertaining to health; and a culture of self-reliance that can inhibit the use of formal service systems.

A companion survey distributed to those invited to the community meetings helped identify health concerns, such as substance abuse (26% of the respondents indicated it to be a concern) and inadequate health care services (noted by 60% of the respondents). Forty percent indicated that health education for the public, particularly in terms of wellness, was a major community need.

Planning: A Model of Health Promotion and Community Development

This section describes the planning process that followed the initial social reconnaissance and outlines the model used for health promotion and community development. The overall strategy for the Kansas Initiative underscored the importance of the following: (a) combining top-down (social planning) and bottom-up (locality development) approaches that include coalition building, leveraging human and fiscal resources, planning, developing model programs and policies, and building local capacity through leadership training and technical assistance; (b) supporting community health initiatives with consultation, technical assistance, and monitoring and feedback on progress and accomplishments; (c) encouraging implementation, evaluation, and maintenance of health promotion and community development efforts; and (d) promoting widespread adoption of model programs and policies within communities (and across the state) and encouraging adaptation of successful programs to fit new contexts and address other health issues.

The Kansas Health Foundation developed a plan for health promotion and disease prevention in the state that draws on identified resources and is consistent with the national Health Objectives for the Year 2000 (U.S. Department of Health and Human Services, 1990). The plan endorsed the establishment of initial prototype projects in areas of health concern and the development of a support system for health promotion initiatives.

Model of Health Promotion and Community Development. Drawing on models of health promotion and community development, this model has four interrelated elements: planning, preventive intervention with targets and agents of change, change in risk and protective factors, and change in ultimate and intermediate health outcomes. Figure 11.1 provides a depiction of the model as it might be used with initiatives to reduce the incidence of substance abuse, cardiovascular disease, adolescent pregnancy, unintentional injuries, or other health goals. Consistent with an outcome orientation, the model is best reviewed by starting with the desired ultimate and intermediate health outcomes.

The *ultimate and intermediate health outcomes* define the mission of the health promotion initiative. Thus, as the case examples will illustrate, Project Freedom has the mission of reducing substance abuse, and Kansas LEAN that of reducing intake of dietary fat. Archival records, such as health statistics, are used to provide a measure of the incidence (new cases) and prevalence (existing cases) of diseases, injuries, and their outcomes. These health statistics may focus on mortality (death) and morbidity (disability). These ultimate health outcomes are usually quite delayed consequences of unhealthy behavior, however. Heart disease, for example, may develop only after decades of smoking and a higher fat diet. Accordingly, more intermediate health outcomes, such as the levels of intake of dietary fat, represent a better target for health promotion initiatives.

Laboratory research and field experiments establish relationships between the ultimate health outcomes of death and disability, and intermediate health outcomes sometimes referred to as behavioral risk factors. The latter denote those behaviors associated with life-style that have been shown to be related to the likelihood of disease or injury. Behavioral risk factor surveys, adolescent health surveys, and other self-report instruments are used to track intermediate health outcomes, such as the self-reported incidence of smoking or dietary fat intake, associated with an ultimate health outcome such as heart disease.

Risk and protective factors, such as peer support or opportunities, affect the likelihood of intermediate outcomes, such as abstinence or unprotected sexual activity. Risk and protective factors include personal factors, such as knowledge, skills, and values and beliefs related to relevant behaviors. They also include environmental factors, such as family and peer support, resources and opportunities, and supportive policies and laws.

Community health initiatives attempt to bring about *community changes*—changes in programs, policies, and practices consistent with the mission. Community changes are immediate health outcomes; they provide the most solid early evidence of the functioning of community health initiatives. Intervention research studies help establish causal relationships between particular community changes and behaviors and outcomes associated with health and avoidance of injury (Fawcett et al., in press–a). The efficacy of a particular community change, such as a police crackdown intended to reduce sales of cigarettes to minors, should not be assumed without experimental evidence. Intervention research results help select for specific changes in risk or protective factors worthy of widespread adoption.

244   STRATEGIES FOR PROMOTING HEALTH

Planning

o Setting community health goals (e.g., reduce substance abuse) consistent with the mission

o Setting community change objectives (e.g., changes in programs, policies, and practices) for each relevant channel of influence

Preventive Intervention

o Universal initiatives for the general population

o High-risk programs for people with multiple risk factors or experiencing critical events

Targets of Change / Agents of Change

Potential Channels of Influence:

o Media
o Families
o Peers
o Schools
o Worksites
o Businesses
o Religious organizations
o Health/mental health organizations
o Social service organizations
o Law enforcement agencies
o Community/civic organizations
o Executive branch of government
o Legislative branch of government

Risk/Protective Factors

Personal Factors

o Knowledge
o Skills
o Values & beliefs
o Degree of health or impairment

Environmental Factors

o Family & peer support
o Models & mentors
o Resources & opportunities
o Positive reinforcement
o Environmental barriers & hazards
o Supportive policies & laws

Ultimate & Intermediate Health Outcomes

Incidence and Prevalence of:

o Substance abuse [negative peer influences, poor academic performance]

o Cardiovascular disease [dietary fat intake, exercise]

o Adolescent pregnancy [abstinence, protected sexual activity]

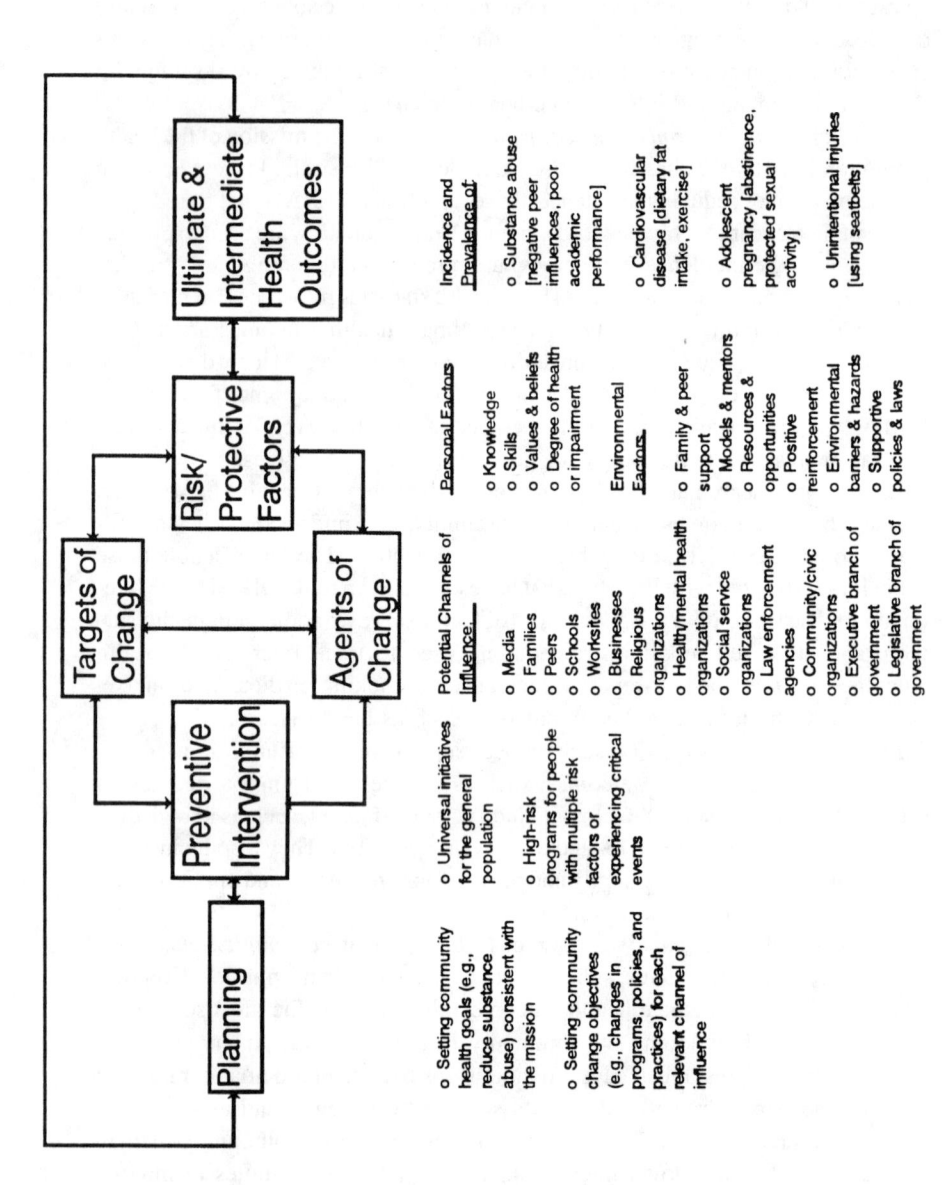

o Unintentional injuries [using seatbelts]

FIGURE 11.1 Model of health promotion and community development.

Preventive interventions attempt to change the behavior of targets of change, such as adolescents, and agents of change, such as parents and teachers, consistent with the mission of the initiative. Targets and agents are reached through various community sectors, known as channels of influence including the media, schools, businesses, religious organizations, and law enforcement agencies. The immediate outcome of preventive interventions is a change in programs, policies, and practices in relevant channels of influence.

Preventive interventions may be launched by state and local coalitions, task forces, or other action groups. They may consist of universal initiatives for the general population, such as adoption of a problem-solving curriculum that may contribute to the health goals of reducing substance abuse and adolescent pregnancy. Preventive interventions also may include high-risk programs for people with multiple risk factors or experiencing critical events, such as youth whose siblings use drugs or experience adolescent pregnancy. A comprehensive intervention to reduce intake of dietary fat, for example, may include universal initiatives to increase awareness and availability of lower-fat alternatives and high-risk programs for people with elevated serum cholesterol.

Planning is an important beginning and end point of this interactive model. The two most important products of the planning process are community health goals and community change objectives. Community health goals refer to specific levels of ultimate and intermediate outcomes that are targeted for attainment at a specified time, such as reducing the estimated pregnancy rate by 50% within 5 years. Community change objectives refer to those changes in programs, policies, or practices assumed to contribute to the mission. Community participation in goal setting is central to the process of health promotion and community development. Ongoing information about community changes helps determine the extent to which these immediate outcomes are produced. Periodic reports on intermediate and ultimate health outcomes informs later determination of which (if any) health concerns warrant new or continued community health initiatives.

Implementation

In the early stages of implementation, the Kansas Health Foundation funded the Work Group on Health Promotion and Community Development at the University of Kansas to provide consultation, technical assistance, and evaluation for selected initiatives. Two community health initiatives were funded initially—Project Freedom, with the mission of reducing adolescent substance abuse, and Kansas LEAN, with the mission of reducing intake of dietary fat. A Health Action Microgrants Program was also piloted to test this approach for supporting small self-help initiatives related to health concerns. Each initiative was conducted as part of a collaborative relationship between the foundation, the work group, and the funded community projects. Following a description of the work group's role, each project is described subsequently.

Work Group on Health Promotion and Community Development. The work group's mission is to develop the capacities of communities to address their health concerns and to contribute to understanding about effective means of health promotion and community development. The work group is a program of the Schiefelbusch Institute of Life Span Studies and the Department of Human Development at the University of Kansas. The work group's students and faculty provide consultation and technical assistance to community health projects associated with the foundation's health promotion and disease prevention initiative. The work group also conducts intervention research studies within the projects, experimentally evaluating intervention prototypes that are candidates for widespread dissemination in the state. Finally, the work group monitors community action, community change, and ultimate and intermediate outcomes of initiatives. This information is fed back to project leadership and foundation program officers to help improve project functioning.

Project Freedom. Project Freedom is a community coalition of more than 300 agencies with the mission of reducing adolescent substance abuse in Wichita (population, 401,000) and in the surrounding Sedgwick County. The coalition set community health goals specifying specific reductions in reported use of tobacco and illegal drugs. Its subcommittees targeted community changes in programs, policies, and practices of relevant channels of influence. These included schools, businesses, legislative bodies, religious organizations, law enforcement agencies, social service organizations, and other channels of influence.

The work group provided consultation during the strategic planning process in which community change objectives were set for each channel. Critical audiences for the coalition—its members, foundation officials, and outside experts on substance abuse—rated the feasibility of the candidate objectives and their importance to the mission of reducing substance abuse. These data were used to refine the final choices of objectives. Similarly, the work group provided technical assistance on the design of specific interventions, also conducting evaluations of their efficacy. The challenge for the coalition is to move beyond its networking, service, and resource generation activities to concentrate on bringing about community changes related to substance abuse and its prevention.

Kansas LEAN. Kansas LEAN is a state and local coalition with the mission of reducing dietary fat intake associated with cardiovascular disease and some cancers. The coalition is comprised of members from the state, county, and city departments of health, the Dillons grocery store chain, Pizza Hut Inc., the State Cooperative Extension Service, a local television station, and a variety of other organizations. This project is patterned after a national program called Project LEAN (Low-Fat Eating for America Now) that was sponsored by the Henry J. Kaiser Family Foundation of Menlo Park, California (Samuels, 1990).

The work group provided similar consultation during strategic planning and the development of specific interventions. In collaboration with program officers and the project director, staff designed and conducted intervention research studies that evaluated promising methods, such as the use of price reductions and product sampling to encourage purchases of lower fat foods in grocery stores and the use of incentives to reduce serum cholesterol levels in health fair participants. Kansas LEAN is similarly challenged to focus on bringing about those community changes that are most likely to contribute to its mission.

Health Action Microgrants Program. The foundation also developed a program of "microgrants," small grants of $500 to $1,000, to stimulate self-help initiatives in health promotion and community development (Paine, Francisco, & Fawcett, in press). The program was designed to remove barriers and provide resources for community change efforts. Microgrant projects consisted of grassroots attempts to change or develop new policies, programs, personal competence, or resources related to the foundation's priorities and consistent with local health concerns. Priority was given to proposed projects in which those affected by the health concern, such as teenaged mothers in the case of adolescent pregnancy, were significantly involved in project planning and implementation.

Awards for the first cycle of microgrant funding in Douglas County illustrate the types of grassroots initiatives that can be supported: (a) a teen speakers' bureau to deliver programs intended to help prevent adolescent pregnancy, (b) a program of fee reduction for mammograms directed by older women who had previously experienced breast cancer, (c) an innovative nutrition program for recovering alcoholics, and (d) a coalition of health consumers that was working to address identified health concerns in the county. This prototype grantmaking program was replicated successfully by Project Freedom in its own "minigrant" program. The health action microgrants program is unique in its commitment to attracting and supporting grassroots, self-help initiatives in health promotion.

Monitoring and Evaluation

As detailed elsewhere (Francisco, Paine, & Fawcett, 1993), the monitoring and evaluation system designed for the Kansas Initiative has two primary purposes: (a) to improve the management of health action groups, and (b) to provide information on group process and outcome that can be used to evaluate a project's success. The objective is not to make a single, post hoc judgment on an action group's effectiveness but rather to provide ongoing information that can be used for improvement.

The monitoring and evaluation system consists of three interrelated activities: (a) monitoring key measures of coalition process and outcome, (b) obtaining feedback from clients on the importance of the coalition's objectives and accomplishments, and (c) using the information to improve group functioning and accomplishments.

Monitoring Key Measures of Coalition Process and Outcome. The method system provides data on seven key measures: the number of members recruited, planning products, financial resources generated, dollars obtained, services provided, community actions taken, and community changes produced.

Members recruited refers to new members, affiliates, or partners of the coalition. Planning products consist of new objectives, bylaws, committees, and other results of planning activities. Financial resources generated reflect instances of grants, donations, and professional services received by the group. Dollars obtained refer to the dollar amounts of grants and other monies received. Services provided refer to classes, workshops, newsletters, screenings, and other informational or service programs provided by the coalition for members of the community.

Community actions are those actions taken by group members to bring about changes in the community related to the group's health goals and community change objectives. If a coalition on substance abuse, for example, is trying to discourage merchants from selling alcohol to minors, group members might write letters to the editor, make telephone calls to the mayor's office, or arrange meetings with police officials. Community changes are those changes in programs (e.g., new services established), policies (e.g., modified city ordinance), or practices (e.g., enhanced enforcement) of governmental bodies, agencies, or businesses that are related to the group's health goals and community change objectives. The efforts of a coalition on infant health, for example, might result in a new outreach program for immunizations or new policies that remove barriers to prenatal care.

Coalitions associated with the Kansas Initiative, such as Project Freedom and Kansas LEAN, use event logs to monitor important events and outcomes related to the group's mission. Coalition leaders, committee chairpeople, and other active group members complete the logs. Accuracy and completeness is verified by interviews with group members and by minutes from group meetings. This information is gathered and summarized each month, and fed back in quarterly reports.

The level of these seven key measures of process and outcome are charted in cumulative records to provide a picture of the group's level of activity and accomplishment over time. The graphs show trends that may suggest the need for various kinds of technical assistance and support. For example, consistently high levels of activity or upward trends may suggest strong group motivation and no need for additional consultation. Alternatively, low levels of activity or downward trends may suggest the need for a review of group goals, methods, or membership so as to improve the level of community activation and change.

In addition, archival records and surveys are used to assess progress on ultimate and intermediate health outcomes. With Kansas LEAN, for example, data from Behavior Risk Factor Surveys are used to establish a baseline for self-reported intake of dietary fat. For Project Freedom, survey data on drug use among in-school youth and archival records, such as for single nighttime vehicle accidents, provide some indication about outcomes. Data sources for different initiatives vary greatly in their accuracy and sensitivity, with those initiatives dealing with illegal behavior such as substance abuse posing the greatest challenges for measuring outcome.

Obtaining Feedback on the Coalition's Objectives and Outcomes. Key client audiences—including members of the coalition, funding partners, and health experts—are given the opportunity to assess the importance of community health goals and community outcomes resulting from the group's efforts. Information obtained from these client surveys is used to help guide adjustments in the group's health goals and objectives, and attempts to achieve them.

Using the Information. The information obtained from monitoring and evaluation system has several important uses. These include (a) to provide an occasion for the group to celebrate accomplishments, (b) to provide corrective feedback when actions or outcomes occur at too low a rate, (c) to help establish relationships between changes in the environment and changes in behaviors associated with health outcomes., and (d) to justify requests for continued or enhanced funding from the foundation or other local sources. This management information is designed to strengthen group process, enhance the level of accomplishment, and promote institutionalization of successful projects.

Support System for Program Maintenance and Dissemination

Chavis, Florin, and Felix (1993) argued for the importance of "enabling" systems—intermediate support organizations and resources networks—in nurturing community development efforts. The support system for the Kansas Initiative has six functions: (a) promoting interest, (b) providing consultation and technical assistance, (c) removing barriers and providing resources, (d) monitoring and evaluating outcomes, (e) rewarding accomplishments, and (f) promoting adoption of successful innovations. Figure 11.2 outlines these general functions and related activities.

To promote local interest in its community health initiatives, the Kansas Health Foundation used a variety of mechanisms including the social reconnaissance process, information gathered on community health concerns, and announcements of available resources and grants. These mechanisms helped involve community members in setting the agenda for local change and offered incentives for coordinated action. The work group's consultation and technical assistance helped with setting goals and objectives, planning actions, and leadership development. By brokering resources, arranging opportunities for peer support, and

250 STRATEGIES FOR PROMOTING HEALTH

Promote Interest	Provide Consultation & Technical Assistance	Remove Barriers and Provide Resources	Monitor and Evaluate Outcomes	Reward Accomplishments	Promote Adoption of Successful Innovations
Conduct a social reconnaissance	Help set community health goals	Broker material resources	Monitor key measures of process and outcome	Award continuation grants	Identify successful innovations and key early adopters
Provide information on community health concerns	Help set community change objectives	Provide social support for leadership	Provide feedback on levels of activation and accomplishment	Provide awards for exemplary projects	Provide support for active dissemination
Announce available resources and grants	Help with action planning	Provide microgrants for self-help initiatives	Conduct intervention research	Enhance public recognition	Monitor for quality assurance
Provide information on successful health promotion innovations	Leadership development	Award coalition grants	Monitor adoption of innovations	Provide incentives for goal attainment	Award dissemination grants
					Submit manuscripts for publication

FIGURE 11.2 Functions and activities of a support system for health promotion and community development.

administering microgrants and other programs, the Kansas Health Foundation helped remove barriers and provide resources for its health-promotion initiatives.

As described earlier, the work group helped monitor and evaluate outcomes using data-gathering and feedback systems and intervention research studies. The Kansas Health Foundation attempted to reward accomplishments of participating projects by continuation grants, awards, and incentives for goal attainment. Finally, the Kansas Health Foundation and work group tried to promote adoption of successful innovations by identifying successful innovations and key early adopters, providing support for active dissemination, monitoring the quality of replicated programs, and other dissemination activities.

Conclusion

To be successful, community health initiatives must encourage active involvement of key people of influence, individuals, grassroots groups, and other interested citizens. Through community involvement, specific health concerns are identified, community change objectives are set, and barriers that can subvert program success are noted. Permitting community control of health promotion initiatives serves to mobilize the local human and material resources that are necessary for sustained change efforts. These grassroots efforts should result in programs small enough to manage, and large and durable enough to produce a significant impact on community conditions supportive of health. Ongoing evaluations assess the Kansas Initiative's success in promoting community activation and change, and their effects on longer term health outcomes.

FUTURE DIRECTIONS

A comprehensive approach to health promotion and community development, such as the Kansas Initiative, faces several challenges. First, it must assist local communities in identifying their health concerns and setting agendas for action. This may require widespread use of social reconnaissance, health concerns assessment, or other methodologies to promote interest and ownership of local health concerns. Second, it must create mechanisms for identifying and creating projects that can produce changes in local communities related to health outcomes. Perhaps resource inventories and networks can be established to help identify and support potential partners. Third, community health initiatives must develop a system for monitoring coalition process and outcome. These data can be used to improve the management of local projects and to elicit support for continuance.

Fourth, a comprehensive initiative must develop a support system necessary to assist local programs in being successful and surviving for the time required to meet its health goals. Consultation and technical assistance and monitoring and feedback systems may be particularly helpful. Finally, a long-term health promotion initiative must produce evidence of effectiveness and program satisfaction to help ensure its own survival. This is important because support must be maintained over the extended time necessary to meet the initiative's community health goals.

Changes in intermediate health objectives, such as a reduction in smoking or intake of dietary fat, and ultimate health objectives, such as a reduction in heart disease, can take a long time—perhaps 5, 10, or 15 years, or more. Community changes—changes in programs, policies, and practices related to the group's mission—can be observed in a shorter time frame. By carefully tracking these more immediate community outcomes over time and obtaining information about relevant risk factors and health indicators for the same period, it may be possible to establish linkages between community changes and intermediate outcomes.

However, such attempts to contribute to the science of health promotion and community development face several challenges. First, community health initiatives usually consist of multiple program components implemented by different agents, in a variety of channels of influence, and unfolded over long periods. This makes it difficult to specify the independent variable and determine the timing of its implementation. Second, field conditions do not often permit the degree of methodological rigor needed for clear demonstrations of experimental control. For example, the absence of adequate comparison groups may preclude use of control group designs; also, a paucity of opportunities for staggered replication of the intervention across groups may limit use of time-series designs to demonstrate experimental control. Finally, there are several aspects of the social context, such as level of competent leadership and history of success in community change efforts, that may affect the immediacy, magnitude, and durability of program success. Accordingly, it is difficult to ascertain the generality of program effects without multiple replications in a variety of community contexts, and information on durability requires longitudinal studies in several communities.

Comprehensive community health initiatives reflect tensions between top-down (social planning) and bottom-up (locality development) approaches. Top-down approaches use experts to inform choices of health-promotion goals and means. For example, foundations typically use epidemiological data and expert consultants to develop their own health goals and grantmaking priorities. By embracing a community development approach, a granting agency pledges to respect the importance of full participation by individuals, families, and communities in promoting and protecting their own health. However, what if a local health coalition elects to shift its efforts to a health goal not addressed by the funding agency or to use a change tactic inconsistent with the funding agency's polices or values? The degree to which collaborating communities ultimately choose their own health goals and select their intervention strategies will provide an indication of the ultimate balance between top-down and bottom-up methods.

Callahan (1990, p. 40), a medical ethicist, posed some basic questions that affect the nature of health care and health-promotion programs in a society: "What kind of life should we live? What do we want to do with the life that good health can give us?" Implicit in the strategy of health promotion and community development is the valuing of citizen action, of neighbors working together to improve the world that affects us. Collaborative approaches to health promotion contribute to health goals and community empowerment. In so doing, they offer a glimpse of the connectedness that is part of the essence of a good life.

ACKNOWLEDGMENTS

This research was supported by a grant from the Kansas Health Foundation (#9004041) to the Work Group on Health Promotion and Community Development at the University of Kansas, Lawrence, Kansas. The authors wish to thank our collaborators: Mary K. Campuzano, senior program officer of the Foundation; Steve Coen, program officer of the Foundation; Judy Johnston, Director of Kansas LEAN; and Jim Copple and Barbara Bradley, former executive director and associate director of Project Freedom.

REFERENCES

Ashton, J., Grey, P., & Barnard, K. (1986). Healthy cities: WHO's new public health initiative. *Health Promotion International, 1*, 55–60.
Blackburn, H., Luepker, R., Kline, F. G., Bracht, N. Carlaw, R., Jacobs, D., Mittelmark, M., Stauffer, L., & Taylor, H. L. (1984). The Minnesota Heart Health Program: A research and demonstration project in cardiovascular disease prevention. In J. D. Matarazzo, S. M. Weiss, J. A. Herd, N. E. Miller, & S. M. Weiss (Eds.), *Behavioral health: A handbook of health enhancement and disease prevention* (pp. 1171–1178). New York: John Wiley.
Braithwaite, R. L., & Lythcott, N. (1989). Community empowerment as a strategy for health promotion for black and other minority populations. *Journal of the American Medical Association, 261*, 282–283.
Breslow, L. (1990). A health promotion primer for the 1990's. *Health Affairs, 9*, 6–21.
Callahan, D. (1990). *What kind of life?: The limits of medical progress.* New York: Simon & Shuster.
Chavis, D. M., Florin, P., & Felix, M. R. J. (1993). Nurturing grassroots initiatives for community development: The role of enabling systems. In T. Hizrahi & J. D. Morrison (Eds.), *Community organization and social administration: Advances, trends, and emerging principles.* New York: Haworth.
Cuoto, R. A. (1990). Promoting health at the grass roots. *Health Affairs, 9*, 145–151.
Epp, J. (1986). Achieving health for all: A framework for health promotion. *Health Promotion, 1*, 419–428.
Farquhar, J. W., Fortman, S. P., Flora, J. A., Taylor, C. B., Haskell, W. L., Williams, P. T., Maccoby, N., & Wood, P. D. (1990). Effects of communitywide education on cardio-

vascular disease risk factors: The Stanford Five-City Project. *Journal of the American Medical Association, 264,* 359–365.

Farquhar, J. W., Fortman, S. P., Maccoby, N., Haskell, W. L., Williams, P. T., Flora, J. A., Taylor, C. B., Brown, B. W., Solomon, D. S., & Hulley, S. B. (1985). The Stanford Five-City Project: Design and methods. *American Journal of Epidemiology, 122,* 323–334.

Fawcett, S. B. (1990). Some emerging standards for community research and action: Aid from a behavioral perspective. In P. Tolan, C. Keys, F. Chertok, & L. Jason (Eds.), *Researching community psychology: Issues of theory and methods* (pp. 674–675). Washington, DC: American Psychological Association.

Fawcett, S. B. (1991). Some values guiding community research and action. *Journal of Applied Behavior Analysis, 24,* 621–636.

Fawcett, S. B., Seekins, T., & Jason, L. A. (1987). Policy research and child passenger safety legislation: A case study and experimental evaluation. *Journal of Social Issues, 43,* 133–148.

Fawcett, S. B., Suarez-Balcazar, Y., Balcazar, F. E., White, G. W., Paine, A. L., Blanchard, K. A., & Embree, M. G. (in press–a). Conducting intervention research: The design and development process. In J. Rothman & E. J. Thomas (Eds.), *Intervention research: Creating effective methods for professional practice.* New York: Haworth.

Fawcett, S. B., White, G. W., Balcazar, F. E., Suarez-Balcazar, Y., Mathews, R. M., Paine, A. L., Seekins, T., & Smith, J. F. (in press–b). A contextual-behavioral model of empowerment: Case studies with people with disabilities. *American Journal of Community Psychology.*

Fortman, S. P., Williams, P. T., Hulley, S. B., Haskell, W. L., & Farquhar, J. W. (1981). Effect of health education on dietary behavior: The Stanford Three Community Study. *American Journal of Clinical Nutrition, 34,* 2030–2038.

Francisco, V. T., Paine, A. L., & Fawcett, S. B. (1993). A methodology for monitoring and evaluating community coalitions. *Health Education Research: Theory and Practice, 8*(3).

Green, L. W. (1986). The theory of participation: A qualitative analysis of its expression in national and international health policies. *Advances in Health Education and Promotion, 1,* 211–236.

Green, L. W., Kreuter, M. W., Deeds, S. G., & Partridge, K. B. (1980). *Health education planning: A diagnostic approach.* Mountain View, CA: Mayfield.

Green, L. W., & Raeburn, J. M. (1988). Health promotion: What is it? What will it become? *Health Promotion, 3,* 151–159.

Green, L. W., & Kreuter, M. W. (1991). *Health promotion planning: An educational and environmental approach.* (2nd ed.). Mountain View, CA: Mayfield.

Hunt, M. K., Lefebvre, R. C., Hixson, M. L., Banspach, S. W., Assaf, A. R., & Carleton, R. A. (1990). Pawtucket Heart Health Program point-of-purchase nutrition education program in supermarkets. *American Journal of Public Health, 80,* 730–732.

Lasater, T., Abrams, D., Artz, L., Beaudin, P., Babrera, L., Elder, J., Ferreira, A., Snow, R., & Charleton, R. (1984). Lay volunteer delivery of a community-based cardiovascular risk factor change program: The Pawtucket experiment. In J. D. Matarazzo, S. M. Weiss, J. A. Herd, N. E. Miller, & S. M. Weiss (Eds.), *Behavioral health: A handbook of health enhancement and disease prevention* (pp. 1166–1170). New York: John Wiley.

Minkler, M. (1989). Health education, health promotion, and the open society: An historical perspective. *Health Education Quarterly, 16,* 17–30.

O'Donnell, M. (1986). Definition of health promotion. *American Journal of Health Promotion, 1,* 4–5.

Paine, A. L., Francisco, V. I., & Fawcett, S. B. (in press). Implementing a health-action microgrants program. *American Journal of Public Health*.

Perry, C. L., Klepp, K., & Sillers, C. (1989). Communitywide strategies for cardiovascular health: The Minnesota Heart Health Program youth program. *Health Education Research: Theory & Practice, 4*, 87–101.

Puska, P. (1984). Community-based prevention of cardiovascular disease: The North Karelia Project. In J. D. Matarazzo, S. M. Weiss, J. A. Herd, N. E. Miller, & S. M. Weiss, *Behavioral health: A handbook of health enhancement and disease prevention* (pp. 1140–1153). New York: John Wiley.

Puska, P., Nissinen, A., Tuomilehto, J., Salonen, J. T., Koskela, K., McAlister, A., Kottke, T. E., Maccoby, N., & Farquhar, J. W. (1985). The community-based strategy to prevent coronary heart disease: Conclusions from the ten years of the North Karelia Project. *Annual Review of Public Health, 6*, 147–193.

Research Triangle Institute. (1990). *Development of a planned approach to community health (PATCH) process evaluation model*. Atlanta: Centers for Disease Control.

Rothman, J., & Tropman, J. E. (1987). Models of community organization and macro practice perspectives: Their mixing and phasing. In F. M. Cox, J. L. Erlich, J. Rothman, & J. E. Tropman (Eds.), *Strategies of community organization: Macro practice* (pp. 3–25). Itasca, IL: Peacock.

Samuels, S. E. (1990). Project LEAN: A national campaign to reduce dietary fat consumption. *American Journal of Health Promotion, 4*, 435–440.

United States Department of Health and Human Services. (1989). *United States health profile*. Washington, DC: U.S. Government Printing Office.

United States Department of Health and Human Services. (1991). *Healthy people 2000: National health promotion and disease prevention objectives* (DHHS Publication No. PHS 91–50213). Washington, DC: U.S. Government Printing Office.

Williams, R. M. (1989). Rx: Social reconnaissance. *Foundation News*, 24–29.

Wolff, T., & Huppert, M. E. (1987). Community coalition development: Community empowerment in areas of high unemployment. *Massachusetts Area Health Education Center Coalition Sampler*.

World Health Organization. (1978). *Alma Alta 1978: Primary health care*. Geneva: Author.

World Health Organization. (1986). The Ottawa charter for health promotion. *Health Promotion, 1*, iii–v.

World Health Organization. (1988). *WHO Healthy Cities Project: An update*. Geneva: Author.

Index

A

Acquired immune deficiency syndrome (AIDS), 125–143
  incidence of, 125
  media campaigns on, 185, 188
  in Third World Populations, 134
Acquired immune deficiency syndrome (AIDS) prevention, 118, 125–143. *See Also* HIV *entries*
  behavior change interventions, 138–140
  case example, 136–142
  "clinical" versus "community" behavior change interventions, 136
  description of problem, 125–129
  future directions, 142–143
  logistical and or application issues, 141–142
  objectives and stages of media-based prevention program, 183–184
  recruiting and assessing participants for AIDS prevention project, 137–138
  study outcomes, 140–141
Adolescent mothers. *See* Teenage pregnancy
Adolescents
  alcohol use by, 75, 76, 80
  automobile accidents of, 76
  erotophobia in, 105
  risk-taking among, 100
  sex guilt in, 105
  sexual activity of, 100
  social morbidities of, 99
  as target audience for HIV prevention, 197–198
African-American adolescents, 22, 23
  in sex education classes, 104
  sexual activity of, 100
African-American females
  birth rates of, 101
  early parenthood in, 116
  long-term follow-up of teenage mothers among, 102
  motivation to delay parenthood in, 109
  risk factors for pregnancy in, 109
African-American mentors, 26
AIDS. *See* Acquired immune deficiency syndrome
Alcohol, adolescents' use of, 75, 76, 80
Analysis of variance (ANOVA) statistical techniques, 209
Automobile accidents
  adolescents and, 76
  drinking age and, 91
  driver education in high school and, 150
  incidence of, 149
  intervention approaches for, 149–150

B

Behavior, factors influencing, 9
Behavioral approaches to prevention, current trends in, 6–8
Behavioral community interventions, failure of, 7
Behavioral community research, 4–5
Behavioral methods, 36
Behavioral promotion of health and mental health, future directions in, 8–10
Behavioral psychologists, 3–4, 6
  collaboration with other professions/ disciplines, 7, 9
Behavioral research, traditional goals of, 9
Behavioral Skills Training Program (BST), 40–41
Behavioral systems framework, 193–196
  representation of, 194f
Behavior change intervention, in AIDS prevention, 138–140
  risk behavior education, 138–139
  self-esteem and relationship issues, 140
  self-management training, 139
  sexual assertiveness training, 139–140
Bereavement, support programs for, 212–213
Birth control, sex education classes and, 104
Boy Scouts of America's "Prepared for Today" program, 61

C

Caregivers, contingencies for, 55–56, 57–58
Change, process of, 7
Child abuse, 33–45. *See also* Child physical abuse, Child sexual abuse
  case example, 42–43
  consequences of, 34–35
  future directions of, 43–45
  incidence of, 33–34
  perpetrator characteristics, 34
  response to problem, 35
  sex and age of victim, 34
Child Abuse Potential Inventory (CAPI), 37–38
Childhood injury prevention
  active methods of prevention, 55–63
  from automobile deaths, 54
  barriers to implementing prevention programs, 63–65
  beliefs about present interventions, 63–64
  case example, 65–68
  child's role in, 58–62, 62–63
  cost-benefit analysis, 64–65
  evaluation challenges, 65
  future directions, 68–70
  grassroots initiatives dedicated to, 69
  industry-sponsored programs, 69
  multiple-level intervention, 69
  passive methods of prevention, 53–55
  public attitudes on, 63
  "rules" on establishing interventions, 65–68
Child physical abuse, 35–39
  "at risk" children and parents, 37–38
  multidimensional nature of, 37
  Project 12-Ways, 38–39
  three factors of, 38–39
Children's Support Group (CSG), 21
Child safety restraints, 54, 70
Child sexual abuse, 39–42
  parents teaching children about, 42–43
  prevention of, 39–42
Chronic illness, support for caregivers and persons suffering from, 215–217
Cocaine, adolescents' use of, 75, 78
Cognitive-behavioral modification procedures, 139
Cognitive-behavioral skills, 19
Cognitive-behavioral training, 23
Community-based safety education, 62
Community development and health promotion, 233–253

advocacy and community change, 240
collaborative relationships, 238–239
comprehensive community health initiative requirements, 251–253
description of problem, 233–235
functions and activities of support system for, 250f
future directions, 251–253
Health Action Microgrants Program, 247
Healthy Cities/Healthy Communities project, 238
intervention and dissemination, 239–240
Kansas Initiative, 240–252
Kansas LEAN, 243, 246–247, 248
large-scale community demonstration projects, 236–237
locality development, 234
model of, 244f
monitoring and evaluation, 247–249
North Karelia Project, Finland, 236–237
PATCH programs, 236
PRECEDE model, 235
PRECEDE-PROCEED model, 235
Project Freedom, 243, 246, 248, 249
research goals and methodology, 239
social planning, 234
social reconnaissance model, 238
social reconnaissance process, 241–251
support system for, 249–251
Work Group on Health Promotion and Community Development, 245, 246
Community psychology model, 5
Condoms, heterosexuals use of, 135
Contextualism, as term, 9
Contextual issues, 9
Contraception
five steps of, 105
programs providing access to, 106–109

D

Design sensitivity, 195
Developmental psychology, 9
Diffusion of innovation model, 189
Divorce Adjustment Program, 21–22
Divorce, children of, 214
Divorce and separation, support programs for, 213–214
"Dram shop" laws, 156–157
Dual-career families, 60
DUI (driving under the influence)
applying behavioral science principles to prevention of, 169–170
consequences of, 166
drinking environment, 159–161
measuring BAC (blood alcohol content), 165–166
server intervention training programs, 157

E

"Ecobehavioral," definition of, 38
Ecological psychology, 9
Erotophobia/erotophilia, 105–106
Evaluation process, subjective variables in, 7
Exercise, social support for, 218

F

Family ecosystem, 38
Family planning programs, 106–107, 117

G

"Gatekeepers," 27
Gay men
behavior changes in, 129–130
community-level interventions for, 131
high risk behavior among, 130
HIV prevention programs for, 129–132
intervention strategies for, 130–131

Guttmacher Institute, 117

H

HAPI, 70
Health promotion, definition of, 233
Health-promotion interventions, 215–218
  caregivers and persons suffering from chronic illness, 215–217
Health promotion through community development. *See* Community development and health promotion
Healthstart, Inc., 107–108
Heterosexuals
  condom use by, 135
  HIV prevention programs for, 134–136
"Hierarchy of effects" model, 186, 187f
Hispanic adolescents, birth rates of, 101
HIV. *See* Human immunodeficiency virus
Home Accident Prevention Inventory, 56
Human immunodeficiency virus (HIV), 125
  changing HIV high risk behavior, 136–137
  curtailing infection with, 125–126
  epidemiology of, 126
  HIV prevention programs for gay men, 129–132
  HIV prevention programs for heterosexuals, 134–136
  HIV prevention programs for IVDUs, 132–134
  IVDUs and, 126, 127
  pattern 1 and 2 risk, 126–127
  risk behavior for, 127–129
  teens as target audience for prevention of, 197–198

I

Implementation issues, 26–28
  collaboration, 26–27
  sources of resistance, 27–28
Incentives, 161–162
Individual deficit model, 78
Information model, 77–78
Interactive information system, 192
Internal control, 7
Interventions
  target audience of, 3
  time point of, expanding, 3–4
Intravenous drug users (IVDUs), 126, 127
  HIV prevention program for, 132–134
IVDUs. *See* Intravenous drug users

J

Johns Hopkins School of Medicine, 108

K

Koop, C. Everett, Surgeon General, 119

L

Life Skills Training (LST), 19, 82–84

M

Main effect model, 206
  testing for, 208–209, 209f, 210
Marijuana, adolescents' use of, 75, 76, 80
Media-based preventive interventions, 181–201
  background of project, 196–198
  behavioral systems framework, 193–196
  case example, 196–200
  description of problem, 181–183
  effective media-based behavior change, 191–196
  future directions, 200–201
  ineffectiveness of, 184–191
  media forms and delivery systems, 182
  methodological problems, 190–191
  modeling, 196

myth of sanctity of interpersonal influence, 188–189
objectives and stages of program, 183–184
for parents and children together, 196
"safer sex" spots on network television, 189–190
school-based prevention programs, 196–197
self-fulfilling prophecy of, 185–186
sexually explicit programs, 196–197
social marketing/formative research, 198–200
teens as targets for HIV prevention, 198
Three-Community Study, 192
underevaluation of conceptual and strategic bases, 184–185
unrealistic goals of, 189–190
video cassette recorders (VCRs) in home, 196, 197
"weak effects" model, 185–186
Mentors
guidebook for, 24–25
"Method," as term in childhood injury prevention, 52
The Midwestern Prevention Project, 85
Minnesota Heart Health Program, 85, 237
Minnesota Smoking Prevention Program (MSPP), 81, 86–88
peer leader training for, 88
summary of, 87T
support for, 86–88
teachers and, 88
Monitoring the Future Study, 75, 76
Multilevel interventions, 8

N

National Cancer Institute, 71
National Center on Child Abuse and Neglect, 33
National Highway Traffic Safety Administration, 168
National Longitudinal Survey of Youth, 100
National Rifle Association, 64
National Safety Council, 168
National Traffic Safety Administration, 152
North Karalia Project, Finland, 85, 236–237

P

Parent Mentor Program, 26
Parents
implementing support programs for, 220–223
as personal safety instructors, 42–43
support programs for, 211–212
Parent support groups, 211–212
clash of cultures in conducting, 221–222
cost-effectiveness of, 220
evaluation issues, 222–223
labor-intensive nature of, 220–221
provided by professionals, 221
targeting at-risk populations, 222
Participant modeling (PM), 40
Pawtucket Heart-Health Program, 237
Perry Preschool Program, 119
Personal or spiritual health, 77
Personal safety skills, 40–41
Person-centered interventions, 3
Person–environment transactions, 3
Physical abuse, 35–39. See also Child physical abuse
interventions for, 36
risk factors for, 36
Physical health, 76
support groups for, 217–218
Planned Approach to Community Health (PATCH), 236
Poison Prevention Packing Act, 53
Postponing Sexual Involvement curriculum, 106
Prevention
active methods of, 55–63
current trends in behavioral approaches to, 6–8
passive methods of, 53–55
primary, 4
secondary, 4

[Prevention cont.]
  theoretical foundation of, 5
Preventive programs, transmitting information about, 8–9
Primary prevention, 4, 181–182
Problem-solving models, and teenage sexuality, 106
Project Alert, 82
Project Burn Prevention, 57
Project SMART, 81
Project 12-Way, 38–39, 56
Psychological health, 77
Psychoneuroimmunology, 10

R

Reciprocity, in relationships, 224–225
Referent power, 223–224
Refrigerator Safety Act, 53
Road safety, 149–170
  activator-behavior-consequence framework (ABC model), 152
  activators for, 155–158
  air bags, 151
  automatic shoulder belts, 151
  behavioral factors causing vehicle collisions, 153–154
  belt use law (BUL), 154, 155
  case example, 167–169
  commitment and goal setting, 158
  components of successful safety-belt program, 168
  consequences for DUI, 166
  consequence techniques for improving, 162–166
  defining target behaviors for, 152–154
  description of problem, 149–151
  designing behavior change interventions for, 152
  direct and delayed rewards of, 163
  direct and immediate rewards of, 162–163
  DO RITE process for, 152, 167, 168
  drinking environment, 159–161
  DUI (driving under the influence of alcohol), 155–156
  education on, 156–157
  environmental factors and, 158–162
  feedback for, 164–165
  future directions, 169–170
  group rewards for, 164
  incentive and disincentives, 161–162
  indirect rewards for, 163–164
  manual lap belts, 151
  policy, 155–156
  reminder strategies, 157–158
  safety-belt reminder systems, 158–159
  safety belt use and injury prevention, 152–153
Role playing
  in studying media-based prevention and families, 198–199
  in teaching personal safety skills, 40

S

Safe Child Program, 41–42
School-based health clinics, 107, 117
  successes of, 113
Schools and health promotion
  changing environments of, 20–21
  ethical issues, 25–26
  evaluation, 25
  future directions, 28–29
  implementation issues, 26–28
  middle and high school levels, 19
  motivation, 23–24
  preschoolers and kindergartners, 19
  program description, 23–24
  program rationale, 22–23
  on settings for interventions in social competency, 17–18
  skills-based social competence programs, 18–20
  targeting at-risk youth, 21–22
School Transitional Environmental Program (STEP), 20
School transitions, social support for, 214–215
Secondary prevention, 4, 181–182
Self-efficacy, 7
Self-evaluation, 24
Self-management model, 23
Self-management strategy, 24–25

INDEX

Self-management training, 139
Self-monitoring, 24
Self-reinforcement, 24
"Senior Gleaners," 219
Server intervention training programs, 157
Sex guilt, 105
Sex knowledge, 105
Sexual abuse, definition of, 33. *See also* Child sexual abuse
Sexual assertiveness training, 139–140
Sexuality education programs, 103–104
Single Parent's Support Group, 22
Skill-based programs, teenage pregnancy and, 104–106
Smoking
  by adolescents, 75, 76, 80
  price of cigarettes and, 91
  social support for stopping, 218
Social competence
  schools as setting for implementing interventions in, 17–18
  skills training, 18–20
Social health, 76–77
Social influences model
  application of, 80–84
  Life Skills Training (LST), 82–84
  on smoking prevention, 81
Social learning model, 37
Social-learning theory, 36, 78
Social psychology, 9
Social-situational model, 36
Social support, 205–225
  analysis of variance (ANOVA) statistical techniques, 209
  beneficial aspects of, 205
  bereavement, 212–213
  chronic illness, 215–217
  description of problem, 205–206
  divorce and separation, 213–214
  functional support, 208
  future directions, 223–225
  health-promotion interventions, 215–216
  implementing parent support programs, 220–223
  life-transition interventions, 211–215
  measurement of support, 206–207
  methodological criticism of research on, 207
  models of support, 206
  parenting, 211–212
  physical health, 217–218
  referent power, 223–224
  school transitions, 214–215
  social support theory, 206–207
  structural equation modeling (SEM), 209
  structural support, 208
  testing models of, 208–211
  women and, 219
Social validity, 7
Society, four levels of, 118
Stanford Five-City Project, 192, 237
Stress-buffering model, 206
  testing for, 208–209, 209f, 210, 214
Structural equation modeling (SEM), 209
Substance abuse, 75–93
  advertising and mass media and, 92
  alcohol prevention, 81–82
  application of social influences model and, 80–84
  availability of substances to adolescents, 91
  case example, 86–88
  on community level, 84–86
  description of problem, 75–77
  dissemination and refinement of information, 89–90
  drug use prevention, 81–82
  enforcement of existing laws, 92
  functions of, 79
  future directions, 89–93
  health domains affected by, 76
  peer leaders in prevention programs, 80
  population-level changes in behavior, 92
  psychosocial risk factors in adolescents, 79
  "scare tactics" on effects of, 78
  smoking prevention, 81

[Substance abuse *cont.*]
  social environment and, 78–79, 90–93
  social influences model of school health education, 78–80
Symbolic modeling (SM), 40

T

"Tactic," as term, 52
Target population, 6
  personal control of, 7
Teenage pregnancy prevention, 99–119. *See also* Adolescents
  adoption as parenting, 102
  birth rates of ethnic groups, 101
  case example, 110–116
  community feedback and data dissemination, 115–116
  community entry of programs on, 111–112
  conflicting messages about sex and, 105
  description of problem, 99–102
  ethnicity and, 116
  future directions, 116–119
  goal identification program design, 112–113
  implementation of programs, 113–114
  incidence of, 100–101
  life options approaches, 109–110
  long-term prognostic indicators for, 102
  Perry Preschool Program, 119
  personal and social problems associated with, 101–102
  Postponing Sexual Involvement curriculum, 106
  poverty and, 116
  prenatal programs associated with, 101
  programs providing access to contraceptives, 106–109
  risk factors for, 109
  sexual attitudes in young men versus young women, 117
  sexuality education programs, 103–104
  skill-based programs, 104–106
  society's messages about sex and, 117
  Teen Outreach program, 109–110
  Teens Learning to Cope (TLC Program), 110–111
Teens Outreach program, 109–110
  multicomponent community-wide programs for preventing, 110
Teens Learning to Cope Program, 110–111
  community entry of, 111–112, 113
  evaluation, 114–115
  feedback and communication, 115–116
  goal identification and program design, 112–113
  implementation of, 113–114
They Help Each Other Spiritually (THEOS), 213
Three-Community Study, 192
TLC program. *See* Teens Learning to Cope Program
Traditional delivery model, 5
Transactional model of mutual influence, 36

U

U.S., child mortality rate in, 51
U.S. Department of Transportation, 170
University of Michigan Transportation Research Institute, 153
University of South Carolina School of Public Health, 110

W

"War on drugs," 77
Weight reduction, social support for, 217
White teenagers, birth rates of, 101
Widow-to-Widow program, 212–213
World Health Organization, 234, 238